THE
8086
BOOK

D5

THE
8086
BOOK

Russell Rector - George Alexy

OSBORNE/McGraw-Hill
Berkeley, California

Published by

Osborne/McGraw-Hill
2600 Tenth Street
Berkeley, California 94710

For information on translations and book distributors outside of the U. S. A. ,
please write OSBORNE/McGraw-Hill at the above address.

The 8086 Book

    7890 DODO 8987654

ISBN 0-931988-29-2

Cover design by Joseph Mauro.

Contents

Figures

Figures (Continued)

Figures (Continued)

Tables

Introduction

This book focuses on three topics: general programming concepts and practices, the 8086 microprocessor with its assembly language, and logic design using the 8086 microprocessor. The discussion of general programming concepts and practices is relevant to any microprocessor, but the rest of the book is specific to the 8086. As such, this book becomes a how-to text for the 8086.

The prime source for the 8086 microprocessor is:

INTEL CORPORATION
3065 Bowers Avenue
Santa Clara, California 95051

The domestic second source is:

Advanced Micro Devices
901 Thompson Place
Sunnyvale, CA. 94086

The discussion of general programming concepts and practices begins by looking at the relationship between the programmer and a computer, since this is ultimately what determines the nature of any design project. Why do some programmers work with machine language while others program in assembly language or perhaps higher level languages? Different types of applications call for different types of programming. In each case good programming practices should be cultivated. A set of rules is described to achieve this goal, and two examples are used to illustrate programming projects.

The description of the 8086 microprocessor itself covers assembly language programming and hardware design.

For the assembly language programmer, the 8086 CPU architecture and the microprocessor's assembly language instruction set are described in detail.

For the hardware designer, timing and bus considerations are described for all signals normally input to the microprocessor or output by it. Single-bus and multi-bus architectures are covered. The standard Intel Multibus is described in detail.

WHAT THIS BOOK ASSUMES YOU KNOW

This book assumes that you have a working knowledge of general microprocessor concepts, and the ideas presented in *An Introduction to Microcomputers: Volume 1 — Basic Concepts,* 2nd Revision, by A. Osborne, Osborne/McGraw-Hill, 1980. Accordingly, this book does not cover any elementary material such as binary arithmetic, buffers, or CPU architecture fundamentals.

The 8086 microprocessor and its immediate support parts are described in great detail within this book. The 8089 I/O Processor is referred to, but it is not described in detail. For a detailed description of this part, see *The 8089 I/O Processor Handbook,* by A. Osborne, Osborne/McGraw-Hill, 1980.

Programming

ASSEMBLY LANGUAGE

What is the function of assembly language in a microcomputer system? How does it differ from machine language or higher level language programming? This chapter will answer these questions by assessing the various roles that assembly language plays.

In a very general sense, all microcomputer systems take the following form:

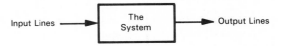

where the *input lines* are used to provide information to *the system*, and the *output lines* are used to transmit information from the system. Generally, the system consists of the following:

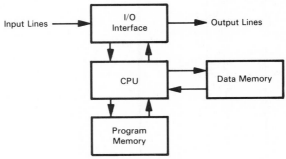

The *Central Processing Unit (CPU)* takes data, through the *I/O interface*, from the input lines; the CPU manipulates this data by executing instructions from its *program memory*. Results are output via the output lines. The CPU stores transient data in the *data memory*.

The CPU, the I/O interface, and the physical memories are the hardware portions of the system. The data that resides in the program memory is the software portion of the system or the program. Elements of the 8086 assembly language are combined to form an 8086 assembly language program, which is processed and stored in the program memory. Thus, the assembly language is used to specify the program that resides in the program memory.

To understand the concept of a program, consider an elementary point-of-sale terminal that has the following components:

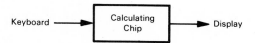

As keystrokes are entered, the *calculating chip* performs operations that convert each keystroke into a machine-acceptable code. The code could represent a number to be manipulated or a calculation to be performed. By interpreting the codes, the calculating chip performs required operations and indicates the results on the *display*.

The calculating chip accomplishes these operations by performing a sequence of tasks. For example, the calculating chip might perform the following sequence of tasks to determine whether or not a key has been pressed.

1.   Read in keyboard status byte

2.   Extract bit 3 from status byte
     (If bit 3 is 0, no key has been depressed. If bit 3 is 1, a key has been depressed.)

3.   Test bit 3
     (If bit 3 is 0, return to step 1. If bit 3 is 1, proceed to step 4.)

4.   Perform the next task. This might be a command to clear the key depressed bit or a command to disable the keyboard.

The complete set of tasks performed by the calculating chip, which would include all the translation and calculation operations, is known as the *algorithm*. An algorithm is composed of an ordered sequence of well-defined tasks that has a starting point and a criterion for stopping. Algorithms are usually expressed in the form of the example above, that is, English sentences that describe the tasks to be performed. Unfortunately, the CPU cannot respond to English sentences like "Read in Keyboard Status Byte." There must be a translation from the algorithm, which is composed of English sentences, into a form interpretable by the CPU, which will consist of a sequence of binary CPU instructions. The set of CPU instructions that is used to implement an algorithm is known as the *object program*.

The CPU executes instructions by analyzing units of information that consist of binary digits, namely digits that are either 1 or 0. Simple CPUs have two cycles, instruction fetch and instruction execute. In the instruction fetch cycle, the CPU generates the address of the location that contains the next instruction (unit of information) to be executed; the CPU requests that the memory provide it with the unit of information at that location. The memory produces the appropriate information. During the ensuing instruction execute cycle, the CPU analyzes the information and performs the appropriate action.

For example, assume the following data is present in an Intel 8086 system in order to perform the tasks shown in the previous example (Addresses and Instructions in binary).

Addresses	Instruction
0000	11100100
0001	00001010
0010	00100100
0011	00001000
0100	01110101
0101	11111010

If the 8086 begins executing at location 0000, it will read in the first instruction, located at 0000, and analyze it. The CPU determines that the instruction is an input instruction and that the next location, 0001, contains the device address from which the data should be read. Therefore the device code is 00001010. If the device at device code 00001010 produces the keyboard status byte, executing this 8086 instruction will read the keyboard status byte into the 8086's AL register. After executing the instruction at 0000, the next instruction executed will be the instruction at 0010. The instruction at 0010 uses information at 0011 to perform an AND with AL. This extracts bit 3, as in the second task in the previous example. The instruction at 0100 and 0101 determines whether bit 3 is 1 or 0, then takes appropriate action.

The CPU operates with 1s and 0s. People, however, are not as adept at using 1s and 0s. Therefore an intermediate step is provided between the CPU's 1s and 0s and people. This step is assembly language. Instead of directly entering 1s and 0s to the computer, people write programs in assembly language. Assembly language programs are converted to the appropriate 1s and 0s by a program known as the *assembler*. The user's program written in assembly language is known as the *source program*.

For example, instead of creating a program out of the 1s and 0s, as shown above, these lines of 8086 assembly code (source code) could be input to the assembler:

```
TOP:    IN      AL,0AH
        AND     AL,08H
        JNZ     TOP
```

The assembler converts the code to the 1s and 0s (object code) of the previous example.

Assembly language consists of a set of instructions that can be converted by the assembler into all the combinations of 1s and 0s that are executable by the system.

For example, the 8086 assembly language instruction:

```
AND     AL,08H
```

is converted by the assembler into these two bytes of object code:

```
00100100
00001000
```

This object code is interpreted by the 8086 CPU as an instruction to AND the contents of the AL register with the word 00001000.

For several reasons, assembly language programming will be more efficient than programming in binary code. First, it is clearly easier to write assembly code using assembly language instructions like AND, ADD, or XOR, rather than writing instructions like 01001000, 10100010, or 01110000. Second, the possibility for errors when entering CPU language instructions is unreasonably high. When writing assembly language, if errors are made, they will usually be caught by the assembler.

PROGRAMMING TASKS

Now consider the relationship between the programmer and the microcomputer system. To make a microcomputer system work, these are the tasks that programmers commonly perform:

1. Specification of the system. A specification includes a general discussion of all the functions that the system will provide, plus a description of the character of the inputs and outputs the system will handle.

2. Design of a computer program that implements the specification on a given system. This requires that the specification be translated into a series of steps that will allow the proposed system to cope with the particular application.

3. Implementation of the program design using a particular computer language. This phase contains three separate tasks: coding, debugging, and integration.

4. Testing of the complete system. Sets of test data are input to the system. The test data is designed to exercise program logic and hardware components.

5. Documentation of the system. Adequate documentation requires a description of how the entire system works, an operator's guide to the system, and complete documentation of the programs.

6. Maintenance of the system. A plan must exist for updating the system should new requirements or new equipment be necessary.

The above list is always used when programming any complex system. There exist, however, a limited number of cases where a 250-page specification, including three subsections on system expansion, a 50-page operator's guide, and a rigorous testing procedure are not necessary. These programs would appear in the following kinds of situations:

1. A serial I/O channel has failed. The hardware person is pointing a finger at the software, the software person finds it impossible to believe that such a squalid piece of hardware is not at fault. Hopefully, the solution is a short program that initializes the channel, then stands around reading and displaying data every time the serial I/O channel indicates data is available. It should be relatively easy to establish whether the hardware is working; if the hardware is working, there can be little doubt about what is not working.

2.   A small number of non-trivial calculations need to be made. Fortunately, a FORTRAN system is available. Hopefully, the solution is a 20-statement FORTRAN program that will produce the desired results.

In both of the above cases, very little specification or program design is committed to paper; these steps are performed in the programmer's head. No documentation is likely to be produced in these cases, and it is doubtful that maintenance will be necessary. It would be very wise, however, to remember that these cases are the exception to the rule.

The preceding list of tasks is used very effectively in environments where there are multiple numbers of programmers. Some programmers execute steps 1 and 2 exclusively, some programmers only perform the implementation process, some dedicate most of their time to testing program systems, others restrict their activities to documentation and/or maintenance, and still others perform some abstruse combination of tasks. In this way, programmers develop specialized skills that may allow for greater productivity. In most assembly language scenarios, however, the assembly language programmer is called upon to execute all of the above tasks. This book emphasizes an assembly language approach to the 8086, so a general discussion of all of these tasks follows.

SPECIFICATION OF THE SYSTEM

When the acquisition of a microcomputer system is initially considered, it results from one of two kinds of analysis:

1.   There is a specific problem that needs to be faced. For example, an aerospace manufacturer is producing a missile guidance system which needs an on-board computing system meeting certain size and speed requirements.

2.   There is a specific market for a new microcomputer system. For example, small businesses that could not previously afford computerized accounting will buy when microcomputer-based business systems prices fall low enough.

In either case, it is important to specify the exact function that the contemplated system will perform. In the first case, the nature of the problem will probably limit the system to performing a specific function. In the second case, it is easy to get carried away with the specification. For a small business system it is necessary to define precisely what accounting functions will be performed and exactly how many records of various types will be allowed in the system. Otherwise the microcomputer system could be assigned more tasks than the hardware has the capacity to handle.

Referring back to our simplistic model of a microcomputer system earlier in this chapter, the specification will define the following:

·   The inputs received by the system

·   The computation performed by the system

·   The outputs created by the system

Inputs

The specification of a microcomputer system's inputs depends a great deal on the level of programming being performed. An applications programmer, writing in BASIC, is very unlikely to be concerned with the type of commands that are given to a disk controller; rather, he will be concerned with the type of data on the disk, how records are laid out in a disk file, how the operating system constricts his manipulation of the disk file, etc. Since this book concerns itself with assembly language programming, and since any reasonable discussion of data base manipulation techniques would be beyond the scope of this book, we will emphasize the specification of the inputs and outputs at the hardware level.

At the hardware level, three parameters define the characteristics of an input channel. They are:

1. The data path width. Input may arrive one bit at a time from a processor controller error system. A parallel or serial I/O channel will input eight bits at a time. A floppy disk controller may transmit 1024 bits (128 bytes) of information upon request.

2. Data transfer speed and type (synchronous or asynchronous). Data may arrive every 200 microseconds from a real time clock. A serial I/O channel may input data asynchronously, every 10 milliseconds. An A/D converter in a control system may transfer data at an undetermined rate, but not faster than once every 500 milliseconds.

3. Accompanying control information. A floppy disk may generate an interrupt when data is available. A keyboard subsystem may set a status bit when data is available. An A/D converter may require that the system read input data and compare it with prior data to determine if new data is available.

After these parameters have been accounted for, it is important to specify how the input channels will be implemented.

An input channel usually has these three types of ports:

1. Data ports. These ports contain the data that will be passed to the processing section of the system.

2. Status ports. These ports contain information that indicates when data is available, whether or not errors have occurred at this channel, and other information concerning the outside world.

3. Control ports. These ports are typically used to initialize the channel's mode of operation and to control the way in which the channel represents itself to the outside world.

All three ports are not always present. In some cases, only the data port is present; in some cases, the channel is automatically initialized when power is applied, therefore rendering the control port unnecessary.

Computation

When specifying the computation section for a microcomputer system, there are three major areas of concern:

1. Processing raw data from the input section. This can take the form of a translation into a code more readily usable by the system (e.g., from ASCII to binary), separating a block of data into its component parts (e.g., a sector of data from a diskette into the file header, header checksum, data, and data checksum).

2. The actual algorithm implemented by the system. While a complete description of the actual algorithm is usually formed in the Program Design, this part of the specification should list all the major functions the system will perform.

3. Processing data for the output section. This processing may include translation of data to a form usable by the output devices (for example, translation of binary data into EBCDIC).

Outputs

Specification of to a microcomputer system's outputs requires an analysis very similar to the one performed for the input section. There are three major parameters for each output channel:

1. The number of bits to be transmitted by the channel.

2. Data transfer speed at the output channel.

3. Accompanying control information that tells the system when the transmitter is demanding more data, or is available to handle more data.

After these parameters have been accounted for, it is necessary to specify how the channel will be controlled. As with input channels, output channels usually have three ports of importance:

1. Data ports. These ports receive the data to be transmitted to the outside world.

2. Status ports. These ports contain information that indicates when data may be transmitted to the data ports, whether or not errors have occurred in the channel, and other information about the outside world.

3. Control ports. These ports are typically used to initialize the channel's mode of operation and to control the way in which the channel presents itself to the outside world.

As with input channels, all of these ports may not be necessary to control an output channel.

While performing the specification process for each of the three major sections, there are a number of useful techniques to remember:

1. In each section, make a list of the possible error conditions that could occur and the system's response to the error.

2. In each section, make a list of all functions that the section is to handle; e.g., make a list of all the input channels, all the computational functions, and all the output channels. Upon completion of a particular section, cross-check the section with your list, hopefully ensuring that all possibilities for the system have been recognized.

The first specification written is not necessarily the last; unless the problem at hand is fairly simple, it will almost certainly not be the last. The Program Design task and the Implementation task may reveal that certain functions cannot be performed given the selected hardware configuration. In this event, it may be necessary to modify the specification so that the hardware configuration is changed or the offending functions are modified so that the given hardware configuration can accomplish them.

PROGRAM DESIGN

Program Design involves taking the words in the specification and writing a sequence of English language steps that describe the method that will implement the specification. Ideally, these English language steps will provide a clear, simple description of what the system will accomplish. At this point, it may not be immediately obvious that a simple description is available for all systems. For example, one would not expect to find a concise description of IBM's DOS/VS operating system. While this may be true for the entire system, in the ideal situation a simple description should be available for each individual part of the system (for example, a printer driver or a multiword subtraction routine). When considering the number of parts in a very large system, one gets a glimmer of the program designer's task: breaking a large specification into a very large number of much smaller modules.

While engaged in the Program Design task, keep these suggestions in mind:

1. In the future the program may have to expand to provide more capabilities. Therefore the program should have built-in expansion facilities. Such facilities would include system subroutines, expandable tables and lists of data, a convenient, well-documented method for adding more functions to the system, and data structures that are reasonably flexible.

2. In a typical design, there is more than one method for accomplishing any given function. In some cases, limitations of the machine force one solution to be used. In other cases, time constraints force another solution. Since these factors, namely machine and time limitations, may not be well-known until the Implementation task, where the actual coding takes place, it is often wise to pursue alternate methods of solving a particular problem during the design stage. The benefits of finding alternatives at this stage are twofold: first, should the cited limitations prevent one solution, the other will already be available, and second, you may discover a more efficient solution in the process.

3. During the design, it is very important to specify what effect a particular module will have on other modules, and equally important to specify what effect other modules will have on that module. This interface between modules becomes important when debugging and integrating program modules.

When Program Design is complete, use the design to review the specification. Cross-checking the design with the specification may reveal flaws or omissions in the design and/or the specification. Be aware of the fact that the design should be reviewed on a regular basis. While the Implementation and Testing tasks are being performed, new information could become available that may force a reevaluation of the Program Design.

IMPLEMENTATION

The Implementation task consists of taking the English language algorithm specified in the Program Design task and making it work on a specific microcomputer system. There are two distinct efforts that go into the Implementation task:

1. Coding. This is the process of converting the English language steps created during the Program Design task into a particular computer language.

2. Debugging and Integrating. This is the process of removing errors from Program Design modules that have been converted by the coding phase into computer language, then integrating these modules into a working system.

Coding

The conversion of the Program Design into a particular computer language can be one of a programmer's easier tasks. If the Program Design function has been done correctly, each separate module will be described by a set of concise English language statements. Keep the following suggestions in mind while coding:

1. Try to use standard subroutines or programs whenever possible. Subroutines are very useful in that they can usually be debugged individually. After removing the bugs from the subroutines it is much easier to debug the main line of code. In addition, standard subroutines make it much easier to add new features to a system.

2. Document the code as clearly as possible. In addition to comment statements which describe individual modules or sections of code, labels which have mnemonic significance are of tremendous value. Some assemblers limit the opportunity to do this, as they restrict the number of characters in a label to six or fewer. In most cases, however, the ability to give extraordinary mnemonic value to the labels for both program and data areas is present and should be exercised to the fullest.

After each of the program design modules has been translated into the appropriate computer language, a series of checks should be made to ensure that the Coding task has been performed correctly and to avoid potential difficulties while performing the Debugging task. This series of checks, sometimes referred to as desk checking, is part of the Coding procedure, but also shares many elements with the Debugging task.

Checks that should be made include:

1. Ensure that the code contains all of the program design modules.

2. Ensure that all decisions included in the program design are included in the code. Check the logic at all of the decision points to ensure that the branches will be performed in the correct manner.

3. Ensure that each program design module has been provided with enough information to allow it to run correctly. This check can be performed for each module by determining what this module expects other modules to supply in terms of:

    -   The contents of the registers
    -   The contents of data structures
    -   The state of I/O devices used by this module
    -   Status settings

4. Ensure that each module provides subsequent modules with the correct information. This check can be performed for each module by determining what this module must supply to other modules in terms of:

    -   The contents of the registers
    -   The contents of data structures
    -   The state of I/O devices used by subsequent modules
    -   Status settings

5. Ensure that code has been entered into this module to handle the following situations:

    -   Errors
    -   Special cases
    -   Boundary cases
    -   Trivial cases

After these checks have been completed, the Debugging process begins.

Debugging and Integration

The Debugging and Integration task consists of removing errors from the code and then integrating debugged modules into a final working system. The functions performed during the Debugging task are very similar to the functions performed during desk checking. The Debugging task is different in that the task is performed while examining code that is running on the system hardware or a simulator for the system hardware. There are a series of tools used in the debugging process that are not available while desk checking. These tools are usually, but not always, provided by a software module called the Debugger. Typical features provided by a Debugger include:

- A Single Step facility. This facility allows a user to execute individual instructions following the program logic.

- Examine/Alter the contents of a memory location or a register. This facility allows the user to view memory/register contents and optionally alter them.

- A Breakpoint facility. This facility allows the user to interrupt the execution of the program which is being debugged, depending upon some condition. Typical breakpoint conditions include reference to a particular address, for either operand reference or instruction fetch.

When debugging a program, the following suggestions should be kept in mind:

1. Begin the debugging process by debugging commonly used or system subroutines. If the lowest-level routines in a software system are known to be functioning appropriately, discovering the source of an error is simplified, as it can be assumed that either the mainline code is in error or it is using the system subroutines in an incorrect fashion.

2. If it is possible, attempt to debug each area of the specification individually. It is appropriate to debug each section of the Input portion of the specification individually, followed by each section of the Computation portion of the specification, followed by each section of the Output portion of the specification. When sections of the specification are debugged individually, it is possible to view each section without interference from other portions of the system. Theoretically, when all of the individual modules have been debugged, the Integration phase will only need to debug the way in which the program modules interface to each other.

When all of the individual modules have been debugged, the Integration phase begins. In this phase, individual modules are combined into a subsystem and then debugged as a subsystem. For example, all the program design modules which affect the input portion of the program can be combined and debugged. As each subsystem is debugged, it can then be combined with other subsystems until the final system is debugged. As noted above, the only function that should be performed by the Integration phase is to ensure that the interface between modules (and eventually subsystems) is handled correctly.

At any one of the stages of Implementation, it may be necessary to return to the Program Design or even the Specification task. Consider these examples:

1. During the Coding stage, it becomes obvious that the code necessary to provide the specified functions will require more memory than has been provided for in the hardware design. First, return to the Program Design task to determine if alternate methods would allow for the use of less memory space. If this doesn't solve the problem, it is time to go back to the Specification task and reconfigure the system in some fashion.

2. During the Debugging phase, it is noticed that the system cannot respond quickly enough if an attempt is made to run all the devices the system is supposed to control. Note that this difficulty might not be obvious in the early stages of Debugging, since the input and output portions of the specification will typically be debugged separately until Integration is performed. In this case, return to the Coding task to see if the execution time for the input or output code can be reduced. If this fails, return to the Program Design task to determine if a more efficient algorithm is available. If, horror of horrors, this fails, return to the Specification stage to revamp the system.

TESTING

The Testing task consists of thoroughly exercising the system by introducing special sets of data and verifying that the correct results are produced. This task is very common in environments where there are large numbers of programmers. For example, before any self-respecting software house releases a new version of an operating system, the new system will have been thoroughly scrutinized. Before an automobile manufacturer releases a version of an on-board computer system, rigorous tests will have been performed. But testing is often overlooked in situations where few assembly language programmers exist. A major reason for the neglect of testing is that it can be very time consuming and therefore very expensive; in addition, it is not a well understood art.

Hopefully a significant portion of the Testing task can be accomplished during the debugging phase of the Implementation task. During the debugging section, for example, each module will be tested by executing the module using data that results in boundary conditions, thereby exercising the module's ability to make decisions. As an example, suppose a module is coded to perform one function if the first byte of a data block is in the range 30_{16} to 39_{16} inclusive, another function if the first byte is in the range 41_{16} to 46_{16} inclusive, and a third function if the byte is not in either of the ranges. Typical test data might well include blocks with a first byte of:

$$2F_{16}$$
$$30_{16}$$
$$39_{16}$$
$$3A_{16}$$
$$40_{16}$$
$$41_{16}$$
$$46_{16}$$
$$47_{16}$$
$$00_{16}$$
$$FF_{16}$$

These blocks would test the system's ability to distinguish between different types of data.

When deciding upon test data to submit to the system, keep the following suggestions in mind:

1. Three basic types of data to enter are:

    · The typical stream of data that the system normally would encounter

    · A series of boundary conditions that exercise the system's ability to perform decisions correctly

    · A random selection of data containing both legitimate and illegitimate data

2. The data should be presented to the system at the following speeds:

    · The typical data rate that the system would normally encounter

    · The fastest data rate at which the system is supposed to function

    · A random selection of data rates

DOCUMENTATION

The Documentation task consists of writing down all information pertinent to the system. There are three basic elements in the documentation of a system:

1. Documentation of the program. As was noted in the discussion of the Implementation task, it is very important to explain how the code works, module by module, and in some cases why the code works the way it does. This sort of documentation allows new readers of the code to easily familiarize themselves with the code. In addition, if they desire to alter the code, good documentation may allow reasonable, informed decisions on how the alteration should be made. Program documentation helps refresh the memory of the original coder, who may be examining a program written in the distant past.

2. A System Guide. The System Guide should include a description of the program's design, a description of how to modify the program, and a brief summary of what the system expects to see in the outside world; i.e., what is driving the input lines and what is receiving the data on the output lines. Hopefully, a System Guide will be fairly simple to put together, as the major elements should have been written up, at least in note form, during the previous tasks.

3. A User's Guide. This may be the most important piece of documentation. If the code is very well documented, and if a superlative System Guide has been written, then other programmers may be able to modify or improve the program; but if there is no User's Guide, it may be impossible for anyone to use the program, in which case no one will care to modify or improve the code, and all the effort will have been wasted. User's Guides are especially important in systems where external users may write programs that interface with the system. In this case, it is of extreme importance to notify users, typically through an update of the User's Guide, of any revisions or additions to the system.

MAINTENANCE

The Maintenance task consists of altering the program to accommodate new equipment or new processing requirements; in essence, keeping the program functioning in a changing environment. The Maintenance task can be simple or complex, depending on the change in the environment. Examples of simple tasks include:

1.   A new piece of hardware is being installed in the system, replacing an outmoded piece of equipment. The I/O interface is remarkably similar to the old hardware; in fact, the change involves only the transposition of a few status lines. In this case, the Maintenance task would involve altering a few lines of code in the program, debugging the code using the new hardware, and writing the appropriate additions to the documentation.

2.   System output is going to a diskette file which will, at some later time, be processed by a more sophisticated system. A new operating system release on the more sophisticated system requires that two previously unused bytes in a diskette file be used for some more significant purpose. Since this possibility was considered during the Program Design phase, the Maintenance task in this case will only require minor alterations to the Computation section of the Specification task and the associated Program Design, Implementation, and Documentation tasks.

More complex tasks might include:

1.   A new piece of hardware is being added to the system. In contrast to the previous example, this equipment is nothing like other system equipment; in fact, it makes new demands on the interrupt structure, the timing of the system, and the processing abilities of the system. In this case, the Maintenance task may require extensive effort in each one of the programming tasks that has been identified.

2.   The marketing department has decided to attach a veritable phalanx of 80-megabyte disk drives to your microprocessor based system. The Maintenance task in this case would probably include all of the programming tasks from Specification to Documentation, or conceivably an orderly removal of the appropriate marketing personnel from the gene pool.

The ability to perform the Maintenance task with relative ease is directly proportional to the care which was taken in the Program Design and Implementation stages. If the Program Design stage left no easy way to add features or provided no general system modules, then additions to the system will probably prove difficult at best. If, during the Implementation process, no reasonable documentation on the hows and whys of the program were provided, introducing new elements of the Program Design into the code will be very tortuous indeed.

Some Program Examples

A SORT PROGRAM

Consider the specification and program design tasks for a sort program module. This program reads data records from a file on a tape drive, sorts keys extracted from the records, then writes a key file to the tape following the data file. The actual code for this program is presented in Chapter 6.

In this exmple, a very simple I/O interface will be assumed. A general block diagram for the I/O interface is shown here:

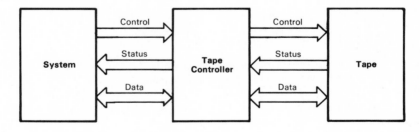

The tape controller transfers 128-byte blocks of data to and from the tape. The controller adds parity bits (for a 9-track tape) and a checksum to a block written to the tape. The controller processes this error-detecting information when a read operation is performed and sets error bits accordingly.

Transfers to and from the tape are performed as follows:

1. The system requests a read or write operation.

2. The system waits for the controller to be ready to transfer a byte of data.

3. The system transfers a byte to/from the controller's data port.

4. If 128 bytes have been transferred, the tape controller sets a flag indicating that the entire block has been transmitted. If the transfer is not complete, the system returns to step 2.

The tape controller will be run with a very simple command structure. The following command byte is sent to the tape controller's command port to initiate action by the tape controller:

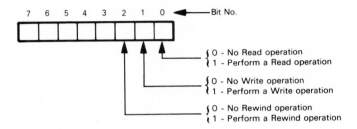

After the system sends a command to the tape controller, the system reads a status byte from the controller. This byte is of the following form:

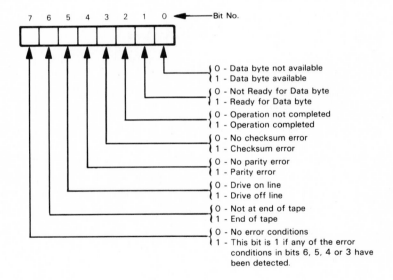

If the system has issued a command for a read operation or a write operation, the appropriate bit (bit 0 for a read operation or bit 1 for a write operation) is sampled. If the tape controller is ready to send/receive data, the system performs a read or write operation from the tape controller's data port. After 128 read/write operations, bit 2 will become a 1, signalling the completion of the operation.

If the system has issued a command for a rewind operation, bit 2 of the status port will indicate that the rewind operation has been completed.

INPUTS

Given the previous description of the characteristics of the tape controller, input parameters may be specified as follows:

1. Data path width. Data arrives from the tape controller one byte at a time. Each read command from the system allows a 128-byte block to be read from the tape.

2. Data transfer speed. In this example, the data will be arriving synchronously. After the Data Byte Available bit goes high, the data may be input at the maximum CPU rate.

3. Accompanying control information. In this example, the tape controller does not interrupt the system. The system reads the tape controller status port to determine if data is available.

COMPUTATION

In this section of the specification, the following elements will be considered:

· The format of the data records that are read from the tape

· The method by which the keys will be sorted

· The format of the data records that are written to the tape.

INPUT RECORD FORMAT

Each data record read from the tape will consist of 128 bytes. There are three fields of interest in each data record read from the tape:

1. Record number. This is a two-byte field which uniquely identifies the record. Record numbers may be in the range 0000_{16} - $FFFE_{16}$. Record numbers $FFFF_{16}$ designates an end-of-file record.

2. Key. This is a ten-byte field. This field may contain data describing the record, and does not have to be unique to the particular record. In this example, we will assume that these ten bytes represent an individual's last name.

3. Data. The remaining 116 bytes in a record contain data.

These three fields are organized in the following manner for all records:

Byte No.	0		Record number (high-order)
	1		Record number (low-order)
	2		Key (most significant byte)
	.	.	.
	.	.	.
	.	.	.
	11		Key (least significant byte)
	12		Data
	.	.	.
	.	.	.
	.	.	.
	127		Data

Note that the size of the data record is conveniently equal to the size of the block that is read from the tape.

SORT METHOD

The sorting method used will be the diminishing increment sort, or Shell sort. This is a commonly used sort algorithm which is described in detail in *Sorting and Searching*, by D.W. Knuth. The collating sequence used will be the ASCII collating sequence. The keys will be sorted in ascending order.

The basic philosophy of the diminishing increment sort is to sort progressively larger sublists using a straight insertion technique until the final pass, when the entire list is sorted using straight insertion. The advantage of this sort is that as the sublists are sorted, the entire list becomes more ordered. Therefore, when the entire list is sorted during the final pass, fewer exchanges are necessary, and that reduces execution time. For example, consider this 10-element list:

10   13   8   14   19   11   6   13   7

The first sorting pass might sort the following lists:

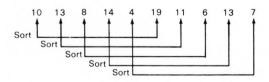

into   10 11 6 13 4 19 13 8 14 7

The second pass might sort the following lists:

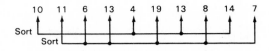

into   4 7 6 8 10 11 13 13 14 19

And the final pass would sort the entire list.

The basic algorithm is:

Given: N records. In this case, the records are 12 bytes long and consist of a record number and a key field.

There are two variables of interest in this algorithm.

Increment: In the diminishing increment sort, a set of increments is chosen that will help determine the number of elements in a sublist. In this case, the increments will be

$$N/2, N/4, \ldots, 1$$

We will call the variable that contains N/2, then N/4, then finally 1 (for the final pass, which sorts the entire list) the increment.

Subsort counter: For each value of increment, i.e., for each sorting pass, this variable counts from (N − Increment) to N. This determines the number of sorts that are performed in each pass.

The algorithm operates as follows:

1. Set Increment = N
    Do Steps 2 through 12 until Increment = 0.

2. Increment = Increment/2
    Sort each sublist using a straight insertion sort.

3. Subsort counter = N − Increment
    Do Steps 4 through 12 until Subsort counter = N + 1

4. Subsort counter = Subsort counter + 1

5. Keytemp = Key (Subsort counter)

6. Recordtemp = Record (Subsort counter)

7. Index = Subsort counter − Increment

8. Compare Keytemp with Key (Index)
    If Keytemp ≥ Key (Index), then go to Step 12 else go to Step 9

9. Record (Index + Increment) = Record (Index)

10. Index = Index − Increment

11. If Index > 0, then go to Step 8 else go to Step 12

12. Record (Index + Increment) = Recordtemp

OUTPUT RECORD FORMAT

Each data record written to the tape consists of 12 bytes. There are two fields of interest in each data record written to the tape:

1. Record number. This is a two-byte field which is identical to the record number field in the input record format.

2. Key. This is a ten-byte field which is identical to the key field in the input record format.

These records are organized as follows:

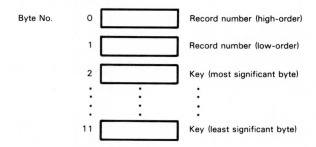

Note that 128, the number of bytes in a tape block, is not a multiple of 12, the number of bytes in an output record. Therefore some algorithm must be used to pack the output records into a tape block. This algorithm is discussed later, in the program design section.

OUTPUTS

Given the previous description of the tape controller's characteristics, output parameters may be specified as follows:

1. Data path width. Data is sent to the tape controller one byte at a time. Each write command from the system allows a 128-byte block to be written to the tape.

2. Data transfer speed. In this example, the data is sent synchronously. After the Ready for Data Byte bit goes high, data may be sent to the controller at the maximum CPU rate.

3. Accompanying control information. In this example, the tape controller does not interrupt the system to signify that it is ready for data. The system reads the tape controller status port to determine if the tape controller is ready for data.

ERROR PROCESSING

In this example, the only errors of concern are tape errors. These errors will be processed by the read/write tape subroutine. This processing will be discussed in Chapter 6.

PROGRAM DESIGN

By examining the task that the program will perform, it appears that there are three major functions that will comprise the program:

- Reading records from the tape and extracting the key from each record

- Sorting the keys

- Writing the sorted keys back to the tape.

None of the above modules is very complex, therefore flowcharts will be used to describe each of them.

Read from Tape

The module that reads the tape contains only one decision point. As the module is reading records from the tape, it examines each record to ascertain whether or not the record is an end-of-file record (record number = $FFFF_{16}$). If an end-of-file record is detected, control is passed to the sort module; otherwise the record number and key will be extracted from the record and saved in a temporary area where they will be processed by the sort module. The next record is then read from the tape.

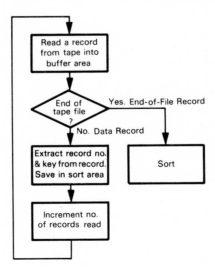

Sort

The sort module implements the sorting algorithm given in the specification.

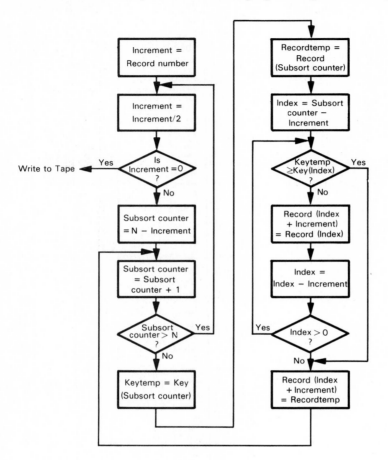

Write to Tape

The module which writes the key file to the tape is not as straightforward as the module which reads from the tape. There are two decision points in this module. The first decision has to do with filling a tape block. Since it would not be very efficient in terms of tape space to write a 128-byte block for each 12-byte record, records are organized in a buffer until 128 or more bytes have been saved. When 128 bytes have been saved, the decision point allows the buffer to be flushed to the tape. The second decision point involved decrements the number of records. When all of the output records have been moved, an end-of-file record (record number = $FFFF_{16}$) is appended to the buffer and then written to tape.

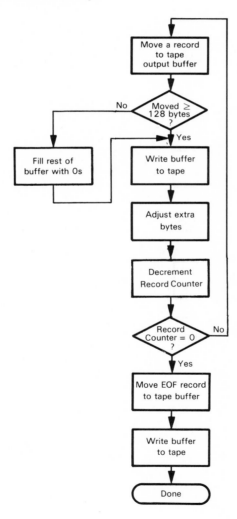

The 8086 Assembly Language Instruction Set

The 8086 is Intel's first 16-bit microprocessor. When introduced in 1978 it was significantly more powerful than any prior microprocessor.

The 8086 assembly language instruction set is upward compatible with 8080A — but at the source program level only. That is to say, every 8080A assembly language instruction can be converted into one or more 8086 assembly language instructions. There is no reason why anyone would try to convert 8086 assembly language instructions, one at a time, into one or more 8080A assembly language instructions, but if you did, you would soon become hopelessly tangled in conflicting memory allocations and special translation rules. That is why we say that the 8086 and 8080A assembly language instruction sets are "upward" compatible.

The 8086 and 8080A assembly language instruction sets are not compatible at the object code level, which means that 8080A programs stored in read-only memory are useless in an 8086 system.

The 8085 and 8080A assembly language instruction sets are identical, with the exception of the 8085 RIM and SIM instructions. The 8085 RIM and SIM instructions cannot be translated into 8086 instructions. This is because the RIM and SIM instructions use the serial I/O logic of the 8085, which has no 8086 counterpart. Without the RIM and SIM instructions the 8085 and 8080A assembly language instruction sets are identical; therefore the 8086 assembly language instruction set must also be upward compatible with the 8085 assembly language instruction set — apart from the RIM and SIM instructions.

The 8085 and 8080A assembly language instruction sets are object code compatible — with the exception of the 8085 RIM and SIM instructions. That is to say, a program existing in read-only memory could be used with one microprocessor or the other.

The 8080A assembly language instruction set is a subset of the Z80 assembly language instruction set. That is to say, the Z80 will execute an 8080A object program — but the reverse is not true. The 8080A cannot execute Z80 programs when the full Z80 instruction set is used. The 8086 assembly language instruction set is not upward compatible with the Z80 assembly language instruction set.

As a historical note, it is worth mentioning that the 8008 microprocessor, which preceded the 8080A, was also compatible only at the source program level. That is to say, there is an 8080A assembly language instruction for every 8008 assembly language instruction, but the two microprocessor object code sets are not the same.

The various instruction set compatibilities that we have described may be illustrated as follows:

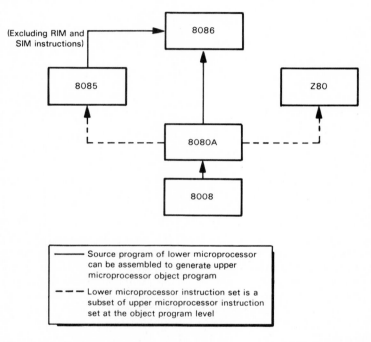

These are the most interesting innovations to be found in 8086 hardware design:

1. 8086 Central Processing Unit logic has been divided into an Execution Unit (EU) and a Bus Interface Unit (BIU). These two halves operate asynchronously. The Bus Interface Unit handles all interfaces with the external bus; it generates external memory and I/O addresses and has a 6-byte instruction object code queue. Whenever the EU needs to access memory or an I/O device, it makes a bus access request to the Bus Interface Unit. Providing the Bus Interface Unit is not currently busy, it acknowledges the bus access request from the EU. When the Bus Interface Unit has no active pending bus access requests from the EU, it performs instruction fetch machine cycles to fill the 6-byte instruction object code queue. The CPU takes its instruction object codes from the front of the queue. Thus instruction fetch time is largely eliminated.

2. The 8086 has been designed to work in a wide range of microcomputer system configurations, ranging from a simple one-CPU system to a multiple-CPU network. To support this wide flexibility, a number of 8086 pins output alternate signals. This may be illustrated as follows:

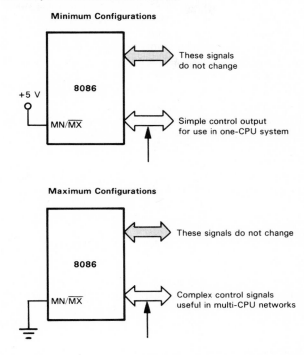

Minimum Configurations

These signals do not change

+5 V

8086

MN/$\overline{\text{MX}}$

Simple control output for use in one-CPU system

Maximum Configurations

These signals do not change

8086

MN/$\overline{\text{MX}}$

Complex control signals useful in multi-CPU networks

The same pins output these two sets of signals, based on a level of MN/$\overline{\text{MX}}$. This wholesale reallocation of signals was a highly imaginative and innovative first for the microprocessor industry.

3. The 8086 has built-in logic to handle bus access priorities in multi-CPU configurations. (This is not a new concept; National Semiconductor's SC/MP has had it for years.)

4. In multi-CPU configurations, each 8086 CPU can have its own local memory, while simultaneously sharing common memory. The common memory may be shared by all CPUs, or by selected CPUs.

5. The 8086 has been designed to compete effectively in program intensive applications that have been the domain of the minicomputer. Up to a million bytes of external memory can be addressed directly. All memory addressing is base relative; this memory addressing technique naturally generates relocatable object programs. (Relocatable object programs can be moved from one memory address space to another and re-executed without modification.) Also, since the 8086 utilizes stack-relative addressing, re-entrant programs are easily written. (Re-entrant programs can be interrupted in mid-execution and re-executed. For example, a subroutine which calls itself is re-entrant; a

program which can be interrupted in mid-execution by an external interrupt, and then re-executed within the interrupt service routine, is also re-entrant.)

6.   The 8086 uses prefix instructions that modify the interpretation of the next instruction's object code.

The 8086, like its predecessor, the 8080A, is really one component of a multiple-chip microprocessor configuration.

In addition to the 8086 microprocessor itself, you must have an 8284 Clock Generator/Driver. You could create the required clock signal using alternative logic, but it would be neither practical nor economical to do so.

The third device necessary in some 8086 microprocessor configurations is the 8288 Bus Controller.

You will usually have an 8288 Bus Controller between an 8086 and its system bus (or busses), just as you will usually have an 8228 System Bus Controller between an 8080A and its system bus. In the case of the 8086, however, you can dispense with the 8288 Bus Controller in single-bus configurations — and pay no penalty for it.

Chapters 6, 7, 8, and 9 discuss basic 8086 hardware, single-CPU configurations, the Multibus* and multi-CPU configurations.

AN I/O DRIVER

Next we will specify a program module which interfaces a system to a serial input/output channel. We will also look at design tasks associated with creating this program module.

The following is a general block diagram for a serial input/output channel:

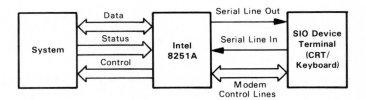

In this example, the serial input/output (SIO) channel is an Intel 8251A Programmable Communication Interface. It is assumed that the 8251A is connected to a communications terminal; the communications terminal has a CRT on which it displays data transmitted by the system. Data from a keyboard is transmitted by the channel to the system. Data is not buffered at the terminal on input or output. Data is transmitted and received asynchronously.

---

* Multibus is a registered trademark of Intel Corporation.

The program module, which will also be referred to as the driver, connects operating system software with the 8251A. This may be illustrated as follows:

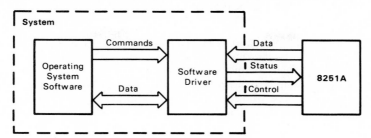

Operating system software sends commands and/or data to the I/O driver program module; this can be handled in a variety of ways. They include:

1. Placing the command or data in a register. For example, one register could be assigned to holding commands, while data passes through another register.

2. Using a task block. The task block could contain the command and data or the command and a pointer to the data. The task block could be located at a fixed memory location, or it could be pointed to by one of the registers.

3. Via the stack. System software could push the equivalent of a task block (i.e., commands and data/pointers) onto the stack.

Selecting one of the above techniques is usually a processor-dependent decision. Since the present discussion is not processor-dependent, the rationale for selecting a parameter passing technique will be deferred to a later chapter.

INPUTS

The SIO device used in this example is an Intel 8251A. This device requires the following input specifications:

1. Data path width. The 8251A allows 5-, 6-, 7-, or 8-bit characters. In this example, an 8-bit data path is required by the device for commands and status. To allow for a future system using a different size data path, the program design will allow the size of the data path to be specified.

2. Data transfer speed. In this example, the data will be transferred asynchronously. Only the maximum data transfer rate can be specified. In this example, 9600 baud is specified as the maximum data transfer rate.

3. Handshaking protocol. In this example the SIO channel does not interrupt the microprocessor, rather the microprocessor polls the channel to determine if data is available.

Next the I/O driver must consider actual I/O channel operations. In addition to data transfer, controls must be transmitted to the I/O channel, in this case an 8251A, and status must be received from it.

A data port is configured as follows:

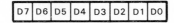

Data is known to be available at this I/O port when an appropriate status bit has been set to 1. In the case of the 8251, the RxRDY (Receiver Ready) bit of the status port must be set to 1.

The 8251A is initialized to a known state by writing information to the control port. At least two bytes of control information are necessary to initialize the 8251A. Control information is sent in the following sequence:

1. Mode Select Byte
2. Sync Character (Synchronous mode only)
3. Sync Character (Synchronous mode only)
4. Command Select Byte

In this example, the 8251A will be operating in the asynchronous mode, therefore a two-byte initialization sequence is needed; it is:

1. Mode Select Byte
2. Command Select Byte

The format for the Mode Select Byte is:

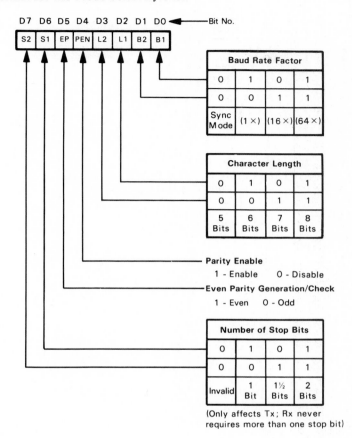

Parity Enable
1 - Enable   0 - Disable

Even Parity Generation/Check
1 - Even   0 - Odd

(Only affects Tx; Rx never
requires more than one stop bit)

The format for the Command Select Byte is:

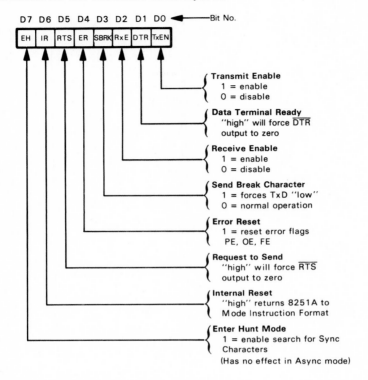

Given the preceding specifications, the Mode Select Byte will be:

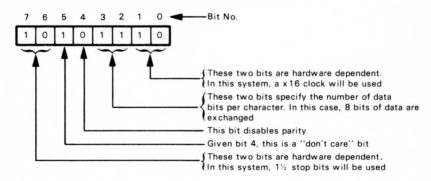

The initial Command Select Byte will be:

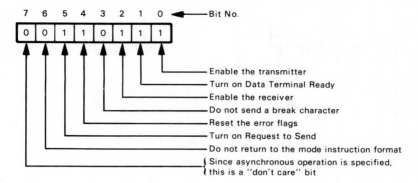

Additional features of 8251A programming are discussed during the implementation section in Chapter 6.

The status port supplies information on the state of the 8251, and the state of the device to which it is connected.

When a byte is read from the status port, the following information is transferred to the system.

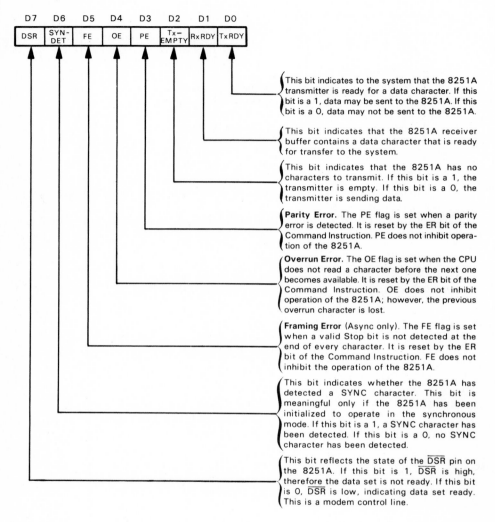

This bit indicates to the system that the 8251A transmitter is ready for a data character. If this bit is a 1, data may be sent to the 8251A. If this bit is a 0, data may not be sent to the 8251A.

This bit indicates that the 8251A receiver buffer contains a data character that is ready for transfer to the system.

This bit indicates that the 8251A has no characters to transmit. If this bit is a 1, the transmitter is empty. If this bit is a 0, the transmitter is sending data.

Parity Error. The PE flag is set when a parity error is detected. It is reset by the ER bit of the Command Instruction. PE does not inhibit operation of the 8251A.

Overrun Error. The OE flag is set when the CPU does not read a character before the next one becomes available. It is reset by the ER bit of the Command Instruction. OE does not inhibit operation of the 8251A; however, the previous overrun character is lost.

Framing Error (Async only). The FE flag is set when a valid Stop bit is not detected at the end of every character. It is reset by the ER bit of the Command Instruction. FE does not inhibit the operation of the 8251A.

This bit indicates whether the 8251A has detected a SYNC character. This bit is meaningful only if the 8251A has been initialized to operate in the synchronous mode. If this bit is a 1, a SYNC character has been detected. If this bit is a 0, no SYNC character has been detected.

This bit reflects the state of the $\overline{\text{DSR}}$ pin on the 8251A. If this bit is 1, $\overline{\text{DSR}}$ is high, therefore the data set is not ready. If this bit is 0, $\overline{\text{DSR}}$ is low, indicating data set ready. This is a modem control line.

COMPUTATION

What sort of functions should the driver provide? Will data be translated on input and/or output? These are the functions a real I/O driver will provide:

1. Initialize the channel. When power is applied to the system, the 8251A powers up in an unknown state. The I/O driver will put the channel into a known state.

2. Input a single character. When this function is requested, the driver reads the status port and waits until data is available. When data is available, the driver reads the data port and passes the information back to the system.

3. Output a single character. When this function is requested, the system must pass the character to be output, or a pointer to that character, to the driver. The driver reads the status port and waits until the transmitter is available. When the transmitter is available, the driver will transfer the specified character to the data port.

4. Check the channel's status. Perhaps the system does not need to read a character, rather it needs to know if a character is available. Under such circumstances the system will read the status port contents.

5. Send control information to the channel. The system may need to alter the state of the channel, for example, to allow the channel to check for parity errors.

6. Input a series of characters from the channel. You may wish to input characters until some terminating condition is detected. For example, a carriage return may constitute a terminating condition, or a fixed number of characters may have to be input. Five numeric characters constitute a ZIP Code, for example. The I/O driver will read data from the channel. This involves waiting for data to be available, then reading the information present at the data port saving the data in some designated place in memory, then testing to determine if the terminating condition has been reached.

7. Output a series of characters to the channel. The system may wish to output a series of characters until a terminating condition is detected. Possible termination conditions might include either the detection of a predetermined end-of-string character or the output of a specific number of characters. The I/O driver will test for the termination condition; if the terminating condition is not detected, the I/O driver will load data from a specified memory location, and send the data to the channel.

OUTPUTS

The 8251A uses the control information to define the channel's output characteristics. These output specifications need to be defined:

1. Data path width. The 8251A allows data units to consist of either 5, 6, 7, or 8 bits. In this system, 8 data bits will be transmitted.

2. Data transfer speed. In this case, the maximum data rate will be 9600 baud.

3. Handshaking protocol. In this example, the 8251A will not interrupt the system, rather the system reads the 8251 Status register to determine whether the 8251A is ready to transmit more data.

We have already described the Data and Control/Status ports of the 8251A. Data may be sent to the channel when the TxRDY bit (Transmitter Ready) of the Status register is 1.

PROGRAM DESIGN

In this section, none of the specific modules will be complex. Given this fact, we will use flowcharts to describe each module of the I/O driver.

Initialization

The Initialization routine contains only one major decision point. If the standard initialization is requested, a pointer to a standard initialization sequence will identify the information which must be sent to the control port. As an alternative, a "custom" initialization sequence may be executed; in this case the user will have to provide the initialization sequence and a pointer to it.

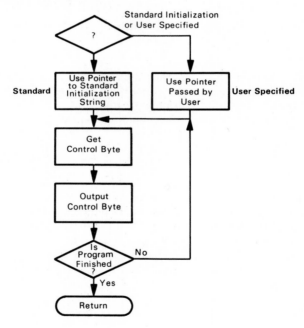

Input a Single Character

The single-character input routine flowchart is illustrated below; it calls a read channel status routine, waits for data to become available, reads the data from the data port, and returns.

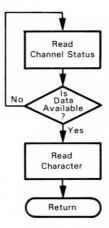

Two considerations not included in the design of the single-character input routine are:

- Handling of 8251 errors. When the read channel status routine is called, the error bits within the 8251 Status register can be examined. If an 8251 error is detected, an appropriate error code is returned to the I/O driver by the single-character input routine.

- Timeout errors. The driver initializes an appropriate register/memory location to serve as a timeout clock, then decrements the contents of this location each time the read channel status routine is called. If the contents of the timeout register/memory location decrement to zero, a timeout error code is returned to the calling routine.

If these considerations are added to the single-character input routine, the flowchart must be modified as follows:

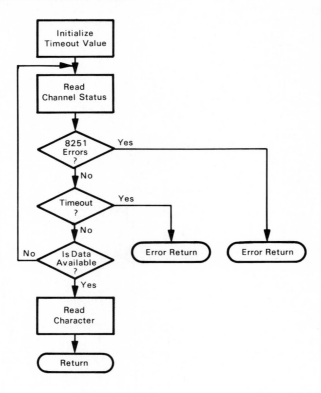

Output a Single Character

The single-character output routine flowchart is illustrated below; it calls a read channel status routine, waits for the transmitter to be available, writes a character to the data port, then returns.

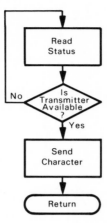

As with the input routine, error and timeout considerations are not included in the initial design, as illustrated above. In the case of the 8251A, there are no error conditions to check for since the 8251A reports no transmission errors in its Status register. But a timeout check could be included and would modify the program flowchart as follows:

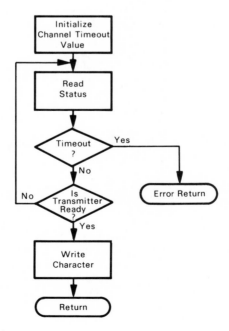

Check Channel Status and Send Control Information

The read channel status routine and the send control information routine each require a very simple flowchart. They may be illustrated as follows:

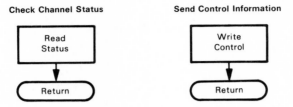

Input a Series of Characters

A multiple-character input routine utilizes the single-character input routine to read data. On return from the single-character input routine, a check for errors is made. If the single-character input routine detects an error, this error is passed back to the calling routine. After saving the character in a location specified by the calling program, the multi-character input routine looks for a termination condition. If the routine has either read the number of characters specified by the calling program or has read a termination character, the multiple-character input routine will return to the calling program.

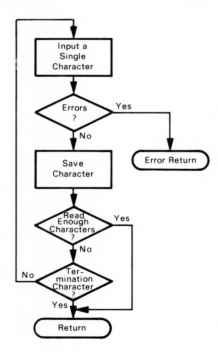

Output a Series of Characters

The multiple-character output routine loads a character from a user specified location. If the character is the termination character, the multi-character output routine returns to the calling program. Otherwise, the character is sent to the single-character output routine. When the single-character output routine returns, a check for timeout is made. If a timeout was detected, it is passed back to the calling routine. The multiple-character output routine then checks to see if it has output the specified number of characters; if it has, it returns to the calling program.

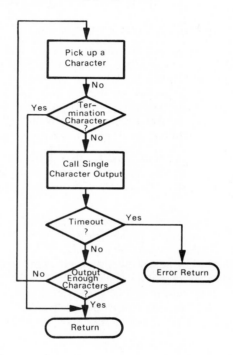

THE 8086 INSTRUCTION SET

The 8086 instruction set has a complexity that is typical for the new generation of 16-bit microprocessors. The 8086 instruction set consists of approximately 70 basic instructions, with up to 30 addressing modes available for memory reference instructions.

Any description of a CPU's instruction set should include these basic types of information:

1. What is the CPU configuration; i.e., what registers and statuses are available? What is the primary use for each register?

2. What instructions are available? Obviously, there must be some comprehensive listing of the instruction set with an associated discussion of each instruction's function. This listing may be organized in any one of a number of ways. In this chapter, we list the instructions alphabetically to help you find individual instructions. In the next chapter we list instructions according to function (e.g., all the arithmetic operations are discussed in one section) which allows you to examine instructions by type or group.

3. What data types does the CPU handle? A simple CPU may require all data to be handled in one form, perhaps as bytes. A more flexible CPU may give you the option of addressing data as individual bits, bytes, 16-bit words, and 32-bit long words.

4. What operand source and destination addressing options are allowed? A simple microprocessor may allow memory to be addressed only by instructions that move data between memory and CPU registers, while all operations on data require operands to reside in CPU registers. A more complex microprocessor may allow one operand to be fetched from memory while the other operand resides in a CPU register. In some cases, the CPU may allow both operands to reside in memory. Available memory addressing options must be evaluated when determining the significance of memory operands.

5. What addressing modes are available for which instructions? Knowing which addressing modes are available for a given instruction is a key to the effective utilization of the instruction set. However, should we attempt to describe each possible addressing mode for each instruction, this book would only be available in 15 volume sets. Therefore, a section on Addressing Modes precedes the listing of the instruction set.

6. How do various groups of instructions affect the CPU's status register? To evaluate any sort of conditional expression in assembly language, you must know how to translate the conditional into assembly language. Knowing how instructions affect status flags allows a programmer to write conditional expressions in assembly language.

7. In certain cases, other information may be important; e.g., the number of cycles that a particular instruction takes to execute or the number of program memory bytes the instruction occupies. In this case, each instruction's description will specify the number of cycles required for execution. The number of bytes each instruction requires, however, is in some cases very dependent on the addressing mode specified.

For our discussion of the 8086 instruction set, we will proceed in the following order:

1. Discussion of the 8086 registers and the 8086 Status register, and discussion of how status is affected by various groups of instructions. The Status register is also referred to as the Flags register or the Program Status Word.

2. Discussion of the 8086 addressing modes.

3. Discussion of each 8086 instruction. This section will be preceded by a summary of the symbols and terms used to describe each instruction.

8086 REGISTERS AND FLAGS

The 8086 has four 16-bit general purpose registers, two 16-bit Pointer registers, two 16-bit Index registers, one 16-bit program counter, four 16-bit Segment registers and one 16-bit Flags register. These registers may be illustrated as follows:

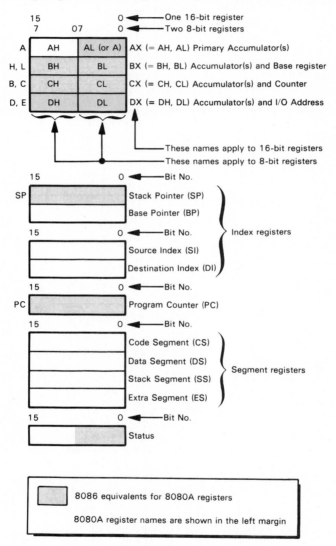

GENERAL PURPOSE REGISTERS

The general purpose registers may be referenced as two separate 8-bit registers. This may be illustrated as follows:

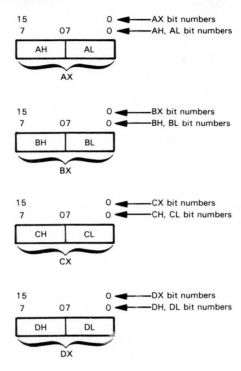

This is an advantage in that instead of performing a 16-bit operation on 8-bit quantities, which may take more time and memory space than an 8-bit operation, an 8-bit operation may be performed. For example, if you want to initialize a register with 200_{10} and then decrement it to 0 based on subsequent events, an 8-bit register will certainly suffice.

The general purpose registers can be used as operands in all the 8- or 16-bit arithmetic/logical operands.

The AX register serves as the primary accumulator. This register has two unique characteristics. All I/O operations are performed through this register, and operations utilizing immediate data typically require less memory space when performed on this register. In addition, some string operations and arithmetic instructions require use of this register.

The AL register generally corresponds to the 8080 A register.

The BX register is referred to as the Base register. This is the only general purpose register which is used in the calculation of 8086 memory addresses. All memory references which use this register in the calculation of the memory address use the DS register as the default segment register. The BX register generally corresponds to the 8080A HL register; the BH register corresponds to the 8080 H register and the BL register corresponds to the 8080 L register.

The CX register is referred to as the Count register. This register is decremented by string and loop operations. CX is typically used to control the number of iterations a loop will perform. It is also used for multiple bit shifts and rotates. This register generally corresponds to the 8080 BC register.

The CH register corresponds to the 8080 B register. The CL register corresponds to the 8080 C register.

The DX register is referred to as the Data register, mostly for mnemonic reasons. This register provides the I/O address for some I/O instructions, a function no other 8086 register performs. This register generally corresponds to the 8080A DE register.

The DH register corresponds to the 8080 D register. The DL register corresponds to the 8080 E register. The D register is also used for arithmetic operations, including multiplication and division.

POINTER REGISTERS

The Pointer registers are used to access data in the stack segment. They may be used as operands in all 16-bit arithmetic/logical operations.

The SP register, referred to as the stack pointer, allows the implementation of a stack in memory. All references to the SP for memory addressing use the SS register as the Segment register. This register generally corresponds to the 8080 SP register.

The BP register, referred to as the base pointer, allows data to be accessed in the stack segment. Typically, this register is used to reference parameters that have been passed via the stack.

INDEX REGISTERS

The Index registers are used to access data in data memory. The Index registers are used extensively by the string operations. They may be used as operands in all the 16-bit arithmetic/logical operations.

SEGMENT REGISTERS

The Segment registers are included in all memory addressing calculations. Each Segment register defines a 64K block of memory in the 8086 memory addressing space, which is referred to as the Segment register's current segment; e.g., the DS register defines a 64K segment referred to as the current data segment.

The CS register is also known as the Code Segment register. During each instruction fetch, the program counter contents are added to the CS register contents in order to compute the memory address for the instruction to be fetched.

The DS register is also known as the Data Segment register. Every data memory reference is taken relative to the Data Segment register, with three exceptions:

1. Stack addresses are computed using the stack pointer.

2. Data memory addresses computed using the BP register are taken relative to the stack segment.

3. String operations (which use the DI register in the address calculation) are taken relative to the extra segment.

The SS register is also called the Stack Segment register. All data memory references that use the SP or BP register in the address calculation are taken relative to the SS register. Therefore all stack-oriented instructions (e.g., PUSH, POP, CALL, RET, and INT) use the SS register as the Segment register.

The ES register is also referred to as the Extra Segment register. String operations compute memory addresses using the DI register that are taken relative to the ES register.

The use of segment registers is typically implied by the instruction, however a mechanism will be discussed later which allows the implied Segment register to be overridden in most circumstances.

FLAGS REGISTER

The 8086 has one 16-bit Flags register, also referred to as a Status register or Program Status Word. This register may be illustrated as follows:

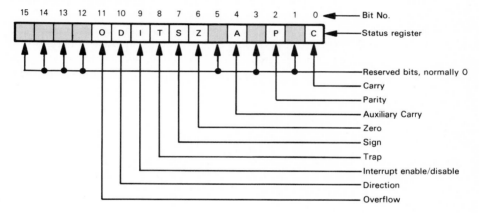

The Carry, Auxiliary Carry, Overflow, and Sign statuses are quite standard.

The Carry status reflects carries out of the high-order bit following arithmetic operations. Carry is also modified by certain shift and rotate instructions.

The Overflow status is the Exclusive-OR of the carries into and out of the high-order bit following arithmetic operations. It implies a magnitude overflow in signed binary arithmetic.

The Sign status equals the high-order bit following an arithmetic operation. On the assumption that signed binary arithmetic is being performed, a Sign status of 0 specifies a positive result, whereas a Sign status of 1 specifies a negative result.

The Auxiliary Carry status is identical to the 8080A status with the same name. It represents carries out of bit 3 in an 8-bit data unit.

Subtract instructions use twos complement arithmetic in order to subtract the minuend from the subtrahend. However, the Carry status is inverted. That is to say, following a subtract operation, the Carry status is set to 1 if there was no carry out of the high-order bit, and the Carry status is reset to 0 if there was a carry out of the high-order bit. The Carry status therefore indicates a borrow.

The Parity status is set to 1 when the low-order eight bits of any data operation result has an even number of 1 bits. An odd number of 1 bits causes the Parity status to be reset to 0.

The Zero status is set to 1 when the result of a data operation is zero; it is set to 0 when the result of a data operation is not zero.

The Direction status determines whether string operations will auto-increment or auto-decrement the contents of Index registers. If the Direction status is 1, then the SI and DI Index registers' contents will be decremented; that is to say, strings will be accessed from the highest memory address down to the lowest memory address. If the Direction status is 0, then the SI and DI Index registers' contents will be incremented; that is to say, strings will be accessed beginning with the lowest memory address.

The Interrupt status is a master interrupt enable/disable. This status must be 1 in order to enable interrupts within the 8086. If this status is 0, then all interrupts will be disabled.

The Trap status is a special debugging aid that puts the 8086 into a "single step" mode. The single step mode is described in detail together with 8086 interrupt logic, since it depends on this interrupt logic for its existence.

The Carry, Auxiliary Carry, Parity, Sign, and Zero statuses are also found in the 8080A. The Overflow, Direction, Interrupt, and Trap statuses are new in the 8086.

HOW INSTRUCTIONS AFFECT THE FLAGS REGISTER

The list below identifies tables that describe individual instructions and how they affect the Flags register. For example, to determine how the ADD instruction affects the flags, consult Table 3-2.

Instruction Mnemonic	Table	Instruction Mnemonic	Table
AAA	3-4	LODS	3-1
AAD	3-10	LOOP instructions	3-1
AAM	3-10	MOV	3-1
AAS	3-4	MOVS	3-1
ADC	3-2	MUL	3-6
ADD	3-2	NEG	3-2
AND	3-1	NOT	3-1
CALL	3-1	OR	3-7
CBW	3-1	OUT	3-1
CLC	3-9	POP	3-1
CLD	3-9	POPF	3-12
CLI	3-9	PUSH	3-1
CMC	3-9	PUSHF	3-1
CMP	3-2	RCL	3-8
CMPS	3-2	RCR	3-8
CWD	3-1	REP	3-1
DAA	3-5	RET	3-1
DAS	3-5	ROR	3-8
DEC	3-3	SAHF	3-9
DIV	3-11	SAR	3-7
ESC	3-1	SBB	3-2
HLT	3-1	SCAS	3-2
IDIV	3-11	SHL	3-7
IMUL	3-6	SHR	3-7
IN	3-1	STC	3-9
INC	3-3	STD	3-9
INT	3-13	STI	3-9
INTO	3-13	STOS	3-1
IRET	3-12	SUB	3-2
Jump-on-Conditions	3-1	TEST	3-7
JCXZ	3-1	WAIT	3-1
JMP	3-1	XCHG	3-1
LAHF	3-1	XLAT	3-1
LDS	3-1	XOR	3-7
LEA	3-1		
LES	3-1		
LOCK	3-1		

No Effect

The instructions in Table 3-1 have no effect on any of the 8086 statuses.

Table 3-1. Instructions that Have No Effect on the 8086 Flags Register

CALL	LOOP instructions
CBW	MOV
CWD	MOVS
ESC	NOT
HLT	OUT
IN	POP
Jump-on-Conditions	PUSH
JCXZ	PUSHF
JMP	REP
LAHF	RET
LDS	STOS
LEA	WAIT
LES	XCHG
LOCK	XLAT
LODS	

Effect on all Arithmetic Flags

The instructions in Table 3-2 affect all six of the 8086 arithmetic flags: Overflow, Carry, Arithmetic, Zero, Sign, and Parity.

Table 3-2. Instructions that Affect All 8086 Arithmetic Flags

ADC	NEG
ADD	SBB
CMP	SCAS
CMPS	SUB

Effect on all Arithmetic Flags Except Carry

The instructions in Table 3-3 affect all the 8086 arithmetic flags except for Carry. Overflow, Arithmetic, Zero, and Parity are all affected.

Table 3-3. Instructions that Affect all 8086 Arithmetic Flags
except Carry

DEC	INC

Effect on all Arithmetic Flags (AF and CF are Meaningful)

The instructions in Table 3-4 affect all the 8086 arithmetic flags. However, only the values for AF and CF are meaningful. The values for Overflow, Zero, Parity, and Sign are unknown.

Table 3-4. Instructions that Affect AF and CF

AAA	AAS

Effect on all Arithmetic Flags (Overflow is Undefined)

The instructions in Table 3-5 affect all the 8086 arithmetic flags. However, the Overflow flag is not meaningful. Carry, Arithmetic, Zero, Sign, and Parity are all meaningful.

Table 3-5. Instructions that Leave Overflow Undefined

DAA	DAS

Effect on all Arithmetic Flags (CF and OF are Meaningful)

The instructions in Table 3-6 affect all the 8086 arithmetic flags. The Carry and Overflow flags are not affected in the normal manner. Consult the instructions for a description of how these flags are set. All other arithmetic flags are undefined.

Table 3-6. Instructions that Affect All Arithmetic Flags, Leaving CF and OF Meaningful

IMUL	MUL

Effect on all Arithmetic Flags (AF is Undefined)

The instructions in Table 3-7 affect all the 8086 arithmetic flags. Carry and Overflow are cleared to 0. AF is undefined. Zero, Parity and Sign are set in the normal manner.

Table 3-7. Instructions that Affect All Arithmetic Flags,
Leaving AF undefined

AND OR SAR SHL	SHR TEST XOR

Effect on CF and OF Only

The instructions in Table 3-8 affect only the Carry and Overflow flags. The Arithmetic, Zero, Sign, and Parity flags are not altered.

Table 3-8. Instructions that Affect Carry and Overflow
Flags Only

RCL RCR	ROR

Effect on Specific Flags

The instructions in Table 3-9 are used to affect specific flags. For example, STI is used to set the Interrupt flag to 1.

Table 3-9. Instructions that Affect Specific Flags

CLC - Clear Carry CLD - Clear Direction CLI - Clear Interrupt CMC - Complement Carry	SAHF - Move AH to 8080 flags STC - Set Carry STD - Set Direction STI - Set Interrupt

Effect on Parity, Sign, and Zero

The instructions in Table 3-10 affect the Parity, Sign, and Zero flags. The Carry, Overflow, and Arithmetic flags are undefined following execution of these instructions.

Table 3-10. Instructions that Affect Parity, Sign and Zero Flags

AAD	AAM

Leave all Arithmetic Flags Undefined

The instructions in Table 3-11 leave all arithmetic flags undefined.

Table 3-11. Instructions that Scramble the Flags

DIV	IDIV

Restore all Flags from Stack

The instructions in Table 3-12 pop data from the stack into all the 8086 flags.

Table 3-12. Instructions that Restore All the 8086 Flags from the Stack

IRET	POPF

Effect on IF and TF Only

The instructions in Table 3-13 clear the Interrupt and Trap flags. The INTO instruction only affects these flags if the Overflow flag is 1.

Table 3-13. Instructions that Clear the Interrupt and Trap Flags

INT	INTO

The DIV and IDIV instructions affect IF and TF only following a divide error.

8086 ADDRESSING MODES

There are two major topics of interest concerning 8086 addressing modes:

1.   How the memory address is formed.

2.   What addressing modes are available.

All 8086 memory addresses are computed by summing the contents of a Segment register and an effective memory address. The effective memory address is computed via a variety of addressing modes, as it would be for any other microprocessor. The selected Segment register contents are left-shifted four bits, then added to the effective memory address to generate the actual address output as follows:

```
Segment Register contents:    X X X X X X X X X X X X X X X X 0 0 0 0
Effective memory address:   + 0 0 0 0 Y Y Y Y Y Y Y Y Y Y Y Y Y Y Y Y
Actual address output:        X X X Z Z Z Z Z Z Z Z Z Z Z Z Z Y Y Y Y
```

X, Y and Z represent any binary digits.

Thus a 20-bit memory address is computed — which allows 1,048,576 bytes of external memory to be addressed directly.

An 8086 address is therefore composed of two distinct addresses: the Segment register contents, referred to as the segment address, and the effective memory address, referred to as the offset address.

The segment registers of the 8086 are unlike any other microprocessor registers. They act as base registers which can point to any memory location that lies on an address boundary that is an even multiple of 16 bytes. Using arbitrary memory addresses, this may be illustrated as follows:

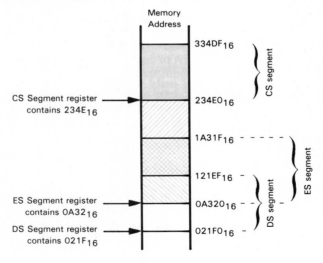

As illustrated above, each segment register identifies the beginning of a 65,536-byte memory segment. Since the 8086 has four segment registers, there will at any time be four selected 65,536-byte memory segments. The actual address output will always select a memory location within one of these four segments. For example, if an actual address output is the sum of the DS Segment register and an effective memory address, then the actual address output must select a memory location within the DS segment; that is to say, within the address range $021F0_{16}$ through $121EF_{16}$ in the illustration above. Likewise, an actual address output which is the sum of the CS Segment register and an effective memory address must select a memory location within the CS segment, which in the illustration above will lie in the address range $234E0_{16}$ through $334DF_{16}$.

No restrictions are placed on the contents of segment registers. Therefore 8086 memory is not divided into 65,536-byte pages, nor do the four segment registers have to specify non-overlapping memory spaces. Each segment register identifies the origin of a 65,536-byte memory segment which may lie anywhere within addressable memory, and may or may not overlap with one or more other segments.

8086 addressing modes can be divided into two distinct types:

1. Program memory addressing modes.

2. Data memory addressing modes.

We will discuss each of these topics, then at the end of this section show how they are implemented on the 8086.

PROGRAM MEMORY ADDRESSING MODES

Whenever an instruction fetch is performed, the address of the memory location from which the instruction is fetched is computed as the sum of an offset taken from the program counter (also called the PC register) and a segment taken from the CS register. Normally, the PC register contents are incremented as instructions are executed. However, Jump and Call instructions may modify the PC register contents in one of three ways:

1. Program relative addressing. An 8-bit or 16-bit displacement provided by the instruction in the form of immediate data is added to the PC register as a signed binary number. This does not alter the CS register contents. Therefore it is termed an intrasegment operation.

2. Direct addressing. New 16-bit addresses present in the instruction in the form of immediate data are loaded into the program counter and the CS register. This is referred to as an intersegment operation.

3. Indirect addressing. Any of the data memory addressing options (which we will describe next) may be used to read data from data memory. However, the data input is interpreted as a memory address by the Jump or Call instruction. You have two indirect addressing options. A single 16-bit data word may be read, in which case it is loaded into the program counter and the Jump or Call references a memory location within the current CS segment. You can also read two 16-bit data words: the first is loaded into the program counter and the second is loaded into the CS Segment register. Thus you can Jump or Call any addressable memory location using indirect addressing.

DATA MEMORY ADDRESSING MODES

The 8086 offers a wide variety of addressing; we will condense it into six basic options. These options are:

1. Immediate
2. Direct
3. Direct, Indexed
4. Implied
5. Base Relative
6. Stack

Immediate Memory Addressing

In this form of addressing, one of the operands is present in the byte(s) immediately following the instruction object code (op-code). If addressing bytes follow the op-code, then the immediate data will follow the addressing bytes. For example:

ADD   AX, 3064H

requests the Assembler to generate an ADD instruction which will add 3064_{16} to the AX register. This may be illustrated as follows:

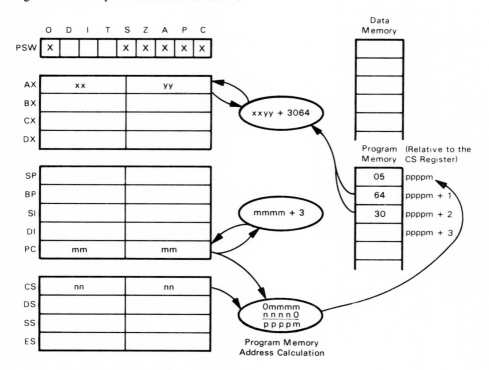

X, Y, M, P, and N all represent any hexadecimal digits.

Note that the 16-bit immediate operand, when stored in program memory, has the low-order byte preceding the high-order byte. This is consistent with the way the 8080A stores immediate operands in program memory. In addition, this is consistent with the way the 8086 stores 16-bit operands in data memory. When a 16-bit store is performed, the low-order 8 bits of data are stored into the low-order memory byte, and the high-order 8 bits of data are stored into the succeeding memory byte.

In this example, the two bytes immediately following the op-code for the ADD to AX instruction are added to the AX register.

Direct Memory Addressing

The 8086 implements straightforward direct memory addressing by adding a 16-bit displacement, provided by two object code bytes, to the Data Segment register. The sum becomes the actual memory address. This may be illustrated as follows:

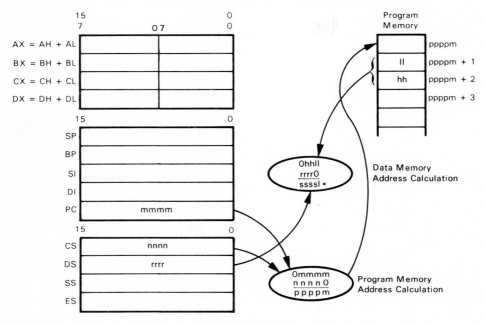

H, L, M, N, P, R and S all represent any hexadecimal digits.

* Actual data memory address output for direct memory addressing.

Note that a 16-bit address displacement, when stored in program memory, has the low-order byte preceding the high-order byte. This is consistent with the way the 8080A stores addresses in program memory.

DS must provide the segment base address when addressing data memory directly, as illustrated above.

Direct, Indexed Memory Addressing

Direct, indexed addressing is allowed by specifying the SI or DI register as an index register. You have the option of adding an 8-bit or 16-bit displacement to the contents of the specified index register in order to generate the effective address.

A 16-bit displacement is stored in two object code bytes; the low-order byte of the displacement precedes the high-order byte of the displacement, as illustrated for direct memory addressing. If an 8-bit displacement is specified, then the high-order bit of the low-order byte is propagated into the high-order byte to create a 16-bit displacement. This may be illustrated a follows:

Displacements: 10110101   01101011

Sign extended: 1 1 1 1 1 1 1 1 0 1 1 0 1 0 1   0 0 0 0 0 0 0 0 1 1 0 1 0 1 1

We may now illustrate direct, indexed addressing as follows:

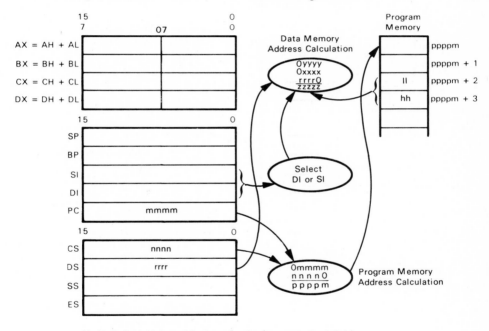

M, N, P, R, X, H, L, and Z all represent any hexadecimal digits.

YYYY is the 16-bit or 8-bit displacement taken from program memory.

XXXX is the index taken from either the DI or SI register.

Implied Memory Addressing

Implied memory addressing is implemented on the 8086 as a degenerate version of a direct, indexed memory addressing. If you do not specify a displacement when using the direct, indexed addressing mode, then you have, in effect, implied memory addressing via the SI or DI register. This may be illustrated as follows:

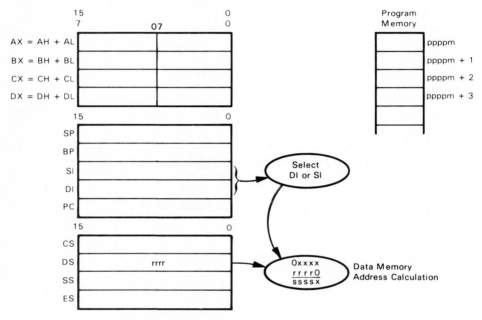

(You may substitute CS, SS or ES for DS by executing an additional 1-byte instruction.)

X, R and S represent any hexadecimal digits.

Base Relative Addressing

The 8086 implements base relative addressing in two ways:

- Data memory base relative addressing, which is within the DS segment (data memory)

- Stack base relative addressing, which is in the SS segment (stack memory)

Data memory base relative addressing uses the BX register contents to provide the base for the effective address. All of the data memory addressing options thus far described, with the exception of immediate addressing, are available with base relative data memory addressing. In effect, base relative data memory addressing merely adds the contents of the BX register to the effective memory address which would otherwise have been generated. Here, for example, is an illustration of base relative direct addressing:

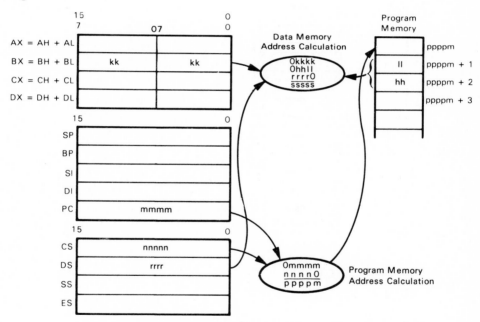

(You may substitute CS, ES or SS for DS by executing an additional 1-byte instruction.)

Simple, direct addressing, which we described earlier, always generated a 16-bit displacement. Base relative, direct addressing allows the displacement, illustrated above as HHLL, to be a 16-bit displacement, an 8-bit displacement with sign extended, or no displacement at all.

Base relative implied memory addressing simply adds the contents of the **BX** register to the selected Index register in order to compute the effective memory address. This may be illustrated as follows:

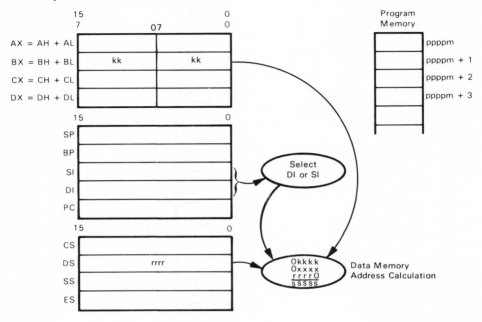

Base relative, direct, indexed data memory addressing may appear to be complicated, but in fact it is not. We simply add the contents of the BX register to the effective memory address, as computed for normal direct, indexed addressing. Thus, base relative, direct, indexed data memory addressing may be illustrated as follows:

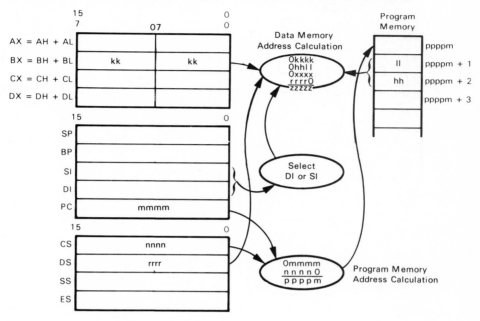

The index xxxx in the illustration above is optional. Base relative, direct memory addressing is also available. In this instance neither SI nor DI will contribute to the address computation, and 0xxxx must be removed from the illustration.

Stack Memory Addressing

The 8086 also has stack memory addressing variations of the base relative, data memory addressing options just described. In this case, however, the BP register is used as the base register. Here, for example, is base relative, direct stack addressing:

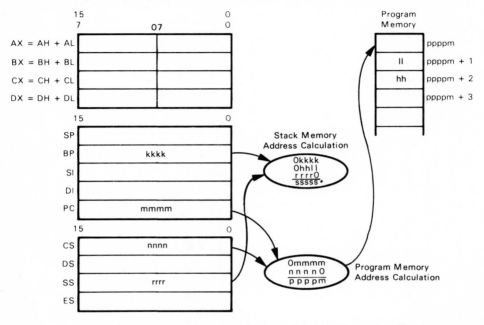

• Actual Stack memory address output for base relative, direct memory addressing

In the illustration above, the displacement HHLL is present, either as a 16-bit displacement or as an 8-bit displacement with sign extended. Base relative stack memory addressing requires a displacement be specified, even if zero.

ADDRESSING MODE BYTE

The 8086 obviously offers an extensive selection of addressing modes. The next question is: how are these addressing modes implemented in the object code? The 8086 specifies most data memory addressing modes in an instruction's object code using one byte of object code, known as the addressing mode byte. The addressing mode byte may have one or two additional displacement bytes associated with it. The addressing mode byte is always the second byte of the instruction object code, unless a prefix instruction has been included prior to the initial object code. The addressing mode byte may be illustrated as follows:

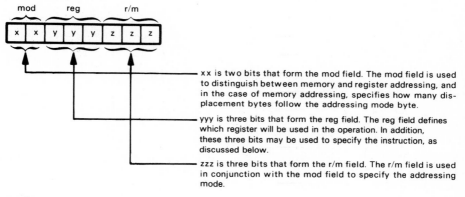

xx is two bits that form the mod field. The mod field is used to distinguish between memory and register addressing, and in the case of memory addressing, specifies how many displacement bytes follow the addressing mode byte.

yyy is three bits that form the reg field. The reg field defines which register will be used in the operation. In addition, these three bits may be used to specify the instruction, as discussed below.

zzz is three bits that form the r/m field. The r/m field is used in conjunction with the mod field to specify the addressing mode.

mod =

00   Memory addressing mode. r/m specifies the exact addressing option. There are no displacement bytes.

01   Memory addressing mode. r/m specifies the exact addressing option. There is one displacement byte. This displacement byte is viewed as a signed number in the range $+127$ to -128. When this number is used in the memory address calculation, the number is sign extended to 16 bits. In this case, the addressing mode bytes can be illustrated as follows:

where mod = 01 and disp is the 8-bit signed displacement value.

10   Memory addressing mode. r/m specifies the addressing option. There are two displacement bytes. The first displacement byte is the low-order eight bits of the displacement. The second displacement byte is the high-order eight bits of the displacement. When this number is used in the memory address calculation, the number is treated as an unsigned 16-bit number. In this case, the addressing mode bytes can be illustrated as follows:

| mod reg r/m | disp low | disp high |

where mod = 10, disp low is the low-order eight bits of the displacement, and disp high is the high-order eight bits of the displacement.

11   register addressing mode. r/m specifies a register. Used in conjunction with the w bit to determine if an 8- or 16-bit register is selected.

reg   reg is used in conjunction with another bit, the w bit, in the selection of the register to be used in the operation. The w bit, which is part of the instruction op-code, selects whether an 8- or 16-bit operation is performed.

reg	w = 0	w = 1
000	AL	AX
001	CL	CX
010	DL	DX
011	BL	BX
100	AH	SP
101	CH	BP
110	DH	SI
111	BH	DI

Certain instructions — those which require only a single register or memory operand (NOT, NEG, etc.), have one implied operand (MOV immediate, DIV, MUL, etc.), or use addressing modes to calculate a target address (JMP, CALL, etc.) — use the reg field as an extension to the opcode byte to specify the desired instruction. See the description of ADC on page 3-59 as an example.

r/m   r/m specifies the addressing mode in conjunction with mod, as follows:

r/m	mod - 00	mod - 01	mod - 10	mod - 11	
				w = 0	w = 1
000	BX + SI	BX + SI + DISP	BX + SI + DISP	AL	AX
001	BX + DI	BX + DI + DISP	BX + DI + DISP	CL	CX
010	BP + SI	BP + SI + DISP	BP + SI + DISP	DL	DX
011	BP + DI	BP + DI + DISP	BP + DI + DISP	BL	BX
100	SI	SI + DISP	SI + DISP	AH	SP
101	DI	DI + DISP	DI + DISP	CH	BP
110	Direct Address	BP + DISP	BP + DISP	DH	SI
111	BX	BX + DISP	BX + DISP	BH	DI

This table is self-explanatory, with the exception of Direct Address. When mod is 00 and r/m is 110, the offset address is taken directly from the two bytes that follow the addressing mode byte. This can be illustrated as follows:

mod reg r/m		addr-low		addr-high

where mod is 00, r/m is 110, addr-high is the high-order 8 bits of the offset address and addr-low is the low-order 8 bits of the offset address.

SEGMENT OVERRIDE

Every addressing mode has a standard default segment register. In most cases you can select an alternative segment register by using a segment override prefix. To use the prefix, place the following byte in front of the instruction whose default segment register assignment is to be overriden.

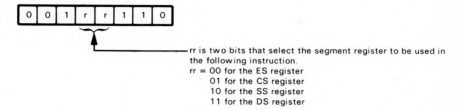

rr is two bits that select the segment register to be used in the following instruction.
rr = 00 for the ES register
01 for the CS register
10 for the SS register
11 for the DS register

In three cases, the segment override may not be used. They are:

1. Stack reference instructions (e.g., PUSH and CALL) that use the stack pointer (SP register) to compute the offset always use the SS register as the segment register.

2. String instructions that use the DI register always use the ES register as the segment register. In a string operation where both SI and DI are used (e.g., MOVS or CMPS), a segment override prefix, if present, overrides the SI offset's segment register.

3. Segment override prefixes cannot be used with program memory addressing. All instruction fetches are relative to the CS Segment register.

MEMORY ADDRESSING TABLES

Memory addressing modes and memory addressing byte information can be combined and summarized as follows:

r/m =	mod = 00	mode = 01	mod = 10
000	Base Relative Indexed BX + SI	Base Relative Indexed BX + SI + DISP	Base Relative Direct Indexed BX + SI + DISP
001	Base Relative Indexed BX + DI	Base Relative Direct Indexed BX + DI + DISP	Base Relative Direct Indexed BX + DI + DISP
010	Base Relative Indexed Stack BP + SI	Base Relative Direct Indexed Stack BP + SI + DISP	Base Relative Direct Indexed Stack BP + SI + DISP
011	Base Relative Indexed Stack BP + DI	Base Relative Direct Indexed Stack BP + DI + DISP	Base Relative Direct Indexed Stack BP + DI + DISP
100	Implied SI	Direct, Indexed SI + DISP	Direct, Indexed SI + DISP
101	Implied DI	Direct, Indexed DI + DISP	Direct, Indexed DI + DISP
110	Direct Direct Address	Base Relative Direct Stack BP + DISP	Base Relative Direct Stack BP + DISP
111	Base Relative BX	Base Relative Direct BX + DISP	Base Relative Direct BX + DISP

Note that two operand instructions will very frequently access one operand out of memory, while the other operand is in a CPU register. Also, both operands will frequently be accessed out of CPU registers. The 8086 does not allow both operands to be accessed out of memory, with the exception of several special data string manipulation instructions. The following options are available:

Source Operand	Destination Operand	Result
CPU Register	CPU Register	CPU Register
Memory Location	CPU Register	CPU Register
CPU Register	Memory Location	Memory location

INSTRUCTION SET MNEMONICS

In the following section, each 8086 assembly language instruction is discussed. The format for each description is composed of six distinct parts:

1. The instruction mnemonic and the various operands associated with it. Variable operands are signified by lower-case letters. The mnemonic itself and any fixed operands are signified by capital letters. Here is an example:

2. A description of the instruction's operation.

3. The machine language encoding of the instruction.

4. An example of the instruction's operation. This is not present for some very simple instructions.

5. A diagram of the instruction's execution, which shows the effect the instruction has on the 8086 flags, registers, and memory.

6. A Notes section that includes assorted information such as short examples of how the instruction might be used, or related instructions that might be more effective in particular instances.

ABBREVIATIONS

These are the abbreviations used for the operands described with the mnemonics:

ac
: Either the AL register, if an 8-bit operation is specified, or the AX register, if a 16-bit operation is specified. This will be represented in an 8086 assembly language instruction by AL or AX.

addr
: An 8086 address composed of two 16-bit addresses, a 16-bit offset address and a 16-bit segment address. Typically, this is represented by a label in an 8086 assembly language instruction.

count
: Either 1 or the contents of the CL register. This will be represented by 1 or CL in an 8086 assembly language instruction.

data
: 8 or 16 bits of immediate data. This can appear as any of a wide selection of numeric representations or expressions in an 8086 assembly language statement.

disp
: 8-bit signed binary displacement used by the Jump and Jump-on-Condition instructions. Invariably this will be represented by a label in an 8086 assembly language instruction.

disp 16   16-bit binary displacement used by the Call, Jump, and Return instructions. When used in the Call and Jump instructions, this is almost always represented by a label. The Return instruction will typically use a numeric expression to represent disp 16. Its use with the Return instruction will be shown.

mem   Memory operand. The addressing mode used to select the operand is specified by the addressing mode byte. This will typically be represented by a label, in which case the assembler will select the appropriate addressing mode byte, or a sequence of symbols that allows the selection of a specific addressing mode byte.

mem/reg   Memory or register operand. Consult descriptions for mem and reg.

port   An I/O port. This will be represented by a numeric representation or an expression. The port number must be beween 0_{16} and FF_{16}.

reg   Register AH, AL, BH, BL, CH, CL, DH, or DL if an 8-bit operation is specified; register AX, BX, CX, DX, SP, BP, SI, or DI if a 16-bit operation is specified.

segreg   Register CS, DS, ES, or SS.

These are the abbreviations used in describing the instruction's encoding.

c   One bit used in the shift and rotate instructions selecting either 1 or the contents of the CL register to be the number of shifts/rotates to be performed.

> c = 0,   Shift/rotate once
> c = 1,   shift/rotate the number of times
>   specified by the CL register.

d   One bit used to specify the direction in which an operation is performed.

disp   8 bits used as a signed binary displacement by the Jump and Jump-on-Condition instructions.

jj   Two hexadecimal digits, used to represent immediate data or part of a 16-bit displacement.

kk   Two hexadecimal digits, used to represent immediate data or part of a 16-bit displacement.

mod reg r/m   8-bit addressing mode byte that is described in earlier in this chapter.

rrr   Three bits selecting one of the 8086 general-purpose registers
IF

an 8-bit operation is specified	16-bit operation is specified
rrr = 000 for AL	rrr = 000 for AX
001 for CL	001 for CX
010 for DL	010 for DX
011 for BL	011 for BX
100 for AH	100 for SP
101 for CH	101 for BP
110 for DH	110 for SI
111 for BH	111 for DI

s

One bit indicating whether or not immediate data is to be sign extended. If a 16-bit operation with immediate data is specified, it is possible that the immediate operand can be expressed using just one byte of program memory space. s is interpreted as follows:

> s = 0,   Two bytes are necessary for the immediate data, no sign extension is performed.
>
> s = 1,   One byte of immediate data is present. To form the sixteen bits of immediate data necessary for the operation, sign extend the high-order bit of the immediate data byte.

ss

Two bits selecting one of the 8086 segment registers.

> ss =   00 for ES
>   01 for CS
>   10 for SS
>   11 for DS

v

One bit indicating the location to which a software interrupt should be vectored. If $v = 0$, then the interrupt service routine is located at the address specified at location $0000C_{16}$, otherwise the address is determined by the succeeding byte.

w

One bit indicating whether an 8- or 16-bit operation is performed.

> w = 0   8-bit operation
> w = 1   16-bit operation

xxx

Three don't care bits.

yy

Two hexadecimal digits indicating the I/O port number to be used by the instruction.

The following symbols are used in the example use of instructions:

H

This will appear at the end of a group of digits to specify that the digits be treated as hexadecimal digits.

[ ]

These are used to indicate the contents of the memory location addressed by the expression inside the brackets. Suppose that the BX register contains $054A_{16}$. The expression

> [BX]

refers to the memory location that has an offset address of $054A_{16}$ in the current data segment.

g,h,j,k,m,n,p,
q,r,s,t,u,v,w,
x,y,z

Are all used to represent one hexadecimal digit. For example,

> jjkk

is used to represent a 16-bit data element;

> ppppm

is used to represent a 20-bit address.

EA   Effective address. EA appears in calculations for the number of
                execution cycles required by individual instructions. EA specifies
                addressing mode execution cycles, which must be added as
                follows:

Direct Addressing	ADD 6 cycles
Direct, Indexed Addressing	ADD 9 cycles
Implied Addressing	ADD 5 cycles
Base Relative Addressing	ADD 5 cycles
Base Relative Direct Addressing	ADD 9 cycles
Base Relative Indexed Addressing	ADD 7 or 8 cycles *
Base Relative Direct Indexed Addressing	ADD 11 or 12 cycles *

Additional addressing mode cycles must be added as follows:

A segment Override Prefix is present	ADD 2 cycles
A 16-bit word is addressed and the word resides at an odd memory address	ADD 4 cycles

* BP + SI and BX + DI modes
require one more clock than
BP + DI and BX + SI modes.

8086 ASSEMBLY LANGUAGE INSTRUCTIONS
ORGANIZED ALPHABETICALLY

AAA

Adjust Result of ASCII Addition

This instruction is used to adjust a result in the AL register, assuming this result was generated by adding two ASCII characters as operands. The adjustment is performed in the following manner:

1. If the low-order four bits of the AL register are between 0 and 9 *and* the AF flag is 0, then go to Step 3.

2. If the low-order four bits of the AL register are between A and F *or* the AF flag is 1, then add 6 to the AL register, add 1 to the AH register, and set the AF flag to 1.

3. Clear the high-order four bits of the AL register.

The encoding for this instruction is:

AAA
37

For example, suppose that the AX register contains 0535_{16} and the BL register contains 39_{16}. Executing the sequence

ADD   AL,BL
AAA

would result in AX containing 0604_{16}. The ADD instruction results in

$$
\begin{array}{rcl}
35_{16} & = & 0011 \quad 0101 \\
39_{16} & = & \underline{0011 \quad 1001} \\
       &   & 0110 \quad 1110
\end{array}
$$

6E being stored into AL. The AAA instruction performs steps 2, 3, and 4 of the adjustment algorithm, which results in the AF and CF flags being set to 1, 04 being stored into the AL register, and the AH register being incremented to 06.

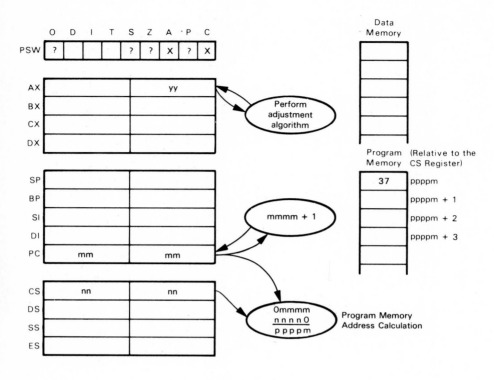

AAA
Number of cycles: 4

Notes:

1.   Note that this instruction would also work if the two operands were one-digit BCD numbers. Why one should desire to do this sort of operation is left up to the reader.

2.   To perform corrections on the addition of two packed BCD digits, refer to the DAA instruction.

3.   As a result of this instruction, the values of the Overflow, Parity, Sign, and Zero flags are undefined.

AAD

Adjust AX Register for Division

This instruction assumes that the AH and AL registers contain unpacked BCD operands. This instruction converts this information into a binary operand in the AL register. The algorithm for conversion assumes that the tens digit is in the AH register and the units digit is in the AL register. The AAD algorithm is as follows:

1. Multiply the contents of the AH register by $0A_{16}$.

2. Add AH to AL.

3. Store 00_{16} into the AH register.

4. Set the flags in the following manner:

   Carry, Overflow, Arithmetic: undefined
   Parity: based on the AL register
   Zero: based on the AL register
   Sign: based on the high-order bit of the AL register

The encoding for this instruction is:

AAD
⌣
D5 0A

Suppose that the AX register contains 0604_{16}. After the instruction

AAD

has executed, the AX register will contain 0040_{16}. The flags will be set as follows:

Carry: undefined
Overflow: undefined
Arithmetic: undefined
Sign: high-order bit of AL register is 0, set Sign to 0
Zero: AL register is non-zero, set Zero to 0
Parity: one 1 bit in AL register, set Parity to 0

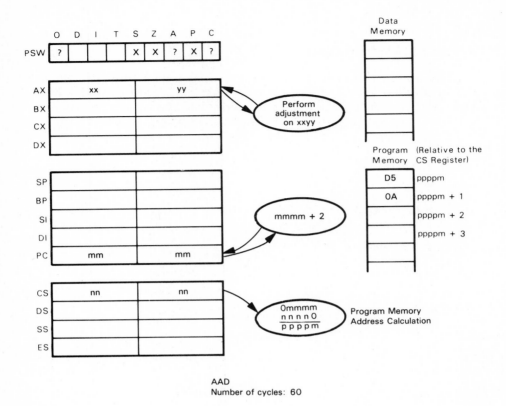

AAD
Number of cycles: 60

Notes:

1. This instruction can also be used to adjust ASCII operands for division. For example, consider the case where the AX register contains 3537_{16}. After the instructions

```
AND   AX,0F0FH
AAD
```

have executed, the AX register will contain 0039_{16}.

AAM

Adjust Result of BCD Multiplication

This instruction adjusts a result in the AL register, assuming that a multiplication has been performed with two unpacked BCD numbers as operands. The adjustment is performed as follows:

1. Divide the AL register by $0A_{16}$. Store the quotient in the AH register. Store the remainder in the AL register.

2. Set the flags in the following manner:

    Carry, Overflow, and Arithmetic: undefined
    Parity: based on the AL register
    Sign: based on the high-order bit of the AL register
    Zero: based on the AL register

The encoding for this instruction is:

AAM
⌣
D4 0A

Suppose that the AL register contains 07_{16} and the BL register contains 09_{16}. After the sequence of instructions

        MUL   AL,BL
        AAM

the AX register will contain 0603_{16}. The MUL instruction results in $3F_{16}$ being stored into the AL register. Performing steps 1 and 2 of the adjustment algorithm results in 0603_{16} in the AX register, and the flags are set in the following manner:

    Carry: undefined
    Overflow: undefined
    Arithmetic: undefined
    Sign: high-order bit of AL is 0, set Sign to 0
    Zero: the AL register is non-zero, set Zero to 0
    Parity: two 1 bits in the AL register, set Parity to 1

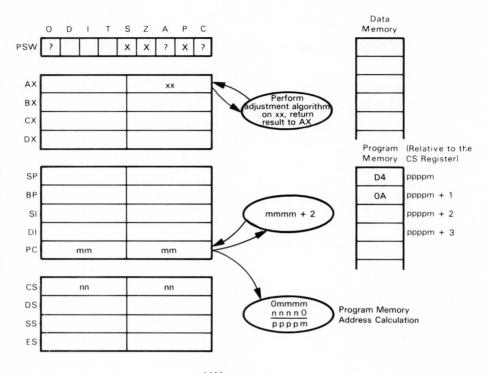

AAM
Number of cycles: 83

AAS

Adjust Result of ASCII Subtraction

This instruction adjusts a result in the AL register, assuming that a subtraction has been performed with two ASCII characters as operands. The adjustment is performed as follows:

1. If the low-order four bits of the AL register are between 0 and 9 *and* the AF flag is 0, then go to Step 3.

2. If the low-order four bits of the AL register are between A and F *or* the AF flag is 1, then subtract 6 from the AL register, subtract 1 from the AH register, and set the AF flag to 1.

3. Clear the high-order four bits of the AL register.

4. Set the CF flag to the value of the AF flag.

The encoding for this instruction is:

$$\underset{\underbrace{}}{\text{AAS}}$$
$$\text{3F}$$

For example, suppose that the AX register contains 0438_{16}. After the sequence of instructions

```
SUB   AL,35H
AAS
```

has executed, the AX register will contain 0403_{16}. The SUB instruction results in

$$
\begin{array}{r}
38_{16} = 0011 \quad 1000 \\
\text{Twos comp of } 35_{16} = 1100 \quad 1011 \\
\hline
0000 \quad 0011
\end{array}
$$

03_{16} being stored into AL. The AAS instruction performs steps 1 and 3 of the adjustment algorithm, which in this case does not modify the AX register. The AF and CF flags are set to 0.

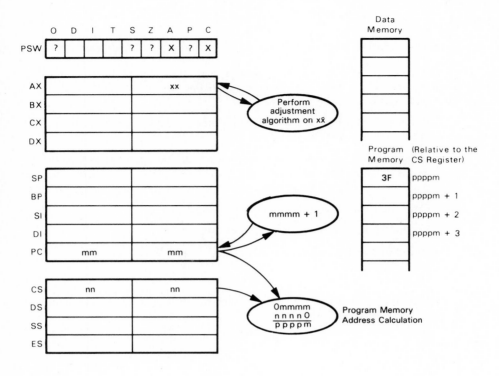

AAS
Number of cycles: 4

Notes:

1. To adjust the results of an ASCII addition, consult the AAA instruction. To adjust the results of packed BCD addition and subtraction, consult the DAA and DAS instructions.

2. The values of the Parity, Zero, Sign, and Overflow flags are undefined following the execution of this instruction.

ADC   ac,data

Add Immediate Data With Carry to AX or AL Register

This instruction is used to add the immediate data present in the succeeding pro-gram memory bytes and the Carry status to the AL (8-bit operation) or AX (16-bit operation) register.

The encoding for this instruction is:

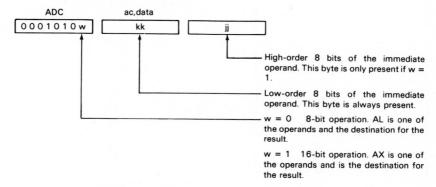

Consider, for example, the case where the AX register contains $4F3D_{16}$ and the Carry status is 1. After the instruction

ADC   AX,0FD81H

is executed, the AX register will contain $4CBF_{16}$ and the Carry status will be 1.

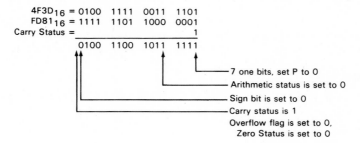

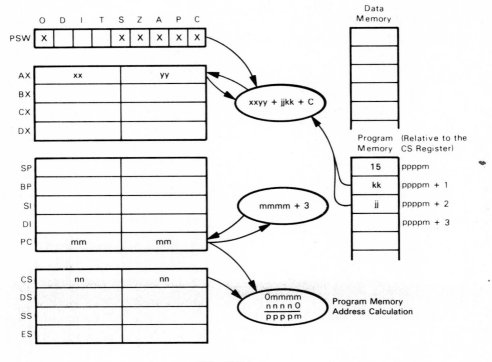

ADC   AX,jjkk
Number of cycles: **4**

Notes:

1. This instruction performs the same function as the 8080 instruction ACI data. In addition, this instruction offers a 16-bit Add With Carry Immediate option.

ADC   mem/reg,data

Add Immediate With Carry to Register or Memory Location

This instruction is used to add immediate data present in the succeeding program memory byte(s) and the Carry status to the specified register or memory location. An 8-bit or 16-bit operation may be specified.

The encoding for this instruction is:

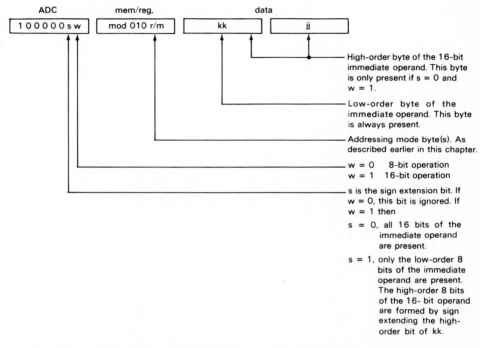

ADC	mem/reg,		data
1 0 0 0 0 0 s w	mod 010 r/m	kk	jj

High-order byte of the 16-bit immediate operand. This byte is only present if s = 0 and w = 1.

Low-order byte of the immediate operand. This byte is always present.

Addressing mode byte(s). As described earlier in this chapter.

w = 0   8-bit operation
w = 1   16-bit operation

s is the sign extension bit. If w = 0, this bit is ignored. If w = 1 then

s = 0, all 16 bits of the immediate operand are present.

s = 1, only the low-order 8 bits of the immediate operand are present. The high-order 8 bits of the 16- bit operand are formed by sign extending the high-order bit of kk.

Suppose that the DS register contains $E400_{16}$, the SI register contains 0040_{16}, the word at memory location $E4040_{16}$ is $6B90_{16}$, and the Carry status is 0. After the instruction

ADC   [SI], 2D31H

executes, the word at memory location $E4040_{16}$ will contain $98C1_{16}$ and the Carry status will be 0.

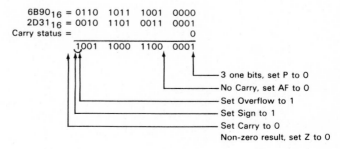

```
     6B90₁₆ = 0110  1011  1001  0000
     2D31₁₆ = 0010  1101  0011  0001
Carry status =                       0
              ─────────────────────────
              1001  1000  1100  0001
```

3 one bits, set P to 0
No Carry, set AF to 0
Set Overflow to 1
Set Sign to 1
Set Carry to 0
Non-zero result, set Z to 0

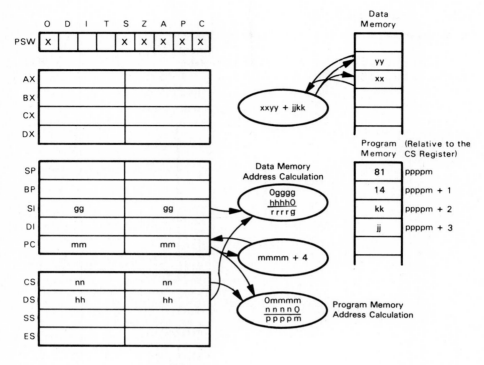

ADC   [SI], jjkk

Number of cycles: Immediate to memory: 17 + EA
Immediate to register: 4

Notes:

1. This instruction is not normally used to ADC immediate data to the AL or AX register. The instruction ADC ac,data is provided for that purpose.

2. Segment registers may not be specified as operands in this instruction.

ADC   mem/reg₁, mem/reg₂

Add Data With Carry From: • **Register to Register**
                              • **Register to Memory**
                              • **Memory to Register**

Add the contents of the register or memory location specified by mem/reg₂ and the Carry status to the contents of the register or memory location specified by mem/reg₁. An 8- or 16-bit operation may be specified. Either mem/reg₁ or mem/reg₂ may be a memory operand, but one of the operands must be a register operand.

The encoding for this instruction is:

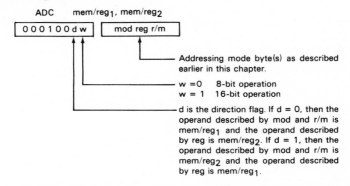

Suppose that the AX register contains 0211_{16}, the BX register contains 0084_{16}, the DS register contains $1C00_{16}$, the Carry status is 1, and the contents of the memory word at $1C084_{16}$ are $00A4_{16}$. After the instruction

ADC   AX,[BX]

has executed, the AX register will contain $02B6_{16}$ and the flags will be set as follows:

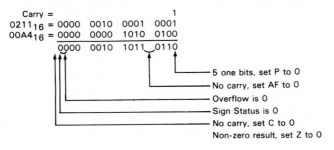

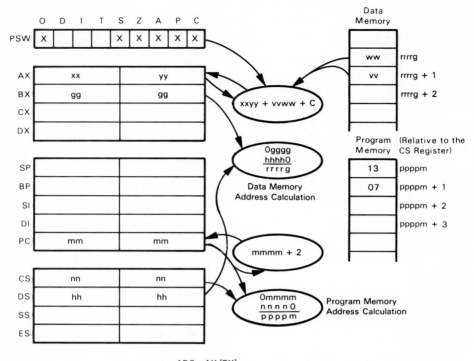

ADC   AX,[BX]
Number of cycles: Memory to register: 9 + EA
                  Register to memory: 16 + EA
                  Register to register: 3

Notes:

1. This instruction is not normally used to ADC to the AX or AL registers. The ADC ac,data instruction accomplishes that function in fewer bytes.

ADD   ac,data

Add Immediate Data to AX or AL Register

This instruction is used to add the immediate data present in the succeeding program memory byte(s) to the AL (8-bit operation) or AX (16-bit operation) register. The encoding for this instruction is:

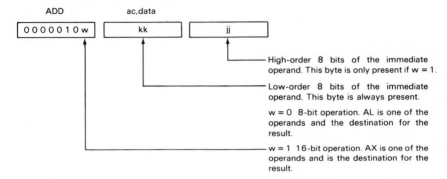

Suppose that the AX register contains 4064_{16} and the Carry status is 1. Executing an

ADD   AX,0F0FH

instruction will result in the accumulator containing $4F73_{16}$.

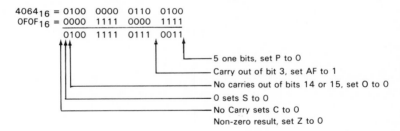

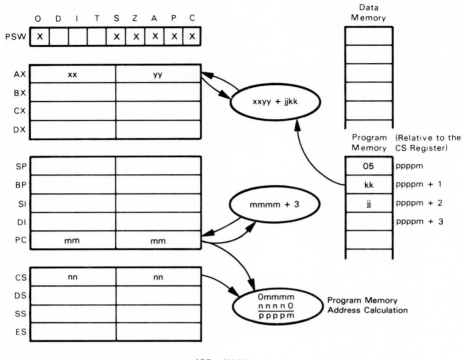

ADD   AX,jjkk
Number of cycles: 4

Notes:

1. This instruction performs the same function as the 8080 instruction ADI data. This instruction has the additional capability of adding 16-bit immediate data elements.

ADD   mem/reg,data

Add Immediate Data to Register or Memory Location

This instruction is used to add the immediate data present in the succeeding program memory byte(s) to the specified register or memory location. An 8- or 16-bit operation may be specified.

The encoding for this instruction is:

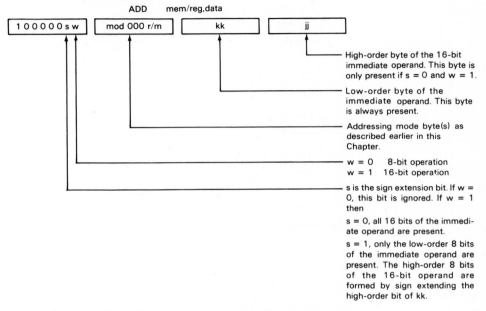

For example, if the DX register should contain 4652_{16} and the instruction

ADD   DX,0F0F0H

is executed, then the DX register contents will be altered to 3742_{16}.

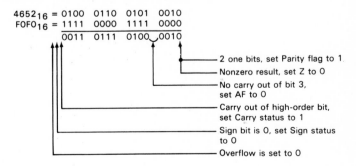

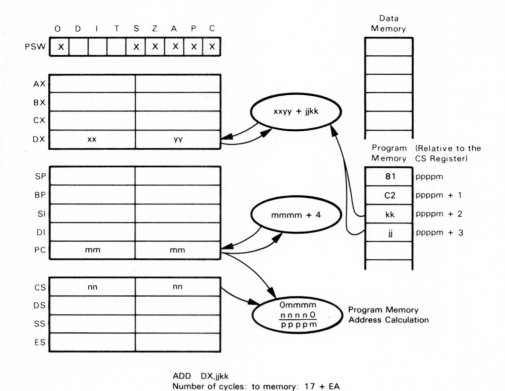

ADD   DX,jjkk
Number of cycles: to memory: 17 + EA
                   to register: 4

Notes:

1. This instruction is not normally used to ADD to the AX or AL registers. The ADD ac,data instruction accomplishes that function in fewer bytes.

ADD   mem/reg₁, mem/reg₂

Add: 1. Register to Register
     2. Register to Memory
     3. Memory to Register

Add the contents of the register or memory location specified by mem/reg₂ to the contents of the register or memory location specified by mem/reg₁. An 8- or 16-bit operation may be specified. Either mem/reg₁ or mem/reg₂ may be a memory operand, but one of the operands must be a register operand.

The encoding for this instruction is:

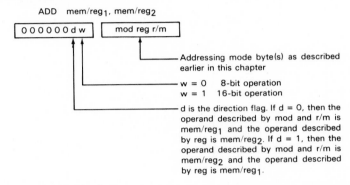

Suppose that the CX register contents are 0029_{16} and the contents of the SI register are $04ED_{16}$. After the instruction

ADD   SI,CX

has executed, the SI register contents and the statuses will be altered as follows:

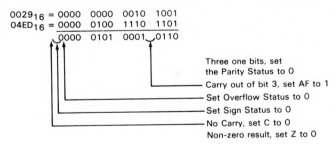

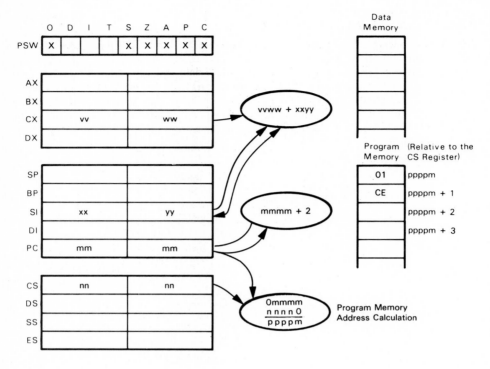

ADD   SI,CX
Number of cycles: Register to Register: 3
                  Register to Memory: 16 + EA
                  Memory to Register: 9 + EA

AND   ac,data

AND Immediate Data with the AL or AX Register

This instruction is used to AND immediate data present in the succeeding program memory byte(s) with the AL (8-bit operation) or AX (16-bit operation) register contents.

The encoding for this instruction is:

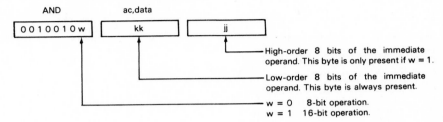

As an example, consider the case where the AL register contains $C3_{16}$. After the instruction

AND   AL,7FH

executes, the AL register will contain 43_{16}.

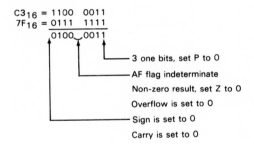

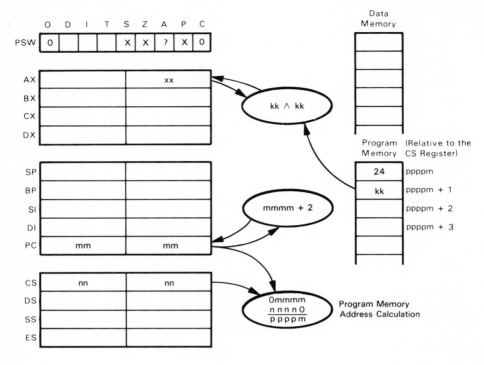

AND   AL,kk
Number of cycles: 4

Notes:

1. This instruction performs the same function as the 8080 instruction ANI data. However, it also allows a 16-bit operation.

2. If you desire to AND immediate with any of the other general purpose registers or with some memory location, consult the AND mem/reg,data instruction.

AND   mem/reg,data

AND Immediate Data with Register or Memory Location

AND immediate data present in the succeeding program memory byte(s) with the specified register or memory location. An 8- or 16-bit operation may be specified.

The encoding for this instruction is:

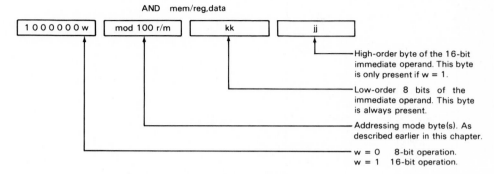

AND   mem/reg,data

Consider the case where the BX register contains 0104_{16}, the DS register contains 0000_{16}, and the byte at memory location 00104_{16} is 47_{16}. After the instruction

> AND   [BX],52H

has executed, memory location 00104_{16} will contain 42_{16}.

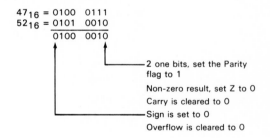

$47_{16} = 0100\ 0111$
$52_{16} = 0101\ 0010$

0100 0010

- 2 one bits, set the Parity flag to 1

Non-zero result, set Z to 0

Carry is cleared to 0

- Sign is set to 0

Overflow is cleared to 0

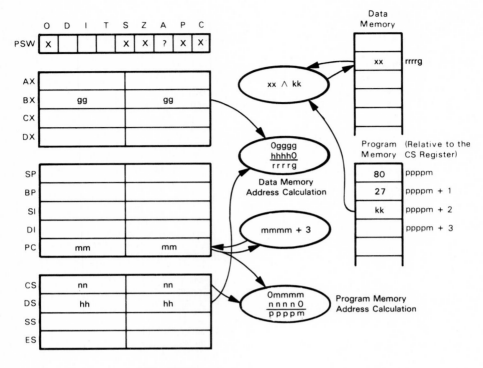

AND   [BX],kk
Number of cycles: Immediate to memory: 17 + EA
Immediate to register: 4

Notes:

1.   This instruction is not normally used to AND data with the AX or AL registers. The instruction AND ac,data is provided for this function.

AND   mem/reg₁, mem/reg₂

AND: · **Register with Register**
        · **Register with Memory**
        · **Memory with Register**

AND the contents of the register or memory location specified by mem/reg₂ with the contents of the register or memory location specified by mem/reg₁, returning the result to mem/reg₁. An 8- or 16-bit operation may be specified. Either mem/reg₁ or mem/reg₂ may be a memory operand, but one of the operands must be a register operand.

The encoding for this instruction is:

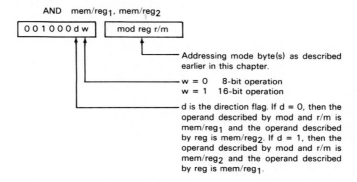

As an example, consider the case where the DL register contains 06_{16}, the DS register contains $B000_{16}$, the BX register contains 0010_{16}, the SI register contains 0006_{16}, and the byte at memory location $B0016_{16}$ contains $F1_{16}$. After the instruction

                    AND   DL, [BX + SI]

has executed, the DL register will contain 00 and the flags will be set as follows:

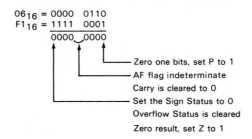

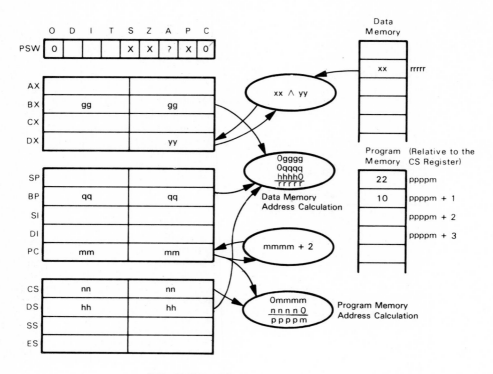

AND   DL, [BX + SI]
Number of cycles: Memory to Register: 9 + EA
                  Register to Memory: 16 + EA
                  Register to Register: 3

CALL   addr

CALL the Subroutine Specified in the Operand (Intersegment)

Store the contents of the CS and PC registers on the top of the stack, i.e., push the address of the instruction following the CALL onto the top of the stack. Place the contents of the succeeding four memory bytes into the PC and CS registers. Place the bytes in the following manner:

1. Store the second and third bytes of this instruction into the PC register.

2. Store the fourth and fifth bytes of this instruction into the CS register.

The encoding for this instruction is:

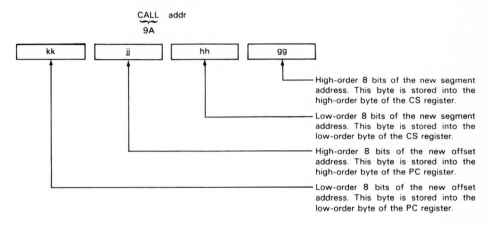

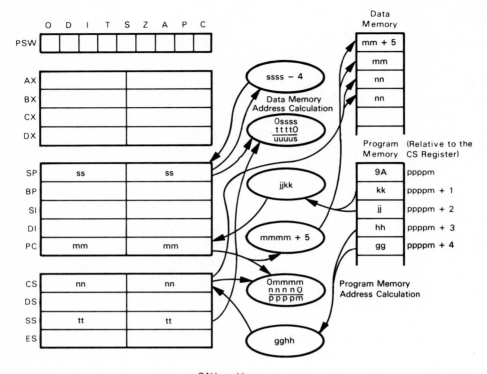

CALL   addr
Number of cycles: 28

Notes:

1.   There are four types of CALLs:

CALL addr: this instruction, intersegment CALL
CALL mem: intersegment indirect CALL
CALL disp: intrasegment CALL
CALL mem/reg: intrasegment indirect CALL

CALL   disp16

CALL the Subroutine Specified in the Operand (Intrasegment)

Push the address of the instruction following the CALL onto the top of the stack. Add the contents of the next two program memory bytes, treating them as a 16-bit unsigned displacement, to the program counter. Continue execution from this point.

The encoding for this instruction is:

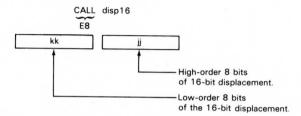

As an example, consider the following instruction sequence:

```
        CALL    SUBR
        AND     AL,7FH
        —
        —
        —
SUBR    PUSH    AX
```

After the CALL instruction has executed, the address of the AND instruction will have been pushed onto the stack, and the PUSH instruction at SUBR will be executed next.

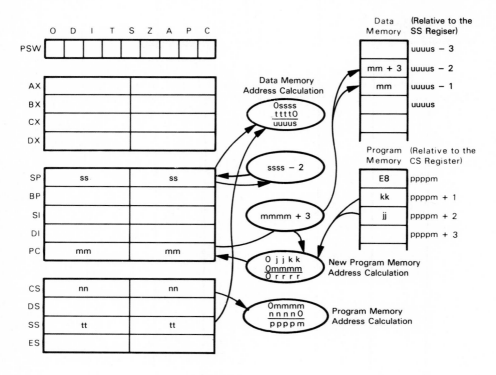

CALL   jjkk
Number of cycles:19

Notes:

1.   There are four types of CALLs:

CALL disp: this instruction, intrasegment CALL
CALL mem/reg: intrasegment indirect CALL
CALL address: intersegment CALL
CALL mem: intersegment indirect CALL

CALL   mem

CALL the Subroutine Specified by the Operand (Intersegment)

Store the contents of the CS and PC registers on the top of the stack, i.e., push the address of the instruction following the CALL onto the stack. Move the word at the specified memory location into the PC register; move the succeeding word into the CS register. Continue execution from this point.

The encoding for this instruction is:

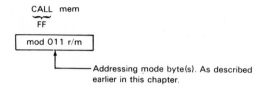

Suppose the DS register contains 0400_{16}, the SI register contains 0004_{16}, the memory word at 04004_{16} is 0100_{16} and the memory word at 04006_{16} is $0FE0_{16}$. After the instruction

CALL   [SI]

has executed, the PC register will contain 0100_{16} and the CS register will contain $0FE0_{16}$. Execution will continue from location $0FF00_{16}$.

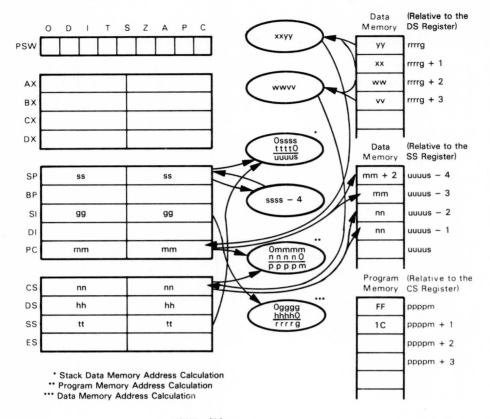

* Stack Data Memory Address Calculation
** Program Memory Address Calculation
*** Data Memory Address Calculation

CALL [SI]
Number of cycles: 37 + EA

Notes:

1. There are four types of CALLs:

    CALL mem: this instruction, intersegment indirect CALL
    CALL addr: intersegment CALL
    CALL mem/reg: intrasegment indirect CALL
    CALL disp: intrasegment CALL

2. If mod = 11, this operation is undefined.

CALL   mem/reg

Call the Subroutine Specified by the Operand (Intrasegment)

Store the address of the instruction following the CALL on the top of the Stack. If the specified operand is a register, move the contents of the register to the PC register. If the specified operand is a memory location, move the contents of the specified memory location to the PC register. Continue execution from this point.

The encoding for this instruction is:

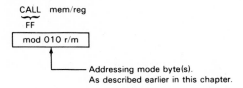

Consider the case where the PC register contains $FF00_{16}$, the DS register contains 0100_{16}, the BX register 0026_{16}, and the word at memory location 01026_{16} is 0240_{16}. After the instruction

CALL   [BX]

has executed, the PC register will contain 0240_{16}. Execution will continue at this location.

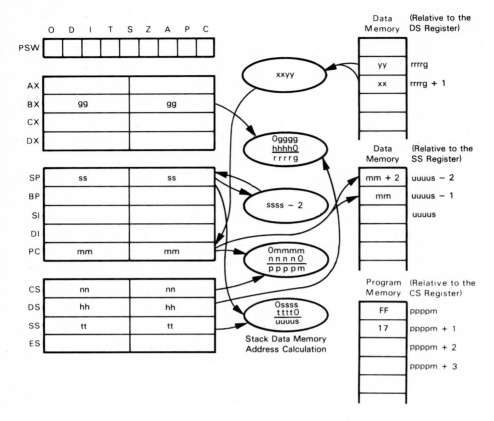

CALL   [BX]   Intrasegment indirect through memory (as illustrated above)
Number of cycles: 21 + EA

CALL BX   Intrasegment indirect through register
Number of cycles: 16

Notes:

1.   There are four types of CALLs:

CALL mem/reg: this instruction, intrasegment indirect CALL
CALL disp: intrasegment CALL
CALL mem: intersegment indirect CALL
CALL addr: intersegment CALL

CBW

Sign Extend the AL Register into the AH Register

If the high-order bit of the AL register is 1, store FF_{16} into the AH register, otherwise store 00_{16} into the AH register.

The encoding of this instruction is:

$$\underbrace{CBW}_{98}$$

As an example, if the AL register contains $4F_{16}$, the executing instruction

CBW

will store 00_{16} into the AH register.

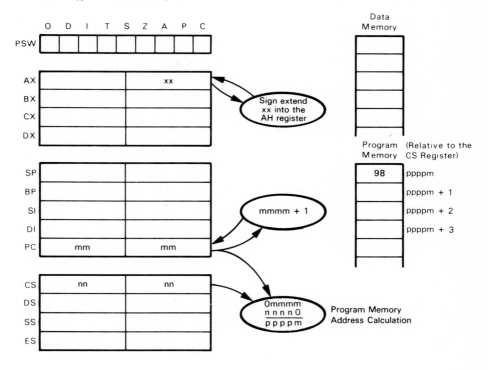

CBW
Number of cycles: 2

Notes:

1. No statuses are affected.

2. The value in the AL register should represent a number between $+127$ and -128, i.e., AL should contain a signed 8-bit value.

3. This instruction can be used for extending the AL register before a 16-bit IMUL or IDIV instruction.

CLC

Clear the Carry Status

This instruction sets the Carry status to 0. No other statuses or registers are affected.

The encoding for this instruction is

$$\underbrace{CLC}_{F8}$$

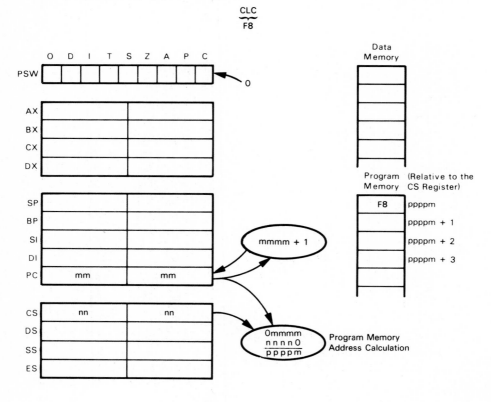

CLC
Number of cycles: 2

CLD

Clear the Direction Flag

This instruction sets the DF flag to 0. This has the effect of making the string operations perform auto-increment on the pointers used by the string operations. No other statuses or registers are affected.

The encoding for this instruction is:

$$\underbrace{\text{CLD}}_{\text{FC}}$$

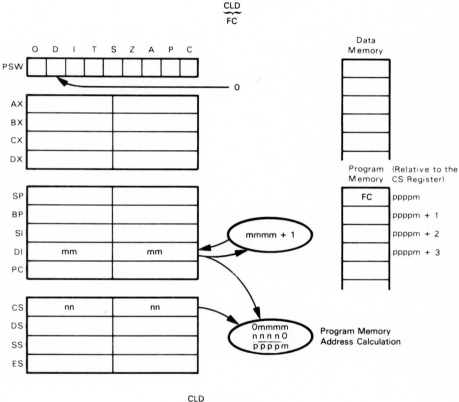

CLD
Number of cycles: 2

CLI

Clear the Interrupt Flag

Set the Interrupt flag to 0. This has the effect of disabling all interrupts except non-maskable interrupts, which occur on the NMI line.

The encoding for this instruction is:

$$\underset{\text{FA}}{\underbrace{\text{CLI}}}$$

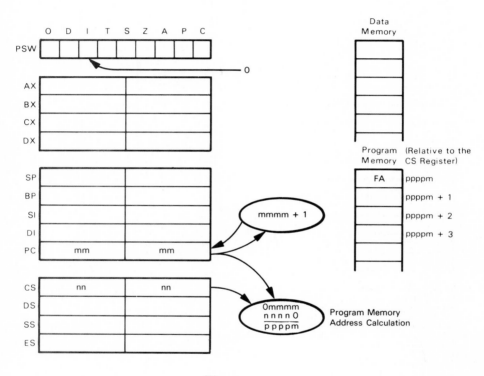

CLI
Number of cycles: 2

Notes:

1. This instruction performs the same function as the 8080 instruction DI.

2. Remember that when the 8086 acknowledges an interrupt request, the interrupts are automatically disabled.

CMC

Complement the Carry Status

Complement the Carry status. No other statuses or registers are affected.
The encoding for this instruction is:

CMC
‿
F5

For example, if the Carry status were 0 and the instruction

CMC

were executed, the Carry status would be set to 1.

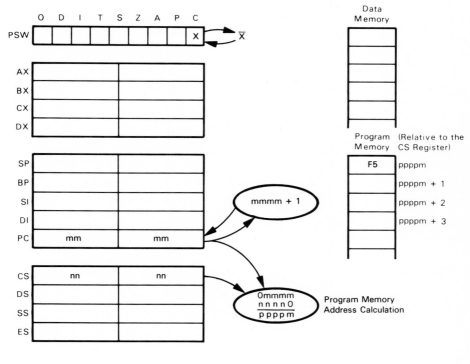

CMC
Number of cycles: 2

Notes:

1. This instruction performs the same function as the 8080 instruction CMC.

CMP ac,data

Compare Immediate Data with Accumulator

This instruction is used to compare immediate data present in the succeeding program memory byte(s) with the AL register (8-bit operation) or the AX register (16-bit operation). The comparison is performed by subtracting the data in the immediate byte(s) from the specified register and using the result to set the flags. The result of this operation is not stored in the specified register, thus no registers are affected, only the statuses.

The encoding for this instruction is:

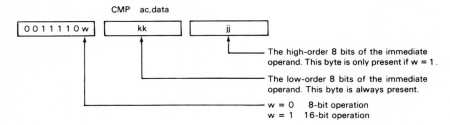

CMP   ac,data

The high-order 8 bits of the immediate operand. This byte is only present if w = 1.

The low-order 8 bits of the immediate operand. This byte is always present.

w = 0   8-bit operation
w = 1   16-bit operation

Consider the case where the AL register contains 20_{16}. After the instruction

CMP   AL,0DH

has executed, the AL register will still contain 20_{16}, but the statuses will be modified as follows:

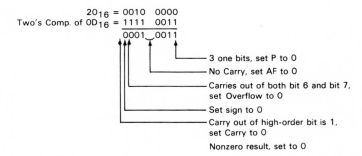

$$20_{16} = 0010\ 0000$$
Two's Comp. of $0D_{16} = 1111\ 0011$
$$0001\ 0011$$

3 one bits, set P to 0
No Carry, set AF to 0
Carries out of both bit 6 and bit 7, set Overflow to 0
Set sign to 0
Carry out of high-order bit is 1, set Carry to 0
Nonzero result, set to 0

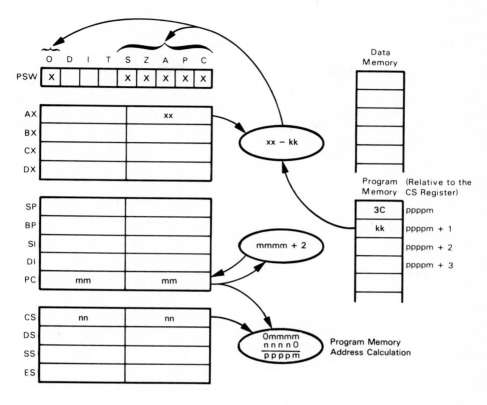

CMP   AL,kk
Number of cycles: 4

Notes:

1. If you desire to compare immediate data with any of the other general purpose registers or with the contents of some memory location, consult the CMP mem/reg, data instruction.

2. This instruction performs the same function as the 8080 instruction CPI data. In addition, this instruction allows for 16-bit comparisons.

CMP   mem/reg,data

Compare Immediate Data with Register or Memory

This instruction compares the immediate data present in the succeeding program memory byte(s) with the specified register or memory location. The comparison is performed by subtracting the data in the immediate bytes from the specified memory location or register, and using the result to set the flags. The result of this operation is not stored in the specified register or memory location, thus no registers or memory locations are affected, only the statuses. An 8-bit or 16-bit operation may be specified.

The encoding for this instruction is:

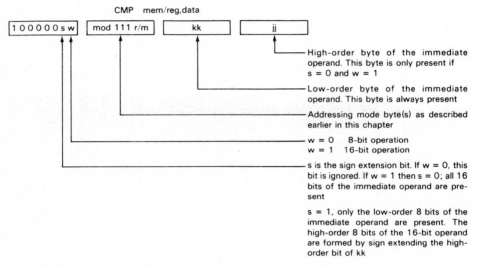

CMP   mem/reg,data

| 1 0 0 0 0 0 s w | mod 111 r/m | kk | jj |

High-order byte of the immediate operand. This byte is only present if s = 0 and w = 1

Low-order byte of the immediate operand. This byte is always present

Addressing mode byte(s) as described earlier in this chapter

w = 0   8-bit operation
w = 1   16-bit operation

s is the sign extension bit. If w = 0, this bit is ignored. If w = 1 then s = 0; all 16 bits of the immediate operand are present

s = 1, only the low-order 8 bits of the immediate operand are present. The high-order 8 bits of the 16-bit operand are formed by sign extending the high-order bit of kk

Suppose that the SI register contains $01BA_{16}$. After the instruction

CMP   SI, 0200H

has executed, the SI register will still contain $01BA_{16}$, but the statuses will be modified as follows:

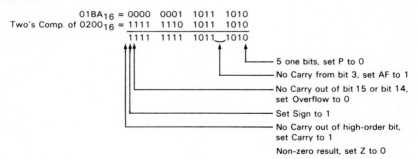

$01BA_{16}$ = 0000 0001 1011 1010
Two's Comp. of 0200_{16} = 1111 1110 1011 1010

1111 1111 1011 1010

5 one bits, set P to 0

No Carry from bit 3, set AF to 1

No Carry out of bit 15 or bit 14, set Overflow to 0

Set Sign to 1

No Carry out of high-order bit, set Carry to 1

Non-zero result, set Z to 0

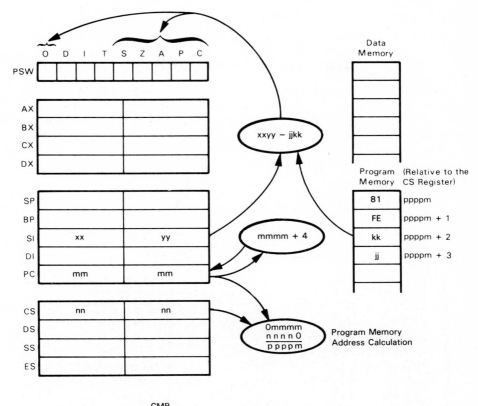

CMP
Number of cycles: Register operand: 4
                   Memory operand: 10 + EA

Notes:

1. This instruction is not typically used to CMP immediate data with the AX or AL register. The instruction CMP ac,data is provided for this purpose.

CMP   mem/reg₁, mem/reg₂

Compare: • **Register with Register**
       • **Register with Memory**
       • **Memory with Register**

     Compare the data in the register or memory operand specified by mem/reg₂ with the data in the register or memory operand specified by mem/reg₁. The comparison is performed by subtracting the data specified by mem/reg₂ from the data specified by mem/reg₁ and using the result to set the flags. Neither mem/reg₁ nor mem/reg₂ is affected by this operation. An 8- or 16-bit operation may be specified.

     The encoding for this instruction is:

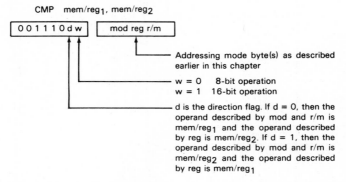

     Suppose that the DH register contains 05₁₆ and the CL register contains 06₁₆. After the instruction

CMP   CL,DH

has executed, neither the CL nor DH register will be affected; however, the flags will be set as follows:

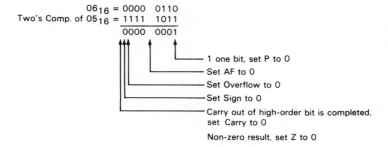

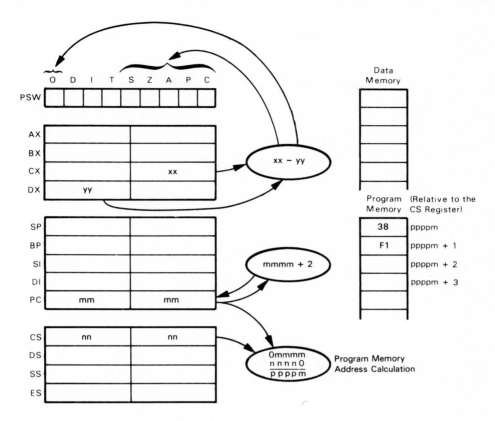

CMP   CL,DH
Number of cycles: Register with register: 3
　　　　　　　　　Memory with register: 9 + EA
　　　　　　　　　Register with memory: 16 + EA

CMPS/CMPSB/CMPSW

Compare Memory with Memory

Compare the contents of the memory location addressed by the SI register with the contents of the memory location addressed by the DI register. The comparison is performed by subtracting the contents of the memory location addressed by the DI register from the contents of the memory location addressed by the SI register and using the result to set the flags. Neither of the memory locations used in the subtraction is affected. The SI and DI registers are incremented/decremented depending on the value of the DF flag. An 8- or 16-bit operation may be specified.

The encoding for this instruction is:

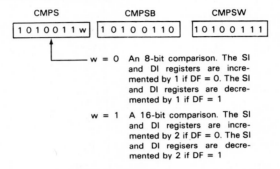

CMPS   CMPSB   CMPSW

`1 0 1 0 0 1 1 w` `1 0 1 0 0 1 1 0` `1 0 1 0 0 1 1 1`

w = 0   An 8-bit comparison. The SI and DI registers are incremented by 1 if DF = 0. The SI and DI registers are decremented by 1 if DF = 1

w = 1   A 16-bit comparison. The SI and DI registers are incremented by 2 if DF = 0. The SI and DI regisers are decremented by 2 if DF = 1

Suppose that the DF flag is 1, the DS register contains 0600_{16}, the SI register contains 0108_{16}, the ES register contains 0060_{16}, the DI register contains 0188_{16}, the word at memory location 06108_{16} is 4544_{16} and the word at memory location 00788_{16} is 4544_{16}. After the instruction

CMPSW

has executed, the SI register will contain $010A_{16}$, the DI register will contain $018A_{16}$ and the flags will be set as follows:

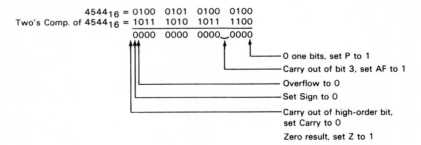

$$4544_{16} = 0100 \quad 0101 \quad 0100 \quad 0100$$
$$\text{Two's Comp. of } 4544_{16} = 1011 \quad 1010 \quad 1011 \quad 1100$$
$$\overline{0000 \quad 0000 \quad 0000 \quad 0000}$$

0 one bits, set P to 1

Carry out of bit 3, set AF to 1

Overflow to 0

Set Sign to 0

Carry out of high-order bit, set Carry to 0

Zero result, set Z to 1

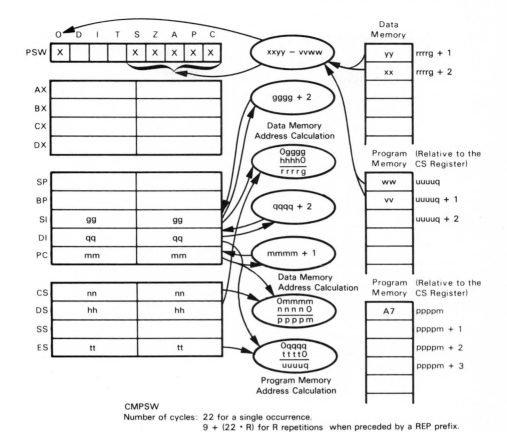

CMPSW
Number of cycles: 22 for a single occurrence.
9 + (22 · R) for R repetitions when preceded by a REP prefix.

Notes:

1. The REP prefix and/or the LOCK prefix may be used with this instruction. If the LOCK prefix and the REP prefix are both used in conjunction with the instruction, certain problems may occur. For a discussion of this enervating subject, please consult Chapter 4.

2. The default segment register for the operand addressed by SI is DS. The segment register may be changed using a segment override prefix. The default segment register for the operand addressed by DI is ES. This segment register assignment may not be overridden.

3. Intel assemblers provide the generalized form plus specific byte and word forms. For the generalized form, the assembler must have certain information to allow it to determine whether an 8-bit or 16-bit comparison will be performed. For a discussion of how this is done, please consult the end of this chapter.

4. The execution time for CMPS with a REP prefix may be illustrated as follows:

$$\underbrace{\text{REP}}_{2 \,+} \quad \underbrace{\text{CMPS}}_{9 \,+\, 22(R)}$$

If R = 10 words, then the execution time is 231 clock cycles.

CWD

Sign Extend the AX Register Into the DX Register

If the high-order bit of the AX register is 1, store $FFFF_{16}$ into the DX register, otherwise store 0000_{16} into the DX register.

The encoding for this instruction is:

$$\underset{99}{\underbrace{\text{CWD}}}$$

Suppose that the AX register contains $B001_{16}$. After the instruction

CWD

has executed, the DX register will contain $FFFF_{16}$.

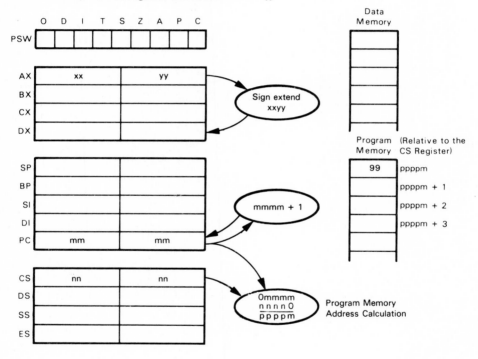

CWD
Number of cycles: 5

Notes:

1. No statuses are affected.

2. This instruction is useful when performing divisions. If a 16-bit divisor is to be used, it is necessary to have a 32-bit dividend. If the only significant bits are in the AX register, this instruction extends the sign bit into the DX register to make a 32-bit dividend. Note that this technique works best for the IDIV instruction.

DAA
Decimal Adjust Accumulator After Addition

Convert the contents of the AL register into binary coded decimal form. This instruction should be used only after adding two BCD numbers, i.e., look upon ADD DAA or ADC DAA as compound, decimal arithmetic instructions which operate on BCD source operands to generate BCD answers.

The algorithm for the conversion is:

1. If the AF flag is 1 *or* the low-order four bits of the AL register are A through F, then add 06_{16} to the AL register and set the AF flag to 1.

2. If the CF flag is 1 *or* the high-order four bits of the AL register are greater than 9, then add 60_{16} to the AL register and set the CF flag to 1.

The encoding for this instruction is:

$$\underset{27}{\underbrace{\text{DAA}}}$$

Suppose the AL register contains 28_{16} and the BL register contains 68_{16}. After the instructions

```
ADD   AL,BL
DAA
```

have executed, the AL register will contain 96_{16}, not 90_{16}.

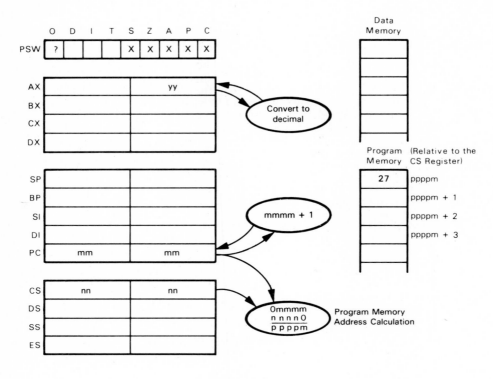

DAA
Number of cycles: 4

Notes:

1. This instruction is useful for the addition of two packed BCD operands. For adjusting the subtraction of two packed BCD operands, consult the DAS instruction. For adjusting the result of ASCII addition and subtraction, consult the AAA and AAS instructions.

DAS

Decimal Adjust Accumulator After Subtraction

This instruction converts the contents of the AL register into binary coded decimal form. This instruction should only be used after subtracting two BCD numbers, i.e., look upon SUB DAS or SBB DAS as compound decimal arithmetic instructions which operate on BCD source operands to generate BCD answers.

The algorithm for the conversion is:

1. If the AF flag is 1 *or* the low-order four bits of the AL register are between A and F, then subtract 06_{16} from the AL register and set the AF flag to 1.

2. If the CF flag is 1 *or* the high-order four bits of the AL register are greater than 9, then subtract 60_{16} from the AL register and set the CF flag to 1.

The encoding for this instruction is:

$$\underset{\overbrace{}}{\text{DAS}}$$
$$2F$$

Suppose that the AL register contains 86_{16} and the AH register contains 07_{16}. After the sequence of instructions

```
SUB   AL,AH
DAS
```

has executed, the AL register will contain 79_{16}. The SUB instruction results in the AL register containing $7F_{16}$.

$$
\begin{array}{r}
86_{16} = 1000 \quad 0110 \\
\text{Two's Comp. of } 07_{16} = \underline{1111 \quad 1001} \\
0111 \quad 1111
\end{array}
$$

Carry out is complemented, set C to 0

Since the low-order 4 bits of the AL register equal F_{16}, the first step of the algorithm is performed. The AF flag is set to 1.

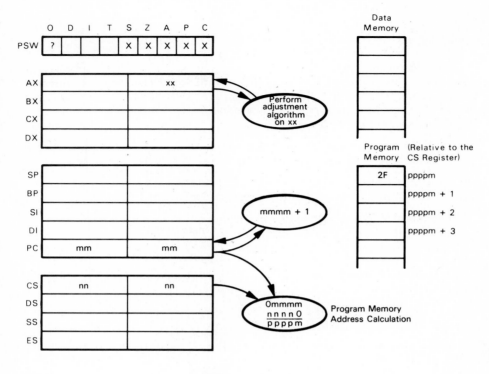

DAS
Number of cycles: 4

Notes:

1. This is a decimal subtraction adjustment algorithm for two packed BCD numbers. Another operation available for adjustment of subtractions is the AAS instruction, which adjusts the results of subtracting ASCII digits.

DEC   mem/reg

Decrement Register or Memory Location

Subtract 1 from the contents of the specified register or memory location. An 8- or 16-bit operation may be specified.

The encoding for this instruction is:

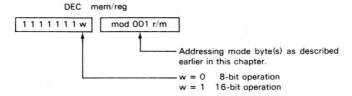

DEC   mem/reg

| 1 1 1 1 1 1 1 w | mod 001 r/m |

Addressing mode byte(s) as described earlier in this chapter.

w = 0   8-bit operation
w = 1   16-bit operation

Suppose that the BH register contains $4F_{16}$. After the instruction

DEC   BH

executes, the BH register contains $4E_{16}$.

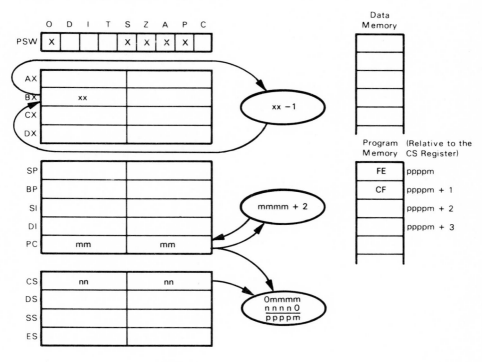

DEC   BH
Number of cycles: Register operand: 3
Memory operand: 15 + EA

Notes:

1. This instruction can perform the same function as the 8080 instruction DCR reg. Note that due to the various addressing modes available and the 8-/16-bit option, this instruction has a good deal more power than the 8080 instruction.

2. Segment registers may not be modified using this instruction.

3. This instruction would not normally be asked to decrement one of the 16-bit registers. The instruction DEC reg performs this function and only occupies one byte of program memory space. This instruction would be used to decrement one of the 8-bit registers or memory.

4. This instruction does not affect the Carry status.

DEC   reg

Decrement Register

Subtract 1 from the contents of the specified register. This is a 16-bit decrement instruction.

The encoding for this instruction is:

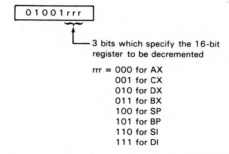

```
01001rrr
```

3 bits which specify the 16-bit register to be decremented

rrr = 000 for AX
      001 for CX
      010 for DX
      011 for BX
      100 for SP
      101 for BP
      110 for SI
      111 for DI

As an example, examine the case where the CX register contains 0200_{16}. Executing a

    DEC   CX

instruction will result in the contents of the CX register being decremented to $01FF_{16}$.

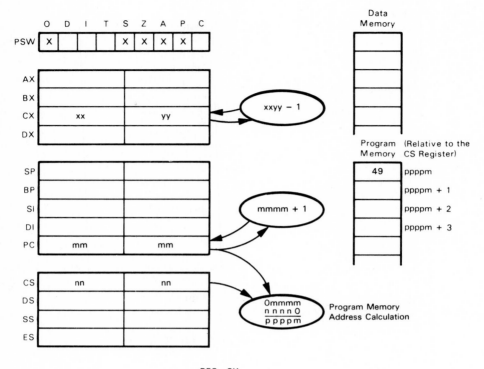

DEC   CX
Number of cycles: 2

Notes:

1. This instruction performs the same function as the 8080 instruction DCX reg.

2. Segment registers may not be decremented using this instruction.

DIV   mem/reg

Divide AH:AL or DX:AX Registers by Register or Memory Location

Divide the AH:AL (8-bit operation) or DX:AX (16-bit operation) register by the contents of the specified 8- or 16-bit register or memory location, considering both operands as unsigned binary numbers. The instruction allows a 16-bit unsigned number to be divided by an 8-bit unsigned number, or a 32-bit unsigned number to be divided by a 16-bit unsigned number. If an 8-bit operation is performed, the 8-bit quotient is returned in the AL register, the 8-bit remainder is returned in the AH register. If the quotient to be returned to the AL register is greater than FF_{16}, then a type 0 (division by zero) interrupt is generated. If a 16-bit operation is performed, the 16-bit quotient is returned to the AX register, the 16-bit remainder is returned to the DX register. If the quotient to be returned to the AX register is greater than $FFFF_{16}$, then a type 0 (division by zero) interrupt is generated.

A division by zero interrupt results in the following actions:

1.   Push the Flags register onto the stack.

2.   Clear the IF and TF flags.

3.   Push the CS register onto the stack.

4.   Load the word at memory location 00002_{16} into the CS register.

5.   Push the PC onto the stack.

6.   Load the word at memory location 00000_{16} into the PC register.

The encoding for this instruction is:

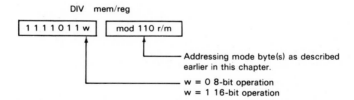

As an example, consider the case where the AX register contains $0F05_{16}$, the DX register contains $068A_{16}$, and the CX register contains $08E9_{16}$. After the instruction

DIV   CX

has executed, the AX register will contain the quotient $BBE1_{16}$, and the DX register will contain the $073C_{16}$. The values of the OF, SF, ZF, AF, PF, and CF flags are undetermined for this operation, i.e., you have no idea what the value of a particular flag will be following DIV.

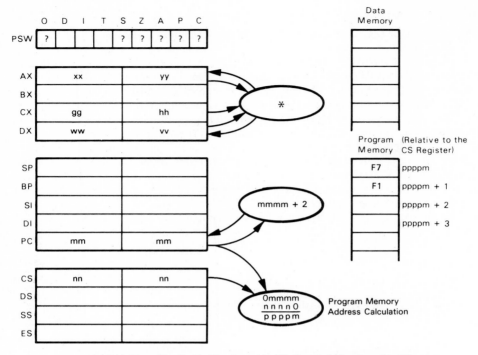

x wwvvxxyy is divided by gghh. Quotient is returned to AX. Remainder is returned to DX

```
DIV   CX
Number of cycles:16-bit memory divide: (150-168) + EA
                  8-bit memory divide: (86-96) + EA
                  16-bit register: 144-162
                  8-bit register: 80-90
```

Notes:

1. The values for all of the arithmetic flags are undetermined after this instruction has executed.

2. If it is necessary to determine whether the DIV instruction will result in a division by 0 interrupt prior to the execution of the DIV instruction, the following instruction sequences will prove helpful.

    16-bit division: Assume that CL contains the divisor.

    ```
    CMP   AH, CL
    JNB   OVERFLOW$HANDLER
    ```

    32-bit division: Assume that BX contains the divisor.

    ```
    CMP   DX,BX
    JNB   OVERFLOW$HANDLER
    ```

    This sort of check would be useful if the divide by zero interrupt handler was not sufficient for your purposes.

3. When the dividend and divisor are the same length, the dividend must first be extended to 16 or 32 bits using a CBW or CWD instruction.

ESC   mem

Access Memory Location

This instruction places the contents of the specified memory location on the data bus. Essentially this instruction performs no operation as far as the 8086 is concerned. This instruction is used to allow other processors to make use of 8086 addressing modes and to receive their instructions from the 8086 instruction stream.

The encoding for this instruction is:

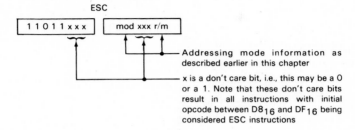

Suppose that the BX register contains $063A_{16}$, the SI register contains 0003_{16}, the DS register contains $FF80_{16}$, and the word at memory location $FFE3D_{16}$ is $C308_{16}$. When the instruction

ESC   [BX + SI]

executes, at the time when the READY line is asserted by the addressed memory device, $C308_{16}$ will be present on the data lines.

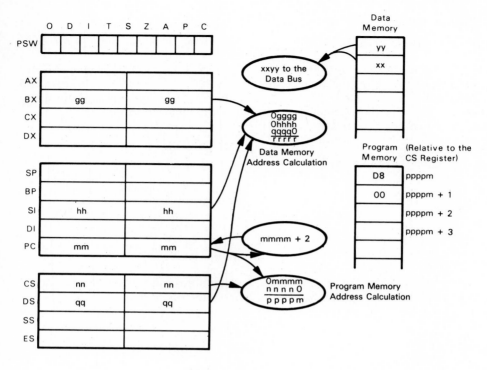

ESC
Number of cycles: 8 + EA

Notes:

1. If mod = 11 (i.e., a register is addressed), this instruction performs no operation.
    CLOCK CYCLES = 2.

HLT

Halt the Processor

When the HLT instruction is executed, program execution ceases. It requires an external interrupt or a reset to restart execution. No registers or statuses are affected.

CAUTION: If interrupts are not enabled by an STI instruction prior to the HLT instruction, the 8086 CPU cannot exit the Halt state except by activation of the hardware Reset or nonmaskable interrupt.

The encoding for this instruction is:

HLT
‿
F4

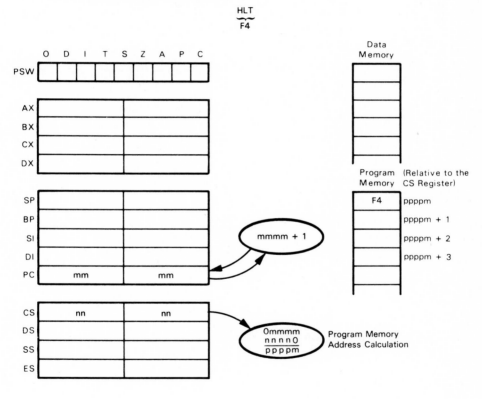

HLT
Number of cycles: 2

IDIV   mem/reg

Divide AH:AL or DX:AX by Register or Memory Location

Divide the AH:AL (8-bit operation) or DX:AX (16-bit operation) register by the contents of the specified 8- or 16-bit register or memory location, considering both operands as signed binary numbers. The instruction allows a 16-bit signed number to be divided by an 8-bit signed number, or a 32-bit signed number to be divided by a 16-bit signed number. If an 8-bit operation is performed, the 8-bit quotient is returned in the AL register; the 8-bit remainder is returned in the AH register. If the quotient to be returned is greater than $7F_{16}$, then a type 0 (division by zero) interrupt is generated. If a 16-bit operation is performed, the 16-bit quotient is returned to the AX register; the 16-bit remainder is returned to the DX register. If the quotient to be returned to the AX register is greater than $7FFFF_{16}$, then a type 0 (division by zero) interrupt is generated.

A division by zero interrupt results in the following actions:

1. Push the Flags register onto the stack.
2. Clear the IF and TF flags.
3. Push the CS register onto the stack.
4. Load the word at memory location 00002_{16} into the CS register.
5. Push the PC onto the stack.
6. Load the word at memory location 00000_{16} into the PC register.

The encoding for this instruction is:

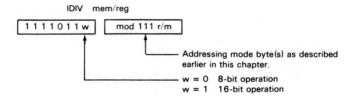

Suppose that the CL register contains $0D_{16}$ and the AX register contains $00A9_{16}$. After the instruction

IDIV   CL

has executed, the AX register will contain $000D_{16}$.

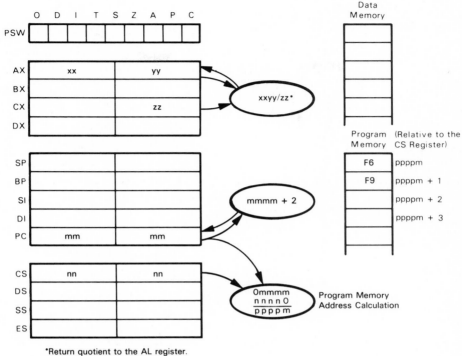

*Return quotient to the AL register.
Return remainder to AH register

IDIV   CL
Number of cycles: 8-bit memory division:
16-bit memory division:
8-bit register division:
16-bit register division:

Notes:

1.   This is the signed number division instruction. Both operands are treated as signed binary numbers in the range:

> 8-bit operation: +127 to −128
> 16-bit operation: +32767 to −32768

For an unsigned division, consult the DIV instruction.

2.   After this instruction executes, the values of the flags are unknown.

3.   When the dividend and divisor are the same length, the dividend must first be converted to 16- or 32-bit form using a CBW or CWD instruction.

IMUL   mem/reg

Multiply AL or AX Register by Register or Memory Location

Multiply the specified register or memory location contents by the AL (8-bit operation) or AX (16-bit operation) register considering both operands as signed binary numbers, i.e., perform a signed multiplication. If an 8-bit operation is performed, the low-order 8 bits of the result will be stored in the AL register, the high-order 8 bits of the result will be stored in the AH register. If a 16-bit operation is performed, the low-order 16 bits of the result are stored in the AX register, the high-order 16 bits of the result are stored in the DX register. In either case, if the high-order half of the result is the sign extension of the low-order half of the result then the Overflow and Carry flags are set to 0, otherwise they are set to 1. (For example, if an 8-bit operation is performed, if the value returned to the AH register is not 00_{16} or FF_{16}, then the Carry and Overflow flags will be 1.) 0 status values mean that AH or DX contains significant digits.

The encoding for this instruction is:

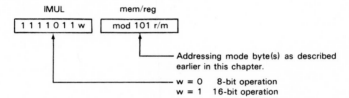

As an example, consider the case where the AX register contains $04E8_{16}$, the DS register contains 0100_{16}, the BX register contains 0006_{16} and the word at memory location 01006_{16} is $4E20_{16}$. After the instruction

IMUL   AX, [BX]

has executed, the AX register will contain $4D00_{16}$, the DX register will contain $017F_{16}$ and the Carry and Overflow statuses will be 1.

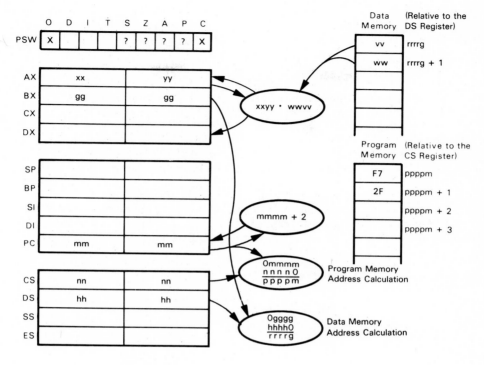

IMUL AX,[BX]
Number of cycles: 8-bit memory multiply: (86 + 104) + EA
16-bit memory multiply: (134 + 160) + EA
8-bit register multiply: 80–98
16-bit register multiply: 128–154

Notes:

1. This is the signed number multiply operation. Both operands are treated as numbers in the range:

    8-bit operation: +127 to −128
    16-bit operation: +32767 to −32768

    For an unsigned multiply operation, consult the instruction MUL.

2. In some cases, it may be more appropriate to use shifts to perform multiplications. These cases would occur when memory conservation is not of paramount importance and speed is necessary.

3. After this instruction has executed, the values of the Sign, Zero, Arithmetic, and Parity flags are undefined.

IN   ac,DX

Input to Accumulator

This instruction loads 8- or 16-bit data elements into the AL (8-bit transfer) or AX (16-bit transfer) register from the I/O port identified by the contents of the DX register.

The encoding for this instruction is:

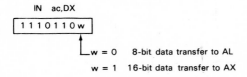

IN   ac,DX

| 1 1 1 0 1 1 0 w |

w = 0   8-bit data transfer to AL

w = 1   16-bit data transfer to AX

No other registers (with the exception of AL or AX) or statuses are affected.

Suppose that the DX register contains 1234_{16}, the I/O buffer at Port 1234_{16} contains 23_{16}, and I/O buffer at Port 1235_{16} contains $F4_{16}$. Executing an

IN   AX,DX

will load 23_{16} into the AL register and $F4_{16}$ into the AH register.

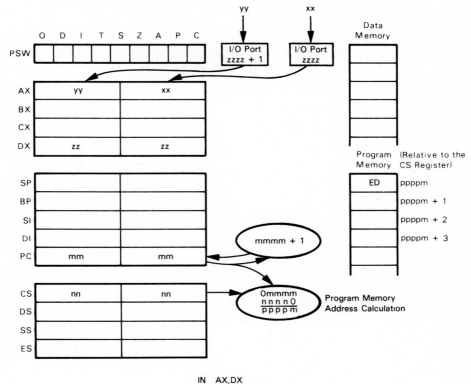

IN   AX,DX
Number of cycles: 8

Notes:

1.   This instruction allows the user to access input ports which have been assigned addresses between 0 and $FFFF_{16}$.

2.   ac may be specified only as AL for 8-bit and AX for 16-bit input.

IN   ac,port

Input to Accumulator

This instruction loads 8- or 16-bit data elements into the AL (8-bit transfer) or AX (16-bit transfer) register from the I/O port identified by the second byte of the instruction.

The encoding for this instruction is:

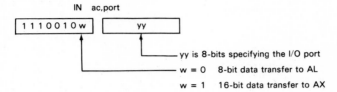

No other registers (with the exception of AL or AX) or statuses are affected. Suppose that the I/O buffer at Port 06_{16} contains 43_{16}. Executing an

IN   AL,06H

instruction will load 43_{16} into the AL register.

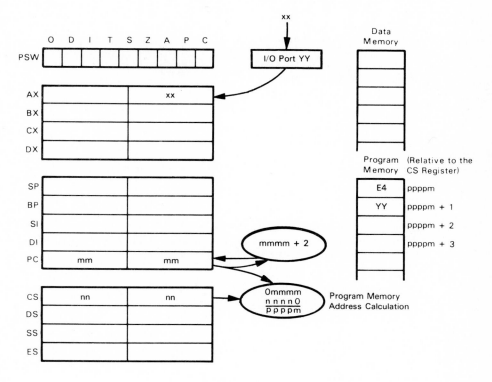

IN   AL,yy
Number of cycles: 10

Notes:

1. This instruction allows the user to access I/O ports which have been assigned addresses between 0 and FF_{16}. To address ports whose addresses are outside this range, consult the instruction IN ac,DX.

2. This instruction performs the same function as the 8080 instruction IN port.

3. ac may be specified only as AL for 8-bit and AX for 16-bit input.

INC   mem/reg

Increment Register or Memory Location

Add 1 to the contents of the specified register or memory location. An 8- or 16-bit operation may be specified.

The encoding for this instruction is:

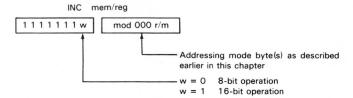

Consider the case in which the DS register contains $F800_{16}$, the contents of the BX register are 0280_{16}, the SI register contains $1E_{16}$, and memory location $F829E_{16}$ contains 64_{16}. After the execution of the instruction

INC   [BX + SI]

location $F829E_{16}$ will contain 65_{16}.

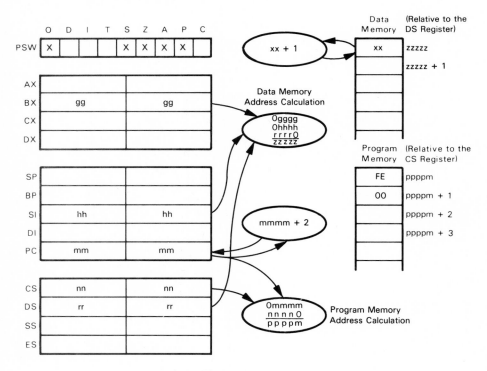

INC   [BX + SI]
Number of cycles: Memory Operand: 15 + EA
Register Operand: 3

Notes:

1. Segment registers may not be incremented by this instruction.

2. This instruction can perform the same function as the 8080 instruction INR reg. Note also that this instruction has a good deal more power than the 8080 instruction.

3. This instruction would not normally be used to increment one of the 16-bit registers. The instruction INC reg performs this function and only occupies one byte of program memory space. This instruction would be used to increment one of the 8-bit registers and memory locations.

4. This instruction does not affect the Carry status.

INC   reg

Increment Register

Add 1 to the contents of the specified register. This is a 16-bit increment instruction.

The encoding for this instruction is:

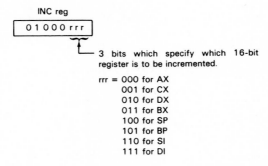

INC reg

```
0 1 0 0 0 r r r
```

— 3 bits which specify which 16-bit register is to be incremented.

rrr = 000 for AX
001 for CX
010 for DX
011 for BX
100 for SP
101 for BP
110 for SI
111 for DI

Consider the case where the contents of the SI register are $00FF_{16}$. Executing an

INC   SI

will result in the contents of the SI register being incremented to 0100_{16}.

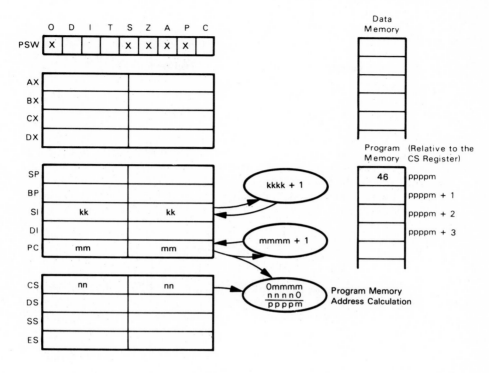

INC SI
Number of cycles: 2

Notes:

1. This instruction performs the same function as the 8080 instruction INX reg.

2. Segment registers may not be incremented using this instruction.

3. This instruction does not affect the Carry status.

INT

Software Interrupt

This instruction performs the following sequence of operations:

1. Push the Flags register onto the stack.

2. Clear the IF and TF flags to 0.

3. Push the CS register onto the stack.

4. Load the word at memory address 00xxx into the CS register. xxx is determined by the low-order bit of the op-code and possibly the second byte of the instruction. If the low-order bit of the op-code is 0, then xxx is $00E_{16}$. If the low-order bit of the op-code is 1, then xxx is equal to 2 plus 4 times the second byte of the instruction. In other words,

$$\text{IF low-order bit} = 0 \quad \text{THEN xxx} = 00E_{16}$$
$$\text{ELSE xxx} = (4*\text{2nd byte}) + 2$$

5. Push the PC register onto the stack.

6. Load the word at memory address 00yyy into the PC register. yyy is determined by the low-order bit of the op-code and possibly the second byte of the instruction. If the low-order bit of the op-code is 0, then yyy is $00C_{16}$. If the low-order bit of the op-code is 1, then yyy is equal to 4 times the second byte of the instruction. In other words,

$$\text{IF low-order bit} = 0 \quad \text{THEN yyy} = 00C_{16}$$
$$\text{ELSE yyy} = 4 * \text{2nd byte}$$

The encoding for this instruction is:

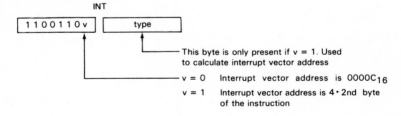

INT

| 1 1 0 0 1 1 0 v | type |

This byte is only present if v = 1. Used to calculate interrupt vector address

v = 0   Interrupt vector address is $0000C_{16}$

v = 1   Interrupt vector address is 4 · 2nd byte of the instruction

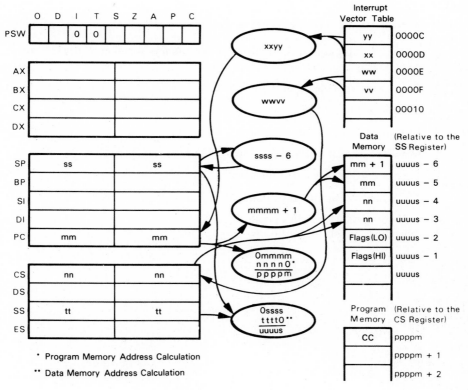

O D I T S Z A P C

PSW [ ][0][0][ ][ ][ ][ ][ ][ ]

AX
BX
CX
DX

SP   ss   ss
BP
SI
DI
PC   mm   mm

CS   nn   nn
DS
SS   tt   tt
ES

Interrupt
Vector Table

xxyy

wwvv

ssss − 6

mmmm + 1

Ommmm
nnnn0*
ppppm

Ossss
ttttO**
uuuus

Interrupt Vector Table:
yy   0000C
xx   0000D
ww   0000E
vv   0000F
     00010

Data   (Relative to the
Memory   SS Register)
mm + 1   uuuus − 6
mm   uuuus − 5
nn   uuuus − 4
nn   uuuus − 3
Flags(LO) uuuus − 2
Flags(HI) uuuus − 1
          uuuus

Program   (Relative to the
Memory   CS Register)
CC   ppppm
          ppppm + 1
          ppppm + 2

* Program Memory Address Calculation

** Data Memory Address Calculation

INT
Number of cycles: 52 if v = 0
                  51 if v = 1

INTO

If Overflow Flag = 1, Perform Type 4 Interrupt

If the Overflow flag is 0, this instruction performs no operation. If the Overflow flag is 1, the following sequence of events occurs:

1. Push the Flags register onto the stack.

2. Set the IF and TF flags to 0.

3. Push the CS register onto the stack.

4. Move the word at memory location 00012_{16} into the CS register.

5. Push the PC register onto the stack.

6. Move the word at memory location 00010_{16} into the PC register.

Continue execution from this point.
The encoding for this instruction is:

INTO
⌣⌣
CE

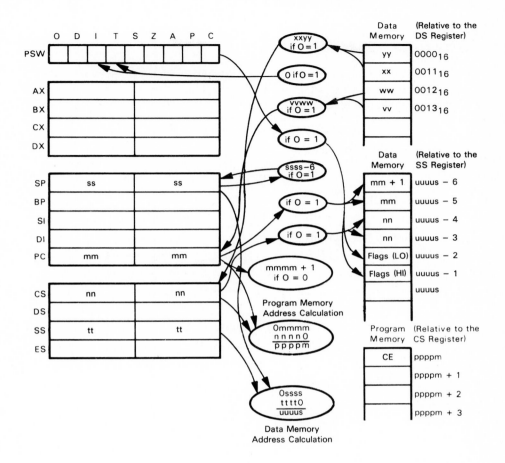

Program Memory
Address Calculation

Data Memory
Address Calculation

INTO
Number of cycles: 53 if overflow set
4 if not

IRET

Return from Interrupt

Pop the two top stack bytes into the program counter; these two bytes provide the offset address for the next instruction to be executed. Pop the next two stack bytes into the CS register; these two bytes provide the code segment address of the next instruction to be executed. Pop the next two stack bytes into the Flags register. Previous program counter, code segment and Flags register contents are lost.

The encoding for this instruction is:

IRET
‿‿
CF

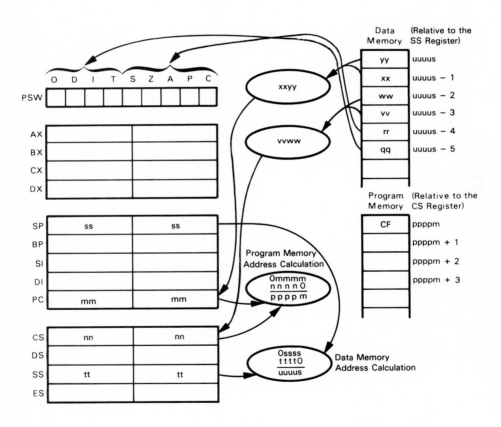

IRET
Number of cycles: 32

JA   disp
JNBE   disp

Jump if Not Below or Equal

This instruction is identical to the JMP disp instruction except that the Jump is executed only if the Carry flag *and* the Zero flag are 0; otherwise the next instruction is executed.

The encoding for this instruction is:

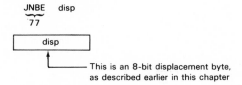

In the following instruction sequence

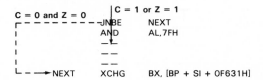

after the JNBE instruction, the XCHG instruction is executed if the Carry flag and the Zero flag are 0. The AND instruction is executed if the Carry flag or the Zero flag is 1.

Number of cycles: Jump is performed: 16
                   Jump is not performed: 4

JAE   disp
JNB   disp

Jump if Not Below/Jump if Above or Equal

This instruction is identical to the JMP disp instruction except that the Jump is executed only if the Carry flag is 0, otherwise the next instruction is executed.

The encoding for this instruction is:

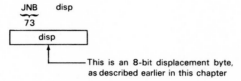

In the following instruction sequence

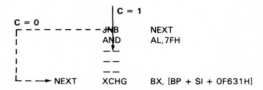

after the JNB instruction, the XCHG instruction is executed if the Carry flag is 0. The AND instruction is executed if the Carry flag is 1.

Number of cycles: Jump is performed: 16
Jump is not performed: 4

JB   disp
JNAE   disp

Jump if Below/Jump if Not Above or Equal

This instruction is identical to the JMP instruction except that the Jump is executed only if the Carry flag is 1.

The encoding for this instruction is:

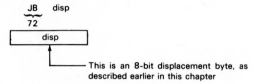

In the following instruction sequence

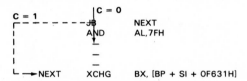

after the JB instruction, the XCHG instruction is executed if the Carry flag is 1. The AND instruction is executed if the Carry status is 0.

Number of cycles: Jump is performed: 16
Jump is not performed: 4

JBE   disp
JNA   disp

Jump if Below or Equal/Jump if Not Above

This instruction is identical to the JMP disp instruction except that the Jump is executed only if either the Carry status *or* the Zero status is 1; otherwise the next instruction is executed.

The encoding for this instruction is:

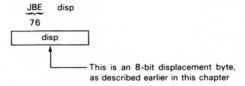

This is an 8-bit displacement byte, as described earlier in this chapter

In the following instruction sequence

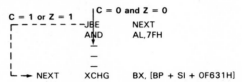

after the JBE instruction, the XCHG instruction will be executed if the Carry status or the Zero status is 1. If both the Carry *and* Zero statuses are 0, then the AND instruction will be executed.

Number of cycles: Jump is performed: 16
Jump is not performed: 4

JCXZ   disp

Jump if CX = 0

This instruction is identical to the JMP disp instruction except that the Jump is executed only if the CX register is 0; otherwise the next instruction is executed.

The encoding for this instruction is:

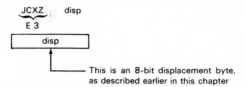

In the following instruction sequence

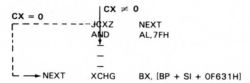

after the JCXZ instruction, the XCHG instruction is executed if the CX register is 0. The AND instruction is executed if the CX register is not 0.

Note that this instruction does not reference the Zero flag to determine if CX is 0; the CX register is referenced directly.

Number of cycles: Jump is performed: 18
Jump is not performed: 6

JE   disp
JZ   disp

Jump if Zero/Jump if Equal

This instruction is identical to the JMP disp instruction except that the Jump is executed only if the Zero status equals 1; otherwise the next instruction is executed.

The encoding for this instruction is:

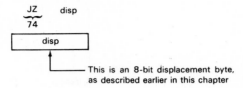

In the following instruction sequence

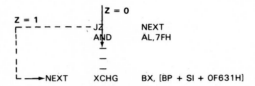

after the JZ instruction, the XCHG instruction is executed if the Zero status equals 1. The AND instruction is executed if the Zero status equals 0.

Number of cycles: Jump is performed: 16
Jump is not performed: 4

JG   disp
JNLE   disp

Jump if Greater/Jump if Not Less nor Equal

This instruction is identical to the JMP disp instruction except that the Jump is executed only if the Zero flag is 0 *and* the Sign flag equals the Overflow flag; otherwise the next instruction is executed.

The encoding for this instruction is:

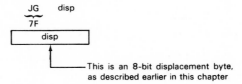

This is an 8-bit displacement byte, as described earlier in this chapter

In the following instruction sequence

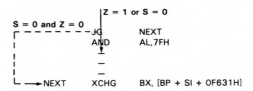

after the JG instruction, the XCHG instruction will be executed if the Zero status is 0 *and* the Sign status equals the Overflow status. If the Zero status is 1 *or* the Sign status does not equal the Overflow status, then the AND instruction is executed.

Number of cycles: Jump is performed: 16
Jump is not performed: 4

JGE disp
JNL disp

Jump if Not Less/Jump if Greater Than or Equal

This instruction is identical to the JMP disp instruction except that the Jump is executed only if the Sign status is equal to the Overflow status; otherwise the next instruction is executed.

The encoding for this instruction is:

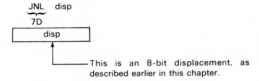

In the following instruction sequence

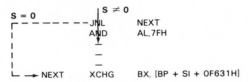

after the JNL instruction, the XCHG instruction is executed if the Sign status is equal to the Overflow status. The AND instruction will be executed if the Sign status is not equal to the Overflow status.

Number of cycles: Jump is performed: 16
Jump is not performed: 4

JL   disp
JNGE   disp

Jump if Less/Jump if Not Greater Than or Equal

This instruction is identical to the JMP disp instruction except that the Jump is executed only if the Sign flag is not equal to the Overflow flag; otherwise the next instruction is executed.

The encoding for this instruction is:

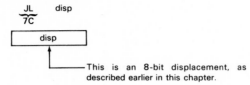

In the following instruction sequence

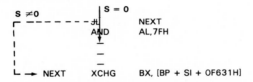

after the JL instruction has executed, the XCHG instruction will be executed if the Sign status is not equal to the Overflow status. The AND instruction is executed if the Sign status and the Overflow status are equal.

Number of cycles: Jump is performed: 16
Jump is not performed: 4

JLE   disp
JNG   disp

Jump if Less or Equal/Jump if not Greater

This instruction is identical to the JMP disp instruction except that the Jump is executed only if the Zero flag is set *or* the Sign flag is not equal to the Overflow flag; otherwise the next instruction is executed.

The encoding for this instruction is:

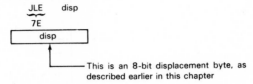

In the following instruction sequence

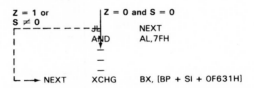

after the JL instruction, the XCHG instruction is executed if the Zero flag is 1 *or* if the Sign flag is not equal to the Overflow flag. The AND instruction is executed if the Zero status is 0 *and* the Sign status equals the Overflow status.

Number of cycles: Jump is performed: 16

Jump is not performed: 4

JMP   addr

Jump to the Instruction Identified in the Operand

Move the contents of the next two program memory bytes into the PC register. Move the contents of the succeeding two program memory bytes (bytes 4 and 5 of the instruction) into the CS register. Continue execution from this point. The previous program counter and Code Segment register contents are lost.

The encoding for this instruction is:

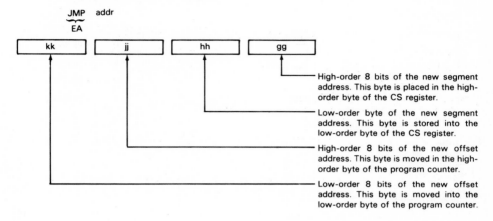

High-order 8 bits of the new segment address. This byte is placed in the high-order byte of the CS register.

Low-order byte of the new segment address. This byte is stored into the low-order byte of the CS register.

High-order 8 bits of the new offset address. This byte is moved in the high-order byte of the program counter.

Low-order 8 bits of the new offset address. This byte is moved into the low-order byte of the program counter.

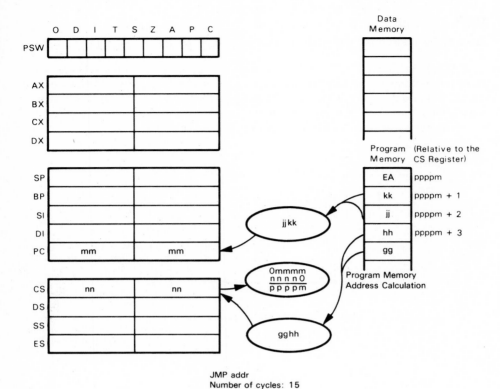

JMP addr
Number of cycles: 15

Notes:

1. The 32 bits of immediate data are the target address and are considered a far label (changes the segment register).

2. The transfer is a direct transfer to a far label.

JMP   disp

Jump to the Instruction Identified in the Operand

This instruction adds the contents of the second object code byte (taken as a signed 8-bit displacement) to the contents of the program counter plus 2; this becomes the offset address of the next instruction to be executed. Previous program counter contents are lost. The Code Segment register contents are unchanged.

The encoding for this instruction is:

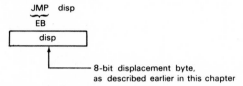

8-bit displacement byte,
as described earlier in this chapter

In the following instruction sequence

```
          JMP      NEXT
          AND      AL,7FH
           —
           —
           —
NEXT      XOR      AL,7FH
```

after the JMP instruction, the XOR instruction will be executed. The AND instruction will never be executed unless a Jump or Call instruction somewhere else in the sequence branches to this instruction.

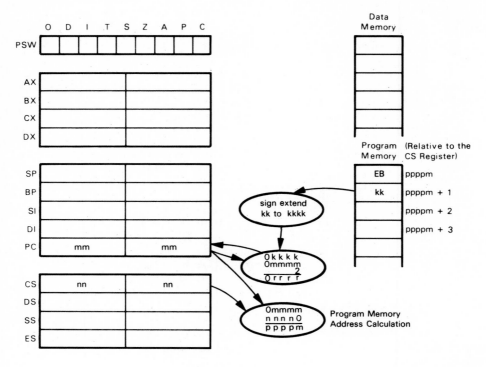

JMP   kk
Number of cycles: 15 clocks

Notes:

1. This instruction uses Program Relative addressing, which is similar to Program Relative Paging as described in *An Introduction to Microcomputers: Volume I — Basic Concepts* (Osborne/McGraw-Hill, 1978). The exception is that the program counter contents are incremented to point to the next instruction before the 8-bit signed displacement is added.

2. This is a self-relative jump within the current segment.

3. The 8-bit displacement is considered a short label displacement.

JMP   disp16

Jump to the Instruction Identified in the Operand

Add the contents of the next two program memory bytes, treating them as a 16-bit unsigned displacement, to the program counter. Continue execution from this point. The previous program counter contents are lost.

The encoding for this instruction is:

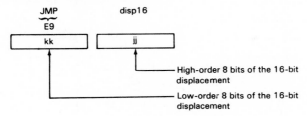

In the following instruction sequence

```
                 JMP    NEXT
       BRICKS    AND    AL,7FH
                  —
                  —
                  —
       NEXT      STOS   BYTE
```

after the JMP instruction has executed, the STOS instruction will be executed. The AND instruction will never be executed unless a CALL or JMP instruction somewhere else in the instruction sequence refers to BRICKS as its operand.

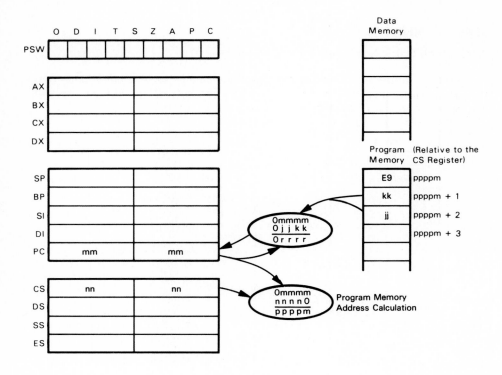

JMP   jjkk
Number of cycles: 15

Notes:

1. This is a self-relative jump within the current segment.

2. The 16-bit displacement is considered a near label (within this segment) displacement.

JMP   mem

Jump to the Instruction Specified by the Operand

Move the word at the specified memory location into the program counter; move the succeeding word into the CS register. Continue execution from this point. Previous program counter and Code Segment register contents are lost.

The encoding for this instruction is:

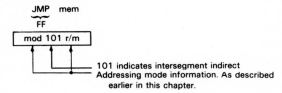

Suppose that the DS register contains 7000_{16}, the DI register contains 0404_{16}, the word at memory location 70404_{16} is 1000_{16}, and the word at memory location 70406_{16} is $7E00_{16}$. After the instruction

JMP far_ptr[DI]

has executed, the program counter will contain 1000_{16} and the CS register will contain $7E00_{16}$. Instruction execution will continue from location $7F000_{16}$.

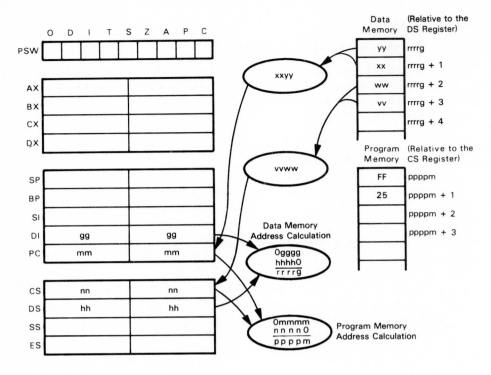

JMP far _ptr[DI]
Number of cycles: 24 + EA intersegment

Notes:

1. Register addressing is not valid for this instruction.

2. This is an intersegment (changes segments) indirect jump through memory, often used for jump tables.

3. The 32-bit target address is considered a far label.

4. The far_ptr directive preceding [DI] tells the assembler to generate the JMP which expects a 32-bit pointer in memory.

JMP   mem/reg

Jump to the Instruction Specified by the Operand

If the specified operand is a register, move the contents of the register into the program counter. If the specified operand is a memory location, move the contents of the memory location into the program counter. Continue execution from this point. Previous program counter contents are lost. The CS register is unchanged.

The encoding for this instruction is:

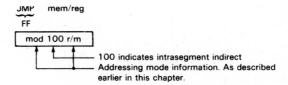

Suppose that the BX register contains $14A9_{16}$. After the instruction

JMP   BX

has executed, the PC will contain $14A9_{16}$ and execution will resume with $14A9_{16}$ as the offset address for the next instruction.

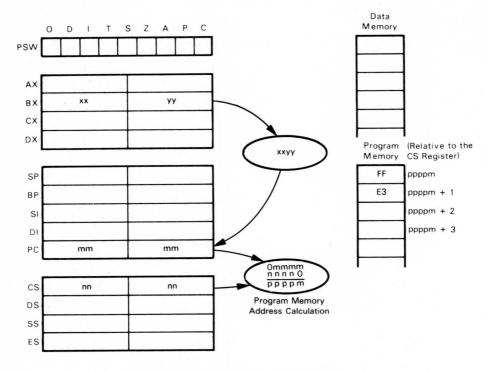

Number of cycles: JMP BX: 11 through registers
JMP [BX]: 16 + EA through memory

Notes:

1. This is an intrasegment (within the segment) indirect jump through either memory or a register.

2. No registers or statuses are affected.

3. The 16-bit target address is considered a near label (within the segment).

4. Absence of far_ptr indicates a 16-bit pointer in memory rather than a 32-bit pointer as in the previous JMP instruction. This assembler convention allows a single mnemonic, JMP, to be used for a variety of binary instruction codes.

JNE   disp
JNZ   disp

Jump if Not Equal/Jump if Not Zero

This instruction is identical to the JMP disp instruction except that the Jump is executed only if the Zero flag is equal to 0; otherwise the next instruction is executed. The encoding for this instruction is:

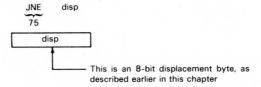

In the following instruction sequence

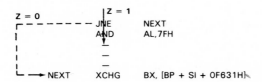

after the JNE instruction, the XCHG instruction will be executed if the Zero flag is 0. The AND instruction will be executed if the Zero flag is 1.

Number of cycles: Jump is performed: 16
Jump is not performed: 4

JNO   disp

Jump on Not Overflow

This instruction is identical to the JMP disp instruction except that the Jump is executed only if the Overflow status is 0; otherwise the next instruction is executed.
The encoding for this instruction is:

This is an 8-bit displacement byte, as described earlier in this chapter

In the following instruction sequence

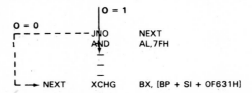

after the JNO instruction, the XCHG instruction is executed if the Overflow status is 0.
The AND instruction is executed if the Overflow status is 1.

Number of cycles: Jump is performed: 16
Jump is not performed: 4

JNP   disp
JPO   disp

Jump if No Parity/Jump if Parity Odd

This instruction is identical to the JMP disp instruction except that the Jump is executed only if the Parity flag is 0; otherwise the next instruction is executed.

The encoding for this instruction is:

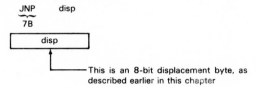

In the following instruction sequence

after the JNP instruction, the XCHG instruction is executed if the Parity flag is 0. The AND instruction is executed if the Parity flag is 1.

Number of cycles: Jump is performed: 16
Jump is not performed: 4

JNS   disp

Jump on Not Sign

This instruction is identical to the JMP disp instruction except that the Jump is executed only if the Sign flag is 0; otherwise the next instruction is executed.

The encoding for this instruction is:

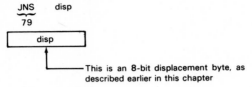

In the following instruction sequence

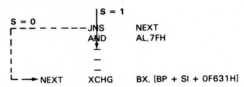

after the JNS instruction is executed, the XCHG instruction executes if the Sign status is 0; otherwise the AND instruction executes.

Number of cycles: Jump is performed: 16
Jump is not performed: 4

JO   disp

Jump if Overflow

This instruction is identical to the JMP disp instruction except that the Jump is executed only if the Overflow flag is 1; otherwise the next instruction is executed.
The encoding for this instruction is:

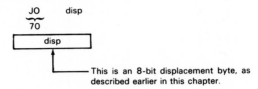

This is an 8-bit displacement byte, as described earlier in this chapter.

In the following instruction sequence

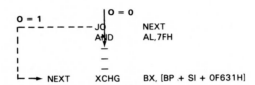

after the JO instruction, the XCHG instruction will be executed if the Overflow status is 1. If the Overflow status is 0, then the AND instruction will be executed.

Number of cycles: Jump is performed: 16
Jump is not performed: 4

JP   disp
JPE   disp

Jump if Parity Even

This instruction is identical to the JMP disp instruction except that the Jump is executed only if the Parity flag is 1; otherwise the next instruction is executed.

The encoding for this instruction is:

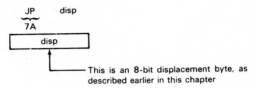

In the following instruction sequence

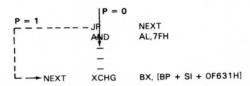

after the JP instruction, the XCHG instruction will be executed if the Parity status is 1. If the Parity status is 0, then the AND instruction will be executed.

Number of cycles: Jump is performed: 16
Jump is not performed: 4

JS   disp

Jump if Sign Status is One

This instruction is identical to the JMP disp instruction except that the Jump is executed only if the Sign status is 1.

The encoding for this instruction is:

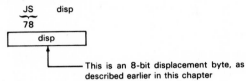

This is an 8-bit displacement byte, as described earlier in this chapter

In the following instruction sequence

after the JS instruction, the XCHG instruction will be executed if the Sign status is 1. If the Sign status is 0, then the AND instruction will be executed.

Number of cycles: Jump is performed: 16
Jump is not performed: 4

LAHF
Load 8080 Flags into AH Register

This instruction moves the low-order eight bits of the Flags register into the AH register. The eight bits that are moved are:

```
 7   6   5   4   3   2   1   0
┌──┬──┬──┬──┬──┬──┬──┬──┐
│SF│ZF│ X│AF│ X│PF│ X│CF│
└──┴──┴──┴──┴──┴──┴──┴──┘
```

where X indicates an undetermined value.

The encoding for this instruction is:

LAHF
⁓
9F

As an example, consider the case where the Carry and Parity flags are 1, the Zero, Sign, and Arithmetic flags are 0. Executing an

LAHF

instruction would move

0 0 X 0 X 1 X 1

into the AH register.

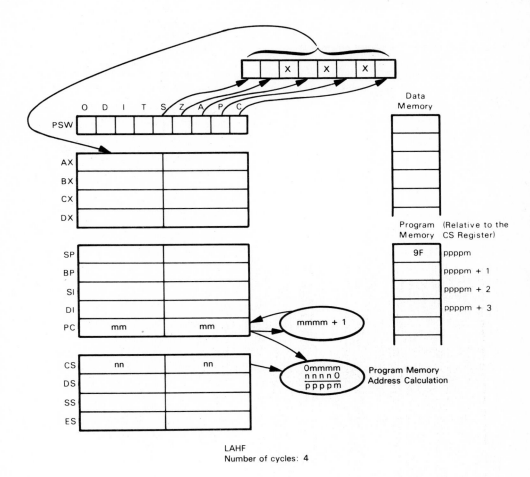

LAHF
Number of cycles: 4

Notes:

1. No statuses are affected. No registers except AH are affected.

2. This instruction is used in conjunction with PUSH AX to emulate the 8080 instruction PUSH PSW.

8086 Code	8080 Code
LAHF	PUSH PSW
PUSH AX	

LDS   reg,mem

Load Register and DS from Memory

Load the contents of the specified memory word into the specified register. Load the contents of the memory word following the specified memory word into the DS register.

This instruction's encoding is:

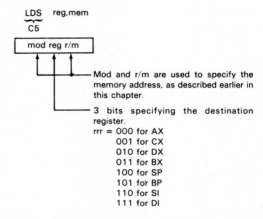

As an example, consider the case where the DS register contains $C000_{16}$, the word at memory location $C0010_{16}$ contains 0180_{16} and the word at memory location $C0012_{16}$ contains 2000_{16}. After the instruction

        LDS   SI, [10H]

has executed, the SI register will contain 0180_{16} and the DS register will contain 2000_{16}.

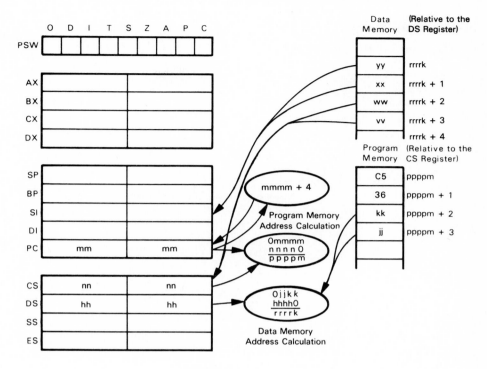

LDS   SI,[jjkk]
Number of cycles: 16 + EA

Notes:

1. No statuses are affected.

2. If mod is 11, then the operation performed by this instruction is undefined.

LEA   reg,mem

Load Register with Offset Address

Load the 16-bit offset address that is used to specify the memory operand into the specified register.

The encoding for this instruction is:

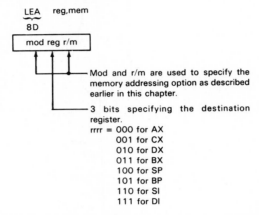

Suppose that the DS register contains 2800_{16}, the BX register contains 0400_{16} and the SI register contains $003C_{16}$. After the instruction

LEA   BX, [BX + SI + 0F62H]

has executed, the BX register will contain $139E_{16}$, which is the sum of the contents of the BX and SI registers and the specified displacement.

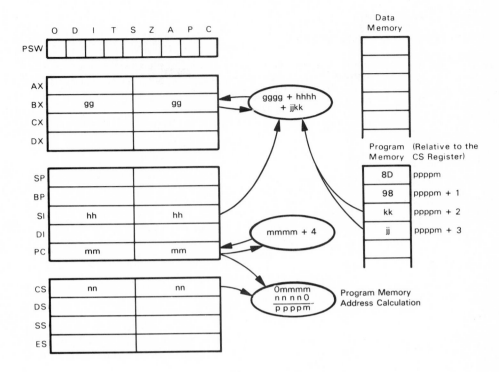

LEA BX, [BX + SI + jjkk]
Number of cycles: 2 + EA

Notes:

1. No statuses are affected.

2. If mod is 11, then the operation performed by this instruction is undefined.

LES   reg,mem

Load Register and ES from Memory

Load the contents of the specified memory word into the specified register. Load the contents of the memory word following the specified memory word into the ES register.

The encoding for this instruction is:

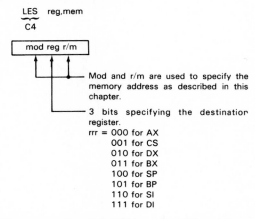

LES reg,mem
⎵
C4

mod reg r/m

Mod and r/m are used to specify the memory address as described in this chapter.

3 bits specifying the destination register.
rrr = 000 for AX
001 for CS
010 for DX
011 for BX
100 for SP
101 for BP
110 for SI
111 for DI

Suppose that the DS register contains $B000_{16}$, the BX register contains $080A_{16}$, the memory word at location $B080A_{16}$ is $05A2_{16}$ and the memory word at $B080C_{16}$ is 4000_{16}. After the instruction

LES   DI,[BX]

has executed, the DI register will contain $05A2_{16}$ and the ES register will contain 4000_{16}.

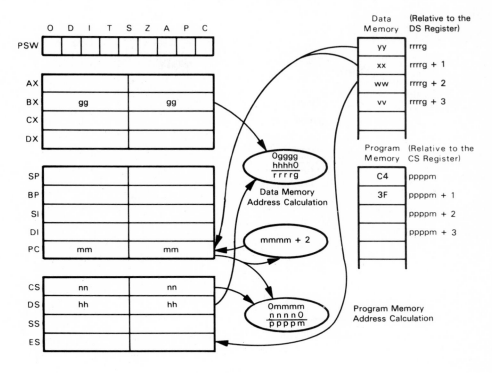

LES   DI,[BX]
Number of cycles: 16 + EA

Notes:

1. No statuses are affected.

2. If mod is 11, then the operation performed by this instruction is undefined.

3. The register specified in this instruction is typically the DI register, since the DI register is the register normally associated with the ES register.

LOCK

Assert Bus Lock Signal

This instruction is used to force the 8086 to output the $\overline{LOCK}$ signal low. The $\overline{LOCK}$ signal is held low for the duration of the next instruction.

This instruction is considered to be a prefix instruction, i.e., it precedes the instruction for which the $\overline{LOCK}$ signal is to be asserted.

The encoding for this instruction is:

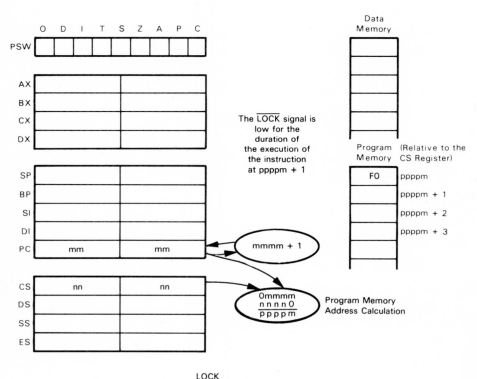

LOCK
Number of cycles: 2

Notes:

1. This prefix may be used to preface any 8086 instruction. If, however, this prefix is used in conjunction with the REP prefix and a string primitive, certain problems may result. For a discussion of this topic, refer to the next chapter.

2. This prefix is very useful in the implementation of test-and-set sequences.

LODS/LODSB/LODSW

Load from Memory into AL or AX Register

Move from the memory location addressed by the SI register to the AL (8-bit operation) or the AX (16-bit operation) register. The SI register is incremented/decremented depending on the value of the DF flag.

The encoding for this instruction is:

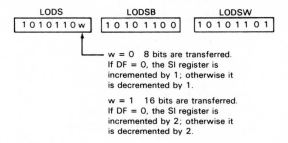

For example, suppose that the DF flag is 0, the SI register contains 0035_{16}, the DS register contains 4008_{16}, and the byte at memory location $400B5_{16}$ is $0F_{16}$. After the instruction

LODSB

has executed, the contents of the AL register will be $0F_{16}$ and the contents of the SI register will be 0036_{16}.

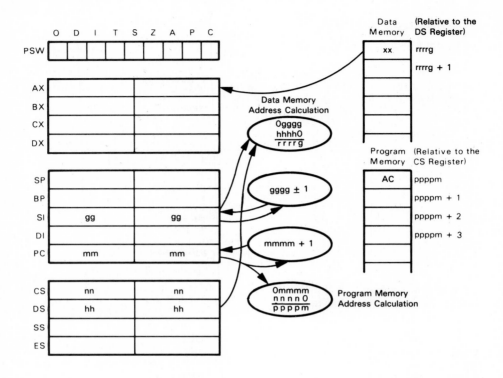

LODSB
Number of cyles: 12 for single occurrence
9 + (13 times repetition if preceded by REP prefix)

Notes:

1. No statuses are affected.

2. The default segment register is the DS register. This may be overridden by the appropriate segment override prefix.

3. Typically, the REP prefix is not used with this instruction.

4. As with other 8086 operations, the generalized form of the instruction requires that some symbol be given to the assembler to allow the assembler to determine whether an 8- or 16-bit operation will be performed. This subject will be discussed later in this chapter.

LOOP   disp

Decrement CX Register and Jump if Not Zero

This instruction decrements the CX register (not affecting the flags) and then functions in the same manner as the JMP disp instruction, except that if the CX register has not been decremented to 0, then the Jump is executed; otherwise the next instruction is executed.

The encoding for this instruction is:

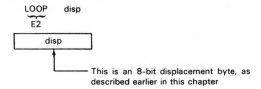

As an example, consider the following sequence of instructions:

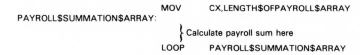

```
                                 MOV      CX,LENGTH$OFPAYROLL$ARRAY
PAYROLL$SUMMATION$ARRAY:
                                   } Calculate payroll sum here
                                 LOOP     PAYROLL$SUMMATION$ARRAY
```

The sequence of instructions between PAYROLL$SUMMATION$ARRAY and the LOOP instruction will be executed LENGTHOFPAYROLL$ARRAY times.

Number of cycles: Jump is performed: 17
Jump is not performed: 5

LOOPZ   disp
LOOPE   disp

Decrement CX Register and Jump if CX=0 and ZF=1

This instruction decrements the CX register (not affecting the flags) and then functions in the same manner as the JMP disp instruction, except that if the CX register has not been decremented to 0 *and* the Zero flag is 1 then the Jump is executed; otherwise the next instruction is executed.

The encoding for this instruction is:

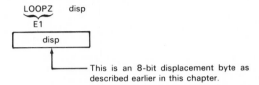

As an example, consider the following sequence of instructions:

```
            MOV     CX,NUMBER$OF$PORTS
            MOV     DX,MAIN$PORT$GROUP
            MOV     BX,REDUNDANT$PORT$GROUP
    TOP:    IN      AX,DX
            INC     DX
            XCHG    BX,DX
            XCHG    AX,BP

            IN      AX,DX
            INC     DX
            XCHG    BX,DX
            CMP     AX,BP
            LOOPE   TOP
            JNZ     PORT$DISPUTE
```

The sequence of instructions between TOP and the LOOPE instruction compare data available at two sets of input ports; one group is pointed to by MAIN$PORT$GROUP, and the other group is pointed to by REDUNDANT$PORT$GROUP. The instruction JNZ PORT$DISPUTE will be executed after one of two scenarios has occurred:

1. A comparison has resulted in the Zero flag being set to 0, in which case the data at the ports is not equal.

2. The instructions between TOP and LOOPE have executed NUMBEROFPORTS times.

The JNZ instruction is used to differentiate between cases 1 and 2.

Number of cycles: Jump is performed: 18
Jump is not performed: 6

LOOPNZ disp
LOOPNE disp

Decrement CX Register and Jump if CX ≠0 and ZF=0

This instruction decrements the CX register (not affecting the flags) and then functions in the same manner as the JMP disp instruction, except that if the CX register has not been decremented to 0 and the Zero flag is 0, then the Jump is executed; otherwise the next instruction is executed.

The encoding for this instruction is:

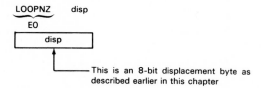

As an example, consider the following sequence of instructions:

```
                         MOV      SI,ELEMENT$TO$MATCH
                         LES      DI
                         MOV      CX,NUMBER OF ENTRIES
SEARCH$FOR$MATCH:        —
                         —           ;SEARCH FOR MATCH
                         —
                         LOOPNE   SEARCH$FOR$MATCH
```

The code between the SEARCHFORMATCH instruction and the LOOPNE instruction will be executed until 1) CX is decremented to 0, or 2) the instruction before LOOPNE sets the Zero flag to 1; e.g., the Zero status might be 1 if a match is found.

Number of cycles: Jump is performed: 19
Jump is not performed: 5

MOV   mem/reg₁, mem/reg₂

Move Data from: · **Register to Register**
· **Memory to Register**
· **Register to Memory**

This instruction is used to move 8- or 16-bit data elements between a register and a register or memory location.

The encoding for this instruction is:

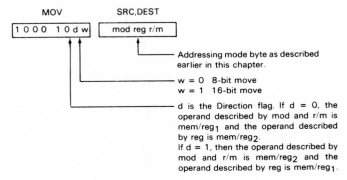

For example, the instruction

MOV   AX,CX

moves the contents of the CX register to the AX register.

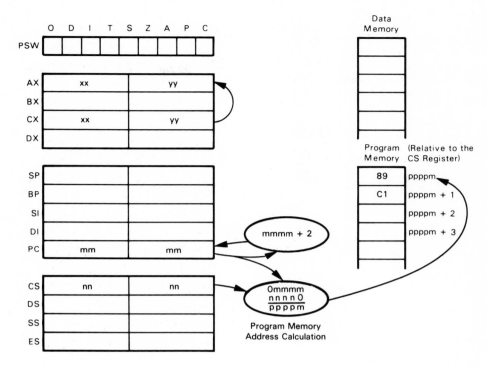

MOV   AX,CX

Number of cycles:
register to register: 2
memory to register: 8 + EA
register to memory: 9 + EA

Notes:

1. Segment registers may not be specified in this instruction. To move data to/from segment registers, consult the MOV segreg,reg or MOV reg,segreg operations.

2. No statuses are affected.

3. This instruction performs the function that the MOV reg,reg instruction accomplished in the 8080 assembly instruction. This instruction does, however, provide for more in the way of flexibility than the corresponding 8080 instruction.

MOV reg,data

Load Immediate Data into Register

This instruction is used to load 8- or 16-bit data elements into a register via immediate addressing.

The encoding for this instruction is:

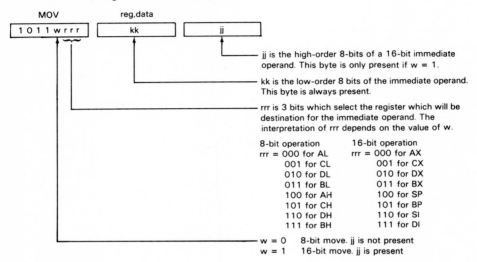

jj is the high-order 8-bits of a 16-bit immediate operand. This byte is only present if w = 1.

kk is the low-order 8 bits of the immediate operand. This byte is always present.

rrr is 3 bits which select the register which will be destination for the immediate operand. The interpretation of rrr depends on the value of w.

8-bit operation	16-bit operation
rrr = 000 for AL	rrr = 000 for AX
001 for CL	001 for CX
010 for DL	010 for DX
011 for BL	011 for BX
100 for AH	100 for SP
101 for CH	101 for BP
110 for DH	110 for SI
111 for BH	111 for DI

w = 0   8-bit move. jj is not present
w = 1   16-bit move. jj is present

For example, the instruction

MOV   CX,3168H

moves the 16-bit quantity 3168_{16} into the CX register.

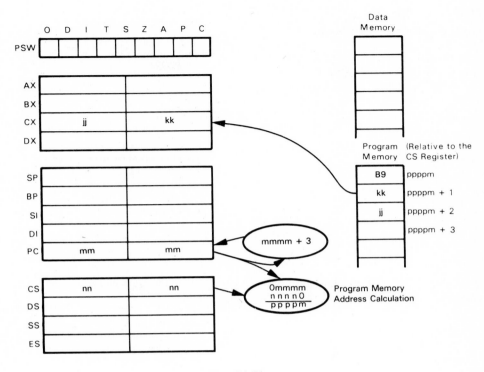

MOV   CX, jjkk
Number of cycles: 4

Notes:

1. Segment registers may not be loaded via this instruction. To load immediate data into a segment register, consult the MOV segreg,mem/reg instruction.

2. This instruction performs the function that MVI (8-bit move immediate) and LXI (16-bit move immediate) instructions perform for the 8080.

3. No statuses are affected.

MOV   ac,mem

Load Accumulator from Memory

This instruction is used to move 8- or 16-bit data elements from a memory location to the accumulator.

The encoding for this instruction is:

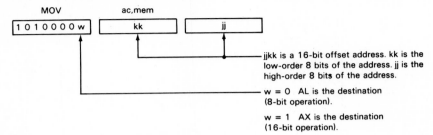

For example, the instruction

MOV   AL,[1064H]

moves the contents of memory location 1064_{16} (relative to the DS register) into the AL register.

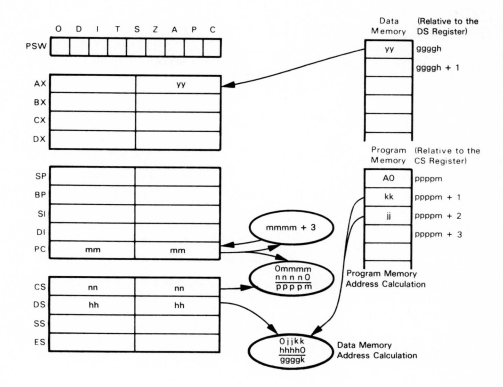

MOV   AL,[jjkk]
Number of cycles: 10

Notes:

1. This instruction performs the same function as the 8080 instruction LDA addr. In addition, this instruction allows a 16-bit load to the AX register.

MOV   mem,ac

Store Accumulator into Memory

This instruction is used to move 8- or 16-bit data elements from the accumulator to a memory location.

The encoding for this instruction is:

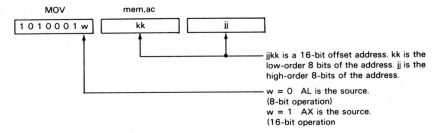

MOV   mem,ac

| 1 0 1 0 0 0 1 w | kk | jj |

jjkk is a 16-bit offset address. kk is the low-order 8 bits of the address. jj is the high-order 8-bits of the address.

w = 0   AL is the source.
(8-bit operation)
w = 1   AX is the source.
(16-bit operation

For example, the instruction

MOV   [1064H],AX

moves the contents of the AX register into memory location 1064_{16} (relative to the DS register). The contents of AL are moved into 1064_{16} and the contents of AH are moved into 1065_{16}.

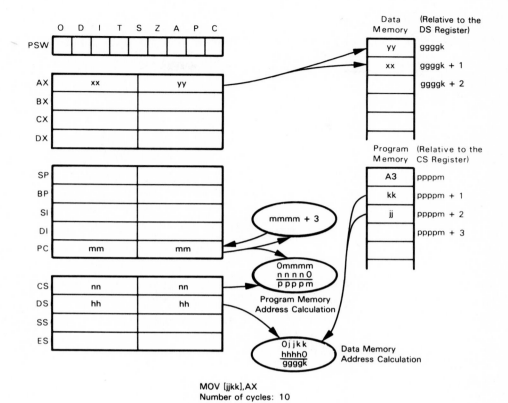

MOV [jjkk],AX
Number of cycles: 10

Notes:

1. No statuses are affected.
2. This instruction performs the same function as the 8080 instruction STA addr. In addition, this instruction allows a 16-bit store of the AX register.

MOV   segreg,mem/reg

Move Memory or Register Data to Segment Register

Move a 16-bit data element from a register or memory location into a segment register.

The encoding for this instruction is:

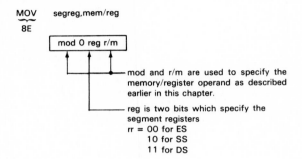

As an example, the instruction

MOV   SS,DX

will move the contents of the DX register into the SS register.

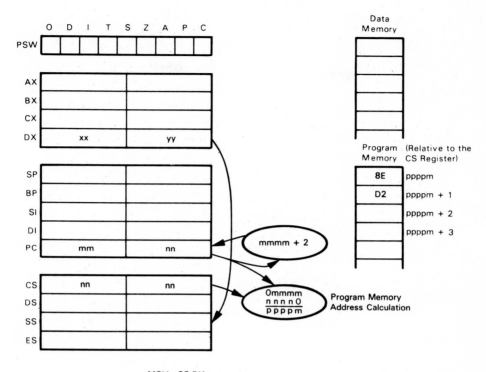

MOV SS,DX
Number of cycles: register to register: 2
                 memory to register: 8 + EA

Notes:

1. If reg=01, then the results of this operation are undefined. This prohibition prevents the user from storing directly into the CS register. Changes to CS should be performed only by JMP, CALL, RET, IRET, and INT — instructions which will also load PC.

2. This instruction is typically used in initialization sequences where the program segment areas are defined.

3. Interrupts are not sampled at the end of this instruction. They are sampled at the end of the instruction following this one. This restriction allows restoring a full 32-bit pointer without interruption, which is critical when SS and SP are loaded.

MOV   mem/reg,segreg

Move Segment Register to Register or Memory

Move a 16-bit data element from a segment register into a register or memory location.

The encoding for this instruction is:

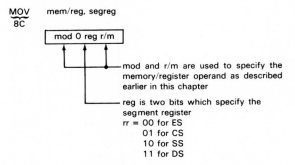

For example, consider the case where the DS register contains 2000_{16}. Executing the instruction

MOV   2000H,DS

would store the byte 00_{16} at location 22000_{16} and 20_{16} at location 22001_{16}.

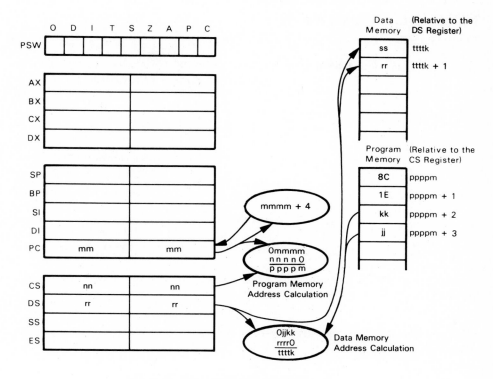

Number of cycles: Register to Register: 2
Register to Memory: 9 + EA

Notes:

1. This is not a general purpose register-to-register MOV; this is for moving segment registers. For a general purpose register MOV, consult MOV mem/reg$_1$,mem/reg$_2$.

MOV   mem/reg,data

Move Immediate Data to Register or Memory

Move the immediate data in the bytes following the op-code to the specified register or memory location. 8- or 16-bit data transfer may be specified.

The encoding for this instruction is:

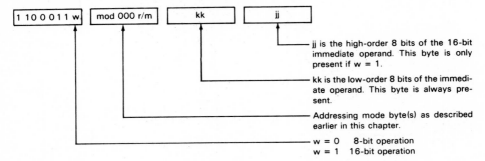

jj is the high-order 8 bits of the 16-bit immediate operand. This byte is only present if w = 1.

kk is the low-order 8 bits of the immediate operand. This byte is always present.

Addressing mode byte(s) as described earlier in this chapter.

w = 0   8-bit operation
w = 1   16-bit operation

For example, consider the case where the DS register contains $D000_{16}$ and the BX register contains 0016_{16}. After the instruction

MOV BX,491FH

has executed, memory location $D0016_{16}$ will contain $1F_{16}$ and memory location $D0017_{16}$ will contain 49_{16}.

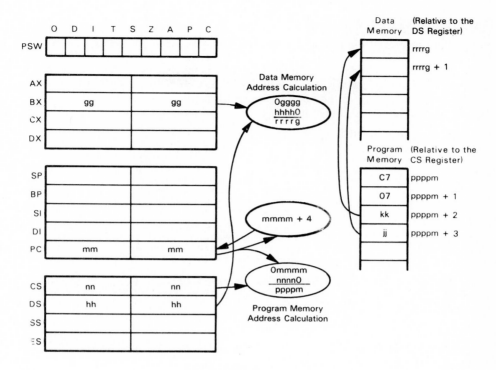

MOV   [BX],jjkk
Number of cycles: 10 + EA

Notes:

1. No statuses are affected.

2. The segment registers may not be specified in this instruction.

3. This instruction is not typically used to move immediate data into the registers. The instruction MOV reg,data is provided for this purpose.

MOVS/MOVSB/MOVSW

Move Byte or Word from Memory to Memory

Move 8 or 16 bits from the memory location pointed to by the SI register to the memory location pointed to by the DI register. The SI and DI registers are incremented/decremented depending on the value of the DF flag.

The encoding for this instruction is:

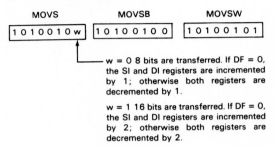

Consider the case where the DF flag is 0, the DS register contains 1000_{16}, the ES register contains 1780_{16}, the SI register contains 0006_{16}, the DI register contains 0006_{16}, and the word at memory location 10006_{16} if $8F0B_{16}$. After the instruction

MOVSW

has executed, memory location 17806_{16} will contain $8F0B_{16}$, the SI register will contain 0008_{16} and the DI register will contain 0008_{16}.

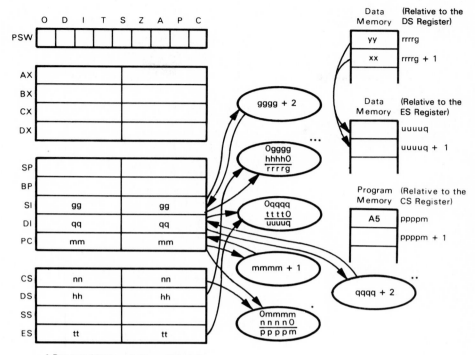

* Program Memory Address Calculation
** Destination Data Memory Address Calculation
*** Source Data Memory Address Calculation

MOVSW
Number of cycles: 18 for single occurrence
9 + (17 times repetition when preceded by REP prefix)

Notes:

1. No statuses are affected.

2. The default segment register for the source operand is the DS register. This segment may be overridden using segment prefixes. The default segment register for the destination operand is the ES register. This segment may not be overridden using segment prefixes.

3. The REP prefix and/or the LOCK prefix may be used with this instruction. Using the REP and the LOCK prefixes in conjunction with this instruction may cause problems. Consult the next chapter for a complete discussion of these potential difficulties.

4. This instruction is very useful for moving blocks of memory. Consider the following sequence of instructions:

    ```
    LES     DI, CURRENT$START$OF$PRINT$BUFFER
    MOV     SI, PAGE$HEADER$MESSAGE
    MOV     CX, PAGE$HEADER$MESSAGE$LENGTH
    REP
    MOVS    BYTE
    ```

    These instructions would move the data from the memory location addressed by PAGE$HEADER$MESSAGE to the memory location addressed by the contents of CURRENT$START$OF$PRINT$BUFFER.

5. For the generalized form of MOVS, how do you specify whether an 8- or 16-bit transfer is to be performed? This will depend on your assembler. For a discussion of this subject, refer to the end of this chapter.

MUL   mem/reg

Multiply AL or AX Register by Register or Memory Location

Multiply the specified register or memory location contents by the AL (8-bit operation) or AX (16-bit operation) register, considering both operands as unsigned numbers, i.e., a simple binary multiplication. If an 8-bit operation is performed, the low-order eight bits of the result are stored in the AL register, the high-order eight bits of the result are stored in the AH register. If a 16-bit operation is performed, the low-order 16 bits of the result are stored in the AX register, the high-order 16 bits of the result are stored in the DX register. In either case, if the high-order half of the result is 0, then the OF and CF flags are set to 0; otherwise they are set to 1 to indicate significant digits in AX or DX.

The encoding for this instruction is:

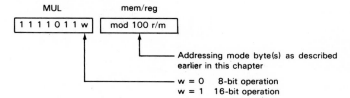

As an example, consider the case where the AX register contains 4514_{16} and the CL register contains 05_{16}. After the instruction

            MUL   AL,CL

has executed, the AX register will contain 0064_{16} and the Carry and Overflow flags will be 0.

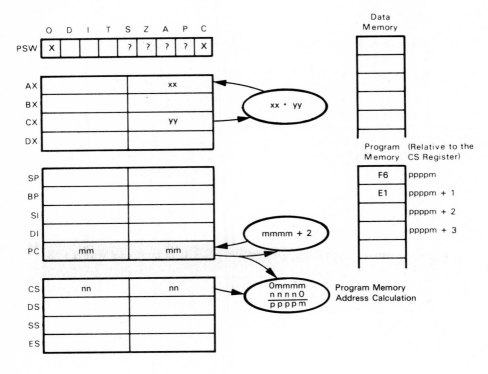

MUL   AL,CL
Number of cycles: 8-bit memory multiply: (76-83) + EA
                    16-bit memory multiply: (124-139) + EA
                    8-bit register multiply: 70-77
                    16-bit register multiply: 118-133

Notes:

1. This is the unsigned number multiply operation. Both operands are treated as unsigned binary numbers in the range:

    8-bit: 0 to 255
    16-bit: 0 to 65535

    For a signed multiply operation, consult the instruction IMUL.

2. In some cases, it may be more appropriate to use shifts to perform multiplications. These cases would occur when memory conservation is not of paramount importance and speed is necessary.

NEG   mem/reg

Negate the Contents of a Register or Memory Location

This instruction performs a twos complement subtraction of the specified operand from zero. The result is stored in the specified operand. An 8- or 16-bit operand may be specified.

The encoding for this instruction is:

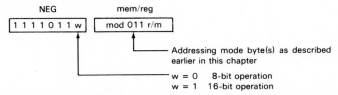

Suppose that the BX register contains 0006_{16}, the DS register contains 1800_{16}, and the contents of memory location 18006_{16} are 47_{16}. After the execution of the instruction

NEG   [BX]

the contents of memory location 18006_{16} will be $B9_{16}$.

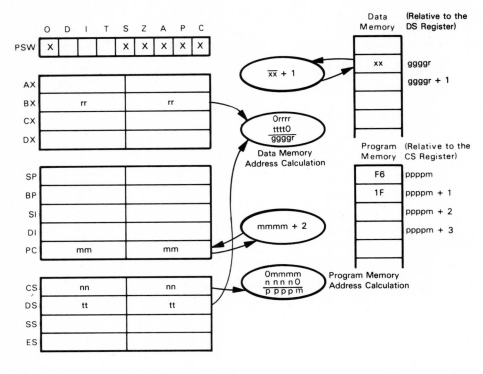

NEG [BX]
Number of cycles: Memory operand: 3
Register operand: 16 + EA

Notes:

1. There is no equivalent instruction in the 8080 assembly language. An equivalent 8080 sequence for this instruction for a 16-bit quantity would be

    ```
    MOV     A,D
    CMA
    MOV     D,A
    MOV     A,E
    CMA
    MOV     E,A
    INX     D
    ```

NOP

No Operation

No operation is performed.
The encoding for this instruction is:

$$\underbrace{\text{NOP}}_{90}$$

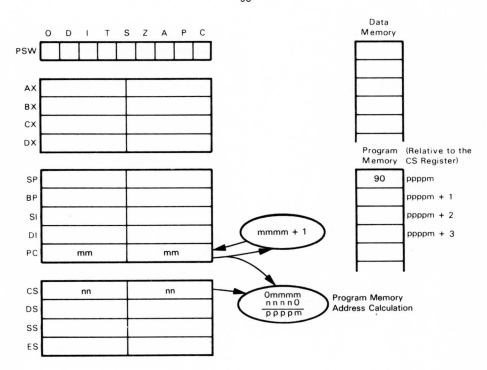

NOP
Number of cycles: 3

NOT   mem/reg

Ones Complement of Register or Memory Location

Complement the contents of the specified register or memory location. The encoding for this instruction is:

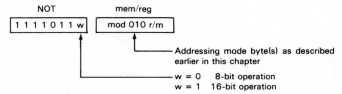

Suppose that the BL register contains FB_{16}. After the instruction

NOT   BL

has executed, the BL register will contain 04_{16}.

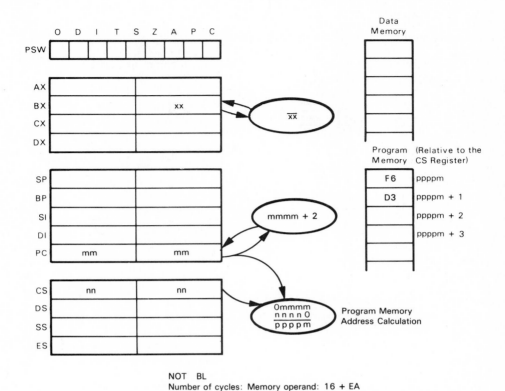

NOT BL
Number of cycles: Memory operand: 16 + EA
Register operand: 3

Notes:

1. No statuses are affected.

2. This instruction performs the same function as the 8080 instruction CMA. This instruction also allows 16-bit complements and complementing of any general purpose register or memory location.

OR   ac,data

OR Immediate Data with the AX or AL Register

OR the immediate data in the succeeding program memory byte(s) with the AL (8-bit operation) or AX (16-bit operation) register.

The encoding for this instruction is:

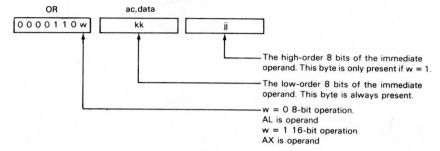

Suppose that the AX register contains 0609_{16}. After the instruction

OR   AX, 3030H

has executed, the AX register will contain 3639_{16}.

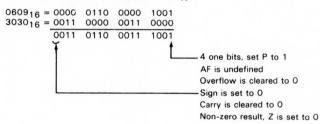

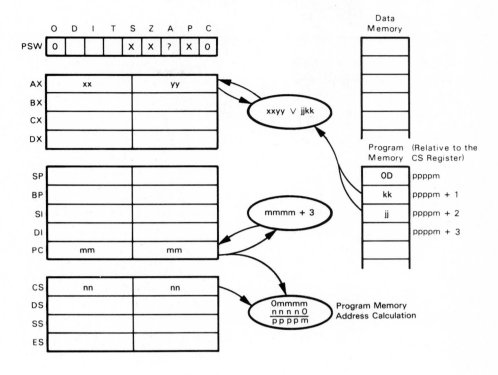

OR   AX,jjkk
Number of cycles: 4

Notes:

1. This instruction performs the same function as the 8080 instruction ORI data. This instruction also has the ability to perform 16-bit operations.

2. If you desire to OR immediate data with any of the other general purpose registers or with some memory location, consult the instruction OR mem/reg,data.

OR   mem/reg,data

OR Immediate Data with Register or Memory Location

OR the immediate data in the succeeding program memory byte(s) with the specified register or memory location. An 8- or 16-bit operation may be specified.

The encoding for this instruction is:

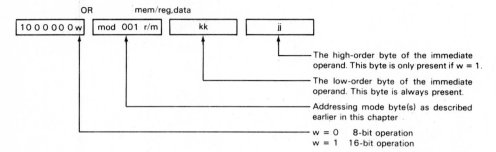

Consider the case where the DS register contains 3800_{16}, the contents of the BX register are 0200_{16}, the DI register contains 0136_{16}, and the word at memory location 38336_{16} is $06B3_{16}$. After the instruction

OR [BX + DI], 0805H

has executed, the word at memory location 38336_{16} will be $0EB7_{16}$.

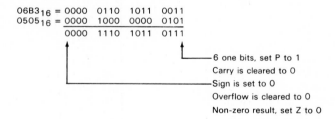

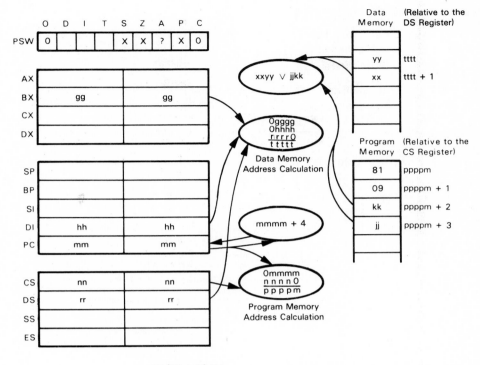

OR [BX + DI], jjkk

Number of cycles: Memory operand: 17 + EA
Register operand: 4

Notes:

1. This instruction is not typically used to OR immediate data with the AX or AL register. The instruction OR ac,data is provided for this purpose.

OR memreg₁, mem/reg₂

OR: · **Register with Register**
· **Register with Memory**
· **Memory with Register**

OR the contents of the register or memory location specified by mem/reg₂ with the contents of the register or memory location specified by mem/reg₁, returning the result to mem/reg₁. An 8- or 16-bit operation may be specified. Either mem/reg₁ or mem/reg₂ may be a memory operand, but one of the operands must be a register operand.

The encoding for this instruction is:

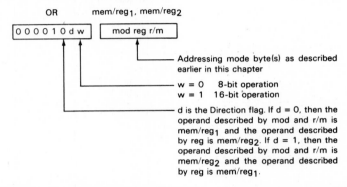

Suppose that the AX register contains 0060_{16}, the DS register contains 4000_{16}, the BX register contains $009A_{16}$, and the word at memory location $4009A_{16}$ contains $012C_{16}$. After the instruction

OR   [BX],AX

has executed, the contents of the word at memory location $4009A_{16}$ will be $016C_{16}$. The flags will be set as follows:

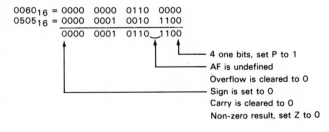

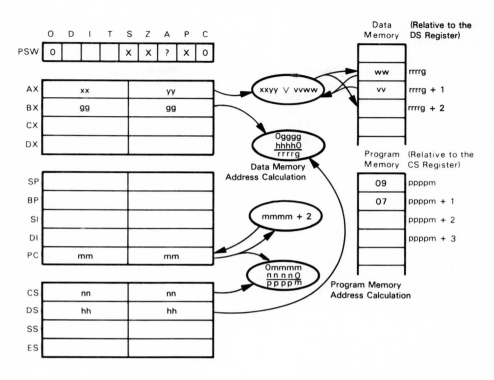

OR [BX],AX

Number of cycles: Register to Memory: 16 + EA
                  Memory to Register: 9 + EA
                  Register to Register: 3

OUT   DX,ac

Output from Accumulator

Output 8- or 16-bit data elements from the AL (8-bit) or AX (16-bit) register to the I/O port identified by the contents of the DX register.

The encoding for this instruction is:

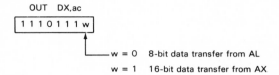

As an example, consider the case where the DX register contains $0FFF2_{16}$ and the AL register 40_{16}. The execution of an

OUT   DX,AL

instruction will result in the quantity 40_{16} being loaded into the I/O buffer at I/O port number $0FFF2_{16}$.

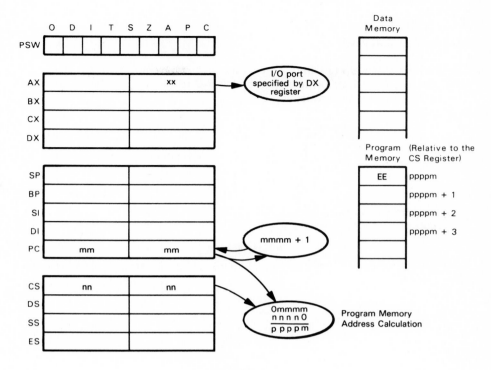

OUT   DX,AL

Number of cycles: 8

Notes:

1. This instruction allows the user to access I/O ports which have been assigned addresses between 0 and $0FFFF_{16}$.

2. No registers or statuses are affected.

OUT   port,ac

Output from Accumulator

This instruction outputs 8- or 16-bit data elements from the AL (8-bit) or AX (16-bit) register to the I/O port identified by the second byte of the instruction.

The encoding for this instruction is:

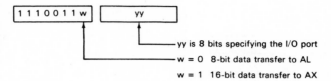

1 1 1 0 0 1 1 w   yy

yy is 8 bits specifying the I/O port
w = 0   8-bit data transfer to AL
w = 1   16-bit data transfer to AX

No registers or statuses are affected.

Suppose that the AX register contains $58A4_{16}$. Executing an

OUT   14H,AX

instruction will transfer $A4_{16}$ to the I/O port addressed at 14_{16} and 58_{16} to the I/O port addressed at 15_{16}.

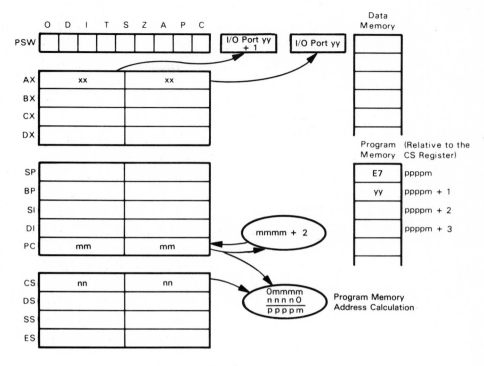

OUT   yy,AX
Number of cycles: 10

Notes:

1. This instruction allows the user to access I/O ports which have been assigned addresses between 0 and FF_{16}. To address ports whose addresses are outside this range, consult the instruction OUT DX,ac.

2. This instruction performs the same function as the 8080 instruction OUT port. Additionally, this instruction allows for 16-bit data transfers in a single instruction (not possible using the 8080 instruction OUT port).

3. To effectively use the OUT instruction, a firm grasp of the hardware configuration is necessary. The way in which the I/O logic has been implemented determines the port addresses that are used to access various hardware functions. It is also possible to design a microcomputer system that accesses external logic using memory reference instructions with specific memory addresses.

POP   mem/reg

Read from the Top of the Stack

Pop the two top stack bytes into the specified memory location or register. This is a 16-bit operation.

The encoding is:

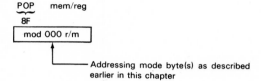

Suppose that the DS register contains $FF00_{16}$, the SI register contains 0008_{16}, the SP register contains $0FEA_{16}$, the SS register contains $2F00_{16}$, and the word stored at location $2FFEA_{16}$ is $3BC5_{16}$. After the instruction

POP [SI]

has executed, the contents of memory location $FF008_{16}$ will be $C5_{16}$ and the contents of memory location $FF009_{16}$ will be $3B_{16}$. SP will be equal to $0FEC_{16}$.

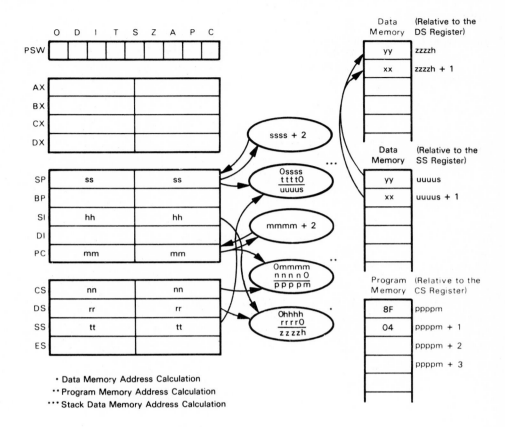

• Data Memory Address Calculation
•• Program Memory Address Calculation
••• Stack Data Memory Address Calculation

POP   [SI]
Number of cycles: Memory operand: 17 + EA
                  Register operand: 8

Notes:

1. This instruction is not typically used to pop data into a register. The instruction POP reg performs this function and only occupies one byte of program memory space.

2. No statuses are affected.

POP   reg

Read from the Top of the Stack

Pop the two top stack bytes into the designated 16-bit register.
The encoding is:

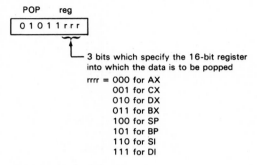

POP   reg

01011rrr

— 3 bits which specify the 16-bit register
into which the data is to be popped

rrrr = 000 for AX
       001 for CX
       010 for DX
       011 for BX
       100 for SP
       101 for BP
       110 for SI
       111 for DI

Ponder, for example, the instruction

POP   BX

This instruction would pop the byte pointed to by the stack pointer (and stack segment) into BL, then increment the stack pointer and pop the addressed byte into BH. Finally, the stack pointer would again be incremented by 1 to point at the new top of stack. This is actually done with a single 16-bit transfer in the 8086.

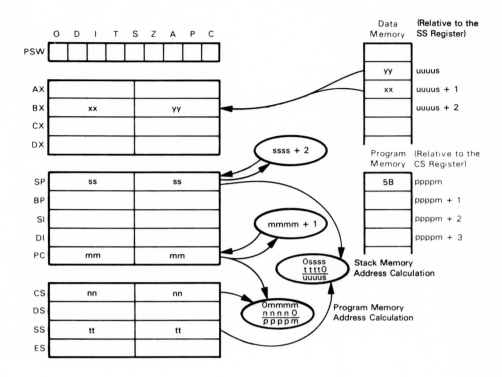

POP   BX
Number of cycles: 8

Notes:

1. This instruction cannot be used to pop data elements into the segment registers. To pop data into segment registers, consider the instruction POP segreg.

2. For this instruction to be meaningful, it is of course necessary to have:

    a. an initialized stack pointer

    b. data already on the stack via a PUSH instruction.

    Naturally, one could use this instruction for the sole purpose of incrementing the SP register by 2; however, this is not recommended.

3. This instruction performs the same function as the 8080 assembly language instruction POP reg.

POP   segreg

Read from the Top of the Stack

This instruction pops the two top stack bytes into the designated 16-bit segment register.

The encoding is:

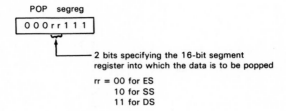

POP   segreg

```
000rr111
```

2 bits specifying the 16-bit segment
register into which the data is to be popped

rr = 00 for ES
     10 for SS
     11 for DS

The instruction

POP   ES

for example, will pop the two top stack bytes into the ES register. Undefined operation if rr = 01.

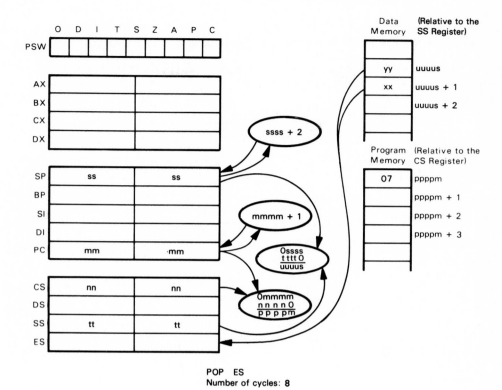

POP   ES
Number of cycles: **8**

Notes:

1. This instruction pops data into the segment registers only. To pop data into the 8086's other registers, consider the instruction POP reg.

2. For a more complete description of the function performed by a POP, consult POP reg.

3. A POP to CS is not legal. Changes to CS should be performed only by JMP, CALL, RET, IRET, and INT — instructions which will also load PC.

4. Interrupts are not sampled at the end of this instruction. They are sampled at the end of the instruction following this one. This restriction allows restoring a full 32-bit pointer without interruption, which is critical when SS and SP are loaded.

POPF

Read from the Top of the Stack into the Flags Register

Pop the two top stack bytes into the Flags register. The first byte popped goes into the low-order byte of the Flags register. The format of the low-order byte of the Flags register is:

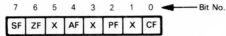

The second byte popped is stored into the high-order byte of the Flags register. The format for this byte is:

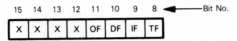

The encoding for this instruction is:

POPF

9D

Consider, for example, the situation where the two top bytes on the stack are 4F (topmost) and 32. Executing the

POPF

instruction will result in the Carry, Parity, Zero, and Interrupt flags being set to 1. All other flags will be set to 0.

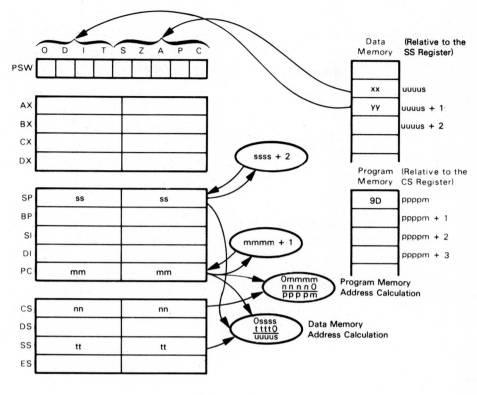

POPF
Number of cycles: 8

Notes:

1. As with all stack operations, it is important that the stack pointer be initialized. In addition, it would be appropriate to have executed a PUSHF instruction, in order to store the value of the flags, before executing a POPF instruction.

2. This instruction performs some of the functions of the 8080 instruction PUSH PSW.

PUSH   mem/reg

Write to the Top of the Stack

This instruction pushes the contents of the specified register or memory location onto the top of the stack. This is a 16-bit push operation.

The encoding is:

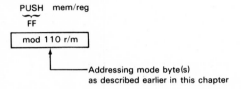

For example, if the DS register contains 2800_{16}, the BX register contains 0400_{16}, the SP register contains 1000_{16}, the SS register contains $2F00_{16}$, and the word stored at memory location 28400_{16} contains $A020_{16}$, then executing the instruction

PUSH   [BX]

will store $A0_{16}$ at memory location $2FFFF_{16}$ and 20_{16} at memory location $2FFFE_{16}$. The SP register will be adjusted to $0FFE_{16}$.

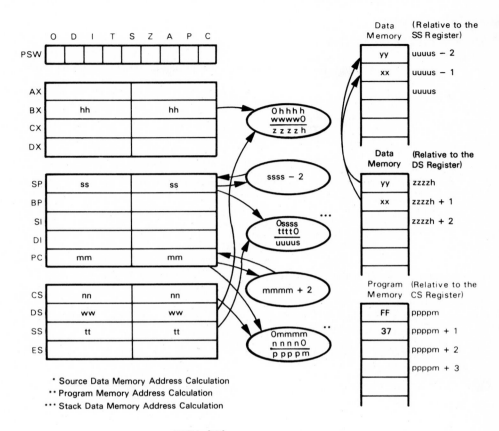

PUSH   [BX]
Number of cycles: memory 16 + EA
register 11

Notes:

1.   This instruction is not typically used to push a register onto the stack. The instruction PUSH reg performs this function and only occupies one byte of program memory space.

2.   No statuses are affected.

PUSH   reg

Write to the Top of the Stack

This instruction pushes the contents of the specified 16-bit register onto the top of stack.

The encoding is:

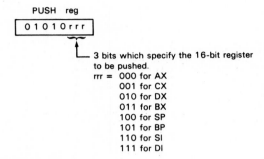

As an example, consider the instruction

PUSH   SI

This instruction would push the 16-bit contents of the SI register onto the stack. This function is performed as follows:

1. Decrement the stack pointer by 1.

2. Store the high-order 8 bits of the specified register into the memory location addressed by the stack pointer and the stack segment.

3. Decrement the stack pointer by 1.

4. Store the low-order 8 bits of the specified register into the memory location addressed by the stack pointer and the stack segment.

The stack pointer is left pointing at the last element stored into the stack, commonly referred to as the top of stack. For the 8086 this is actually one 16-bit transfer.

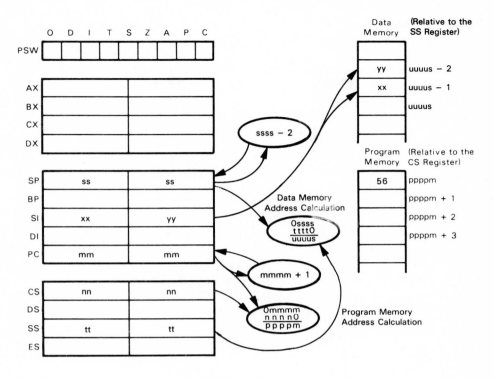

PUSH SI
Number of cycles: 10

Notes:

1. This instruction cannot be used to push the segment registers or the Flags register. To push segment registers, consult the instruction PUSH segreg. To push the Flags register, consult the PUSHF instruction.

2. This instruction is most effective when used after the stack pointer has been initialized. In fact, the only time this instruction should be used is after the initialization of the stack pointer.

3. To retrieve the data from the stack, use the POP instructions.

4. This instruction performs the same function as the 8080 instruction PUSH reg.

PUSH   segreg

Write to the Top of the Stack

This instruction pushes the contents of the specified 16-bit segment register onto the top of stack.

The encoding is:

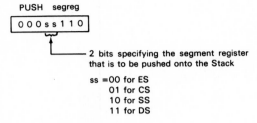

PUSH   segreg

```
000ss110
```

2 bits specifying the segment register
that is to be pushed onto the Stack

ss =00 for ES
    01 for CS
    10 for SS
    11 for DS

Examine, for example, the following instruction

PUSH   DS

This instruction will push the 16-bit contents of the DS register onto the stack. Illegal operation if ss = 01.

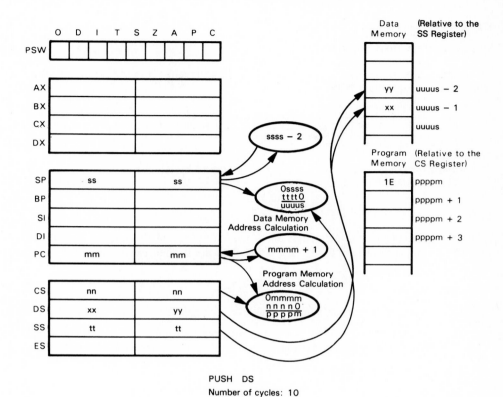

PUSH   DS
Number of cycles: 10

Notes:

1. This instruction can only be used to push the contents of segment registers onto the stack. To push the contents of other registers, consult the PUSH reg and PUSHF instructions.

2. For a more detailed description of the action of the PUSH operation, consult the PUSH reg instruction.

3. Remember that to ensure optimal results, the stack pointer must be initialized.

PUSHF

Write the Flags Register to the Top of Stack

This instruction pushes the contents of the Flags register onto the top of the stack. The format for the Flags register is:

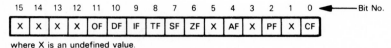

where X is an undefined value.

Bits 15-8 are stored onto the stack first, followed by bits 7-0.
The encoding for this instruction is:

$$\underbrace{\text{PUSHF}}_{\text{9C}}$$

As an example, should the Interrupt, Sign, and Zero flags be 1, while the Overflow, Direction, Trap, Arithmetic, Parity, and Carry flags are 0, then executing a

PUSHF

instruction would

1. Decrement the stack pointer.

2. Store the byte XXXX0010 into the memory location addressed by the stack pointer and Stack Segment register. (X refers to an undefined value.)

3. Decrement the stack pointer.

4. Store the byte 11X0X0X0 into the memory location addressed by the stack stack pointer and Stack Segment register. For the 8086 this is performed as a single 16-bit transfer.

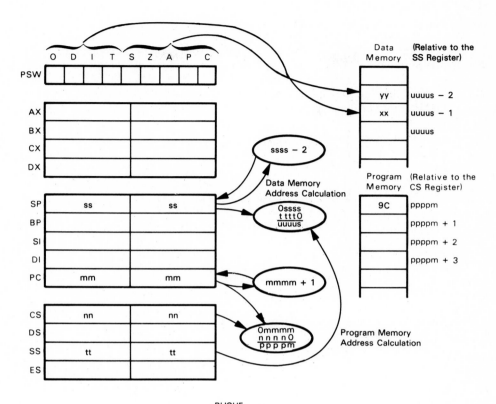

PUSHF
Number of cycles: 10

Notes:

1. Remember that, as with all stack instructions, this instruction works best after the stack pointer has been initialized.

2. This instruction does not perform the same function as the 8080 instruction PUSH PSW. The PUSH PSW instruction pushes the contents of the accumulator as well as the 8080 flags. To emulate PUSH PSW, consult the LAHF instruction.

RCL   mem/reg,count

Rotate Register or Memory Location Left Through Carry

Rotate the contents of the specified register or memory location left by the specified number of bits through the Carry status. The number of bits to rotate, represented by the variable count, is either one or the number contained in the CL register. An 8- or 16-bit operand may be specified.

The encoding for this instruction is:

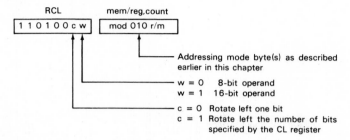

Suppose that the AX register contains $FB00_{16}$ and the Carry status is 0. After the instruction

RCL   AX,1

has executed, the Carry status will be 1 and the AX register will contain $F600_{16}$.

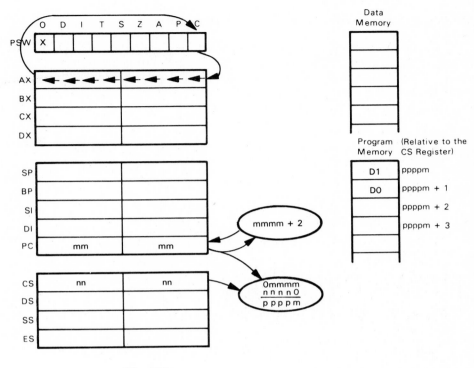

RCL   AX,1

Number of cycles: Register (1-bit rotate): 2
Register (N-bit rotate): 8 + (4 * N)
Memory (1-bit rotate): 15 + EA
Memory (N-bit rotate): 20 + EA + (4 * N)

Notes:

1. This instruction performs the same function as the 8080 instruction RAL. This instruction does, however, allow a great deal more flexibility in that multi-bit rotates are allowed, rotations of 16-bit quantities are allowed, and any register or memory location may be rotated.

2. Note that it is not intuitively obvious whether an 8- or 16-bit rotate is to be performed. The manner in which this is determined depends on your assembler. For a discussion of this entertaining subject, refer to the end of this chapter.

RCR   mem/reg,count

Rotate Register or Memory Location Right Through Carry

Rotate the contents of the specified register or memory location right by the specified number of bits through the Carry status. The number of bits to rotate, represented by the variable count, is either one or the number contained in the CL register. An 8- or 16-bit operand may be specified.

The encoding for this instruction is:

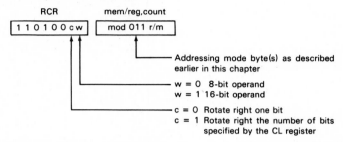

Suppose that the CX register contains $F709_{16}$ and the Carry status is 1. After the instruction

RCR   CX,CL

has executed, the CX register will contain $09FB_{16}$ and the Carry status will be 1.

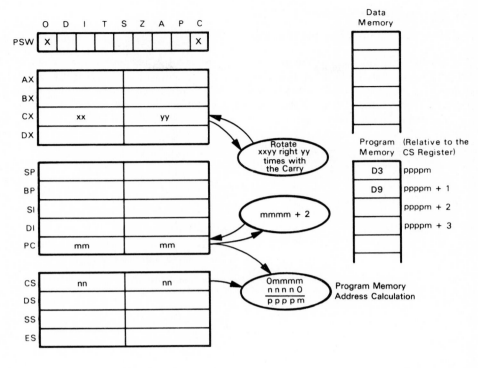

RCR   CX,CL

Number of cycles: Register (N-bit rotate): 8 + (4 · N)
                  Register (1-bit rotate): 2
                  Memory (N-bit rotate): 20 +EA + (4 · N)
                  Memory (1-bit rotate): 15 + EA

Notes:

1. This instruction performs the same function as the 8080 instruction RAR. This instruction does, however, allow a great deal more flexibility in that multi-bit rotates are allowed, rotations of 16-bit quantities are allowed, and any register or memory location may be rotated.

2. Differentiating between an 8- or 16-bit rotation is not obvious when one considers this instruction. For a discussion of this problem, see the end of this chapter.

REP/REPE/REPNE/REPNZ/REPZ

Repeat the Following String Instruction

Repeat the following string instruction until the CX register has been decremented to zero. All string instructions will continue to execute until CX is 0 with the exception of the SCAS and CMPS instructions, which will cease to execute if the value of the ZF flag is equal to the low-order bit of this instruction, the z bit.

The encoding for this instruction is:

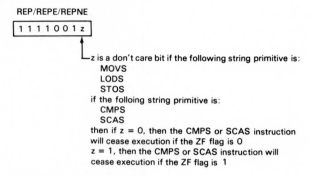

REP/REPE/REPNE

```
1 1 1 1 0 0 1 z
```

z is a don't care bit if the following string primitive is:
MOVS
LODS
STOS
if the folloing string primitive is:
CMPS
SCAS
then if z = 0, then the CMPS or SCAS instruction will cease execution if the ZF flag is 0
z = 1, then the CMPS or SCAS instruction will cease execution if the ZF flag is 1

In the following instruction sequence

```
MOV     SI,IOBUF
LES     DI,ADDR
MOV     CX,COUNT
REP
MOVB
```

COUNT bytes are moved from IOBUF to ADDR by the REP MOVB instruction.

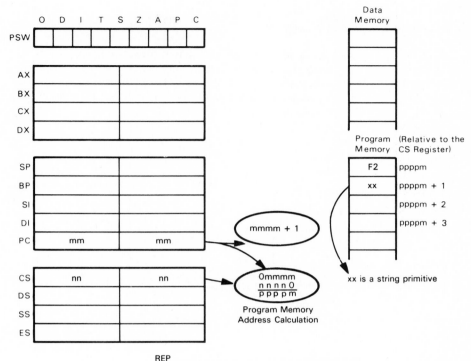

REP

Number of cycles: 2 incurred only for recognition of
the repeat prefix, and <u>not</u> included
with each iteration of the following
string primitive

Notes:

1. The encoding for REPE and REPZ is $F3_{16}$. The encoding for REPNE and REPNZ is $F2_{16}$.

2. REP is referred to as an instruction prefix. Other prefixes include LOCK and SEG. If REP is combined with a LOCK or SEG prefix, certain precautions must be taken. Consult the next chapter for a discussion of these precautions.

RET

Return from Subroutine (Intersegment)

Pop the top two stack bytes into the program counter; these two bytes provide the offset address of the next instruction to be executed. Pop the next two stack bytes into the CS register; these two bytes provide the code segment address of the next instruction to be executed. Previous program counter and Code Segment register contents are lost.

The encoding for this instruction is:

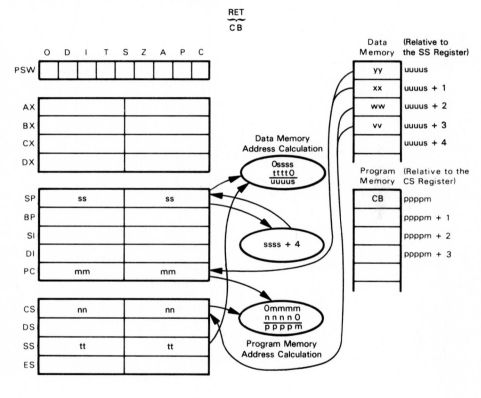

RET
Number of cycles: 24

Notes:

1. Every subroutine should have at least one RET instruction. This instruction is the last instruction executed in the subroutine and returns control to the calling program.

2. This RET instruction corresponds to the two intersegment CALLs, intersegment direct and intersegment indirect.

3. No statuses are affected.

RET

Return from Subroutine (Intrasegment)

Move the contents of the two top stack bytes to the program counter; i.e., pop the stack into the program counter. These bytes provide the offset address of the next instruction to be executed. Previous program counter contents are lost.

The encoding for this instruction is:

$$\underbrace{\text{RET}}_{\text{C3}}$$

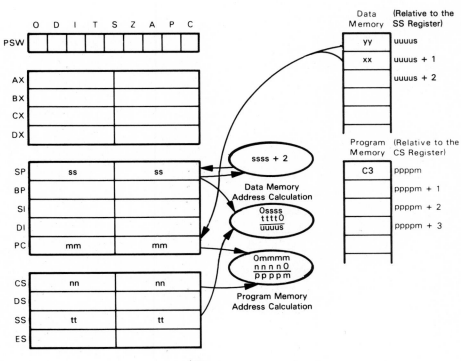

RET
Number of cycles: 16

Notes:

1. This instruction performs the same function as the 8080 instruction RET.

2. Every subroutine should contain at least one RET instruction; this is the last instruction executed within the subroutine and causes execution to return to the calling program. Other methods may be used to return to a calling program; however, typically they are less efficient and more obscure than the straightforward RET instruction.

3. The 8086 offers three other kinds of RETs. These RETs have some correspondence to the CALL instructions. This RET corresponds to CALL disp and CALL mem/reg indirect intrasegment.

4. No statuses are affected.

RET   disp16

Return from Subroutine and Add to Stack Pointer (Intersegment)

Pop the two top stack bytes into the program counter; these two bytes provide the offset address for the next instruction to be executed. Pop the next two stack bytes into the CS register; these two bytes provide the code segment address of the next instruction to be executed. Previous program counter and Code Segment register contents are lost. Add the data in the two succeeding program memory bytes to the stack pointer. This has the effect of adjusting the stack pointer past parameters that might have been placed onto the stack prior to the CALL that corresponds to this RET.

The encoding for this instruction is:

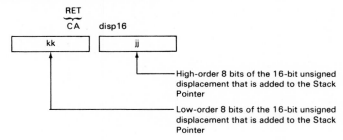

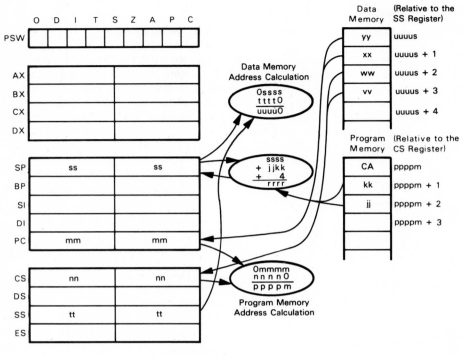

RET   jjkk
Number of cycles: 23

Notes:

1. No statuses are affected.

2. Every subroutine should have at least one RET instruction. This instruction is the last instruction executed in the subroutine and resumes execution in the calling program at the instruction after the corresponding CALL.

3. This RET instruction corresponds to the two intersegment CALLs, intersegment direct and intersegment indirect.

RET disp16

Return from Subroutine and Add to Stack Pointer (Intrasegment)

Pop the stack into the program counter; the two bytes moved provide the offset address of the next instruction to be executed. Previous program counter contents are lost. Add the data in the two succeeding program memory bytes to the stack pointer. This has the effect of adjusting the stack pointer past parameters that might have been placed onto the stack prior to the CALL that corresponds to this RET.

The encoding for this instruction is:

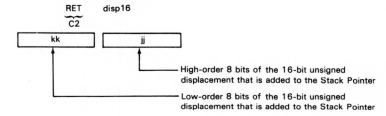

High-order 8 bits of the 16-bit unsigned displacement that is added to the Stack Pointer

Low-order 8 bits of the 16-bit unsigned displacement that is added to the Stack Pointer

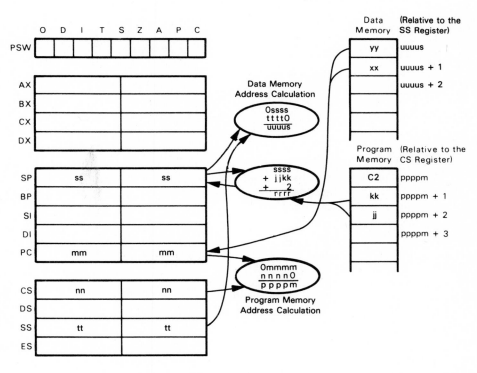

RET jjkk
Number of cycles: 20

Notes:

1. Every subroutine should contain at least one RET instruction; this is the last instruction executed within the subroutine and causes execution to return to the calling program.

2. The 8086 offers three other kinds of RETURN instructions. These RETURNs have some correspondence to the CALL instructions. This RET corresponds to CALL disp and CALL mem/reg indirect intrasegment.

3. No statuses are affected.

ROL   mem/reg,count

Rotate Register or Memory Location Left

Rotate the contents of the specified register or memory location left by the specified number of bits. The number of bits to rotate, represented by the variable count, is either one or the number contained in the CL register.

The encoding for this instruction is:

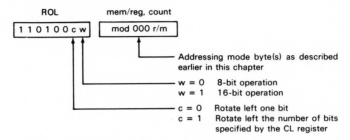

Suppose that the BX register contains $AB1F_{16}$ and the CL register contains 03_{16}. After the instruction

        ROL   BX,CL

has executed, the BX register will contain $58FD_{16}$ and the Carry flag will be set to 1.

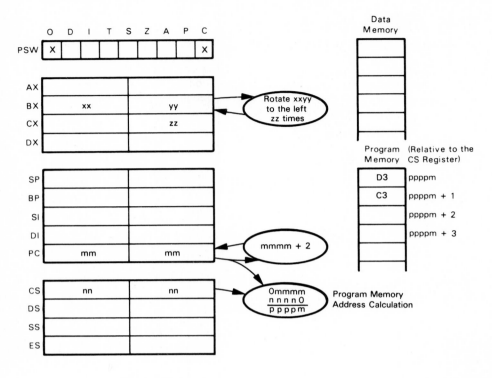

```
ROL   BX,CL
Number of cycles:  Register (N-bit rotate): 8 + (4 · N)
                   Register (1-bit rotate): 2
                   Memory (N-bit rotate): 20 + EA + (4 · N)
                   Memory (1-bit rotate): 15 + EA
```

Notes:

1. This instruction performs the same function as the 8080 instruction RLC. This instruction does, however, allow a great deal more flexibility in that multi-bit rotates are allowed, rotations of 16-bit quantities are allowed, and any register or memory location may be rotated.

2. Whether an 8- or 16-bit quantity is to be rotated is not immediately obvious when considering the syntax of this instruction. The assembler used will have a great deal to do with how this difficulty is solved.

ROR   mem/reg,count

Rotate Register or Memory Location Right

Rotate the contents of the specified register or memory location right by the specified number of bits. The number of bits to rotate, represented by the variable count, is either one or the number contained in the CL register.

The encoding for this instruction is:

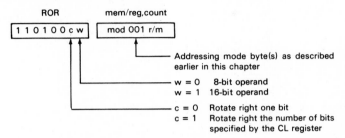

Suppose that the DS register contains $F000_{16}$, the SI register contains $06B2_{16}$ and the byte at memory location $F06B2_{16}$ contains 04_{16}. After the instruction

ROR   [SI],1

has executed, the byte at memory location $F06B2_{16}$ will contain 02_{16} and the Carry and Overflow statuses will be set to 0.

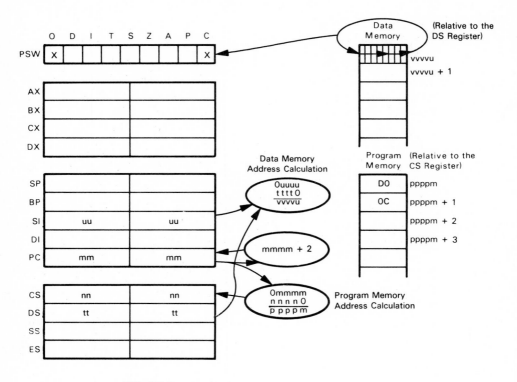

ROR   [SI],1
Number of cycles: Memory (1-bit rotate): 15 + EA
                  Memory (N-bit rotate): 20 + EA + (4 · N)
                  Register (1-bit rotate): 2
                  Register (N-bit rotate): 8 + (4 · N)

Notes:

1. This instruction performs the same function as the 8080 instruction RRC. This instruction does, however, allow a great deal more flexibility in that multi-bit rotates are allowed, rotations of 16-bit quantities are allowed, and any register or memory location may be rotated.

2. Note that whether an 8- or 16-bit quantity is to be rotated cannot be determined from the instruction

SAHF

Store the AH Register into the 8080 Flags

This instruction moves the contents of the AH register into the low-order 8 bits of the Flags register. The bits in the AH register are used as follows:

Bit 7:   Store into the Sign Flag
Bit 6:   Store into the Zero Flag
Bit 5:   Ignore
Bit 4:   Store into the Arithmetic Flag
Bit 3:   Ignore
Bit 2:   Store into the Parity Flag
Bit 1:   Ignore
Bit 0:   Store into the Carry Flag

The encoding for this instruction is:

SAHF
⁓
9E

For example, suppose that the AH register contains $E7_{16}$. Executing an

SAHF

instruction would set the Sign, Zero, Parity, and Carry statuses to 1 while setting the Arithmetic flag to 0.

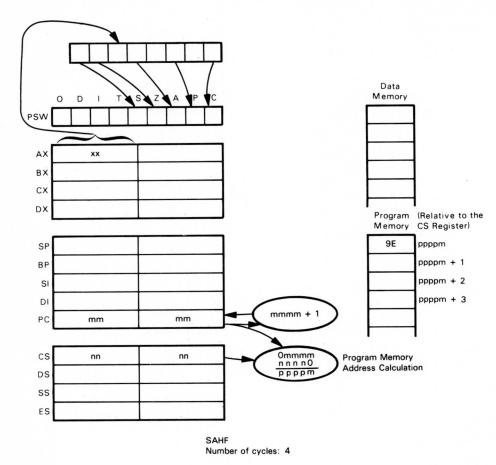

SAHF
Number of cycles: 4

Notes:

1. No registers, other than the Flags register, are affected. The Overflow, Direction, Interrupt, and Trap flags are not affected.

2. This instruction is used along with POP AX to emulate the 8080 instruction POP PSW.

8086 Code	8080 Code
POP AX	POP PSW
SAHF	

Note that for the 8086 sequence to make sense, the sequence

```
LAHF
PUSH  AX
```

must have been used to save the 8080 flags.

SAR   mem/reg,count

Shift Register or Memory Location Right

Shift the contents of the specified register or memory location right by the specified number of bits. The number of bits to shift, represented by the variable count, is either one or the number contained in the CL register. This is an arithmetic right shift.

The encoding for this instruction is:

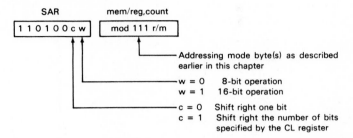

Suppose that the CL register contains 05_{16}, the DI register contains $180A_{16}$, the DS register contains $F800_{16}$ and the word at memory location $F980A_{16}$ contains 0064_{16}. After the instruction

SAR   [DI],CL

has executed, the word at memory location $F980A_{16}$ will be 0003_{16}.

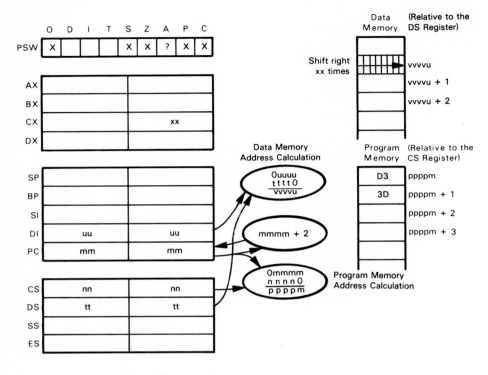

SAR   [DI],CL
Number of cycles: Memory (N-bit shift): 20 + EA + (4 · N)
                  Memory (1-bit shift): 15 + EA
                  Register (N-bit shift): 8 + (4 · N)
                  Register (1-bit shift): 2

Notes:

1. This is an arithmetic right shift as opposed to a logical right shift. The differences are:

Arithmetic right (SAR)	Shift all bits right once. Leave the high-order bit in the same state. This has the effect of sign extending the high-order bit. If a multi-bit shift is performed, sign extend the high-order bit as far as is necessary.
Logical right (SHR)	Shift all bits right once. Shift a zero into the high-order bit. If a multi-bit shift is performed, continue shifting in zeros as necessary.

SBB   ac,data

Subtract Immediate from AX or AL Register with Borrow

Subtract the immediate data in the succeeding program memory byte(s) from the AL (8-bit operation) or AX (16-bit operation) register with borrow. The subtraction is performed using twos complement methodology.

The encoding for this instruction is:

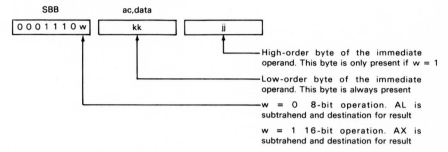

Suppose that the AX register contains $6B3A_{16}$ and the Carry status is 1. After the instruction

$$\text{SBB   AX,4D2CH}$$

has executed, the AX register will contain $1E0D_{16}$.

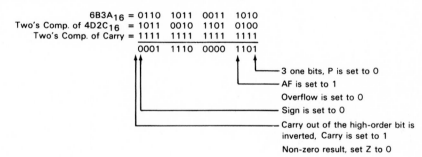

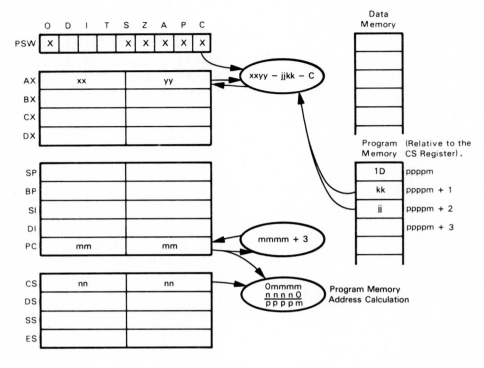

SBB   AX,jjkk
Number of cycles: 4

Notes:

1. This instruction performs the same function as the 8080 instruction SBI data; however, this instruction also allows 16-bit operations.

SBB   mem/reg,data

Subtract Immediate Data from Register or Memory Location with Borrow

Subtract the immediate data in the succeeding program memory byte(s) from the specified register or memory location with borrow. An 8- or 16-bit operation may be specified. The subtraction is performed using twos complement methodology.

The encoding for this instruction is:

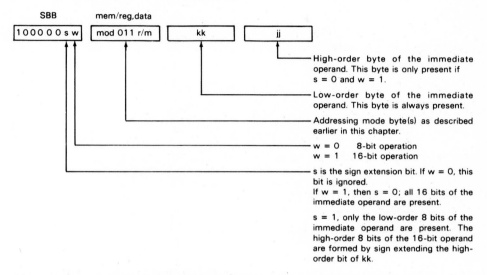

SBB	mem/reg,data		
1 0 0 0 0 0 s w	mod 0 1 1 r/m	kk	jj

High-order byte of the immediate operand. This byte is only present if s = 0 and w = 1.

Low-order byte of the immediate operand. This byte is always present.

Addressing mode byte(s) as described earlier in this chapter.

w = 0   8-bit operation
w = 1   16-bit operation

s is the sign extension bit. If w = 0, this bit is ignored.
If w = 1, then s = 0; all 16 bits of the immediate operand are present.

s = 1, only the low-order 8 bits of the immediate operand are present. The high-order 8 bits of the 16-bit operand are formed by sign extending the high-order bit of kk.

For example, if the Carry Status is 0, the SS register contains $2F00_{16}$, the BP register contains $0F6A_{16}$, the contents of the DI register are 0018_{16}, and the contents of the word at memory location $2FF82_{16}$ are 0400_{16}, then executing a

SBB   [BP + SI], 03F8H

will result in the word at memory location $2FF82_{16}$ being altered to 0008_{16}.

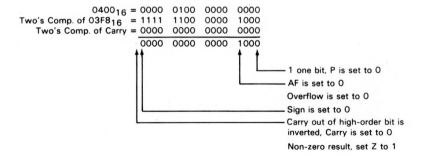

```
              0400₁₆ = 0000  0100  0000  0000
Two's Comp. of 03F8₁₆ = 1111  1100  0000  1000
Two's Comp. of Carry = 0000  0000  0000  0000
                        0000  0000  0000  1000
```

1 one bit, P is set to 0

AF is set to 0

Overflow is set to 0

Sign is set to 0

Carry out of high-order bit is inverted, Carry is set to 0

Non-zero result, set Z to 1

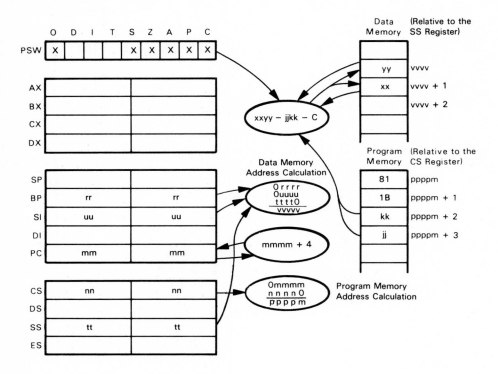

SBB   [BP + SI],jjkk

Number of cycles: Memory operand: 17 + EA
                              Register operand: 4

SBB   mem/reg$_1$, mem/reg$_2$

Subtract: • **Register from Register with Borrow**
          • **Register from Memory with Borrow**
          • **Memory from Register with Borrow**

     Subtract the contents of the register or memory location specified by mem/reg$_2$ and the Carry status from the contents of the register or memory location specified by mem/reg$_1$. An 8- or 16-bit operation may be specified. Either mem/reg$_1$ or mem/reg$_2$ may be a memory operand, but one of the operands must be a register operand.

     The encoding for this instruction is:

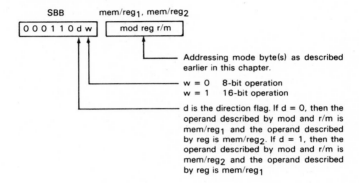

                   Addressing mode byte(s) as described earlier in this chapter.

                   w = 0   8-bit operation
                   w = 1   16-bit operation

                   d is the direction flag. If d = 0, then the operand described by mod and r/m is mem/reg$_1$ and the operand described by reg is mem/reg$_2$. If d = 1, then the operand described by mod and r/m is mem/reg$_2$ and the operand described by reg is mem/reg$_1$

Consider the case where the DL register contains 03_{16}, the BL register contains 64_{16}, and the Carry status is 1. After the instruction

                   SBB   BL,DL

has executed, the BL register will contain 60_{16} and the statuses will be set as follows:

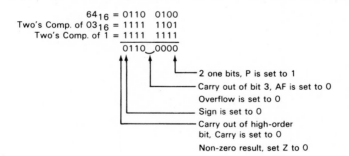

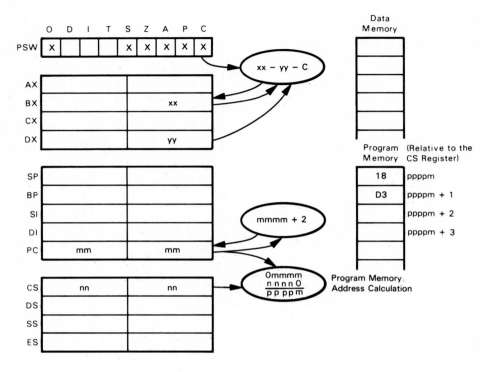

SBB   BL,DL
Number of cycles: Register to register: 3
Register to memory: 16 + EA
Memory to register: 9 + EA

SCAS/SCASB/SCASW

Compare Memory with AL or AX Register

Compare the contents of the memory location addressed by the DI register with the AL (8-bit operation) or AX (16-bit operation) register. The comparison is performed by subtracting the contents of the memory location addressed by the DI register from the AL or AX register and using the result to set the flags. Neither the memory location nor the AX register is affected. The DI register is incremented/decremented depending on the value of the DF flag.

The encoding for this instruction is:

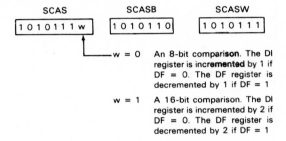

	SCAS		SCASB	SCASW

| 1 0 1 0 1 1 1 w | 1 0 1 0 1 1 0 | 1 0 1 0 1 1 1 |

w = 0   An 8-bit comparison. The DI register is incremented by 1 if DF = 0. The DF register is decremented by 1 if DF = 1

w = 1   A 16-bit comparison. The DI register is incremented by 2 if DF = 0. The DF register is decremented by 2 if DF = 1

Consider the case where the DI register contains 0000_{16}, the ES register contains 1800_{16}, the DF flag is 0, the contents of memory location 18000_{16} are 09_{16}, and the contents of the AL register are $0D_{16}$. After the instruction

SCASB

executes, the DI register will contain 0001_{16} and the flags will be set as follows:

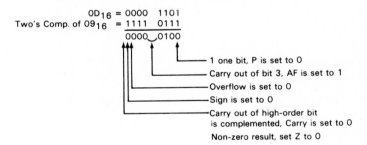

$$0D_{16} = 0000 \quad 1101$$
$$\text{Two's Comp. of } 09_{16} = 1111 \quad 0111$$
$$0000\_0100$$

—— 1 one bit, P is set to 0

—— Carry out of bit 3, AF is set to 1

—— Overflow is set to 0

—— Sign is set to 0

—— Carry out of high-order bit is complemented, Carry is set to 0

Non-zero result, set Z to 0

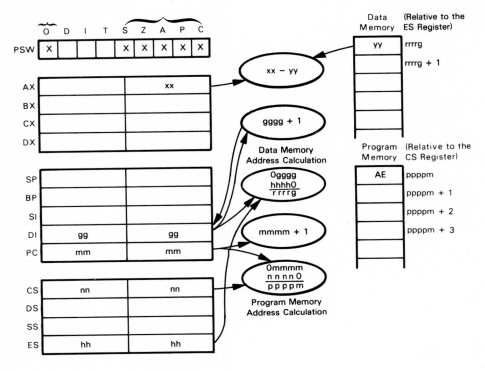

SCASB
Number of cycles: 15 for a single occurrence
9 + (15 times repetition when preceded by REP prefix)

Notes:

1. The REP prefix and/or the LOCK prefix may be used with this instruction. If the REP prefix and the LOCK prefix are used with this instruction, certain problems may result. An analysis of this difficulty is presented in the next chapter.

2. Determination of byte or word operand for the generalized form of SCAS is discussed at the end of this chapter.

SEG   segreg

Override Default Segment Register

Use the specified segment register to compute the data memory address for the instruction this prefix precedes; i.e., use the contents of the specified segment register as the segment address for the data memory address calculation.

The encoding for this instruction is:

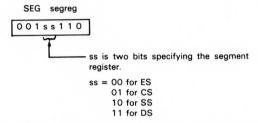

SEG   segreg

$$001ss110$$

ss is two bits specifying the segment register.

ss = 00 for ES
      01 for CS
      10 for SS
      11 for DS

Consider the following situation: the DS register contains 1000_{16}, the ES register contains 2000_{16}, the BX register contains 0008_{16}, the word at memory location 10008_{16} is $FEFE_{16}$, and the word at memory location 20008_{16} is $060A_{16}$. After the instructions

```
SEG  ES
MOV  AX,[BX]
```

have executed, the AX register will contain $060A_{16}$.

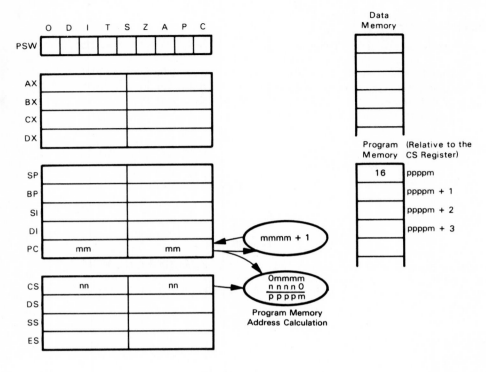

SEG ES
Number of cycles: 2

Notes:

1. The invocation of the segment override prefix is assembler dependent.

   As shown above, the sequence

   ```
   SEG   ES
   MOV   AX,[BX]
   ```

   is used to override DS with ES.
   An alternative used by Intel's assembler is

   ```
   MOV   AX,ES:[BX]
   ```

   — the request for segment override is imbedded in the move instruction. The assembler will generate the override prefix as part of the MOV instruction code generation.

SHL   mem/reg,count
SAL   mem/reg,count

Shift Register or Memory Location Left

Shift the contents of the specified register or memory location left by the specified number of bits. The number of bits to shift, represented by the variable count, is either one or the number contained in the CL register. This is a logical left shift.

The encoding for this instruction is:

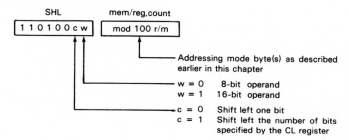

Suppose that the CL register contains 02_{16} and the SI register contains $A450_{16}$. After the instruction

SHL   SI,CL

has executed, the SI register will contain 9140_{16} and the Carry status will be 0.

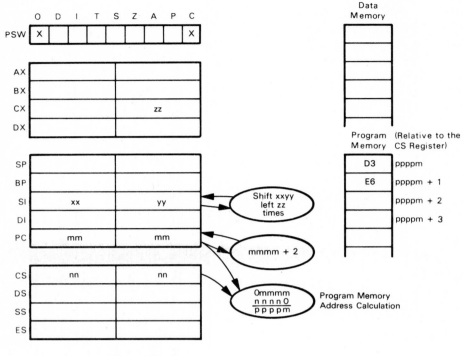

```
SHL   SI,CL
Number of cycles: Register (N-bit shift): 8 + (4 · N)
                  Register (1-bit shift): 2
                  Memory (N-bit shift): 20 + EA + (4 · N)
                  Memory (1-bit shift): 15 + EA
```

Notes:

1. This instruction can be used to perform multiplications in addition to shifts. Since the MUL and IMUL instructions require at least 71 cycles to execute, there are occasions where using shifts to perform multiplication becomes an attractive solution. Typically, these situations arise when optimizing the speed of the code is more of a factor than memory conservation, and when the multiplication to be performed will always be a power of two, or will always be some constant. Consider the following cases:

```
                         CALL    MULT$BY$8
                          ·
                          ·
                          ·
         MULT$BY$8        MOV     CL,3
                          SAL     AX,CL
                          RET
```

The MULTBY8 routine requires 5 bytes of code for the routine and 3 bytes of code for the CALL. Instead of requiring 71 cycles (minimum) to perform the multiply, however, 19 cycles are necessary for the CALL and 32 cycles are necessary for the routine.

```
                      CALL        SAL$THREE$TIMES
                        .
                        .
                        .
SAL$THREE$TIMES       SAL
                      SAL
                      SAL
                      RET
```

This routine requires an additional 2 bytes; however, this routine executes in a mere 14 cycles.

It is clear that selecting routines which only multiply by powers of two will certainly show off the SHL instruction. Consider the case of a multiply by 15.

```
                      CALL        MULT$BY$15
                        .
                        .
                        .
MULT$BY$15            MOV         CL,4
                      MOV         DX,AX
                      SAL         AL,CL
                      SUB         AX,DX
                      RET
```

This routine requires 9 bytes of code and 41 cycles, an additional 19 for the CALL. This is only marginally faster than using the MUL instruction. This routine can work much faster if individual SAL instructions are included.

```
                      CALL        MULT$BY$15
                        .
                        .
                        .
MULT$BY$15            MOV         DX,AX
                      SAL
                      SAL
                      SAL
                      SAL
                      SUB         AX,DX
                      RET
```

In this case, the routine needs only 21 cycles to operate.

2. 8- or 16-bit rotation? This instruction, the way it is expressed in this description, doesn't specify this.

SHR   mem/reg,count

Shift Register or Memory Location Right

Shift the contents of the specified register or memory location right by the specified number of bits. The number of bits to shift, represented by the variable count, is either one or the number contained in the CL register. The bit shifted into the high-order bit is a zero. This is a logical right shift.

The encoding for this instruction is:

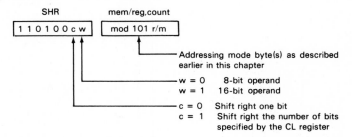

Suppose that the BL register contains $F0_{16}$. After the instruction

         SHR   BL

has executed, the contents of the BL register will be 78_{16}.

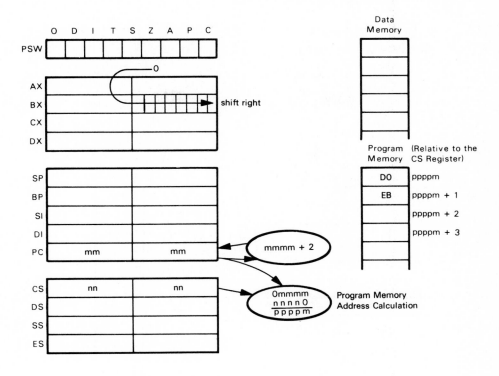

SHR   BL

Number of cycles: Register (1-bit shift): 2
Register (N-bit shift): 8 + (4 · N)
Memory (1-bit shift): 15 + EA
Memory (N-bit shift): 20 + EA + (4 · N)

Notes:

1. This is a logical right shift as opposed to an arithmetic right shift. The differences are

Logical right (SHR)　　Shift all bits right once. Shift a zero into the high-order bit. If a multi-bit shift is performed, continue shifting in zeros as necessary.

Arithmetic right (SAR)　Shift all bits right once. Leave the high-order bit in the same state. This has the effect of sign extending the high-order bit. If a multi-bit shift is performed, sign extend the high-order bit as far as is necessary.

STC

Set the Carry Flag

This instruction is used to set the Carry status to 1. No other statuses or register contents are affected.

The encoding for this instruction is:

$$\underbrace{\text{STC}}_{\text{F9}}$$

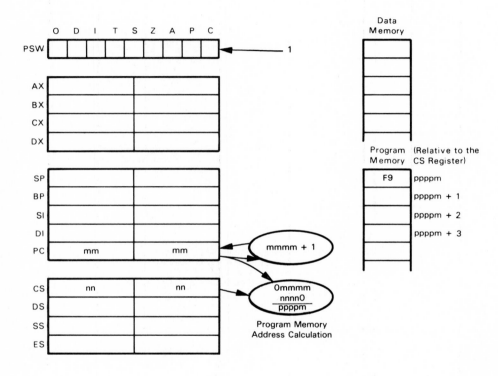

STC
Number of cycles: 2

STD

Set the Direction Flag

This instruction is used to set the Direction flag to 1. No other statuses or register contents are affected. This instruction makes string operations perform auto-decrement on the pointers used by the string operations.

The encoding for this instruction is:

$$\underset{\text{FD}}{\underbrace{\text{STD}}}$$

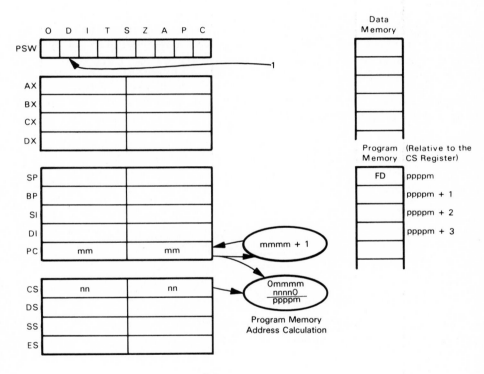

STD
Number of cycles: 2

STI

Set the Interrupt Flag

Set the Interrupt flag to 1 after the execution of the next instruction. This has the effect of enabling interrupts.

The reason for waiting one instruction is as follows. Most interrupt service routines end with the two instructions:

```
STI      ; ENABLE INTERRUPTS
RET      ; RETURN TO INTERRUPTED PROGRAM
```

If interrupts are processed serially, then for the entire duration of the interrupt service routine all interrupts are disabled — which means that in a multi-interrupt application, there is a significant possibility for one or more interrupts to be pending when any interrupt service routine completes execution.

If interrupts were acknowledged as soon as the STI instructions had executed, then the Return instruction would not be executed. Under these circumstances returns would stack up one on top the other and unnecessarily consume stack memory space. This may be illustrated as follows:

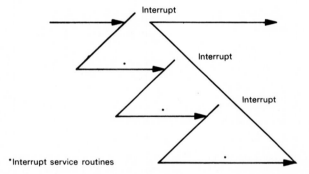

*Interrupt service routines

By inhibiting interrupts for one more instruction following execution of STI, the 8086 CPU ensures that the RET instruction gets executed in sequence:

```
STI      ; ENABLE INTERRUPTS
RET      ; RETURN FROM INTERRUPT
```

It is not uncommon for interrupts to be kept disabled while an interrupt service routine is executing. Interrupts are processed serially:

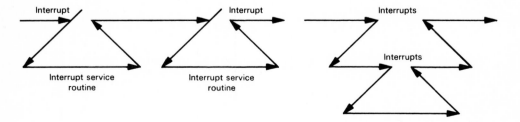

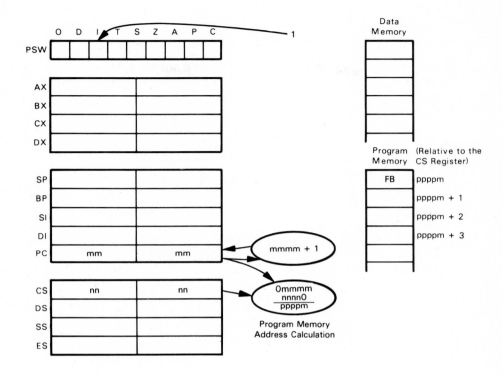

STI
Number of cycles: 2

Notes:

1. This instruction performs the same function as the 8080 instruction EI.

STOS/STOSB/STOSW

Store AL or AX Register Into Memory

Store the AL (8-bit operation) or AX (16-bit operation) register into the memory location addressed by the DI register. The DI register is incremented/decremented depending on the value of the DF flag.

The encoding for this instruction is:

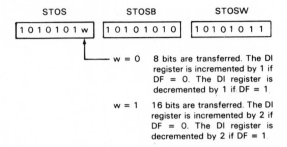

For example, suppose that the DF flag is 1, the DI register contains $000A_{16}$, the ES register contains 2800_{16}, and the AX register contains 0604_{16}. After the instruction

STOSW

has executed, the contents of the word at memory location $2800A_{16}$ will be 0604_{16}, and the DI register will contain 0008_{16}.

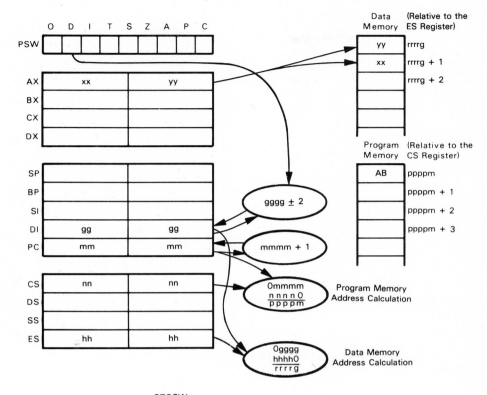

STOSW
Number of cycles: 11 per single occurrence
9 + (10 times repetition when preceded by the REP prefix)

Notes:

1. No statuses are affected.

2. The segment address for this instruction is always contained in the ES register. No segment override prefix may be used for this instruction. If a segment override prefix is present, it will be ignored.

3. This instruction may be preceded by the REP prefix and/or the LOCK prefix. Using the REP and the LOCK prefixes in conjunction with this instruction may cause problems. Consult the next chapter for a complete discussion of these potential difficulties.

4. This instruction is very useful in setting entire buffers or data areas to a particular value. Consider the following instruction sequence:

```
LES       DI,JOB$COSTING$ARRAY
MOV       CX,JOB$COSTING$ARRAY$WORD$LENGTH
MOV       AX,0000H

REP
STOS WORD
```

    After this sequence has executed, the JOB$COSTING$ARRAY will contain all 0's.

5. For the generalized form of STOS, how does the assembler determine whether 8 or 16 bits are to be stored? For a discussion of this problem, consult the last section of this chapter.

SUB   ac,data

Subtract Immediate Data from the AL or AX Register

This instruction is used to subtract immediate data from the AL (8-bit operation) or the AX (16-bit operation) register. The subtraction is performed utilizing twos complement methodology.

The encoding for this instruction is:

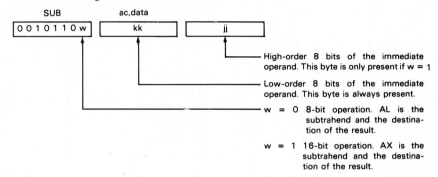

SUB   ac,data

| 0 0 1 0 1 1 0 w | kk | jj |

High-order 8 bits of the immediate operand. This byte is only present if w = 1

Low-order 8 bits of the immediate operand. This byte is always present.

w = 0   8-bit operation. AL is the subtrahend and the destination of the result.

w = 1   16-bit operation. AX is the subtrahend and the destination of the result.

For example, suppose that the AL register contains 61_{16}. After the execution of the instruction

SUB   AL,065H

the contents of the accumulator will be FC_{16}.

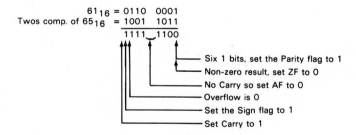

$$61_{16} = 0110\ \ 0001$$
Twos comp. of 65_{16} = 1001   1011
1111   1100

Six 1 bits, set the Parity flag to 1
Non-zero result, set ZF to 0
No Carry so set AF to 0
Overflow is 0
Set the Sign flag to 1
Set Carry to 1

Notice that the resulting Carry is complemented.

Note that FC_{16} is the twos complement representation of -4, which is indeed the result we expect when we subtract 65_{16} from 61_{16}.

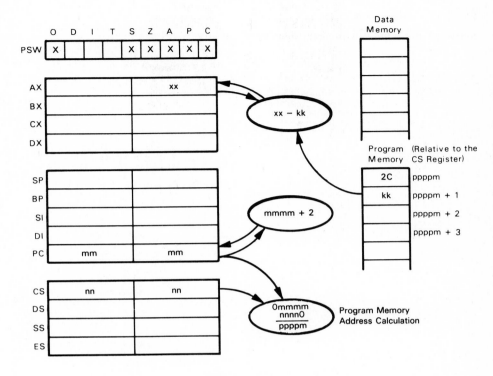

SUB   AL,kk
Number of cycles: 4

Notes:

1.   This instruction performs the same function as the 8080 instruction SUI data. This instruction, however, also allows 16-bit operations.

SUB   mem/reg,data

Subtract Immediate Data from Register or Memory Location

Subtract the immediate data in the succeeding program memory byte(s) from the specified register or memory location. An 8- or 16-bit operation may be specified.

The encoding for this instruction is:

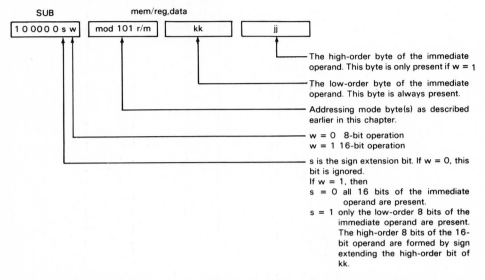

Suppose that the DS register contains 3000_{16}, the SI register contains 0040_{16}, and the word at memory location 30054_{16} contains 4336_{16}. After the instruction

SUB [SI + 14H], 0136H

has executed, the word at memory location 30054_{16} will contain 4200_{16}. The flags will be set as follows:

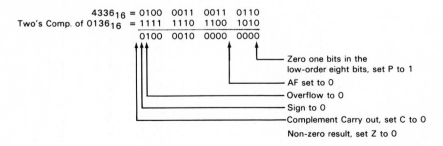

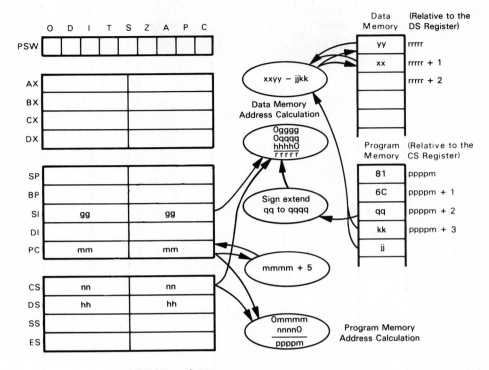

SUB [SI + qq], jjkk
Number of cycles: immediate from memory: 17 + EA
                  immediate from register: 4

Notes:

1. This instruction is not usually applied to subtracting immediate data from the AX or AL register. The instruction SUB ac,data is provided for this purpose.

SUB   mem/reg$_1$, mem/reg$_2$

Subtract: •   **Register from Register**
          •   **Register from Memory**
          •   **Memory from Register**

Subtract the contents of the register or memory location specified by mem/reg$_2$ from the contents of the register or memory location specified by mem/reg$_1$. An 8- or 16-bit operation may be specified. Either mem/reg$_1$ or mem/reg$_2$ may be a memory operand, but one of the operands must be a register operand.

The encoding for this instruction is:

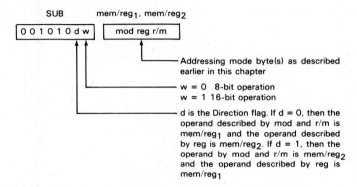

Suppose that the DH register contains 41_{16}, the SS register contains 0000_{16}, the BP register contains $00E4_{16}$, and the byte at memory location $000E8_{16}$ contains $5A_{16}$. After the instruction

SUB   DH,[BP + 4]

executes, the DH register will contain $E7_{16}$, and the statuses will be set as follows:

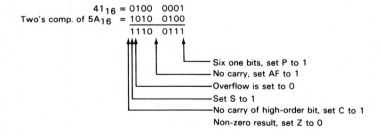

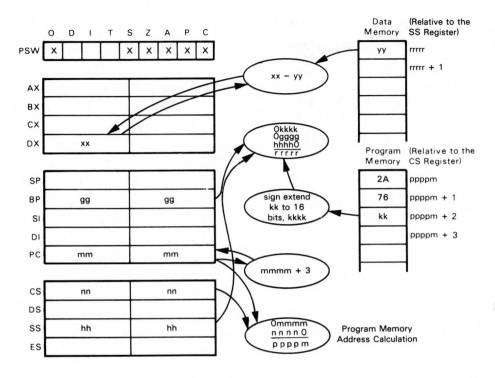

SUB   DH,[BP + kk]

Number of cycles: Memory to Register: 9 + EA
Register to Memory: 16 + EA
Register to Register: 3

TEST   ac,data

Test Immediate Data with AX or AL Register

AND the immediate data in the succeeding program memory byte(s) with the contents of the AL (8-bit operation) or the AX (16-bit operation) register, but do not return the result to the register.

The encoding for this instruction is:

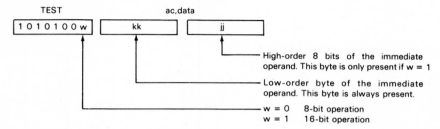

As an example, consider the situation where the AX register contains $73AC_{16}$. After the instruction

TEST   AX,0040H

has executed, the AX register will still contain $73AC_{16}$, but the Flags register will have been altered to reflect the ANDing of $73AC_{16}$ and 0040_{16}.

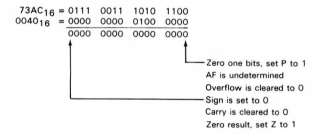

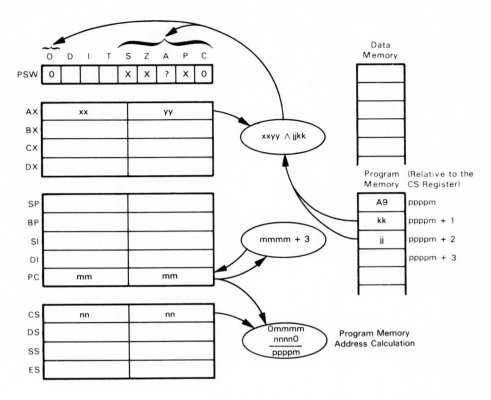

TEST   AX,jjkk
Number of cycles: 4

Notes:

1. If it is desired to TEST the contents of other registers or memory locations, consult the TEST mem/reg,data instruction.

TEST   mem/reg,data

Test Immediate Data with Register or Memory Location

AND the immediate data in the succeeding program memory byte(s) with the contents of the specified register or memory location, but do not return the result to the specified register or memory location. An 8- or 16-bit operation may be specified.

The encoding for this instruction is:

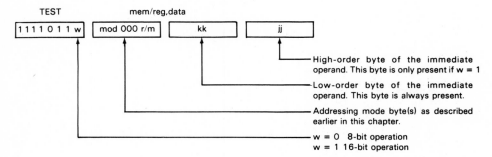

For example, consider the case where the SI register contains $03F6_{16}$. After the instruction

TEST   SI,0400H

executes, the contents of the SI register will be unchanged; however, the flags will be set to reflect the result of ANDing $03F6_{16}$ and 0400_{16}.

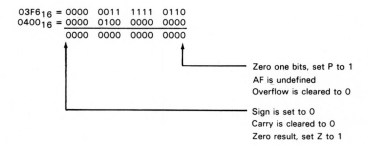

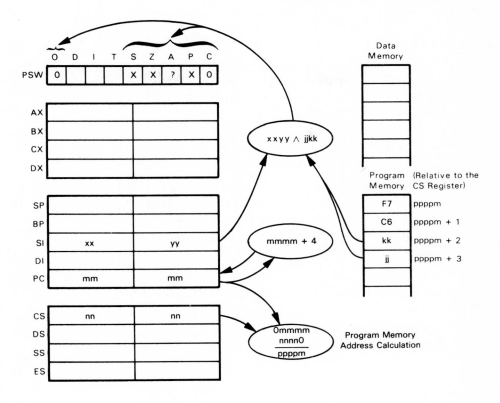

TEST SI,jjkk
Number of cycles: Immediate with register: 5
Immediate with memory: 11 + EA

Notes:

1. Testing the AX or AL register would not be a function normally associated with this instruction, since the TEST ac,data is provided for this purpose.

TEST   reg,mem/reg

Test Register with Memory

AND the contents of the specified register with the contents of the specified register or memory location using the result to set the flags, but not returning the result to the register(s) or memory location. An 8- or 16-bit operation may be specified.

The encoding for this instruction is:

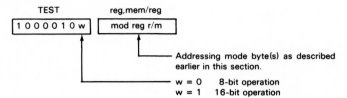

Suppose that the AL register contains 40_{16}, the DS register contains 8800_{16}, and the byte at memory location 88053_{16} is AF_{16}. After the instruction

TEST AL,[+ 53]

has executed, neither the AL register nor the byte at memory location 88053_{16} will be affected; however, the flags will be affected as follows:

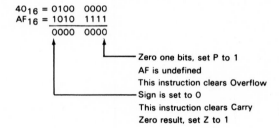

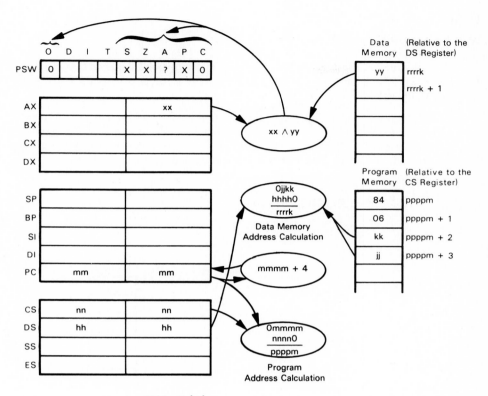

TEST   AL,[kk]

Number of cycles: Register with Memory: 9 + EA
Register with Register: 3

WAIT

Wait for Asserted Signal on Test Pin

This instruction causes the 8086 to enter an idle state if the signal on the $\overline{\text{TEST}}$ pin is not asserted. The 8086 will only leave the idle state if one of two conditions is met. The conditions are:

1. If the interrupts are enabled, an external interrupt will force the 8086 to service the interrupt. The address saved when the 8086 processes the interrupt is the address of the WAIT instruction. Thus, when the interrupt service routine returns, it returns to the WAIT instruction.

2. The $\overline{\text{TEST}}$ signal is asserted.

The encoding for this instruction is:

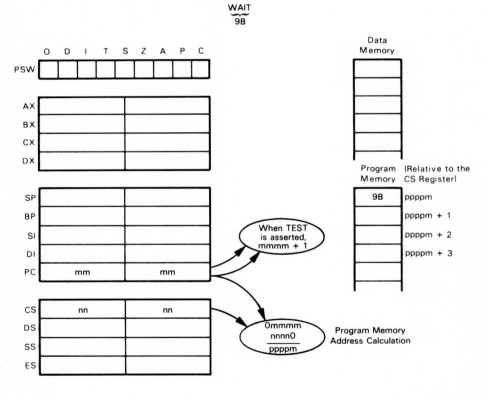

WAIT
Number of Cycles: Minimum = 3

XCHG   reg

Exchange Register's Contents with Accumulator

Exchange the 16-bit contents of the specified register with the contents of the accumulator.

The encoding for this instruction is:

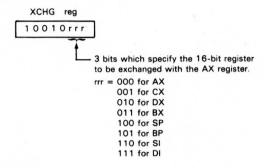

```
XCHG   reg
```
```
1 0 0 1 0 r r r
```

└─ 3 bits which specify the 16-bit register to be exchanged with the AX register.

rrr = 000 for AX
       001 for CX
       010 for DX
       011 for BX
       100 for SP
       101 for BP
       110 for SI
       111 for DI

For example, the instruction

```
XCHG   BX
```

is used to swap the contents of the BX register with the contents of the AX register.

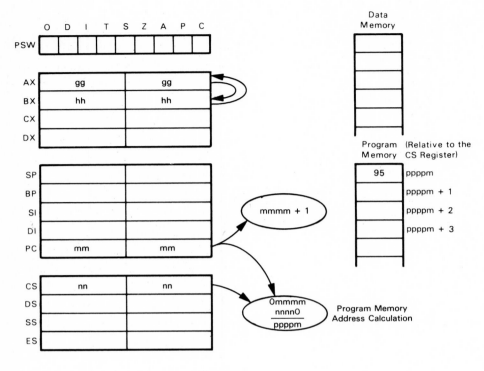

XCHG BX
Number of cycles: 3

Notes:

1. No statuses are affected.

2. The instruction XCHG AX,AX is the instruction which is used as the NOP instruction by the 8086.

XCHG   reg,mem/reg

Exchange Register Data with Register or Memory

This instruction swaps the contents of the register or memory location specified by the mem/reg operand with the contents of the register specified by the reg operand. An 8- or 16-bit transfer may be specified.

The encoding for this instruction is:

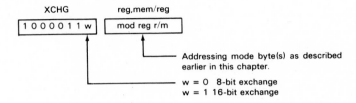

Evaluate the situation where the contents of the BX register are $6F30_{16}$, the SS register contains $2F00_{16}$, the SI register contains 0046_{16}, the BP register contains 0200_{16}, and the word stored at memory location $2F246_{16}$ is 4154_{16}. After the instruction

XCHG   BX,[BP + SI]

executes, the BX register will contain 4154_{16}, memory location $2F246_{16}$ will contain 30_{16} and memory location $2F247_{16}$ will contain $6F_{16}$.

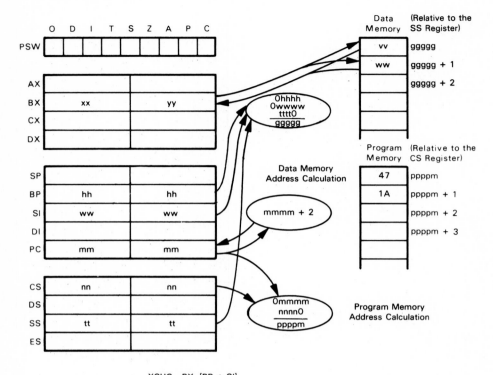

XCHG BX, [BP + SI]
Number of cycles: memory with register: 17 + EA
                  register with register: 4

Notes:

1. No statuses are affected.

2. The segment registers may not be specified in this instruction. There is no instruction to exchange segment registers.

3. Typically, this instruction is not used to exchange a register with the AX register. The instruction XCHG reg is provided for this purpose.

XLAT

Perform Table Lookup via AL and BX Registers

An 8-bit data element is loaded into the AL register. This data element is addressed by using the following algorithm:

1.   Add the 8-bit contents of the AL register to the 16-bit BX register.

2.   Use the result of the addition in step 1 as the offset address for the DS register (assuming that no segment override has been executed).

Instruction encoding for XLAT is:

XLAT
D7

For example, should the AL register contain $0F_{16}$, the BX register 0040_{16}, and the DS register $F000_{16}$, then executing the instruction

XLAT

would load the contents of memory location $F004F_{16}$ into the AL register.

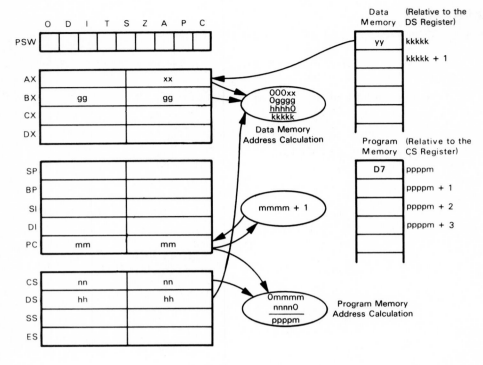

XLAT
Number of cycles: 11

Notes:

1. This instruction is most commonly used in the case where the BX register contains the beginning address of a table and the AL register is used as an index into the table.

XOR   ac,data

XOR Immediate Data with AX or AL Register

This instruction exclusive-ORs 8- or 16-bit data elements with the AL (8-bit) or AX (16-bit) register via immediate addressing.

The encoding for this instruction is:

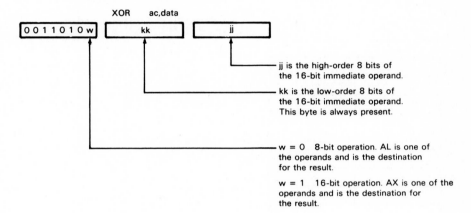

For example, suppose that AX contains $B31C_{16}$. Executing the instruction

XOR   AX,5522H

would result in $E63E_{16}$ being stored into the AX register.

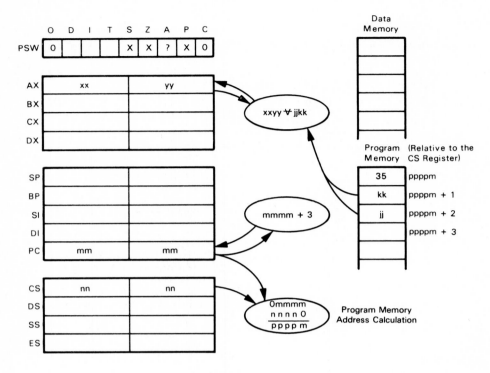

XOR   AX,jjkk
Number of cycles: 4

Notes:

1. This instruction performs the same function as the XRI data instruction in the 8080 assembly language. This instruction, however, also allows 16-bit data units, whereas the 8080 XRI only uses 8-bit data elements.

XOR   mem/reg₁, mem/reg₂

XOR: · **Register with Register**
· **Register with Memory**
· **Memory with Register**

Exclusive-OR the contents of the register or memory location specified by mem/reg₂ with the contents of the register or memory location specified by mem/reg₁, returning the result to mem/reg₁. An 8- or 16-bit operation may be specified. Either mem/reg₁ or mem/reg₂ may be a memory operand, but one of the operands must be a register operand.

The encoding for this instruction is:

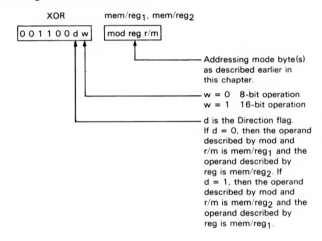

Suppose that the AX register contains $07B7_{16}$, the DS register contains 9080_{16}, the SI register contains $040E_{16}$, and the word at memory location $90C0E_{16}$ is $A6F0_{16}$. After the instruction

XOR   AX,[SI]

has executed, the AX register will contain $A147_{16}$. The flags will be set as follows:

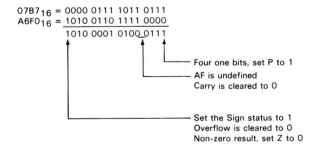

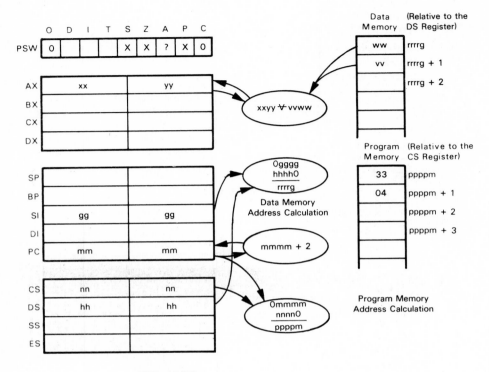

XOR   AX,[SI]

Number of cycles: Memory to Register: 9 + EA
                  Register to Memory: 16 + EA
                  Register to Register: 3

XOR   mem/reg,data

XOR Immediate Data with Register or Memory Location

XOR the immediate data in the succeeding program memory byte(s) with the specified register or memory location. An 8- or 16-bit operation may be specified.

The encoding for this instruction is:

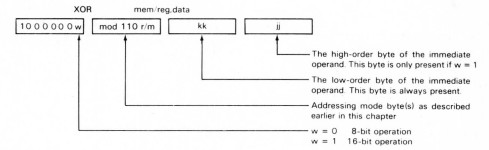

Consider the case where the DS register contains 3800_{16}, the contents of the BX register are 0200_{16}, the DI register contains 0136_{16}, and the word at memory location 38336_{16} is $06B3_{16}$. After the instruction

$$XOR [BX + DI], 0805H$$

has executed, the word at memory location 38336_{16} will be $0EB6_{16}$.

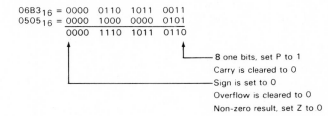

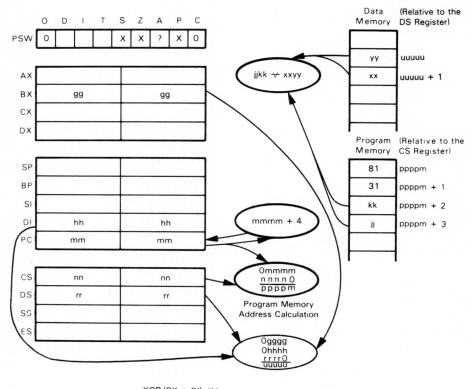

XOR [BX + DI], jjkk

Number of cycles: Memory operand: 17 + EA
Register operand: 4

Notes:

1. This instruction is not typically used to XOR immediate data with AX or AL register. The instruction XOR ac,data is provided for this purpose.

ASSEMBLER-DEPENDENT MNEMONICS

Some 8086 assembler mnemonics do not expressly define whether an 8-bit or 16-bit operation is to be performed. All instructions which have one of the 8086 registers as an operand can use the register to determine whether an 8-bit or 16-bit operation is required. For example, if the instruction is

        XOR   AX,0804H

a 16-bit operation is clearly in order. Some instructions, however, can perform an 8-bit or 16-bit operation, yet may not specify a register. These instructions include two basic types: the string operations, e.g., CMPS, LODS, and instructions which can have a single memory operand, e.g., MUL, NOT.

Assemblers can deal with this difficulty in one of three ways. These are:

1. A character can be added to the mnemonic that will indicate whether a word or byte operation is specified. For example, MUL can be specified as

            MULB   8 × 8-bit multiplication, or
            MULW   16 × 16-bit multiplication

    In the case of the string operations, the character, be it B (for Byte) or W (for Word) follows the last character of the mnemonic. For example, the instruction CMPS is replaced by:

            CMPSB 8-bit comparison
            CMPSW 16-bit comparison

2. The operand for the string operations can be WORD or BYTE. For example, the MOVS instruction can be:

            MOVS BYTE   8-bit move
            MOVS WORD   16-bit move

    In addition, this strategy can be applied to the single memory operand instructions. For example,

            NOT   SI   ,BYTE
            NOT   SI   ,WORD

3. The programmer defines all his data areas and symbols as WORD or BYTE elements. The assembler retains this information and then when a reference is made to the data area/symbol, the assembler determines whether an 8- or 16-bit operation is necessary. For example,

            TOUCH$TONE$OUTPUT$BYTE   DB 00H   ;DB means define byte
            TIMER   DW 0000H   ;DW means define word

    When the following operations are performed

            NOT TOUCH$TONE$OUTPUT$BYTE
            INC TIMER

    an 8-bit operation is assembled for the NOT operation and a 16-bit operation is specified for the INC operation. Note that a particular assembler may use more than one of these options to perform its function.

For string instructions, although the object code level instruction does not contain operands, the generalized source form of the instruction must specify operands. This requirement allows the assembler to determine whether byte or word operations are required. For example, consider the

LODS

instruction. The source operand address is specified by the DS and SI registers while the destination is the AX or AL register. The mnemonic LODS alone provides insufficient information to determine the operand type (byte or word). However,

ID_NUMBER DB 5
.
.
.
LODS ID_NUMBER

provides data typing information which allows the assembler to automatically construct the byte load form of LODS. This notation also enhances readability and maintainability of the code since the programmer specifies what is being loaded.

4

8086 Instruction Groups

This chapter contains another discussion of the 8086 instruction set. In contrast to the discussion presented in Chapter 3, where each instruction was described individually, this chapter discusses groups of instructions. The 8086 instructions are grouped according to the functions they perform. These groups are:

- Data Movement Instructions
- Arithmetic Instructions
- Logical Instructions
- String Primitive Instructions
- Program Counter Control Instructions
- I/O Instructions
- Interrupt Instructions
- Rotate and Shift Instructions

DATA MOVEMENT INSTRUCTIONS

The 8086 instructions which perform data movement are shown in Table 4-1. 8086 data movement instructions can be divided into three general categories:

Instructions which move data from register to register or between memory locations and registers.

1. Instructions which move data from register to register or between memory locations and registers.

2. Instructions which move data onto and off of the stack.

3. Instructions which move multiple bytes from one memory location to another.

The first and second types of instructions will be discussed in this section. Multiple byte instructions, which are created using instructions called string primitives, will only be discussed peripherally in this section; they will be discussed in detail later in this chapter.

Data movement instructions are used in following types of routine:

1. A routine to move the contents of BUFFER$A to BUFFER$B.

2. A routine to initialize the contents of BUFFER$A.

3. A routine to translate the contents of BUFFER$A.

Table 4-1. 8086 Data Movement Instructions

Mnemonic	Operands	Object Code	Bytes	Clocks	O	D	I	T	S	Z	A	P	C	Operation Performed
MOV	mem/reg₁, mem/reg₂	100010dw mod rrr r/m (DISP) (DISP)	2, 3 or 4	reg - reg: 2 mem - reg: 8 + EA reg - mem: 9 + EA										$[mem/reg_1] \leftarrow [mem/reg_2]$* An 8- or 16-bit data element is moved from the memory location or register specified by mem/reg₂ into the memory location or register specified by mem/reg₁.
MOV	mem/reg, data	1100011w mod 000 r/m (DISP) (DISP) kk jj (if w = 1)	3, 4, 5 or 6	10 + EA										$[mem/reg] \leftarrow data$ Move 8- or 16-bit immediate data into the memory location or register specified by mem/reg.
MOV	reg, data	1011wrrr kk jj (if w = 1)	2 or 3	4										$[reg] \leftarrow data$ Move 8- or 16-bit immediate data into the register specified by reg.
MOV	ac, mem	1010000w kk jj	3	10										$[ac] \leftarrow [mem]$ Move data from the memory location specified by mem into the AL (8-bit operation) or the AX (16-bit operation) register.
MOV	mem, ac	1010001w kk jj	3	10										$[mem] \leftarrow [ac]$ Move data from the AL (8-bit operation) or AX (16-bit operation) register into the memory location specified by mem.
MOV	segreg, mem/reg	8E mod 0 ss r/m (DISP) (DISP)	2, 3 or 4	reg - reg: 2 mem - reg: 8 + EA										$[segreg] \leftarrow [mem/reg]$ Move 16 bits of data from the memory location or register specified by mem/reg into the selected segment register. If ss = 01, this operation is undefined.
MOV	mem/reg, segreg	8C mod 0 ss r/m (DISP) (DISP)	2, 3 or 4	reg - reg: 2 mem - reg: 9 + EA										$[mem/reg] \leftarrow [segreg]$ Move the contents of the selected segment register into the specified memory location or register.
XCHG	mem/reg₁, mem/reg₂	1000011w mod rrr r/m (DISP) (DISP)	2, 3 or 4	reg - reg: 4 reg - mem: 17 + EA										$[mem/reg_1] \longleftrightarrow [mem/reg_2]$* Exchange the 8- or 16-bit contents of the memory location specified by mem/reg₁ with the contents of the memory location or register specified by mem/reg₂.

* This does not imply mem ← mem

Table 4-1. 8086 Data Movement Instructions (Continued)

Mnemonic	Operands	Object Code	Bytes	Clocks	Status O	D	I	T	S	Z	A	P	C	Operation Performed
XCHG	reg	10010rrr	1	3										[AX] ←→ [reg] Exchange the contents of the AX register with the contents of the selected register.
XLAT		D7	1	11										[AL] ← [[AL] + [BX]] Load the data byte addressed by summing AL with BX into the AL register.
LDS	reg,mem	C5 mod rrr r/m (DISP) (DISP)	2, 3 or 4	16 + EA										[reg] ← [mem], [DS] ← [mem + 2] Load 16 bits of data from the memory location specified by mem into the selected register. Load 16 bits of data from the memory location following the memory location specified by mem into the DS register.
LEA	reg,mem	8D mod rrr r/m (DISP) (DISP)	2, 3 or 4	2 + EA										[reg] ← mem (offset portion of address) Move the 16 bits which are the offset portion of the memory address into the selected register.
LES	reg,mem	C4 mod rrr r/m (DISP) (DISP)	2, 3 or 4	16 + EA										[reg] ← [mem], [ES] ← [mem + 2] Load 16 bits of data from the memory location specified by mem into the selected register. Load 16 bits of data from the memory location following the memory location specified by mem into the ES register.
PUSH	mem/reg	FF mod 110 r/m (DISP) (DISP)	2, 3 or 4	reg: 11 mem: 16 + EA										[SP] ← [SP] − 2, [[SP]] ← [mem/reg] Decrement SP by 2. Store the 16-bit contents of the memory location or register specified by mem/reg onto the top of the stack.
PUSH	reg	01010rrr	1	10										[SP] ← [SP] − 2, [[SP]] ← [reg] Decrement SP by 2. Store the 16-bit contents of the specified register onto the top of the stack.
PUSH	segreg	000ss110	1	10										[SP] ← [SP] − 2, [[SP]] ← [segreg] Decrement SP by 2. Store the 16-bit contents of the specified register onto the top of the stack.
PUSHF		9C	1	10										[SP] ← [SP] − 2, [[SP]] ← [FLAGS] Decrement SP by 2. Store the contents of the FLAGS register onto the top of the stack.

Table 4-1. 8086 Data Movement Instructions (Continued)

Mnemonic	Operands	Object Code	Bytes	Clocks	O	D	I	T	S	Z	A	P	C	Operation Performed
POP	mem/reg	8F mod 000 r/m (DISP) (DISP)	2, 3 or 4	reg: 8 mem: 17 + EA										[mem/reg] ← [[SP]], [SP] ← [SP] + 2 Move the 16 bits at the top of the stack into the memory location or register specified by mem/reg. Increment SP by 2.
POP	reg	01011rrr	1	8										[reg] ← [[SP]], [SP] ← [SP] + 2 Move the 16 bits at the top of the stack into the specified register. Increment SP by 2.
POP	segreg	000ss111	1	8										[segreg] ← [[SP]], [SP] ← [SP] + 2 Move the 16 bits at the top of the stack into the specified segment register. Increment SP by 2. If ss = 01, this operation is undefined.
POPF		9D	1	8	X	X	X	X	X	X	X	X	X	[FLAGS] ← [[SP]], [SP] ← [SP] + 2 Move the 16 bits at the top of the stack into the FLAGS register. Increment SP by 2.
LAHF		9F	1	4										Transfer the 8080 flags to the AH register.
SAHF		9E	1	4					X	X	X	X	X	Transfer the AH register to the 8080 flags.

BUFFER-TO-BUFFER MOVE ROUTINES

Two elementary buffer-to-buffer move routines are shown in Figures 4-1 and 4-2 for 8-bit and 16-bit data elements, respectively. These routines assume that the SI register contains the address of BUFFER$A, the DI register contains the address of BUFFER$B, and the CX register contains the number of data elements to move.

```
MOVE$BYTES:     MOV     AL,[SI]             ;LOAD BYTE FROM SOURCE
                MOV     [DI],AL             ;STORE BYTE INTO DESTINATION
                INC     SI                  ;ADJUST POINTERS
                INC     DI
                DEC     CX                  ;DECREMENT # TO MOVE
                JNZ     MOVE$BYTES          ;LOOP IF NOT DONE
                RET
```

Figure 4-1. 8-Bit Buffer-to-Buffer Move

```
MOVE$WORDS:     MOV     AX,[SI]             ;LOAD WORD FROM SOURCE
                MOV     [DI],AX             ;STORE WORD INTO DESTINATION
                                            ;ADJUST POINTERS
                INC     SI
                INC     SI
                INC     DI
                INC     DI
                DEC     CX                  ;DECREMENT # TO MOVE
                JNZ     MOVE$WORDS          ;LOOP IF NOT DONE
                RET
```

Figure 4-2. 16-Bit Buffer-to-Buffer Move

The instruction sequences illustrated in Figures 4-1 and 4-2 move data in the Data Segment. The BX register can be used in place of the SI or DI register in these routines.

The routines as illustrated are simple to follow, but they are not very efficient. String primitive operations, which are described later in this chapter, may provide much more efficient buffer-to-buffer move routines; also, the LOOP instruction improves the efficiency of any decrement and branch program logic.

Initializing Registers for Buffer-to-Buffer Moves

There are many ways of initializing registers that are used by instruction sequences such as the buffer-to-buffer move routines. The initialization methods depend on how the addresses and the count are obtained. An additional factor is the number of registers that need to be initialized; for example, in most cases, the DS register will already be initialized.

The buffer beginning addresses and the byte or word count for the buffer to buffer move routine can be held in a block of memory words pointed to by a register. Consider the following eight-byte memory block:

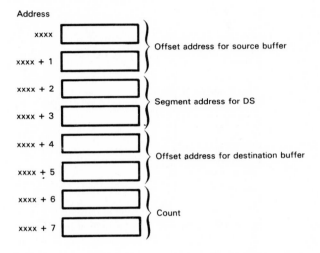

Memory byte pairs hold four addresses, as illustrated above.

The block of memory words illustrated above is frequently referred to as a parameter block; the individual data values in the block are parameters.

The DI register could be loaded with the starting address of this block (xxxx in the illustration above) to provide the parameters for the initialization sequence.

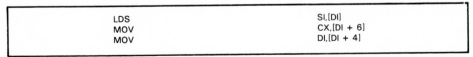

```
LDS        SI,[DI]
MOV        CX,[DI + 6]
MOV        DI,[DI + 4]
```

Figure 4-3. Buffer Move Register Initialization

The BX register can be used instead of the DI register, if more convenient.

When a string primitive instruction is used, the parameter block may have to be expanded as shown below to include a segment address which is loaded into the ES register:

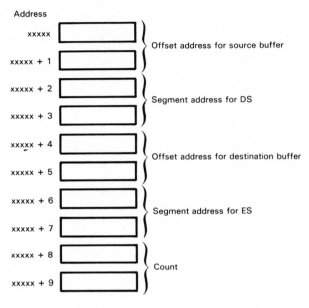

This technique allows data to be moved from any location to any other in the one million-byte memory space. If segments are not specified, data is moved within the current segments only.

Again loading the DI register with the beginning address for this block (xxxxx in the illustration above), the initialization sequence becomes.

```
LDS          SI,[DI]
MOV          CX,[DI + 8]
LES          DI,[DI + 4]
```

Figure 4-4. Alternate Buffer Move Register Initialization

If one of the buffers is always in a fixed location in memory, the address of the fixed buffer can be specified as immediate data. Consider the following instruction sequence.

```
MOV          SI,ADDR$FOR$BUFFER$A
MOV          AX,SEGADDR$FOR$BUFFER$A
MOV          DS,AX
MOV          CX,[DI + 4]
LES          DI,[DI]
```

Figure 4-5. Buffer Move Register Initialization Using Immediate Data

In the first instruction, the immediate data ADDRFORBUFFER$A is moved into the SI register. The second instruction moves the immediate data SEGADDRFORBUFFER$A into the AX register. This instruction is necessary because the 8086 has no instructions which move immediate data into a Segment register. (An exception is an inter-segment Jump instruction which loads a 16-bit segment address into the Code Segment register.) The third instruction moves the segment address into the DS register. Recall that oft times, the DS register is already set to the desired value and no modification is necessary. The fourth and fifth instructions are used to load the count and destination buffer address into the appropriate registers. These instructions require that DI point to a block of the following form:

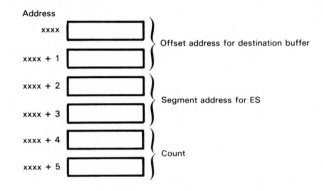

Parameters (in this case address and count information) can be passed to a routine via the stack. For the buffer-to-buffer move this may be illustrated as follows:

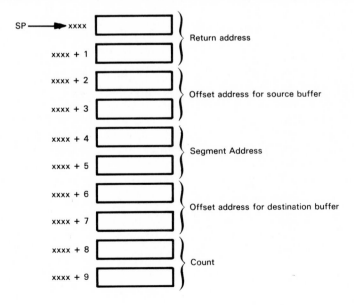

The following instruction sequence initializes registers.

```
POP      BX           ;POP RETURN ADDRESS
POP      SI
POP      DS
POP      DI
POP      CX
```

Figure 4-6. Buffer Move Register Initialization via Stack
and Pop Instructions

This approach makes it difficult to return from a subroutine using the RET instruction. But the 8086 allows a register to supply the return address. Therefore,

```
JMP      BX
```

could be used instead of RET. If this approach appears intrinsically ugly, or if all the registers are in use, consider the following sequence:

```
PUSH      BP
MOV       BP,SP
MOV       SI, [BP + 4]
MOV       DS,[BP + 6]
MOV       DI, [BP + 8]
MOV       CX,[BP + 10]
```

Figure 4-7. Buffer Move Register Initialization via Stack
and Indirect Addressing

These instructions will perform the desired initializations. The routine may then be terminated with a

```
MOV      SP,BP
POP      BP
RET      8
```

which will move the return address into the program counter and then add 8 to the adjusted stack pointer, thus removing parameters from the stack; these have been pushed by the called routine.

If the buffers are present in the current data segment, the buffer addresses can be loaded using the LEA (Load Effective Address) instruction. The following sequence loads SI and DI using the LEA instruction, then loads the COUNT data from memory into CX using the MOV instruction

```
LEA       SI,BUFFER$A
LEA       DI,BUFFER$B
MOV       CX,COUNT
```

Figure 4-8. Buffer Move Register Initialization
using LEA Instruction

Another example assumes that the first two bytes of BUFFER$A contain the number of bytes in the buffer, and therefore the number of bytes to be moved. Here is the resulting parameter block:

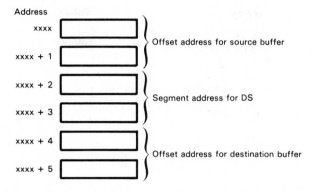

If the DI register points to this parameter block, the following initialization sequence could be used:

```
LDS     SI,[DI]
MOV     DI, [DI + 4]
MOV     CX, [SI]
INC     SI
INC     SI
```

Two buffer initialization routines are shown below. The first routine replicates a 8-bit pattern through a buffer; the second routine replicates a 16-bit pattern through the buffer. Frequently such routines are used to clear a buffer, in which case the 8-bit or 16-bit value will be 0. You will use the first routine to clear a short buffer with an odd byte length; you use the second routine to clear a buffer with an even byte length, or a long buffer with an odd byte length (use a single byte instruction to clear the odd byte). There are occasions when a buffer must be initialized with some non-zero pattern; for example, an ASCII space code might be used to initialize a buffer that is eventually to hold ASCII character strings.

The routines described in Figures 4-9 and 4-10 assume that the DI register points to the destination buffer. The AL or AX register contains the 8-bit or 16-bit value to be replicated through the buffer. The CX register specifies the number of bytes or words in the buffer.

Initializing a Buffer

A buffer initialization routine loads some arbitrary data into a memory buffer.

```
INITIALIZE$LOOP:    MOV     [DI],AL             ;STORE INITIALIZING DATA
                    INC     DI                  ;ADJUST POINTER
                    DEC     CX                  ;DECREMENT AND BRANCH
                    JNZ     INITIALIZE$LOOP     ;If not done
                    RET
```

Figure 4-9. Buffer Initialization (8-Bit Data Elements)

```
INITIALIZE$LOOP:    MOV     [DI],AX             ;STORE INITIALIZING DATA
                    INC     DI
                    INC     DI
                    DEC     CX
                    JNZ     INITIALIZE$LOOP
                    RET
```

Figure 4-10. Buffer Initialization (16-Bit Data Elements)

The BX or SI registers can be used instead of DI in the two buffer initialization programs.

Sometimes the first n bytes of a buffer are used to describe the buffer. For example, the total length of the buffer and displacement to the first empty byte might be stored in the first two buffer bytes. These buffer descriptive bytes must be adjusted when data is written into the buffer.

The buffer initialization routine must itself have registers initialized, as described for the buffer-to-buffer move routines.

In general, the address/count information is delivered to the routine in one of the following ways:

- In a parameter block

- On the stack

- In immediate data

- In an address used by an LEA instruction.

Translating a Buffer

When a buffer is translated, every element in the buffer is converted, using a translation table to make the conversion. The translation table provides a direct replacement value for every initial value that an element can have. For example, if a buffer consists of one-byte elements, then there are 256 possible initial values that each element can have, and similarly there are 256 translated values that the same element can have. The translation table will link each initial value to a translated value. Perhaps the most frequently seen translation table converts between ASCII and EBCDIC characters, each of which is encoded as a byte value. In this case, if a buffer of ASCII characters were translated, the result would be a buffer of equivalent EBCDIC characters.

Consider two ways in which a buffer may be translated:

1. Data within the buffer may be translated and left in the buffer.

2. Data may be translated while being moved from one buffer to another.

The routine in Figure 4-11 translates data without moving it. This routine assumes that the BX register contains the address of a translation table, the SI register contains the address of the buffer to be translated, and the CX register contains the number of data elements to be translated.

```
TRANSLATE$LOOP:   MOV    AL,[SI]            ;LOAD FROM BUFFER
                  XLAT                      ;INDEX INTO TABLE
                  MOV    [SI],AL            ;STORE CONVERTED DATA INTO BUFFER
                  INC    SI                 ;POINT AT NEXT ELEMENT
                  DEC    CX                 ;DECREMENT AND TEST FOR DONE
                  JNZ    TRANSLATE$LOOP
                  RET
```

Figure 4-11. Buffer Translation

The routine in Figure 4-11 assumes that the element being translated maps into a 256-byte table. This assumption allows the XLAT instruction to be used. If the element to be translated is a 16-bit data unit, a larger table may be necessary. The routine in Figure 4-12 maps 16-bit data elements into a 65K-byte table, producing an 8-bit result.

```
TRANSLATE$LOOP:   MOV    DI,[SI]            ;LOAD ELEMENT
                  MOV    AX,[BX + DI]       ;USE ELEMENT AS INDEX
                  MOV    [SI], AX           ;STORE RESULT
                  INC    SI                 ;UPDATE POINTERS
                  INC    SI
                  DEC    CX                 ;DECREMENT AND TEST
                  JNZ    TRANSLATE$LOOP     ;FOR DONE
                  RET
```

Figure 4-12. Translation of 16-Bit Data Elements

```
TRANSLATE$LOOP: MOV    AL,[SI]              ;LOAD ELEMENT FROM SOURCE BUFFER
                XLAT                        ;TRANSLATE DATA
                MOV    [DI],AL              ;STORE CONVERTED DATA IN DESTINATION BUFFER
                INC    SI                   ;UPDATE POINTERS
                INC    DI
                DEC    CX                   ;DECREMENT AND TEST FOR DONE
                JNZ    TRANSLATE$LOOP
                RET
```

Figure 4-13. Buffer-to-Buffer Translation

The routine in Figure 4-13 translates data while moving it from one buffer to another. This routine assumes that the BX register contains the address of the conversion table, the SI register contains the address of the buffer to be translated, the DI register contains the address of the buffer where the translated data will be stored, and the CX register contains the number of data elements to be translated.

The routine in Figure 4-13 assumes that both of the buffers are present in the segment addressed by the DS register.

Many translation routines also check that all the elements in the translated buffer lie between specified boundary values. The routines in Figure 4-11 through 4-13 will be updated to include such a check later in this chapter.

Register initialization for these routines is similar to the initialization methods used by the buffer-to-buffer move routines.

SAVING THE STATE OF THE MACHINE

The 8086 has fourteen 16-bit registers. In most cases having so many registers is very desirable. But when the state of the entire machine must be saved while appropriate processing is performed, and then the state of the machine must be restored, an abundance of registers is less of an asset.

When a hardware or software interrupt occurs, for example, the 8086 saves the contents of the Flags register, the program counter, and the Code Segment register during its interrupt acknowledge sequence. The interrupt service routine must save the complete state of the machine. The following instruction sequence will accomplish this task.

There is no specific order in which the registers must be pushed; however the registers must be restored in the inverse order from which they were pushed. If registers are saved using the sequence illustrated in Figure 4-14, the following sequence must be used to restore the registers.

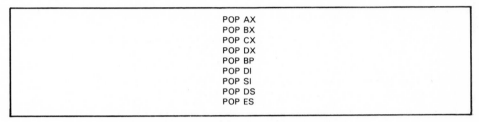

```
PUSH ES
PUSH DS
PUSH SI
PUSH DI
PUSH BP
PUSH DX
PUSH CX
PUSH BX
PUSH AX
```

Figure 4-14. Saving the 8086 Registers

```
POP AX
POP BX
POP CX
POP DX
POP BP
POP DI
POP SI
POP DS
POP ES
```

Figure 4-15. Restoring the 8086 Registers

To save the state of the entire machine requires 11 bytes of code and 110 clock periods. The 110 cycles do not include time the 8086 uses to respond to the interrupt. For hardware interrupts the 8086 requires 62 clock periods to acknowledge the interrupt. For software interrupts the 8086 requires 51 to 53 clock periods to acknowledge the interrupt. These response cycles follow execution of the instruction during which the interrupt occurred. Thus, saving the state of the entire machine may take as many as 172 clock periods, requiring 32.4 microseconds on a 5 MHz 8086. Restoring the state of the machine requires 110 clock periods, plus an additional 24 clock periods for an IRET (Interrupt Return) instruction. Therefore to save and then restore the 8086 machine state may take up to 306 clock periods, or 61.2 microseconds per interrupt.

SEGMENT REGISTER INITIALIZATION

If a program is written to run in conjunction with an operating system, then the operating system will typically initialize segment registers, and subsequently modify their contents, as needed. If a program is written to run without the benefit of an operating system, then the segment registers must be initialized. The instructions shown in Figure 4-16 will initialize the segment registers.

```
MOV     AX, IMM$DATA$FOR$DS        ;LOAD IMMEDIATE DATA INTO AX
MOV     DS, AX
MOV     AX, IMM$DATA$FOR$ES        ;LOAD IMMEDIATE DATA INTO AX
MOV     ES, AX
MOV     AX, IMM$DATA$FOR$SS        ;LOAD IMMEDIATE DATA INTO AX
MOV     SS, AX
```

Figure 4-16. Initializing the ES Register via Immediate Data

Another way to initialize segment registers is to move data directly from memory into the segment registers, as shown in Figure 4-17.

```
MOV     DS, CS: DATA$FOR$DS
MOV     ES, CS: DATA$FOR$ES
MOV     SS, CS: DATA$FOR$SS
```

Figure 4-17. Initializing the ES Register
via Code Segment Locations

The segment prefixes for the second and third instructions may be eliminated if the data for Segment Registers ES and SS are contained in the segment addressed by DS.

The 8086 provides special protection for a particular initialization sequence. When the SS and SP registers are initialized by consecutive MOV instructions, the 8086 will not allow an interrupt to occur between the MOV instructions. Thus,

```
MOV     SS, CS: DATA$FOR$SS
MOV     SP, DATA$FOR$SP
```

is an uninterruptable instruction sequence.

ARITHMETIC INSTRUCTIONS

There are these five types of 8086 arithmetic instructions:

1. Addition instructions

2. Subtraction instructions

3. Multiplication instructions

4. Division instructions

5. Compare instructions

Each of the above categories, except for compare instructions, has variations that allow for ASCII/BCD operations.

ADDITION INSTRUCTIONS

Instructions that perform various types of addition are shown in Table 4-2.

Figures 4-18, 4-19, and 4-20 illustrate the use of various addition instructions. Each of the routines assumes that the numbers or strings to be added are present in the Data Segment, and are ordered as follows:

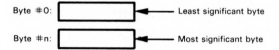

Sum a Pair of Multiword Numbers

The routine in Figure 4-18 assumes that the SI and DI registers contain the starting addresses for the multiword numbers to be added, and the CX register contains the number of words to add. The result is stored in the string pointed to by the DI register.

```
START:              CLC                         ;CLEAR CARRY FOR INITIAL ADDITION
ADDITION$LOOP:      MOV     AX,[SI]             ;LOAD FROM INITIAL STRING
                    ADC     [DI],AX             ;ADD AX TO MEMORY
                    INC     SI                  ;UPDATE POINTERS
                    INC     SI
                    INC     DI
                    INC     DI
                    DEC     CX
                    JNZ     ADDITION$LOOP
                    RET
```

Figure 4-18. Multiword Addition

String primitives and the LOOP instructions can reduce the number of memory locations, and the time required to perform this routine.

Table 4-2. 8086 Addition Instructions

Mnemonic	Operands	Object Code	Bytes	Clocks	O	D	I	T	S	Z	A	P	C	Operation Performed
									Status					
ADC	mem/reg₁, mem/reg₂	000100dw mod rrr r/m (DISP) (DISP)	2, 3 or 4	reg-reg: 3 mem-reg: 9+EA reg-mem: 16+EA	X				X	X	X	X	X	$[mem/reg_1] \leftarrow [mem/reg_1] + [mem/reg_2] + [C]$ Add the 8- or 16-bit contents of the memory location or memory register specified by mem/reg₂ and the Carry status to the 8- or 16-bit contents of the memory location or register selected by mem/reg₁.
ADC	mem/reg. data	100000sw mod 010 r/m (DISP) (DISP) kk jj (if sw = 01)	3, 4, 5 or 6	reg: 4 mem: 17+EA	X				X	X	X	X	X	$[mem/reg] \leftarrow [mem/reg] + data + [C]$ Add the 8 or 16 bits of immediate data and the Carry status to the 8- or 16-bit contents of the memory location or register selected by mem/reg.
ADC	ac, data	0001010w kk jj (if sw = 01)	2 or 3	4	X				X	X	X	X	X	$[ac] \leftarrow [ac] + data + [C]$ Add the 8 or 16 bits of immediate data and the Carry status to the AL (8-bit operation) or AX (16-bit operation) register.
ADD	mem/reg₁, mem/reg₂	000000dw mod rrr r/m (DISP) (DISP)	2, 3 or 4	reg-reg: 3 mem-reg: 9+EA reg-mem: 16+EA	X				X	X	X	X	X	$[mem/reg_1] \leftarrow [mem/reg_1] + [mem/reg_2]$ Add the 8- or 16-bit contents of the memory location or register specified by mem/reg₂ to the 8- or 16-bit contents of the memory location or register selected by mem/reg₁.
ADD	mem/reg. data	100000sw mod 000 r/m (DISP) (DISP) kk jj (if sw = 01)	3, 4, 5 or 6	reg: 4 mem: 17+EA	X				X	X	X	X	X	$[mem/reg] \leftarrow [mem/reg] + data$ Add the 8 or 16 bits of immediate data to the 8 or 16 bit contents of the memory location or register selected by mem/reg.
ADD	ac, data	0000010w kk jj (if w = 1)	2 or 3	4	X				X	X	X	X	X	$[ac] \leftarrow [ac] + data$ Add the 8 or 16 bits of immediate data to the AL (8-bit operation) or AX (16-bit operation) register.
INC	mem/reg	1111111w mod 000 r/m (DISP) (DISP)	2, 3 or 4	reg: 3 mem: 15+EA	X				X	X	X	X		$[mem/reg] \leftarrow [mem/reg] + 1$ Increment by 1 the 8 or 16 bit contents of the memory location or register selected by mem/reg.

Table 4-2. 8086 Addition Instructions (Continued)

Mnemonic	Operands	Object Code	Bytes	Clocks	O	D	I	T	S	Z	A	P	C	Operation Performed
									Status					
INC	reg	01000rrr	1	2	X				X	X	X	X		[reg] ← [reg] + 1 Increment by 1 the 16-bit contents of the specified register.
AAA		37	1	4	?				?	?	X	?	X	ASCII adjust the contents of the AL register after an addition.
DAA		27	1	4	?				X	X	X	X	X	Decimal adjust the contents of the AL register after an addition.

Sum a Pair of Multibyte BCD Numbers

The routine in Figure 4-19 assumes that the SI and DI registers contain the starting addresses for the BCD strings to be added, and the CX register contains the number of BCD bytes in each BCD string. The result is stored in the string pointed to by the DI register.

```
START:                  CLC                             ;CLEAR CARRY FOR INITIAL ADDITION
BCD$ADDITION$LOOP:      MOV     AL,[SI]                 ;LOAD FROM STRING A
                        ADC     AL,[DI]                 ;ADD FROM STRING B
                        DAA                             ;PERFORM BCD ADJUST
                        MOV     [DI],AL                 ;STORE RESULT
                        INC     SI                      ;UPDATE POINTERS
                        INC     DI
                        DEC     CX                      ;DECREMENT AND TEST
                        JNZ     BCD$ADDITION$LOOP       ;FOR DONE
                        RET
```

Figure 4-19. Multibyte BCD Addition

Sum a Pair of Multibyte ASCII Strings

The routine in Figure 4-20 assumes that the SI and DI registers contain the starting addresses for two ASCII strings that are to be added. The CX register contains the number of ASCII bytes in each string. The result will be stored in the string pointed to by the DI register.

```
                        CLC
ASCII$ADDITION$LOOP:    MOV     AL,[SI]                 ;LOAD FROM STRING A
                        ADC     AL,[DI]                 ;ADD STRING B
                        AAA                             ;PERFORM AN ADJUST
                        MOV     [DI],AL                 ;STORE RESULT
                        INC     SI                      ;ADJUST POINTERS
                        INC     DI
                        DEC     CX                      ;DECREMENT AND TEST
                        JNZ     ASCII$ADDITION$LOOP     ;FOR DONE
                        RET
```

Figure 4-20. Multibyte ASCII Addition

The routines in Figures 4-19 and 4-20 can both use the string primitives to reduce the number of bytes and the amount of time required to perform these operations.

For the above addition routines, consider the case where the numbers to be added have the following format:

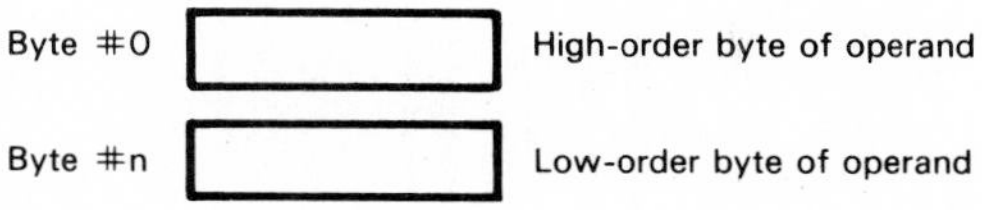

Byte #0		High-order byte of operand
Byte #n		Low-order byte of operand

In this case, addition routines would differ from Figures 4-18 through 4-20 in two major respects:

1. The initialization sequence would differ. The initialization sequences would point registers at the last byte of the multibyte number, instead of the first.

2. The pointers would be decremented, not incremented.

To account for these differences, modified starting addresses must be loaded into appropriate address registers. Subsequently addresses must be decremented.

SUBTRACTION INSTRUCTIONS

Subtraction instructions are shown in Table 4-3.

The subtraction versions of the multibyte addition routines presented in the previous section are easily derived. Creation of these routines is left to the reader as an exercise.

Table 4-3. 8086 Subtraction Instructions

Mnemonic	Operands	Object Code	Bytes	Clocks	O	D	I	T	S	Z	A	P	C	Operation Performed
SUB	mem/reg₁, mem/reg₂	001010dw mod rrr r/m (DISP) (DISP)	2, 3 or 4	reg - reg: 3 mem - reg: 9 + EA reg - mem: 16 + EA	X				X	X	X	X	X	[mem/reg₁] ← [mem/reg₁] – [mem/reg₂] Subtract the 8 or 16 bit contents of the memory location or register specified by mem/reg₂ from the 8 or 16 bit contents of the memory location or register specified by mem/reg₁.
SUB	mem/reg data	100000sw mod 101 r/m (DISP) (DISP) kk jj (if sw = 01)	3, 4, 5 or 6	reg: 4 mem: 17 + EA	X				X	X	X	X	X	[mem/reg] ← [mem/reg] – data Subtract 8 or 16 bits of immediate data from the 8 or 16 bit contents of the memory location or register specified by mem/reg.
SUB	ac,data	0010110w kk jj (if w = 1)	2 or 3	4	X				X	X	X	X	X	[ac] ← [ac] – data Subtract 8 or 16 bits of immediate data from the AL (8-bit operation) or AX (16-bit operation) register.
SBB	mem/reg₁, mem/reg₂	000110dw mod rrr r/m (DISP) (DISP)	2, 3 or 4	reg - reg: 3 mem - reg: 9 + EA reg - mem: 16 + EA	X				X	X	X	X	X	[mem/reg₁] ← [mem/reg₁] – [mem/reg₂] – [C] Subtract the 8 or 16 bit contents of the memory location or register specified by mem/reg₂ and the Carry status from the 8 or 16 bit contents of the memory location or register specified by mem/reg.
SBB	mem/reg, data	100000sw mod 011 r/m (DISP) (DISP) kk jj (if sw = 01)	3, 4, 5 or 6	reg: 4 mem: 17 + EA	X				X	X	X	X	X	[mem/reg] ← [mem/reg] – data – [C] Subtract the 8 or 16 bits of immediate data and the Carry status from the 8- or 16-bit contents of the memory location specified by mem/reg₁.
SBB	ac,data	0001110w kk jj (if w = 1)	2 or 3	4	X				X	X	X	X	X	[ac] ← [ac] – data – [C] Subtract the 8 or 16 bits of immediate data and the Carry status from the AL (8-bit operation) or AX (16-bit operation) register.
DEC	mem/reg	1111111w mod 001 r/m (DISP) (DISP)	2, 3 or 4	reg: 3 mem: 15 + EA	X				X	X	X	X		[mem/reg] ← [mem/reg] – 1 Decrement by 1 the 8 or 16 bit contents of the memory location or register selected by mem/reg.

Table 4-3. 8086 Subtraction Instructions (Continued)

Mnemonic	Operands	Object Code	Bytes	Clocks	Status O	D	I	T	S	Z	A	P	C	Operation Performed
DEC	reg	01001rrr	1	2	X				X	X	X	X		[reg] ← [reg] − 1. Decrement by 1 the 16 bit contents of the specified register.
AAS		3F	1	4	?				?	?	X	?	X	ASCII adjust the contents of the AL register after a subtraction.
DAS		2F	1	4	?				X	X	X	X	X	Decimal adjust the contents of the AL register after a subtraction.
NEG	mem/reg	1111011w mod 011 r/m (DISP) (DISP)	2, 3 or 4	reg: 3 mem: 16 + EA	X				X	X	X	X	X	[reg] ← [reg] + 1. Twos complement the 8 or 16 bit contents of the memory location or register specified by mem/reg.

MULTIPLICATION INSTRUCTIONS

8086 instructions that perform various types of multiplication are shown in Table 4-4.

The routines in Figures 4-21 and 4-22 illustrate typical uses of 8086 multiplication instructions.

32-Bit × 32-Bit Multiply

The routine in Figure 4-21 multiplies two 32-bit unsigned numbers, generating a 64-bit result. This routine operates on a data block having the following form.

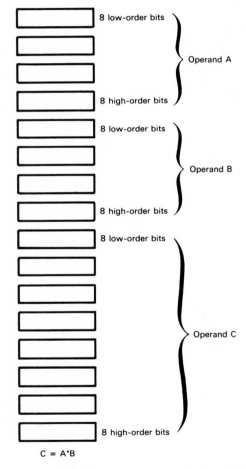

C = A·B

The routine in Figure 4-21 assumes that the BX register points at this block.

Another approach to a task such as this is to add an 8087 numeric coprocessor to the 8086 system. The 8087 performs 32- and 64-bit integer arithmetic as well as single- and double-precision floating point arithmetic.

```
                    MOV     AX, [BX]            ;MULTIPLY LOW-ORDER 16 BITS
                    MUL     [BX + 4]            ;BY LOW-ORDER 16 BITS

                    MOV     [BX + 8],AX         ;SAVE RESULT, WHICH IS IN AX
                    MOV     [BX + 10],DX        ;AND DX

                    MOV     AX, [BX]            ;MULTIPLY LOW-ORDER 16 BITS OF
                                                ;OPERAND A BY HIGH-ORDER 16 BITS
                    MUL     [BX + 6]            ;OF OPERAND B

                    ADD     [BX + 10],AX        ;ADD TO PREVIOUS RESULT
                    ADC     [BX + 12],DX        ;ASSUME RESULT BYTES
                    JNC     NEXT$MUL            ;ARE INITIALLY ZERO
                    INC     [BX + 14]

NEXT$MUL:           MOV     AX,[BX + 2]         ;MULTIPLY HIGH-ORDER 16 BITS OF
                                                ;OPERAND A BY LOW-ORDER 16 BITS
                    MUL     [BX + 4]            ;OF OPERAND B

                    ADD     [BX + 10],AX        ;ADD TO PREVIOUS RESULT
                    ADC     [BX + 12],DX
                    INC     HIGH$ORDER$MUL
                    INC     [BX + 14]           ;SAVE CARRY

HIGH$ORDER$MUL      MOV     AX, [BX + 2]        ;MULTIPLY HIGH-ORDER 16 BITS
                                                ;OF OPERAND A BY HIGH-ORDER 16
                    MUL     [BX + 6]            ;BITS OF OPERAND B

                    ADD     [BX + 12],AX        ;ADD TO PREVIOUS RESULT
                    ADC     [BX + 14],DX        ;ADD TO PREVIOUS RESULT
                    RET
```

Figure 4-21. 32-Bit by 32-Bit Multiplication

ASCII Multiplication

The routine in Figure 4-22 multiplies an ASCII string by a single ASCII digit. The result is a string of unpacked BCD digits. The routine assumes that the ASCII string is organized in the following manner.

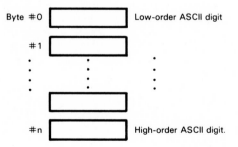

Table 4-4. 8086 Multiplication Instructions

Mnemonic	Operands	Object Code	Bytes	Clocks	O	D	I	T	S	Z	A	P	C	Operation Performed
MUL	reg (8-bit)	11110110 11100 reg	2	70 → 77	X				?	?	?	?	X	if w = 0, [AX] ← [AL] • [mem/reg] if w = 1, [DX] [AX] ← [AX] • [mem/reg] Multiply the 8- or 16-bit contents of the memory location or register specified by mem/reg with the contents of the AL (8-bit operation) or AX (16-bit operation) register. The result is stored in the AX register, in the case of an 8×8-bit operation, or the DX register (high-order 16 bits) and the AX register (low-order 16 bits) in the case of a 16 ×16-bit operation. This is an unsigned multiplication operation. The execution time may vary by 7 clocks for 8-bit operands and 15 clocks for 16-bit operands.
	reg (16-bit)	11110111 11100 reg	2	118 →133										
	mem (8-bit)	11110110 mod 100 r/m (DISP) (DISP)	2, 3 or 4	(76 → 83) + EA										
	mem (16-bit)	11110111 mod 100 r/m (DISP) (DISP)	2, 3 or 4	(124—139) + EA										
IMUL	reg (8-bit)	11110110 11101 reg	2	80 → 98	X				?	?	?	?	X	if w = 0, [AX] ← [AL] • [mem/reg] if w = 1, [DX] [AX] ← [AX] • [mem/reg] Multiply the 8- or 16-bit contents of the memory location or register specified by mem/reg with the contents of the AL (8-bit operation) or AX (16-bit operation) register. The result is stored in the AX register, in the case of an 8 × 8-bit operation, or the DX register (high-order 16 bits) and the AX register (low-order 16 bits) in the case of a 16 × 16-bit operation. This is a signed multiplication operation. The execution time may vary by 18 clocks for 8-bit operands and 26 clocks for 16-bit operands. The variation is data-dependent.
	reg (16-bit)	11110111 11101 reg	2	128 —154										
	mem (8-bit)	11110110 mod 101 r/m (DISP) (DISP)	2, 3 or 4	(86 —104) + EA										
	mem (16-bit)	11110111 mod 101 r/m (DISP) (DISP)	2, 3 or 4	(134—160) + EA										
AAM		D4 0A	2	83	?				X	X	?	X	?	After multiplying two unpacked decimal operands, adjust the product in AX to become an unpacked decimal result.

The routine further assumes that the SI register points at the ASCII string, the DL register contains the multiplier, a single ASCII digit, the DI register points to the memory locations where the result, a BCD string, will be stored, and the CX register contains the number of digits in the multiplicand. The result stored in the BCD string will have the following form.

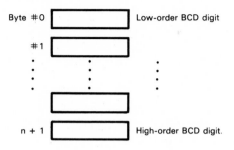

```
                     MOV     [DI], 0                      ;CLEAR INITIAL BYTE OF BCD STRING
                     AND     DL,0FH                       ;AND OFF BITS 4 AND 5 OF MULTIPLIER
MULTIPLY$NEXT$BYTE:  MOV     AL,[SI]                      ;LOAD MULTIPLICAND
                     INC     SI
                     AND     AL,0FH                       ;CLEAR UPPER NIBBLE
                     MUL     DL                           ;MULTIPLY BCD * BCD
                     AAM                                  ;ADJUST RESULT
                     ADD     AL,[DI]                      ;ADD IN BCD
                     AAA
                     MOV     [DI],AL                      ;STORE RESULT
                     INC     DI
                     MOV     [DI],AH
                     DEC     CX                           ;DECREMENT AND TEST FOR DONE
                     JNZ     MULTIPLY$NEXT$BYTE
                     RET
```

Figure 4-22. ASCII Multiplication

DIVISION INSTRUCTIONS

The 8086 instructions that perform various tasks of division are shown in Table 4-5.

The routine in Figure 4-23 illustrates use of the 8086 division instructions.

ASCII Division

The routine in Figure 4-23 divides a string of ASCII digits by a single ASCII digit. The result is a string of BCD digits. The routine assumes that the ASCII string is organized in the following manner.

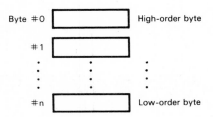

The SI register points to the ASCII string, the DL register contains the divisor, a single ASCII digit, the DI register points to the memory locations where the result, a BCD string, will be stored, and the CX register contains the number of digits in the dividend. The result, stored in the BCD string, will be of the following form.

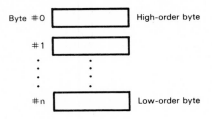

Table 4-5. 8086 Division Instructions

Mnemonic	Operands	Object Code	Bytes	Clocks	O	D	I	T	S	Z	A	P	C	Operation Performed
DIV	reg (8-bit)	11110110 11110 reg	2	80 → 90	?				?	?	?	?	?	if w = 0, [AH] remainder ⎤← [AX]/[mem/reg] [AL] quotient ⎦ if w = 1, [DX] remainder ⎤← [DX]/[AX] [mem/reg] [AX] quotient ⎦ Divide the AX register, in the case of a 16-bit operation, or the DX register (high-order 16 bits) and AX (low-order 16 bits), in the case of a 32-bit operation, by the 8- or 16-bit contents of the memory location or register specified by mem/reg. In the case of a 16 × 8-bit division, the quotient is placed in AL, and the remainder is stored in AH. In the case of a 32 × 16-bit division, the quotient is placed in the AX register, and the remainder is placed in the DX register. This is an unsigned division operation. The execution time may vary by 10 clocks for 8-bit operands and 18 clocks for 16-bit operands. The variation is data dependent.
	reg (16-bit)	11110111 11110 reg	2	144 →162										
	mem (8-bit)	11110110 mod 110 r/m (DISP) (DISP)	2, 3 or 4	(86 →96) + EA										
	mem (16-bit)	11110111 mod 110 r/m (DISP) (DISP)	2, 3 or 4	(150 →168) + EA										
IDIV	reg (8-bit)	11110110 11111 reg	2	101→112	?				?	?	?	?	?	if w = 0, [AH] remainder ⎤← [AX]/[mem/reg] [AL] quotient ⎦ if w = 1, [DX] remainder ⎤← [DX] [AX]/[mem/reg] [AX] quotient ⎦ Divide the AX register, in the case of a 16-bit operation, or the DX register (high-order 16 bits) and AX (low-order 16 bits), in the case of a 32-bit operation, by the 8- or 16-bit contents of the memory location or register specified by mem/reg. In the case of a 16 × 8-bit division, the quotient is placed in AL, and the remainder is stored in AH. In the case of a 32 × 16-bit division, the quotient is placed in the AX register, and the remainder is placed in the DX register. This is a signed division operation. The execution time may vary by 11 clocks for 8-bit operands and 19 clocks for 16-bit operands. The variation is data dependent.
	reg (16-bit)	11110111 11111 reg	2	165→184										
	mem (8-bit)	11110110 mod 111 r/m (DISP) (DISP)	2, 3 or 4	(107→118) + EA										
	mem (16-bit)	11110111 mod 111 r/m (DISP) (DISP)	2,3 or 4	(171→190) + EA										

Status

Table 4-5. 8086 Division Instructions (Continued)

Mnemonic	Operands	Object Code	Bytes	Clocks	Status										Operation Performed
					O	D	I	T	S	Z	A	P	C	
CBW		98	1	2										[AH] ← [AL7] Extend the sign bit of the AL register, bit 7, into the AH register.
CWD		99	1	5										[DX] ← [AX15] Extend the sign bit of the AX register, bit 15, into the DX register.
AAD		D5 0A	2	60	?				X	X	?	X	?	Decimal adjust dividend in AL prior to dividing an unpacked decimal divisor, to generate an unpacked decimal quotient.

```
                        AND      DL,OFH              ;CLEAR HIGH-ORDER NIBBLE
                        XOR      AH,AH               ;CLEAR AH
DIVIDE$NEXT$BYTE:       MOV      AL,[SI]             ;LOAD BYTE FROM ASCII STRING
                        INC      SI

                        AND      AL,OFH              ;CLEAR BITS 4 AND 5
                        AAD                          ;ADJUST USING AH
                        DIV      DL

                        MOV      [DI],AL             ;STORE RESULT
                        INC      DI

                        DEC      CX                  ;DECREMENT AND TEST FOR DONE
                        JNZ      DIVIDE$NEXT$BYTE
                        RET
```

Figure 4-23. ASCII Division

64-Bit Division

Dividing a 64-bit dividend by a 32-bit divisor is not an easy task on the 8086. The DIV and IDIV instructions are not particularly useful when performing this function. To divide a 64-bit number by a 32-bit number, a subtract and shift algorithm must be employed. The construction of such a routine, a nontrivial task, is beyond the scope of the current discussion.

Another approach to a task such as this is to add an 8087 numeric coprocessor to the 8086 system. The 8087 performs 32- and 64-bit integer arithmetic as well as single- and double-precision floating point arithmetic.

COMPARE INSTRUCTIONS

8086 compare instructions are shown in Table 4-6; they execute like subtract instructions, however no result is returned to a register or memory location. The subtract operation is used only to set status flags.

Use of compare instructions is illustrated in Figures 4-24 through 4-26.

Two string primitive instructions, CMPS and SCAS, also perform comparisons. These instructions are discussed with the other primitive instructions later in the chapter.

Table 4-6. 8086 Comparison Instructions

Mnemonic	Operands	Object Code	Bytes	Clocks	Status O	D	I	T	S	Z	A	P	C	Operation Performed
CMP	mem/reg$_1$, mem/reg$_2$	001110dw mod rrr r/m (DISP) (DISP)	2, 3 or 4	reg-reg: 3 mem-reg: 9 + EA reg-mem: 9 + EA	X				X	X	X	X	X	[mem/reg$_1$] – [mem/reg$_2$] Subtract the 8- or 16-bit contents of the memory location or register selected by mem/reg$_2$ from the 8- or 16-bit contents of the memory location or register specified by mem/reg$_1$, use the result to set the flags, then discard the result.
CMP	mem/reg, data	100000sw mod 111 r/m (DISP) (DISP) kk jj (if sw = 01)	3,4,5 or 6	reg: 4 mem: 10 + EA	X				X	X	X	X	X	[mem/reg] – data Subtract the 8 or 16 bits of immediate data from the 8- or 16-bit contents of the memory location or register specified by mem/reg, use the result to set the flags, then discard the result.
CMP	ac,data	0011110w kk jj (if w = 1)	2 or 3	4	X				X	X	X	X	X	[ac] – data Subtract the 8 or 16 bits of immediate data from the AL (8-bit operation) or the AX (16-bit operation) register, use the result to set the flags, then discard the result.

Calculate the Length of a String

The routine in Figure 4-24 determines the number of a characters in a string.

This routine assumes that the SI register addresses the string being scanned and AH contains a character that identifies the end of the string. When this routine finishes executing, the DX register will contain the number of characters between the start of the string and the terminating character.

```
                         MOV    DX,OFFFFH            ;INITIALIZE COUNT TO -1
SCAN$FOR$DELIMITER:      INC    DX                   ;INCREMENT COUNT
                         MOV    AL,[SI]              ;LOAD BYTE FROM STRING
                         INC    SI                   ;UPDATE POINTER
                         CMP    AH,AL                ;COMPARE WITH TERMINATION
                         JNZ    SCAN$FOR$DELIMITER   ;BRANCH IF NOT TERMINATION
                         RET
```

Figure 4-24. Calculate the Length of a String

The string primitive instruction SCAS can be used to reduce the amount of memory and speed of execution of this routine. The SCAS instruction is discussed with the other string primitive instructions later in this chapter.

Find the Largest 8-Bit Unsigned Number in a Sequence

The routine in Figure 4-25 will determine the largest 8-bit unsigned number in a sequence of 8-bit unsigned numbers. This routine assumes that the SI register addresses the sequence of numbers to be scanned, while the CX register contains the number of bytes to be scanned. When this routine has finished executing, AH will contain the maximum value, and DX will point at the maximum value.

```
                      XOR    AH,AH              ;INITIALIZE MAX. NUMBER
SCAN$NEXT$BYTE:       MOV    AL,[SI]            ;LOAD BYTE FROM SEQUENCE
                      CMP    AH,AL             ;COMPARE WITH CURRENT MAX. #
                      JAE    UPDATE$PTR
                      MOV    AH,AL              ;SAVE NEW MAX. NUMBER
                      MOV    DX,SI             ;SAVE LOCATION OF MAX. #
UPDATE$PTR:           INC    SI
                      DEC    CX
                      JNZ    SCAN$NEXT$BYTE
                      RET
```

Figure 4-25. Find the Largest 8-Bit Number

The routine in Figure 4-25 and the routine in Figure 4-26 can be improved by using string primitive instructions.

Find the Largest 16-Bit Number in a Sequence

The routine in Figure 4-26 will determine the largest 16-bit signed number in a sequence of 16-bit signed numbers. This routine assumes that the SI register addresses the series of numbers to be scanned while the CX register contains the number of words to be scanned.

```
                    MOV     BX,8000H        ;INITIALIZE MAX. NUMBER
    SCAN$LOOP:      MOV     AX,[SI]         ;LOAD NUMBER FROM SEQUENCE
                    CMP     BX,AX           ;COMPARE WITH CURRENT MAX. NUMBER
                    JGE     UPDATE$PTR
                    MOV     BX,AX           ;SAVE NEW MAX. NUMBER
                    MOV     DX,SI           ;SAVE LOCATION OF MAX. NUMBER
    UPDATE$PTR:     INC     SI              ;UPDATE PRT.
                    INC     SI
                    DEC     CX              ;DECREMENT AND TEST FOR DONE
                    JNZ     SCAN$LOOP
                    RET
```

Figure 4-26. Find the Largest 16-Bit Number

BUFFER$TRANSLATION

Earlier in this chapter, two buffer translation routines were presented. The following routine includes error checking. The characters in the buffer which is to be translated must lie in the range $20_{16} \leq$ character $\leq 5F_{16}$. This routine assumes that the BX register contains the address of the conversion table, the SI register contains the address of the buffer to be translated, and the CX register contains the number of data elements to be translated.

```
    TRANSLATE$LOOP:     MOV     AL,[SI]             ;LOAD BYTE FROM SOURCE
                        SUB     AL,20H              ;NORMALIZE
                        JB      TRANSLATE$ERROR     ;IF LESS THAN 0, REPORT ERROR
                        CMP     AL,3FH              ;COMPARE WITH NORMALIZED MAX.
                        JA      TRANSLATE$ERROR     ;IF GREATER, REPORT ERROR
                        XLAT                        ;TRANSLATE NORMALIZED VALUE
                        MOV     [SI],AL             ;STORE CONVERTED DATA
                        INC     SI                  ;ADJUST POINTERS
                        DEC     CX
                        JNZ     TRANSLATE$LOOP
                        RET                         ;GOOD RETURN WITH Z=1
    TRANSLATE$ERROR:    RET                         ;ERROR RETURN WITH Z=0
```

Figure 4-27. Buffer Translation with Range Checking

The routine returns with $Z=1$ if there were no translation errors and $Z=0$ for one or more translation errors. Note that the subtraction instruction limits the size of the conversion table to 40_{16} bytes. Data could be validated using two CMP instructions with the BX register addressing a location 20_{16} bytes before the conversion table.

LOGICAL INSTRUCTIONS

The 8086 provides the usual logical functions. These functions are:

AND
NOT
OR
XOR

In addition, the TEST instruction performs an AND operation without altering either of the operands.

The 8086 logical instructions are shown in Table 4-7.

Table 4-7. 8086 Logical Instructions

Mnemonic	Operands	Object Code	Bytes	Clocks	O	D	I	T	S	Z	A	P	C	Operation Performed
AND	mem/reg₁, mem/reg₂	001000dw mod rrr r/m (DISP) (DISP)	2, 3, or 4	reg-reg: 3 mem-reg: 9 + EA reg-mem: 16 + EA	X				X	X	?	X	X	$[mem/reg_1] \leftarrow [mem/reg_1]$ AND $[mem/reg_2]$ AND the 8- or 16-bit contents of the memory location or register selected by mem/reg₂ with the 8- or 16-bit contents of the memory location or register specified by mem/reg₁, leaving the result in the memory location or register specified by mem/reg₁.
AND	mem/reg, data	1000000w mod 100 r/m (DISP) (DISP) kk jj (if w = 1)	3,4,5 or 6	reg: 4 mem: 17 + EA	X				X	X	?	X	X	$[mem/reg] \leftarrow [mem/reg]$ AND data AND the 8 or 16 bits of immediate data with the 8- or 16-bit contents of the memory location or register specified by mem/reg, storing the result in the memory location or register specified by mem/reg.
AND	ac,data	0010010w kk jj (if w = 1)	2 or 3	4	X				X	X	?	X	X	$[ac] \leftarrow [ac]$ AND data AND the 8 or 16 bits of immediate data with the AL (8-bit operation) or the AX (16-bit operation) register, leaving the result in the AL or AX register.
NOT	mem/reg	1111011w mod 010 r/m (DISP) (DISP)	2,3 or 4	reg: 3 mem: 16 + EA										$[mem/reg] \leftarrow [mem/reg]$ Ones complement the 8- or 16-bit contents of the memory location or register specified by mem/reg.
OR	mem/reg₁, mem/reg₂	000010dw mod rrr r/m (DISP) (DISP)	2,3 or 4	reg-reg: 3 mem-reg: 9 + EA reg-mem: 16 + EA	X				X	X	?	X	X	$[mem/reg_1] \leftarrow [mem/reg_1]$ OR $[mem/reg_2]$ OR the 8- or 16-bit contents of the memory location or register specified by mem/reg₂ with the 8- or 16-bit contents of the memory location or register selected by mem/reg, leaving the result in the memory location or register specified by mem/reg₁.
OR	mem/reg, data	1000000w mod 001 r/m (DISP) (DISP) kk jj (if w = 1)	3,4,5 or 6	reg: 4 mem: 17 + EA	X				X	X	?	X	X	$[mem/reg] \leftarrow [mem/reg]$ OR data OR the 8 or 16 bits of immediate data with the 8- or 16-bit contents of the memory location or register specified by mem/reg, leaving the result in the memory location or register specified by mem/reg.

Table 4-7. 8086 Logical Instructions (Continued)

Mnemonic	Operands	Object Code	Bytes	Clocks	O	D	I	T	S	Z	A	P	C	Operation Performed
									Status					
OR	ac,data	0000110w kk jj (if w = 1)	2 or 3	4	X				X	X	?	X	X	[ac] ← [ac] OR data OR the 8 or 16 bits of immediate data with the AL (8-bit operation) or AX (16-bit operation) register, leaving the result in the AL or AX register.
TEST	mem/reg₁, mem/reg₂	1000010w mod rrr r/m (DISP) (DISP)	2,3 or 4	reg-reg: 3 mem-reg: 9 + EA	X				X	X	?	X	X	[mem/reg₁] AND [mem/reg₂] AND the 8- or 16-bit contents of the memory location or register specified by mem/reg₂ with the 8- or 16-bit contents of the memory location or register specified by mem/reg₁, using the result to set the flags, then discarding the result.
TEST	mem/reg. data	1111011w mod 000 r/m (DISP) (DISP) kk jj (if w = 1)	3,4,5 or 6	reg: 5 mem: 11 + EA	X				X	X	?	X	X	[mem/reg] AND data AND the 8 or 16 bits of immediate data with the 8- or 16-bit contents of the memory location or register specified by mem/reg, using the result to set the flags, then discarding the result.
TEST	ac,data	1010100w kk jj (if w = 1)	2 or 3	4	X				X	X	?	X	X	[ac] AND data AND the 8 or 16 bits of immediate data with the AL (8-bit operation) or AX (16-bit operation) register, using the result to set the flags, then discarding the result.
XOR	mem/reg₁, mem/reg₂	001100dw mod rrr r/m (DISP) (DISP)	2,3 or 4	reg-reg: 3 mem-reg: 9 + EA reg-mem: 16 + EA	X				X	X	?	X	X	[mem/reg₁] ← [mem/reg₁] XOR [mem/reg₂] Exclusive-OR the 8- or 16-bit contents of the memory location or register specified by mem/reg₂ with the 8- or 16-bit contents of the memory location or register specified by mem/reg₁, leaving the result in the memory location or register specified by mem/reg₁.
XOR	mem/reg. data	1000000w mod 110 r/m (DISP) (DISP) kk jj (if w = 1)	3,4,5 or 6	reg: 4 mem: 17 + EA	X				X	X	?	X	X	[mem/reg] ← [mem/reg] XOR data Exclusive-OR the 8 or 16 bits of immediate data with the 8- or 16-bit contents of the memory location or register specified by mem/reg, leaving the result in the memory location or register specified by mem/reg.
XOR	ac,data	0011010w kk jj (if w = 1)	2 or 3	4	X				X	X	?	X	X	[ac] ← [ac] XOR data Exclusive-OR the 8 or 16 bits of immediate data with the AL (8-bit operation) or AX (16-bit operation) register, leaving the result in the AL or AX register.

The routine in Figure 4-29 illustrates 8086 logical instructions. Consider the following scenario;

1.   An I/O port is receiving a stream of data blocks. These data blocks are in Signetics hex code.

2.   The I/O port generates an interrupt whenever a character becomes available.

The routine in Figure 4-29 is an interrupt service routine that handles the above scenario via the following steps:

1.   Save the raw information.

2.   Convert the raw information into object code.

3.   Check the checksum.

4.   Set a message "message completed" bit when processing is complete.

The routine in Figure 4-29 performs these functions by implementing the flowchart in Figure 4-28.

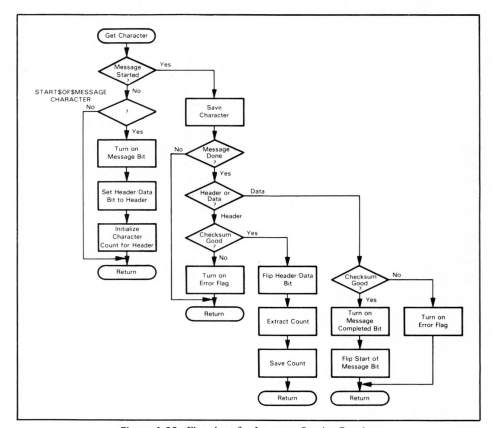

Figure 4-28. Flowchart for Interrupt Service Routine

As illustrated below, the Signetics object code format has the following elements.

1. A gap having any number of non-printing characters, including spaces

2. Start of block character: a colon

3. Address field: four hex characters

4. Count field: two hex characters in range 0 to 1E

5. Block Control Character for address and count fields: two hex characters

6. Data field: twice the value in the count field which is the number of memory locations loaded by the current block

7. Block Control Character: two hex characters

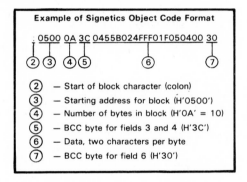

The Block Control Character, otherwise known as a checksum, is created by manipulating the data bytes within a data string. The Signetics object code format includes two Block Control Characters. The first Block Control Character ⑤ applies to the three preceding data bytes, which contain the starting address for the block and the number of bytes in the block. The second Block Control Character ⑦ applies to the string of data bytes in field ⑥

To generate a Block Control Character, the character is first cleared, then repetitively exclusive-ORed with each data byte in the related string. After each exclusive-OR step, the result is left rotated one bit. To illustrate Block Control Character logic, consider the first Block Control Character in the Signetics object format illustration; it is generated from the byte sequence 05 00 0A as follows:

BCC	Data	BCC XOR Data	Left Rotate
00000000	00000101	00000101	00001010
00001010	00000000	00001010	00010100
00010100	00001010	00011110	00111100
			BCC = 3CH

This routine uses four variables in memory, in addition to the buffer written which the data is stored. The variables are:

STATUS$BYTE:

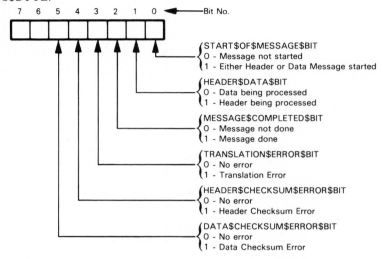

CHARACTER$COUNT:
One byte which contains the number of characters left to be read in either the header or the data block. The start of message code initializes this variables to NUMBEROFHEADER$CHARACTERS, which is equated to 8. When the header has been processed, this variable is initialized to 2* (Number of object code bytes in data block) +2.

OBJECT$BYTE$COUNT:
One byte which contains the number of object code bytes in the data block. This variable is initialized after the header has been processed.

BUFFER$POINTER:
A 16-bit offset address which indicates where the next byte of data from the I/O port should be stored. This variable is initialized by the Start of Message code, which loads immediate data into BUFFER$POINTER. This assumes that the buffer will always be in a fixed position. If it is necessary to vary the location of the buffer, this variable could be initialized by a system or user program.

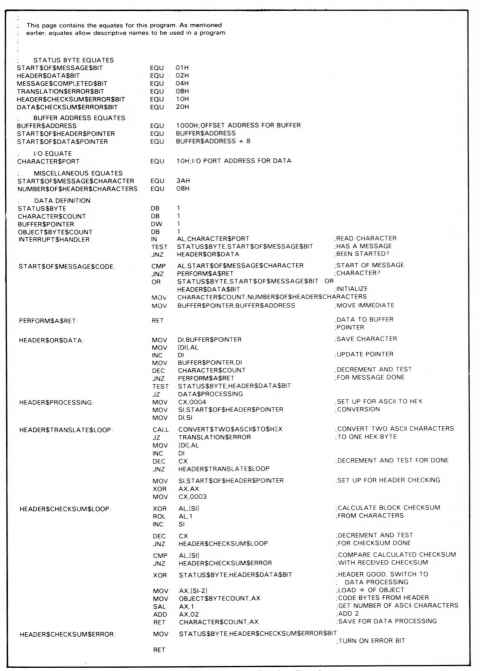

```
;
;   This page contains the equates for this program. As mentioned
;   earlier, equates allow descriptive names to be used in a program.
;
;
;
;     STATUS BYTE EQUATES
START$OF$MESSAGE$BIT              EQU    01H
HEADER$DATA$BIT                   EQU    02H
MESSAGE$COMPLETED$BIT             EQU    04H
TRANSLATION$ERROR$BIT             EQU    08H
HEADER$CHECKSUM$ERROR$BIT         EQU    10H
DATA$CHECKSUM$ERROR$BIT           EQU    20H
;     BUFFER ADDRESS EQUATES
BUFFER$ADDRESS                    EQU    1000H;OFFSET ADDRESS FOR BUFFER
START$OF$HEADER$POINTER           EQU    BUFFER$ADDRESS
START$OF$DATA$POINTER             EQU    BUFFER$ADDRESS + 8
;     I/O EQUATE
CHARACTER$PORT                    EQU    10H;I/O PORT ADDRESS FOR DATA
;     MISCELLANEOUS EQUATES
START$OF$MESSAGE$CHARACTER        EQU    3AH
NUMBER$OF$HEADER$CHARACTERS       EQU    08H
;     DATA DEFINITION
STATUS$BYTE                       DB     1
CHARACTER$COUNT                   DB     1
BUFFER$POINTER                    DW     1
OBJECT$BYTE$COUNT                 DB     1
INTERRUPT$HANDLER:                IN     AL,CHARACTER$PORT                      ;READ CHARACTER
                                  TEST   STATUS$BYTE,START$OF$MESSAGE$BIT       ;HAS A MESSAGE
                                  JNZ    HEADER$OR$DATA                         ;BEEN STARTED?
START$OF$MESSAGE$CODE:            CMP    AL,START$OF$MESSAGE$CHARACTER          ;START OF MESSAGE
                                  JNZ    PERFORM$A$RET                          ;CHARACTER?
                                  OR     STATUS$BYTE,START$OF$MESSAGE$BIT  OR
                                         HEADER$DATA$BIT                        ;INITIALIZE
                                  MOV    CHARACTER$COUNT,NUMBER$OF$HEADER$CHARACTERS
                                  MOV    BUFFER$POINTER,BUFFER$ADDRESS          ;MOVE IMMEDIATE
PERFORM$A$RET:                    RET                                          ;DATA TO BUFFER
                                                                               ;POINTER
HEADER$OR$DATA:                   MOV    DI,BUFFER$POINTER                      ;SAVE CHARACTER
                                  MOV    [DI],AL
                                  INC    DI                                    ;UPDATE POINTER
                                  MOV    BUFFER$POINTER,DI
                                  DEC    CHARACTER$COUNT                        ;DECREMENT AND TEST
                                  JNZ    PERFORM$A$RET                          ;FOR MESSAGE DONE
                                  TEST   STATUS$BYTE,HEADER$DATA$BIT
                                  JZ     DATA$PROCESSING
HEADER$PROCESSING:                MOV    CX,0004                               ;SET UP FOR ASCII TO HEX
                                  MOV    SI,START$OF$HEADER$POINTER             ;CONVERSION
                                  MOV    DI,SI
HEADER$TRANSLATE$LOOP:            CALL   CONVERT$TWO$ASCII$TO$HEX               ;CONVERT TWO ASCII CHARACTERS
                                  JZ     TRANSLATION$ERROR                      ;TO ONE HEX BYTE
                                  MOV    [DI],AL
                                  INC    DI
                                  DEC    CX                                    ;DECREMENT AND TEST FOR DONE
                                  JNZ    HEADER$TRANSLATE$LOOP
                                  MOV    SI,START$OF$HEADER$POINTER             ;SET UP FOR HEADER CHECKING
                                  XOR    AX,AX
                                  MOV    CX,0003
HEADER$CHECKSUM$LOOP:             XOR    AL,[SI]                                ;CALCULATE BLOCK CHECKSUM
                                  ROL    AL,1                                  ;FROM CHARACTERS
                                  INC    SI
                                  DEC    CX                                    ;DECREMENT AND TEST
                                  JNZ    HEADER$CHECKSUM$LOOP                   ;FOR CHECKSUM DONE
                                  CMP    AL,[SI]                                ;COMPARE CALCULATED CHECKSUM
                                  JNZ    HEADER$CHECKSUM$ERROR                  ;WITH RECEIVED CHECKSUM
                                  XOR    STATUS$BYTE,HEADER$DATA$BIT            ;HEADER GOOD, SWITCH TO
                                                                               ;  DATA PROCESSING
                                  MOV    AX,[SI-2]                              ;LOAD # OF OBJECT
                                  MOV    OBJECT$BYTECOUNT,AX                    ;CODE BYTES FROM HEADER
                                  SAL    AX,1                                  ;GET NUMBER OF ASCII CHARACTERS
                                  ADD    AX,02                                 ;ADD 2
                                  RET    CHARACTER$COUNT,AX                     ;SAVE FOR DATA PROCESSING
HEADER$CHECKSUM$ERROR:            MOV    STATUS$BYTE,HEADER$CHECKSUM$ERROR$BIT
                                                                               ;TURN ON ERROR BIT
                                  RET
```

Figure 4-29. Interrupt Service Routine

```
TRANSLATION$ERROR:          MOV    STATUS$BYTE,TRANSLATION$ERROR$BIT   ;TURN ON ERROR BIT
                            RET
DATA$PROCESSING:            MOV    CX,OBJECT$BYTE$COUNT                ;SET UP FOR CONVERSION
                            MOV    SI,START$OF$DATA$POINTER            ;FROM ASCII TO HEX
                            MOV    DI,START$OF$DATA$POINTER-4

DATA$TRANSLATE$LOOP:        CALL   CONVERT$TWO$ASCII$TO$HEX
                            JZ     TRANSLATION$ERROR
                            MOV    [DI],AL
                            INC    DI
                            DEC    CX                                 ;DECREMENT AND TEST FOR
                            JNZ    DATA$TRANSLATE$LOOP                 ;DONE

                            MOV    SI,START$OF$DATA$POINTER -4         ;SET UP FOR CHECKSUM
                            XOR    AX,AX                              ;CALCULATION
                            MOV    CX,OBJECT$BYTE$COUNT

DATA$CHECKSUM$LOOP:         XOR    AL,[SI]
                            ROL    AL,1                               ;CALCULATE CHECKSUM
                            INC    SI
                            DEC    CX
                            JNZ    DATA$CHECKSUM$LOOP
                            CMP    AL,[SI]                            ;COMPARE CALCULATED CHECKSUM
                            JNZ    DATA$CHECKSUM$ERROR                ;WITH RECEIVED CHECKSUM

                            XOR    STATUS$BYTE,START$OF$MESSAGE$BIT    ;TURN ON
                            OR     MESSAGE$COMPLETED$BIT              ;MESSAGE COMPLETED BIT

                            RET                                       ;TURN OFF START OF MESSAGE BIT
DATA$CHECKSUM$ERROR:        MOV    STATUS$BYTE,DATA$CHECKSUM$ERROR$BIT ;TURN ON ERROR BYTE
                            RET
```

Figure 4-29. Interrupt Service Routine (Continued)

Several assumptions have been made by the logic of the program illustrated in Figure 4-28; they include:

1. The state of the machine has been saved and on return will be correctly restored.

2. The segment registers are set to the correct values.

3. Any hardware errors flags set by the I/O port are handled elsewhere.

4. A subroutine named CONVERTTWOASCIITOHEX that converts two ASCII characters pointed to by the DI register into one hex byte and returns the value in AL.

It is reasonable to expect that the first three assumptions are provided for by some sort of system interrupt handler. If this is not the case, these assumptions can be handled by:

1. Using the code shown in Figures 4-14 and 4-15 to save and restore the machine state. Note, however, that this routine does not use the BX, DX, or BP registers. It is not, therefore, necessary to save and restore these registers. The RETURN instruction should be altered to an IRET instruction.

2. Perform an appropriate segment register initialization routine.

3. Read the status port for the input device and set a flag in the status byte to indicate any errors. Bits 6 or 7 could be used for this purpose.

The CONVERTTWOASCIITOHEX routine will be presented later in this chapter.

STRING PRIMITIVE INSTRUCTIONS

8086 string primitive instructions are shown in Table 4-8. Each string primitive instruction performs a sequence of operations normally handled by an instruction loop. The string primitive instruction performs an operation specified by the primitive, then increments or decrements the pointer registers involved in the operation. On each iteration the affected pointer registers can be incremented or decremented, by 1 or 2. Pointer registers will be incremented if the value of the Direction flag in the Flags register is 0; the affected pointers will be decremented if the value of the Direction flag is 1. The affected pointer registers will be incremented or decremented by 1 if the low-order bit of the string primitive operation code is 0. If the low-order bit of the string primitive operation code is 1, the affected pointer registers will be incremented or decremented by 2.

There are these five string primitives;

MOVS - Move 8 or 16 bits of data from memory location to memory location

LODS - Load 8 or 16 bits of data from memory into the AL or AX register

STOS - Store the AL (8-bit operation) or AX (16-bit operation) register into memory

SCAS - Compare the AL (8-bit operation) or AX (16-bit operation) register with memory

CMPS - Compare memory location with memory location

String primitive instructions used fixed addressing modes, as follows:

MOVS - Move data from the memory location addressed by the SI register in the Data Segment to the memory location addressed by the DI register in the Extra Segment.

LODS - Load data from the memory location addressed by the SI register in the Data Segment to the AL or AX register.

STOS - Store the AL or AX register into the memory location addressed by the DI register in the Extra Segment.

SCAS - Compare the AL or AX register contents with the data in the memory location addressed by the DI register in the Extra Segment.

CMPS - Compare the data in the memory location addressed by the SI register in the Data Segment with the data in the memory location addressed by the DI register in the Extra Segment.

Segment override prefixes allow SI to access a segment other than the Data Segment. Segment override prefixes may not be used with the DI register. The DI register must access the Extra Segment.

Table 4-8. String Primitive Instructions

Mnemonic	Operands	Object Code	Bytes	Clocks	O	D	I	T	S	Z	A	P	C	Operation Performed
LODS		1010110w	1	12 9 + 13*										[ac] →[[SI]], [SI] →[SI] ±DELTA Move data into the AL (8-bit operation or AX (16-bit operation) register from the memory location addressed by SI. Increment or decrement SI depending on the value of the Direction Flag. DELTA is 1 if w = 0, 2 if w = 1.
MOVS		1010010w	1	18 9 + 17*										[DI] →[[SI]], [SI] →[SI] ±DELTA [DI] →[DI] ±DELTA Move 8 or 16 bits of data from the memory location addressed by SI to the memory location addressed by DI. Increment or decrement SI and DI depending on the value of the Direction Flag. DELTA is 1 if w = 0, 2 if w = 1.
STOS		1010101w	1	11 9 + 10*										[[DI]] →[ac], [DI] →[DI] ±DELTA Move the contents of the AL (8-bit operation) or AX (16-bit operation) register. Increment or decrement DI depending on the value of the Direction Flag. DELTA is 1 if w = 0, 2 if w = 1.
CMPS		1010011w	1	22 9 + 22*	X				X	X	X	X	X	[[SI]] – [[DI]], [SI] →[SI] ± DELTA [DI] →[DI] ±DELTA Subtract the 8 or 16 bits addressed by the DI register from the 8 or 16 bits addressed by the SI register. Use the result to set the flags, then discard the result. Increment or decrement SI and DI depending on the value of the Direction Flag. DELTA is 1 if w = 0, 2 if w = 1.
SCAS		1010111w	1	15 9 + 15*	X				X	X	X	X	X	[ac] – [[DI]] Subtract the 8 or 16 bits addressed by the DI register from the AL (8-bit operation) or the AX (16-bit operation) register. Use the result to set the flags, then discard the result. Increment or decrement DI depending on the value of the Direction Flag. DELTA is 1 if w = 0, 2 if w = 1.

* If preceded by the Repeat prefix (REP) there are 9 clocks plus the (*) number of clocks for the first transfer and the (*) number of clocks for each subsequent transfer

THE REP PREFIX

REP is a one-byte prefix that converts any string primitive instruction into a reexecuting loop.

String primitive instructions each execute as one iteration of a loop. The source and destination pointer registers SI and DI are assumed, by string primitive instructions, to supply source and/or destination memory addresses; these addresses are automatically incremented or decremented following each execution of the string primitive instruction. This leaves the address(es) pointing to the next location in the string to be accessed. The REP prefix specifies a termination condition which causes the string primitive instruction to continue executing until the termination condition is met.

For the MOVS, LODS, and STOS string primitives, there is a single termination condition. The CX register is treated as a counter; each time the string primitive executes, the CX register contents is automatically decremented by REP prefix logic. When the CX register contents decrements to 0, the instruction following the string primitive is executed.

CMPS and SCAS also use the CX register as a counter in the presence of a REP prefix; and as described for MOVS, LODS, and STOS, the CX register contents decrementing to 0 becomes a termination condition. In addition, CMPS and SCAS set status flags following each iterative execution. The level of the zero status bit serves as an additional termination condition. For this to be possible the CMPS and SCAS string primitives use two forms of the REP prefix:

1. REPZ or REPE which causes a termination if the zero status is set after any iterated execution of the string primitive.

2. REPNZ or REPNE which causes a termination condition if the zero status is reset after any iterated execution.

In summary, the REP prefix surrounds a string primitive instruction's execution with the following steps:

1. Tests the CX register contents. If CX contains 0 proceed to the instruction that follows the string primitive.

2. Service any pending interrupt.

3. Execute the string primitive instruction once. The pointer register addresses are incremented or decremented during this step as a normal part of the string primitive instruction's execution.

4. Decrement the CX register contents.

5a. For MOVS, LODS, or STOS proceed to step 1.

5b. For CMPS or SCAS, compare the zero status with the conditions specified by the REP prefix. If the specified zero status does not exist, then return to step 1; otherwise execute the instruction following the string primitve.

String primitive instructions are very powerful. Sequences such as:

```
MOV   AL,[SI]
INC   SI
```

or

```
MOV   AX,[SI]
INC   SI
INC   SI
```

can be replaced by

```
MOVSB
```

or

```
MOVSW
```

Consider Figure 4-2. If the Direction Flag is set to 0, this sequence of instructions may be replaced by

```
REP   MOVSW
      RET
```

In addition, note that the REP and MOVW instructions are single byte instructions, therefore, a CALL to this routine would be more expensive than inserting

```
REP   MOVSW
```

directly into the program.

Figure 4-9, the buffer initialization routine, can be replaced by

```
REP   STOSB
```

This replacement assumes that the Direction Flag is set to 0.

As an exercise, the reader should look over the other programs given earlier on this chapter and look for examples that can use the string primitives.

Consider a variation of the program illustrated in Figure 4-1 that compares two strings of bytes. Written out completely, the program would appear as follows:

```
COMP$BYTES:    MOV   AL,[SI]          ;LOAD BYTE FROM SOURCE
               CMP   [DI],AL          ;COMPARE WITH DESTINATION
               JZ    EQUAL            ;TEST FOR SIMILAR BYTES
               INC   SI               ;ADJUST POINTERS
               INC   DI
               DEC   CX               ;DECREMENT NUMBER TO MOVE
               JNZ   COMP$BYTES       ;LOOP IF NOT DONE
```

Figure 4-30. 8-Bit Buffer-to-Buffer Compare

CMP compares bytes or words, register-to-register, register-to-memory or memory-to-register. In Figure 4-30 the contents of two memory buffers are compared, looking for identical bytes. Pointer registers SI and DI address the source and destination registers, respectively. Registers SI, DI, and CX have been selected deliberately in Figure 4-30, because these are the registers used by the CMPSB and CMPSW string primitives; this allows the entire program sequence illustrated in Figure 4-30 to be replaced by:

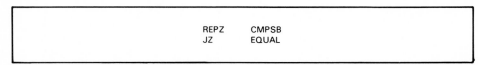

```
REPZ    CMPSB
JZ      EQUAL
```

Figure 4-31. Alternate 8-Bit Buffer-to-Buffer Compare

PROGRAM COUNTER CONTROL INSTRUCTIONS

This group of 8086 instructions unconditionally alter program counter contents, and in some cases they alter Code Segment register contents as well. These instructions are summarized in Table 4-9.

CALL instructions are used to transfer control from a program to a subprogram. The subprogram may reside in the current code segment or in a code segment specified by the instruction. The address of the subprogram may be provided by the instruction as an immediate address, or it may be stored in memory or registers. The four 8086 CALL instructions allow the following possibilities:

	Current Code Segment	Code Segment Specified by Instruction
Immediate Address	CALL disp16	CALL addr
Address in Memory/Register	CALL mem/reg	CALL mem

The CALL disp16 instruction is the only instruction in which a signed 16-bit number is added to the program counter. The other three CALL instructions move data directly from memory or register to the program counter. Prior Code Segment and/or program counter contents are pushed onto the Stack — and are thus saved.

RETURN instructions are used to transfer control from a subprogram back to the program that is called the subprogram. RETURN instructions that terminate a subprogram operate as the inverse of the CALL that invoked the subprogram. When a RETURN instruction is executed, data is popped from the stack into the program counter and, optionally, the Code Segment register. In addition, the RETURN instructions can optionally add a displacement to the stack pointer. This allows a RETURN instruction to adjust the stack pointer so it bypasses parameters that are on the stack for the subprogram to operate on. The four 8086 RETURN instructions allow these options:

	Pop into PC	Pop into CS,PC
Normal Return	RET	RET
Add Displacement to Stack	RET disp16	RET disp16

Note that the 8086 does not provide Call-on-Condition or Return-on-Condition instructions. To implement the corresponding 8080 instruction, the CALL or RETURN instruction must be combined with a Jump-on-Condition instruction. For example, the following 8080 instruction sequence

```
                    CNZ    SUB$PROGRAM    CALL SUB$PROGRAM if ZF = 0
NEXT$INSTRUCTION:   ORA    A
```

is replaced by the 8086 sequence

```
                    JZ     NEXT$INSTRUCTION   ;JUMP TO NEXT$INSTRUCTION if ZF =1
                    CALL   SUB$PROGRAM        ;JUMP TO SUB$PROGRAM if ZF = 0
NEXT$INSTRUCTION:   OR     AX,BX
```

8086 Jump instructions are presented in Table 4-9. 8086 Jump instructions generally offer the same variations as 8086 CALL instructions. An additional Jump instruction is:

```
                    JMP    disp
```

which has two bytes of object code, as opposed to the three-byte JMP disp16 instruction. JMP disp is a relative jump; it adds an 8-bit signed binary displacement to the program counter. This allows program jumps to occur within 1-127 bytes of the Jump instruction. Numerous programming examples given in this chapter use Jump instructions and illustrate their use.

Table 4-9. Program Counter Control Instructions

Mnemonic	Operands	Object Code	Bytes	Clocks	O	D	I	T	S	Z	A	P	C	Operation Performed
CALL	addr	9A kk jj hh gg	5	28										[SP] ← [SP] − 2, [[SP]] ← [PC], [SP] ← [SP] − 2, [[SP]] ← [CS], [PC] ← addr (offset portion), [CS] ← addr (segment portion) Call a subroutine in another code segment space. A new offset address, jjkk, and a new segment address, gghh, are provided.
CALL	disp16	E8 kk jj	3	19										[SP] ← [SP] −2, [[SP]] ← [PC] [PC] ← [PC] + disp16 Call a subroutine in the current code segment.
CALL	mem (SEG + PC)	FF mod 011 r/m (DISP) (DISP)	2,3 or 4	37 + EA										[SP] ← [SP] − 2, [[SP]] ← [PC], [SP] ← [SP] − 2, [[SP]] ← [CS], [PC] ← [mem], [CS] ← [mem + 2] Call a subroutine in another code segment space. The 16 bits contained in the memory location addressed by mem are moved into the PC. The contents of the succeeding memory word are loaded into the CS register.
CALL	mem/reg (PC only)	FF mod 010 r/m (DISP) (DISP)	2,3 or 4	21 + EA (mem) 16 (reg)										[SP] ← [SP] −2, [[SP]] ← [PC] [PC] ← [mem/reg] Call a subroutine in the current code segment. The 16 bits contained in the memory location or register addressed by mem/reg are moved into the PC.
RET		C3	1	16										[PC] ← [[SP]], [SP] ← [SP] + 2 Perform a return to a calling program in the current code segment.
RET		CB	1	24										[PC] ← [[SP]], [SP] ← [SP] + 2, [CS] ← [[SP]], [SP] ← [SP] + 2 Perform a return to a calling program in another code segment.
RET	disp16	C2 kk jj	3	20										[PC] ← [[SP]], [SP] ← [SP] + 2 + disp16 Perform a return to a calling program in the current code segment; adjust the stack pointer by disp16.
RET	disp16	CA kk jj	3	23										[PC] ← [[SP]], [SP] ← [SP] + 2, [CS] ← [[SP]], [SP] ← [SP] + 2 + disp16 Perform a return to a calling program in another code segment; adjust the stack pointer by disp16.

Table 4-9. Program Counter Control Instructions (Continued)

Mnemonic	Operands	Object Code	Bytes	Clocks	O	D	I	T	S	Z	A	P	C	Operation Performed
									Status					
JMP	addr	EA kk jj hh gg	5	15										[PC]← addr (offset portion), [CS] ← addr (segment portion) Jump to another code segment. A new offset address, jjkk, and a new segment address, gghh, are provided.
JMP	disp	EB kk	2	15										[PC] ← [PC] + disp Perform a program relative jump.
JMP	disp16	E9 kk jj	3	15										[PC] ← [PC] + disp16 Jump to a location in the current code segment.
JMP	mem (SEG + PC)	FF mod 101 r/m (DISP) (DISP)	2,3 or 4	24 + EA										[PC] ← [mem], [CS] ← [mem + 2] Jump to a location in another code segment. Move the contents of the memory location addressed by mem into the PC. Move the contents of the succeeding memory location into the CS register.
JMP	mem/reg (PC only)	FF mod 100 r/m (DISP) (DISP)	2,3 or 4	16 + EA (mem) 11 (reg)										[PC] ← [mem/reg] Jump to a memory location in the current code segment. Move the contents of the memory location or register addressed by mem/reg into the PC.

JUMP-ON-CONDITION INSTRUCTIONS

8086 instructions that alter the contents of the program counter based on various conditions are presented in Table 4-10.

Table 4-11 lists the arithmetic comparisons that are commonly used and shows how to derive them with the 8086.

In general, greater or less are adjectives that are applied to signed operations. Above or below are adjectives that are applied to unsigned operations.

The 8086 instructions that decrement the CX register, then optionally alter the contents of the program counter are presented in Table 4-12. These instructions are commonly referred to as LOOP structures. As an exercise, review the previous sections of this Chapter and replace the structure

```
DEC      CX
JNZ      label
```

with

```
LOOP      label
```

Each replacement represents a savings of one byte of object code. In addition, one clock period per execution is saved. For a loop that iterates 100 times per execution, this represents a savings of 100 clock periods, or 20 μs on a 5 MHz 8086.

The JCXZ instruction is unique in this group of instructions in that it does not jump based on the contents of the Flags register, rather the JUMP is performed if the CX register is 0. Since the JCXZ instruction shares an interest in the CX register, along with the LOOP instructions, it is also presented with LOOP instructions in Table 4-12.

LOOP Instruction

The LOOP instruction combines the DEC CX and JNZ instructions. For example, the instruction sequence of Figure 4-1 can be rewritten as:

```
MOVE$BYTES:     MOV      AL, [SI]
                MOV      [DI], AL
                INC      SI
                INC      DI
                LOOP     MOVE$BYTES
```

In all future code sequences, the LOOP instruction will replace the

```
DEC      CX
JNZ      label
```

instruction sequence.

Table 4-10. Jump-on-Condition Instructions

Mnemonic	Operands	Object Code	Bytes	Clocks	Status O	D	I	T	S	Z	A	P	C	Operation Performed
JA	disp	77 kk	2	4/16										If ([C] OR [Z]) = 0, then [PC] ← [PC] + disp. Branch relative if the Carry and Zero flags are 0.
JNBE	disp	same as JA												
JAE	disp	73 kk	2	4/16										If [C] = 0, then [PC] ← [PC] + disp. Branch relative if the Carry flag is 0.
JNC	disp	same as JAE												
JNB	disp	same as JAE												
JB	disp	72 kk	2	4/16										If [C] = 1, then [PC] ← [PC] + disp. Branch relative if the Carry flag is 1.
JC	disp	same as JB												
JNAE	disp	same as JB												
JBE	disp	76 kk	2	4/16										If ([C] OR [Z]) = 1, then [PC] ← [PC] + disp. Branch relative if the Carry flag or the Zero flag are equal to 1.
JNA	disp	same as JBE												
JE	disp	74 kk	2	4/16										If [Z] = 1, then [PC] ← [PC] + disp. Branch relative if the Zero flag is 1.
JZ	disp	same as JE												
JG	disp	7F kk	2	4/16										If ([Z] = 0 AND ([S] = [O])) = 1, then [PC] ← [PC] + disp. Branch relative if the Zero flag is 0 and the Sign flag is equal to the Overflow flag.
JNLE	disp	same as JG												
JGE	disp	7D kk	2	4/16										If [S] = [O], then [PC] ← [PC] + disp. Branch relative if the Sign flag is equal to the Overflow flag.
JNL	disp	same as JGE												
JL	disp	7C kk	2	4/16										If [S] ≠ [O], then [PC] ← [PC] + disp. Branch relative if the Sign flag is not equal to the Overflow flag.
JNGE	disp	same as JL												
JLE	disp	7E kk	2	4/16										If ([S] = [O] AND [Z] = 0) = 1, then [PC] ← [PC] + disp. Branch relative if the Sign flag is equal to the Overflow flag and the Zero flag is 0.
JNG	disp	same as JLE												

Table 4-10. Jump-on-Condition Instructions (Continued)

Mnemonic	Operands	Object Code	Bytes	Clocks	Status O	D	I	T	S	Z	A	P	C	Operation Performed
JNE	disp	75 kk	2	4/16										If [Z] = 0, then [PC] ← [PC] + disp Branch relative if the Zero flag is 0.
JNZ	disp	same as JNE												
JNO	disp	71 kk	2	4/16										If [O] = 0, then [PC] ← [PC] + disp Branch relative if the Overflow flag is 0.
JNP	disp	7B kk	2	4/16										If [P] = 0, then [PC] ← [PC] + disp Branch relative if the Parity flag is 0.
JPO	disp	same as JNP												
JNS	disp	79 kk	2	4/16										If [S] = 0, then [PC] ← [PC] + disp Branch relative if the Sign flag is 0.
JO	disp	70 kk	2	4/16										If [O] = 1, then [PC] ← [PC] + disp Branch relative if the Overflow flag is 1.
JP	disp	7A kk	2	4/16										If [P] = 1, then [PC] ← [PC] + disp Branch relative if the Parity flag is 1.
JPE	disp	same as JP												
JS	disp	78 kk	2	4/16										If [S] = 1, then [PC] ← [PC] + disp Branch relative if the Sign flag is 1.
JCXZ	disp	E3 kk	2	6/18										If [CX] = 0, then [PC] ← [PC] + disp Branch relative if the CX register is 0.

Table 4-11. Signed vs. Unsigned Comparison Instructions

		Signed			Unsigned	
=	.EQ.	JE or JZ	Equal or zero	JE or JZ	Equal or zero
≠	.NE.	JNE or JNZ	Not equal or not zero	JNE or JNZ	Not equal or not zero
>	.GT.	JG or JNLE	(Greater) or not (less or equal)	JA or JNBE	(Above) or not (below or equal)
≥	.GE.	JGE or JNL	(Greater or equal) or (not less)	JAE or JNB	(Above or equal) or (not below)
<	.LT.	JL or JNGE	(Less) or not (greater or equal)	JB or JNAE	(Below) or not (above or equal)
≤	.LE.	JLE or JNG	(Less or equal) or (not greater)	JBE or JNA	(Below or equal) or (not above)

Table 4-12. Loop Instructions

Mnemonic	Operands	Object Code	Bytes	Clocks	Status										Operation Performed
					O	D	I	T	S	Z	A	P	C	
LOOP	disp	E2 kk	2	5/17										[CX] ← [CX] −1, if [CX] = 0, then [PC] ←[PC] + disp Decrement the CX register, not affecting the flags. If the CX register is 0, branch relative.
LOOPE	disp	E1 kk	2	6/18										[CX] ← [CX] − 1, if [CX] ≠ 0, and [Z] = 1, then [PC] ← [PC] + disp Decrement the CX register, not affecting the flags. If the CX register is not 0 and the Zero flag is 1, branch relative.
LOOPZ	disp	same as LOOPE												
LOOPNE	disp	E0 kk	2	5/19										[CX] ← [CX] − 1, if [CX] ≠ 0 and [Z] = 0, then [PC] ← [PC] + disp Decrement the CX register, not affecting the flags. If the CX register is not 0 and the Zero flag is 0, branch relative.
LOOPNZ	disp	same as LOOPNE												
JCXZ	disp	E3 kk	2	6/18										If [CX] = 0, then [PC] ←[PC] + disp Branch relative if the CX register is 0.

PROCESSOR CONTROL INSTRUCTIONS

The 8086 instructions which operate on the Flags register and control various aspects of the 8086's external interface are shown in Table 4-13.

I/O INSTRUCTIONS

8086 instructions that perform input and output functions are shown in Figure 4-14.

Memory mapped addressing on the 8086 has one significant advantage over I/O port addressing. The string primitive instructions allow repeated operations to be performed on memory addresses, depending on how the memory mapped I/O address decoding is performed. Compare Figure 4-32, where I/O port addressing is used, with Figure 4-33, where memory mapped addressing is used. Both of these routines output a block of data. The number of bytes in the block is contained in the CX register. The routine in Figure 4-32 moves the block pointed to by the DI register out to I/O$PORT. The routine in Figure 4-33 moves the block pointed to by the SI register to the memory mapped I/O port addressed by the DI register.

I/O port addresses may be specified directly, or the I/O port address may be held in the DX register. 8-bit addresses are specified directly; 16-bit I/O port addresses are specified via the DX register.

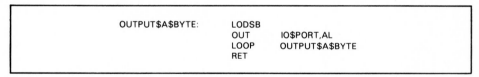

Figure 4-32. Block I/O via I/O Port Addressing

Figure 4-33. Block I/O via Memory Mapped Addressing

Note, a block of memory addresses must be assigned to the memory mapped I/O port since MOVS automatically increments/decrements the addresses in SI and DI.

Table 4-13. Processor Control Instructions

Mnemonic	Operands	Object Code	Bytes	Clocks	O	D	I	T	S	Z	A	P	C	Operation Performed
CLC		F8	1	2									0	[C] ← 0 Clear Carry status.
CMC		F5	1	2									X	[C] ← [C̄] Complement the Carry status.
CLD		FC	1	2		0								[D] ← 0 Clear the Direction flag.
CLI		FA	1	2			0							[I] ← 0 Clear the Interrupt enable status, thereby disabling all interrupts.
STC		F9	1	2									1	[C] ← 1 Set the Carry status.
STD		FD	1	2		1								[D] ← 1 Set the Direction flag.
STI		FB	1	2			1							[I] ← 1 Set the Interrupt flag to 1, thereby enabling interrupts.
NOP		90	1	3										Perform no operation.
ESC	mem	11011xxx mod xxx r/m (DISP) (DISP)	2, 3 or 4	8 + EA										Place the contents of the memory location addressed by mem onto the address/data bus. If mod = 11, perform no operation.
LOCK		F0	1	2										Guarantee this 8086 control of its bus during the execution of the next instruction.
WAIT		9B	1	3 or more										Enter a WAIT state until external logic drives the TEST pin low.
HLT		F4	1	2 or more										Enter a HALT state.

Table 4-14. 8086 I/O Instructions

Mnemonic	Operands	Object Code	Bytes	Clocks	Status										Operation Performed
					O	D	I	T	S	Z	A	P	C	
IN	ac,DX	1110110w	1	8										[ac] ← [PORTDX] Input to the AL register (8-bit operation) or the AX register (16-bit operation) from the I/O port specified by the DX register.
IN	ac,port	1110010w kk	2	10										[ac] ← [port] Input to the AL register (8-bit operation) or the AX register (16-bit operation) from the I/O port specified in the second byte of the instruction.
OUT	ac,DX	1110011w	1	8										[PORTDX] ← [ac] Output the contents of the AL register (8-bit operation) or the AX register (16-bit operation) to the I/O port specified by the DX register.
OUT	ac,port	1110111w kk	2	10										[port] ← [ac] Output the contents of the AL register (8-bit operation) or the AX register (16-bit operation) to the I/O port specified in the second byte of the instruction.

INTERRUPT INSTRUCTIONS

The software interrupt instruction, the interrupt on overflow instruction and the return from interrupt instruction are shown in Table 4-15.

The software interrupt instruction is used for two major purposes:

1. To debug programs. The single byte software interrupt instruction calls a routine whose address is at location $000C_{16}$. Typically this routine is part of a debug package and is used to handle breakpoints.

2. To call subroutines whose address is present in the first 1024 bytes of memory. When the two byte software interrupt instruction is used, any one of 256 subroutines whose address has been placed in the first 1024 bytes of memory may be called.

Software interrupt instructions have the advantage of using one or two bytes of program memory, as compared to five bytes of program memory used by an intersegment CALL. In addition, the software interrupt automatically saves the Flags register onto the stack — a desirable feature in many cases. A minor disadvantage of software interrupts is that if a routine is called via a software interrupt, the routine must return via an IRET instruction, which takes more time than a RET instruction.

Table 4-15. 8086 Interrupt Instructions

Mnemonic	Operands	Object Code	Bytes	Clocks	O	D	I	T	S	Z	A	P	C	Operation Performed
INT		1100110v kk(if V = 1) V = 0 V = 1	 1 2	 52 51			 0	 0						$[SP] \leftarrow [SP] - 2, [[SP]] \leftarrow [FLAGS], [I] \leftarrow 0, [T] \leftarrow 0,$ $[SP] \leftarrow [SP] - 2, [[SP]] \leftarrow [CS], [CS] \leftarrow [SP] - 2,$ $[[SP]] \leftarrow [PC], [CS] \leftarrow [vector (segment part)],$ $[PC] \leftarrow [vector (offset part)]$ If $v = 0$, vector (offset part) $= [0000C_{16}]$ vector (segment part) $= [0000E_{16}]$ If $v = 1$, vector (offset part) $= [(kk * 4)]$ vector (segment part) $= [(kk * 4) + 2]$ Perform a software interrupt.
INTO		CE	1	(O = 1) 53 4 (O = 0)	X		0	0						If $[O] = 1$, then $[SP] \leftarrow [SP] - 2, [[SP]] \leftarrow [FLAGS], IF \leftarrow 0,$ $TF \leftarrow 0, [SP] \leftarrow [SP] - 2, [[SP]] \leftarrow [CS], [CS] \leftarrow [SP] - 2,$ $[[SP]] \leftarrow [PC], [CS] \leftarrow [00012_{16}], [PC] \leftarrow [00010_{16}].$ If the Overflow flag is set, perform a software interrupt via the vector dedicated to overflow processing, otherwise, execute the next sequential instruction.
IRET		CF	1	32	X	X	X	X	X	X	X	X	X	$[PC] \leftarrow [[SP]], [SP] \leftarrow [SP] + 2, [CS] \leftarrow [[SP]], [SP] \leftarrow [SP]$ $+ 2, [FLAGS] \leftarrow [[SP]], [SP] \leftarrow [SP] + 2$ Return from an interrupt service routine.

ROTATE AND SHIFT INSTRUCTIONS

8086 instructions that perform rotates and shifts are shown in Table 4-16.

Rotate and shift instructions are frequently used to perform bit testing operations. These instructions are used by themselves or in conjunction with logical operations to test for various bit patterns. To test the low-order bit of a register, a

```
ROR    reg, 1
```

instruction operates one cycle faster than a

```
AND    reg, 01H
```

instruction or a

```
TEST    reg, 01H
```

instruction. The ROR instruction tests the Carry Status, as opposed to the AND or TEST instructions where the Zero Status is significant. To test the low-order bit of a 16-bit pointer/index register, use:

```
ROR    reg, 1
```

This instruction will save one byte of object code, and operate one cycle faster than a

```
AND    reg. 0001H
```

instruction or a

```
TEST    reg, 0001H
```

instruction. Note, however, that the ROR instruction alters the contents of the register, whereas the TEST instruction is non-destructive.

The high-order bit of an 8-bit register or a 16-bit register can be tested, as described above, by replacing the ROR instructions with ROL instructions.

Rotate and shift instructions perform arithmetic operations. The arithmetic shift operations can be used to perform both multiplication and division. The routine in Figure 4-34 converts two ASCII characters into their hex equivalent. This routine assumes that the SI register points to the two characters (high-order byte first) and returns the result in the AL register. This routine also ensures that the bytes converted lie in the range $0 \leq$ character ≤ 9 or $A \leq$ character $\leq F$. If the character is out of range, the zero status will be 1 on return, otherwise the zero status will be 0.

```
CONVERT$TWO$ASCII$TO$HEX    PROC    NEAR

                            PUSH    CX
                            LODSB                               ;LOAD FROM SI TO AL
                            CALL    CONVERT$ASCII$TO$HEX
                            JZ      TRANSLATION$ERROR

                            MOV     CL,4                        ;SET UP FOR ROTATE
                            SAL     AL,CL                       ;ROTATE FOUR TIMES
                            MOV     AH,AL                       ;SAVE IN AH
                            LODSB
                            CALL    CONVERT$ASCII$TO$HEX
                            JZ      TRANSLATION$ERROR

                            OR      AL,AH                       ;CREATE THE HEX BYTE
                            OR      AH,OFFH                     ;TURN ZF=0
                            POP     CX
                            RET
TRANSLATION$ERROR:          RET                                 ;ZF IS KNOWN TO BE 1

CONVERT$TWO$ASCII$TO$HEX    ENDP

CONVERT$ASCII$TO$HEX        PROC    NEAR

                            SUB     AL,30H
                            JL      TRANNY$ERROR
                            CMP     AL,OAH                      ;IS IT 0 - 9
                            JL      DONE
                            SUB     AL,07H                      ;ADJUST FOR A - F.
                            CMP     AL,10H                      ;IS IT MORE?
                            JGE     TRANNY$ERROR
DONE:                       RET

TRANNY$ERROR:               XOR     AH,AH
                            RET

CONVERT$ASCII$TO$HEX        ENDP
```

Figure 4-34. Routine to Convert Two ASCII Digits to
Their Hex Equivalents

Table 4-16. 8086 Shift and Rotate Instructions

Mnemonic	Operands	Object Code	Bytes	Clocks	O	D	I	T	S	Z	A	P	C	Operation Performed
RCL	mem/reg, count	110100vw mod 010 r/m (DISP) (DISP)	2, 3 or 4	count = 1, reg: 2 mem: 15 + EA count = [CL] reg: 8 + 4·[CL] mem: 20 + EA + 4·[CL]	X								X	Rotate the contents of the memory location or register specified by mem/reg left through the Carry status. The number of bits to rotate is determined by count and will be either 1 (v = 0) or the contents of the CL register (v = 1). The rotation is performed as follows: if w = 0 if w = 1

Table 4-16. 8086 Shift and Rotate Instructions (Continued)

Mnemonic	Operands	Object Code	Bytes	Clocks	Status									Operation Performed
					O	D	I	T	S	Z	A	P	C	
RCR	mem/reg. count	110100vw mod 011 r/m (DISP) (DISP)	2, 3 or 4	count = 1, reg: 2 mem: 15 + EA count = [CL] reg: 8 + 4·[CL] mem: 20 + EA + 4 · [CL]	X								X	Rotate the contents of the memory location or register specified by mem/reg right through the Carry status. The number of bits to rotate is determined by count and will be either 1 (v = 0) or the contents of the CL register (v = 1). The rotation is performed as follows: if w = 0 7 6 5 4 3 2 1 0 if w = 1 15 14 13 2 1 0

Table 4-16. 8086 Shift and Rotate Instructions (Continued)

Mnemonic	Operands	Object Code	Bytes	Clocks	Status									Operation Performed
					O	D	I	T	S	Z	A	P	C	
ROL	mem/reg, count	110100vw mod 000 r/m (DISP) (DISP)	2, 3 or 4	count = 1, reg: 2 mem: 15 + EA count = [CL] reg: 8 + 4·[CL] mem: 20 + EA + 4·[CL]	X								X	Rotate the contents of the memory location or register specified by mem/reg left. Rotate the high-order bit of the operand into the Carry status. The number of bits to rotate is determined by count and will be either 1 (v = 0) or the contents of the CL register (v = 1). The rotation is performed as follows: w = 0 7 6 5 4 3 2 1 0 w = 1 15 14 13 2 1 0

Table 4-16. 8086 Shift and Rotate Instructions (Continued)

Mnemonic	Operands	Object Code	Bytes	Clocks	Status									Operation Performed
					O	D	I	T	S	Z	A	P	C	
ROR	mem/reg, count	110100vw mod 001 r/m (DISP) (DISP)	2, 3 or 4	count = 1, reg: 2 mem: 15 + EA count = [CL] reg: 8 + 4*[CL] mem: 20 + EA + 4* [CL]	X								X	Rotate the contents of the memory location or register specified by mem/reg right. Rotate the low-order bit of the operand into the Carry status. The number of bits to rotate is determined by count and will be either 1 (v = 0) or the contents of the CL register (v = 1). The rotation is performed as follows:

if w = 0

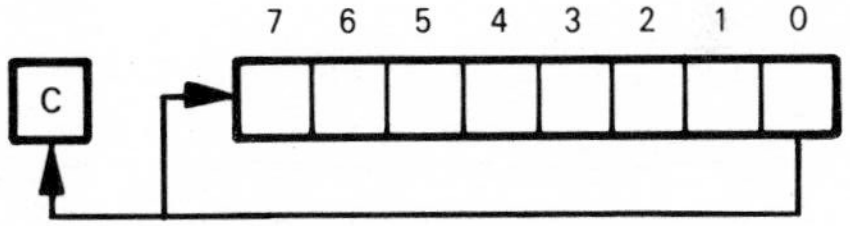

if w = 1

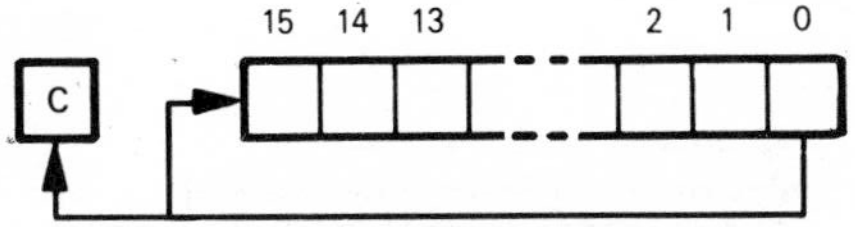

Table 4-16. 8086 Shift and Rotate Instructions (Continued)

Mnemonic	Operands	Object Code	Bytes	Clocks	O	D	I	T	S	Z	A	P	C	Operation Performed
SAL	mem/reg, count	110100vw mod 100 r/m (DISP) (DISP)	2, 3 or 4	count = 1, reg: 2 mem: 15 + EA count = [CL] reg: 8 + 4·[CL] mem: 20 + EA + 4·[CL]	X				X	X	?	X	X	Shift the contents of the memory location or register specified by mem/reg left. Shift a zero into the low-order bit of the operand. The number of bits to shift is determined by count and will be either 1 (v = 0) or the contents of the CL register (v = 1). The rotation is performed as follows: if w = 0 if w = 1
SHL	mem/reg, count	same as SAL												

Status flag columns (left to right): O D I T S Z A P C

Table 4-16. 8086 Shift and Rotate Instructions (Continued)

Mnemonic	Operands	Object Code	Bytes	Clocks	O	D	I	T	S	Z	A	P	C	Operation Performed
SAR	mem/reg, count	110100vw mod 111 r/m (DISP) (DISP)	2, 3 or 4	count = 1, reg: 2 mem: 15 + EA count = [CL] reg: 8 + 4·[CL] mem: 20 + EA + 4·[CL]	X				X	X	?	X	X	Shift the contents of the memory location right. Propagate the sign of the operand by preserving the value of the high-order bit. The number of bits to shift is determined by count and will be either 1 (v = 0) or the contents of the CL register (v = 1). the rotation is performed as follows:

Status header spans: O D I T S, Z A P C

Table 4-16. 8086 Shift and Rotate Instructions (Continued)

Mnemonic	Operands	Object Code	Bytes	Clocks	O	D	I	T	S	Z	A	P	C	Operation Performed
SHR	mem/reg, count	111100vw mod 101 r/m (DISP) (DISP)	2, 3 or 4	count = 1, reg: 2 mem: 15 + EA count = [CL] reg: 8 + 4·[CL] mem: 20 + EA + 4 · [CL]	X				X	X	?	X	X	Shift the contents of the memory location or register specified by mem/reg right. Shift a zero into the high-order bit of the operand. The number of bits to shift is determined by count and will be either 1 (v = 0) or the contents of the CL register (v = 1). The rotation is performed as follows: if w = 0 if w = 1

Status

5

Software Development

There are three tools that greatly assist the software development process. These are:

- An Editor

Editors are used to enter and/or modify source code. The source code is usually saved on some form of mass storage, e.g., floppy disk, hard disk, or in dire emergencies, paper tape. The source code is usually organized on mass storage in the form of a file, referred to as the source file. Editors create and operate on source files in a number of different ways depending on how the source file may be accessed, e.g., a source file residing on magnetic tape is not handled in the same way as a source file residing on floppy disk. Users typically request editor functions by entering commands from a video terminal.

- An Assembler

Assemblers are used to translate source code into object code. An assembler reads the source file that (in most cases) has been generated by the editor, translates the source code, and then writes the object code to mass storage in the form of a file referred to as the object file. An assembler may also produce additional files such as a file that contains the source code and the object code, referred to as the listing file, and a file which contains all the labels and variable names used in the source code, referred to as the symbol file. The listing file is usually printed, and then referred to during the debugging process.

- A Debugger

Debuggers are used to assist in detecting errors in the object code. A debugger is either loaded with the object code generated by the assembler, or it is loaded by itself, at which point the user can request that an object file be loaded from mass storage. A typical debugger allows the user to control the execution of the object code, and to view the contents of memory and registers.

The three programs mentioned above are the major tools essential for the development process. Additional tools which are useful include linkers and loaders. Linkers are used to link multiple subprograms into one program. Linkers resolve external references from subprograms. External references occur when instructions in one module refer to a symbol (label or variable name) that is defined in another module. Loaders are used to bring object code from mass storage into memory.

For the purposes of this discussion, consider a hypothetical system, to be used in the software development process, which contains the following hardware elements:

- CPU

- RAM

- Floppy disk drives

- CRT terminal

- Printer

The connections between these elements are depicted in Figure 5-1.

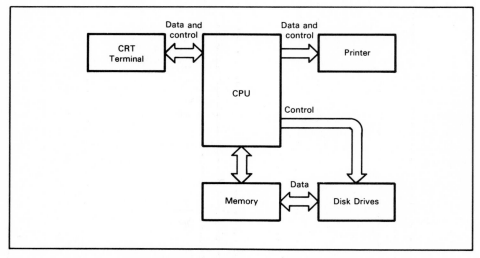

Figure 5-1. Hypothetical Development System

Throughout this discussion of editors, assemblers, and debuggers, it will be assumed that these support programs are executed on the above system. In addition, as each of the support programs is discussed, a hypothetical command language for the support program will be used in examples illustrating typical functions provided by the support program. It should be emphasized that both the system and the command languages are only examples, and will not be found in the real world.

EDITORS

Most editors accomplish their function by performing some combination of the following tasks:

- Reading data from mass storage into memory.

- Operating on the data in memory in response to commands from the user.

- Writing data from memory out to mass storage.

Figure 5-2 shows an example of this operation.

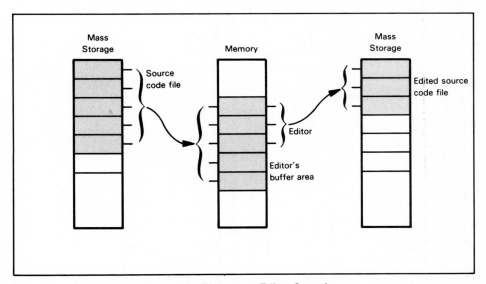

Figure 5-2. Elementary Editor Operation

The following terms are commonly used when describing basic types of editors.

Buffer: data is read from mass storage into a memory area referred to as the buffer. All editing commands operate on the data in the buffer. After the data has been processed it is written from the buffer to mass storage.

Character or Line Pointer: The editor maintains a pointer into the buffer. All user commands are taken as being relative to this pointer. For example, a command to delete four characters would delete four characters after the pointer. Some editors use a pointer that refers to a particular character in the buffer. These editors are referred to as character-oriented editors. Some editors use a pointer that refers to a particular line. These are referred to as line-oriented editors.

EDITOR FUNCTIONS

What sorts of functions should an editor provide?
The editor should provide the following capabilities:

- Read data from mass storage to memory

- Write from memory to mass storage

- Insert data into memory

- Delete data from memory

- Change the position of the character/line pointer in the buffer

- Display the contents of the buffer

- Search the buffer for occurrence of the specified string

- Change the contents of the buffer

- System commands

The sample editor used to illustrate these capabilities will respond to user commands entered at the CRT terminal. A command consists of three fields:

number   command   strings

Number indicates the number of times that a particular command is to be executed. This field is interpreted as a decimal number. This field may be omitted. If this field is omitted, a default value of 1 is assumed.

Command is a single character which indicates the operation to be performed.

Strings is a sequence of characters. Some commands use one or more strings while they are executing. This field may be omitted. Strings are terminated by either a # character or the return character.

All commands are terminated by a carriage return, represented by ⓡ. The following are examples of command strings:

A ⓡ	Append one line to the buffer
10L ⓡ	Move pointer 10 lines down in buffer
CTHE#AN ⓡ	Change the string THE to AN

Read/Write Data to/from Memory

The editor must provide the ability to read or write from the buffer to mass storage. The user should be able to specify the amount of data that is to be transferred. Typical amounts of data would include:

- One or more characters

- One or more lines. For example, transferring one line would move all data until a carriage return is detected. Transferring n lines would move all data until n carriage returns are detected.

- An entire buffer. For a read operation this would involve moving data from mass storage into the buffer until the buffer is full. For a write operation, this would involve moving data from the buffer to mass storage until the entire buffer has been moved to mass storage.

Additional features that might be useful include:

- An operation that transfers data from mass storage and then deletes the data that has been transferred.

- A read or write operation that would transfer data until a specific character is detected. For example, this would allow the user to transfer pages of data, that is to say transfer all information until an end-of-page character (form feed) is detected.

As an example, consider the case where the sample editor command to add lines to the buffer is A. The command

A ⓡ

would add one line to the buffer. The command

10A ⓡ

would add ten lines to the buffer. The command

!A ⓡ

would fill the buffer with information from mass storage. The execution of the command

5A

could be depicted as follows:

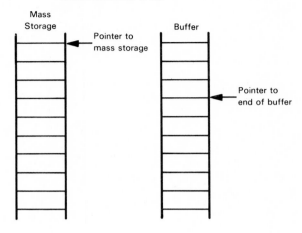

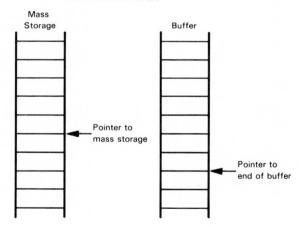

Insert Data into the Buffer

The editor must provide the ability to add data to the buffer. Users typically need to perform one of two types of source code insertion. These are:

- Large amounts of source code must be inserted. This would occur when the source code is first being entered or when a significant revision of the source code is being performed.

- One or two lines of source code must be entered. This would occur when the debugging process is underway and "bugs" are corrected or when the source code is first being entered and the user discovers that one or two lines were inadvertently omitted.

Most editors respond to these two different needs by supplying two different modes of insertion: a mode by which the user may enter unlimited amounts of data, and a mode by which a limited amount of data may be entered by the user.

Consider the case where the sample editor command to insert data is I. Suppose the buffer appears as follows:

```
                            MOV     CX,AX
                            ADD     DX,SP
          Pointer ──────→   JNC     EXIT$STAGE$LEFT
```

If the command

```
          I       SHR     DX,1  (r)
```

is entered, the buffer would be altered to

```
                            MOV     CX,AX
                            ADD     DX,SP
                            SHR     DX,1
                            JNC     EXIT$STAGE$LEFT
```

Delete Data from the Buffer

The editor must provide the ability to remove data from the buffer. The user should be able to specify the amount of source code to be removed. Typical amounts include:

- One or more characters.

- One or more lines. Removing one line will remove the line pointed to by the line pointer or remove all data in the buffer beginning with the character pointed to by the current character pointer until a carriage return is detected. Removing n lines would remove the n lines below the current line pointer or all data from the current character pointer until n carriage returns have been detected.

Consider the case where the sample editor command to delete a line from the buffer is K. Suppose the buffer appears as follows:

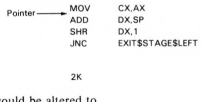

```
          Pointer ──────→   MOV     CX,AX
                            ADD     DX,SP
                            SHR     DX,1
                            JNC     EXIT$STAGE$LEFT
```

If the command

```
                    2K
```

is entered, the buffer would be altered to

```
                            MOV     CX,AX
                            JNC     EXIT$STAGE$LEFT
```

Moving the Character/Line Pointer

The editor must provide the ability to move the character/line pointer to different positions in the buffer. The user should be able to specify the number of characters/lines that the pointer is to be moved. Additional capabilities that might be useful include:

- Move the character/line pointer to the top of the buffer.

- Move the character/line pointer to the end of the buffer.

- Move the character/line pointer to a specific line in the buffer. For example, the user might be able to request that the character/line pointer be moved to line number 11 in the buffer.

Consider the case where the sample editor command to move the character/line pointer up or down in the buffer is L. Suppose the buffer appears as follows:

```
Pointer ──────►  MOV      CX,AX
                 ADD      DX,SP
                 SHR      DX,1
                 JNC      EXIT$STAGE$LEFT
                 TEST     BX,40H
                 JZ       DONT$MESS$WITH$BILL
```

If the command

```
                 4L
```

is entered, the buffer would be unchanged; however, the pointer would point at the JZ DONT$MESS$WITH$BILL instruction. If the command is

```
                 -3L
```

the buffer would again be unchanged; however, the pointer would point at the SHR DX,1 instruction.

Display the Contents of the Buffer

The editor should provide the ability to display the buffer on the user's terminal. The user should be able to specify the number of characters/lines that will be displayed. Additional capabilities that might be useful include:

- If the user has a CRT terminal, then it might be useful to display a full screen of data automatically. In addition, the ability to scroll through the buffer either displaying a line at a time or a full screen at a time could also prove useful.

Consider the case where the sample editor command to display a line from the buffer on the CRT terminal is T. If the buffer contains:

```
                 IN       AL,TOUCH$TONE$DECODER$PORT
Pointer ──────►  CMP      AL,COLUMN$4$DIGIT
                 JNZ      TOUCH$TONE$ENCODE
                 MOV      [DI],MESSAGE$STARTED$CODE
```

and the command

```
                 2T
```

is entered, then the lines

```
CMP     AL,COLUMN$4$DIGIT
JNZ     TOUCH$TONE$ENCODE
```

will be displayed on the CRT terminal.

Search the Buffer for an Occurrence of a String

The editor should provide the ability to search the buffer for the occurrence of a string of characters specified by the user. An additional capability that would be extremely useful would be to search all the source code for the occurrence of a particular string. For example, when the source code is initially entered, typographical errors are often present. Using the search facility in combination with a change facility allows the source code to be corrected with a minimum of difficulty.

Consider the case where the sample editor command to search the buffer is S. If the buffer appears as follows:

```
              IN     AL,TOUCH$TONE$DECODER$PORT
Pointer ───▶  CMP    AL,COLUMN$4$DIGIT
              JNZ    TOUCH$TONE$ENCODE
              MOV    [DI],MESSAGES$STARTED$CODE
```

and the command

```
              S TONE  Ⓡ
```

is entered, the result will depend on whether a character pointer or a line pointer is employed by the editor. In the case of a line pointer, the buffer will be unchanged. However, the position of the line pointer will be altered as follows:

```
              IN     AL,TOUCH$TONE$DECODER$PORT
              CMP    AL,COLUMN$4$DIGIT
Pointer ───▶  JNZ    TOUCH$TONE$ENCODE
              MOV    [DI],MESSAGE$STARTED$CODE
```

In the case of a character pointer, the pointer will be altered as follows:

```
              IN     AL,TOUCH$TONE$DECODER$PORT
              CMP    AL,COLUMN$4$DIGIT
Pointer ────────────────
              JNZ    TOUCH$TONE$ENCODE
              MOV    [DI],MESSAGE$STARTED$CODE
```

Change a String in the Buffer

The editor must provide the ability to change data in the buffer. The user should be able to specify that any string present in the buffer be replaced by a user-specified string. The delete facility can be considered a degenerate case of the change facility, in that the user-specified string is a null string.

Consider the case where the sample editor command to change data in the buffer is C string1#string2, where the command functions by locating the next occurrence of string 1 in the buffer and replacing it with string 2. If the buffer appears as follows:

```
                    IN        AL,TOUCH$TONE$DECODER$PORT
Pointer ────────► CMP        AL,COLUMN$4$DIGIT
                    JNZ       TOUCH$TONE$ENCODE
                    MOV       [DI],MESSAGE$STARTED$CODE
```

and the command:

```
         C CODE#TRANCE  ⓡ
```

is entered, the buffer will be altered to

```
                    IN        AL,TOUCH$TONE$DECODER$PORT
                    CMP       AL,COLUMN$4$DIGIT
Pointer ────────► JNZ       TOUCH$TONE$ENTRANCE
                    MOV       [DI],MESSAGE$STARTED$CODE
```

SYSTEM COMMANDS

The editor must provide commands that allow the user to terminate the edit session in a reasonable manner. Reasonable termination methods might include:

- Move all data in the buffer to mass storage.

- Move all unprocessed source code through the buffer to mass storage. This can be considered a normal termination method.

- Exit the edit immediately without flushing the buffer. This method might be used in the case where unwise or unfortunate user manipulation has catastrophically affected the source code. Depending upon the form of mass storage, the user may be able to restore the source code to its original form.

The above types of commands are necessary components for a rudimentary editor. More sophisticated editors would include other capabilities such as:

1. The concatenation of individual commands into command strings.

2. Multiple iterations of command strings. For example, this would be especially useful for changing all occurrences of a particular string in the source code.

3. More sophisticated file-handling. In this discussion, the concept of files has been avoided. The source code has only been discussed in terms of residing on mass storage. More advanced editors are typically run from a fast mass storage device, e.g., hard-disk, and interface with an operating system which provides powerful data file manipulation capabilities. Indeed, some editors relieve the user of the responsibility of reading and writing from the buffer.

With these editors, the user can scroll throughout the source code without worrying about reading/writing source code; this function is performed by the editor automatically.

4. Arithmetic capabilities. Some editors may also be used as very powerful calculators.

5. The ability to extract a certain portion of the buffer and reserve it for later use. This ability can be extremely useful if it is necessary to rearrange the source code, e.g., 100 lines of source code at the beginning of the file must be moved to the middle of the file.

6. The ability to include "ambiguous" elements in any string operation. For example, the search operation might use A*CDE to search for any five-character string where the first character is A, the last three characters are CDE, and the second character may be ambiguous, i.e., any character.

ASSEMBLERS

Most assemblers perform the following functions:

- Separate assembly language source code into individual statements.

- Break each assembly language statement into its component parts. These parts include labels, assembly language operators, assembler directives, operands for the assembly language operators and comments.

- Process each of the component parts according to the rules of the assembly language. From this process, the assembler generates an object code file and a symbol table.

- Write files to mass storage. These files would include an object code file, a listing file (which is comprised of the object code file and the source code file) and a symbol table file.

Separating the source code into the individual assembly language statements is a fairly easy task since most source code files are organized with one statement per line, i.e., there is one statement between two carriage returns. Some assemblers allow more than one statement per line; these statements are usually separated by a special delimiting character which is treated in a similar fashion to the carriage return.

The function that makes an assembler an extremely useful tool is the processing of the individual assembly language statements. The individual parts of the assembly language statement are:

- Labels. There may or may not be a label present in an assembly language instruction. If a label is present, it is saved in a symbol table along with the current value of the location counter. In more complex assemblers, more information may be saved, depending on the type of operator or directive specified.

- Operators. Operators are either assembly language mnemonics, e.g., ADC, STD, IN, or assembler directives. Assembly language mnemonics are translated by the assembler into object code. Some mnemonics require operands, for the precise object code generated will depend on other information present in the assembly language statement. For example, the ADC instruction can generate hundreds of different object codes, but the ADC AX,DX instruction generates a unique object code.

Assembler directives are used to control several functions the assembler employs to generate the object code file and the listing file. These directives control:

- The location at which the source code is assembled. Programs which will include absolute addresses for program memory location must be aware of where they will reside in memory. Consider the case where the sample assembler's location specifying directive is ORG. If the assembler directive

        ORG   0400H

  is included in the source code, the assembly language statements succeeding this one will be assembled assuming that the program counter was set to 0400H.

- The program's starting address. This is typically saved in the object code. Most assemblers allow the starting address of the program to be specified in the last statement of the source code, the END statement. Assuming that the source assembler uses the END statement to specify the starting address, if the statement

        END   STARTOFPROGRAM

  is the last source code statement, then the assembler will generate an object code that includes the address of STARTOFPROGRAM as the starting address.

- The format of the listing file. Directives which control the listing file format could control the pagination, whether or not certain sections of the source and object code are included in the listing file and the various headings associated with the listing file.

- The initial values for data memory locations.

- Operands. Operands, for assembly language mnemonics or assembly language directives that require operands, can appear in a variety of different forms:
  Register names
  Numbers (in one of a number of different bases)
  Variable names
  Labels
  Strings of ASCII characters
  Expressions (a combination of any of the above in conjunction with arithmetic or logical operators)

- Comments. Comments are used to explain the operation of the program. They are ignored by the assembler, but are essential to any user who is interested in modifying the program.

The translation process that the assembler performs is a fairly straightforward task. When the statement has been broken into its constituent parts, the constituent parts are mapped into series of tables which produce pieces of the object code. These pieces are then assembled into the final object code.

DEBUGGERS

A debugger is a development tool that is used to assist in removing errors from object programs. Debuggers, like editors and assemblers, vary in complexity. The most elementary debuggers contain elements that allow the user to:

- Control Execution
- Display register/memory

Debuggers allow the user to control execution by providing facilities such as:

- A single step facility. A single step facility allows the user to execute the object code one instruction at a time. The user is able to view the registers/memory between each instruction's execution, which, hopefully, is sufficient to allow the user to guarantee that the instructions are performing the desired function. More complex debuggers contain sophisticated forms of the single step routine which allow the user to specify the exact number of instructions to be performed and to specify the registers or memory locations that will be displayed following each instruction's execution.

- A breakpoint facility. A breakpoint facility allows the user to control execution by placing a special code, or in the case of the 8086, a software interrupt instruction, into the object code at locations specified by the user. When the special code is executed, it results in a transfer of control to the debugger, thereby halting the execution of the user's object code. At this point, the debugger replaces the original object code at the location modified to contain the special code and allows the user to view the state of the machine.

Debuggers typically allow the user to display the contents of any portion of memory and the contents of the CPU's internal registers, thus allowing a complete view of the state of the machine.

More complex debuggers allow the user to:

- Alter memory/register contents
- Trace object code execution
- Assemble/disassemble object code
- Read/write from mass storage
- Perform simple arithmetic functions
- Use more sophisticated breakpoints
- Manipulate the symbol table

Typical debuggers provide several facilities toward the alteration of memory/register contents. These would include:

- Examine and optionally alter a memory location

- Fill a sequence of memory locations with a constant

- Move the contents of a block of memory locations to another block of memory locations.

Consider the case where the sample debugger command to fill memory locations with a constant is F $addr_1$, $addr_2$, constant. This command would fill all the memory locations from $addr_1$ to $addr_2$ (inclusive) with constant. For example, if the debugger command

F100,17F,20

were entered, the debugger would enter the constant 20_{16} in all locations from 100_{16} to $17F_{16}$.

Debuggers that allow the user to trace the execution of object code usually implement this function as an extension of the single step facility. The user typically specifies the number of steps to be executed and the kind of information to be displayed, thereby allowing the user to watch (trace) the program's execution.

Some debuggers provide a more sophisticated form of memory display in which the user can specify that the memory contents be displayed as assembly language instructions rather than hexadecimal numbers. For example, instead of

D   400,405

resulting in

400   E4 10 24 40 74 FA

the command

L   400

would display memory locations 400-405 as:

```
400    IN  AL,10
402    AND AL,40
404    JZ  400
```

In addition, some debuggers provide a basic assembler facility that the user may employ to alter the contents of memory. Instead of substituting object code,

```
S404   75,
405    FA
```

the user may substitute source code,

```
A404   JNZ
       400
```

A debugger often provides an elementary ability to read and write data to and from mass storage. Typical capabilities include:

- Read an object code file from mass storage to a series of memory locations specified by the user.

- Write an object code file from memory locations specified by the user to mass storage.

- Basic paper tape handling facilities.

Most debuggers provide hexadecimal arithmetic facilities. The user is commonly able to enter two hexadecimal numbers and have the debugger calculate and display the sum and difference of these two numbers.

Debuggers that possess more sophisticated breakpoint facilities usually provide:

- A pass count for each breakpoint. Each time an instruction is fetched from the breakpoint address, the pass count is decremented. When the pass count reaches zero, the user program is suspended and control is returned to the debugger. The user may then view the state of the machine. This feature is particularly useful when debugging program loops. If, for example, the fifty-third iteration of the loop seems to be causing some difficulty, a breakpoint in the loop can be established with a pass count of fifty-three, and the offending iteration can be viewed at the user's leisure. If a pass count capability is not available, stopping the execution of the user program during the fifty-third iteration is not a trivial task.

- A hardware breakpoint facility that suspends the execution of the user's object code when a memory location is accessed for data. This is very useful for occasions when memory locations are being trashed in an unpredictable fashion. Breaking on a memory access typically allows for the identification of the source of the problem.

Sophisticated debuggers often work with a symbol table created by the assembler. These debuggers allow the user to reference memory locations by name. This feature is very helpful when working with relocatable object code. Instead of calculating the address of a particular variable using a load map and a listing, the variable can be referenced directly by name.

6

Examples of 8086 Assembly Language Programming

This chapter presents two examples of 8086 assembly language programming: a sort program and an I/O driver. The specification and program design efforts for these examples were presented earlier in Chapter 2.

SORT PROGRAM

The sort program is divided into three separate modules. These are:

- Read the tape
- Sort the records
- Write the tape

"Read the tape" calls one subroutine:

Read tape record

"Sort the records" calls these four subroutines:

Move subsort to temp
Compare keys
Compute pointer
Move record

"Write the tape" calls one subroutine:

Write tape record

By reviewing the source code, it becomes obvious that not all the subroutine calls are necessary. For example, the "Read tape record" routine is called by only one statement in the source code. But the source code module is clearer than it would be if the entire "Read tape record" routine were included in the source code at the point at which is was called.

The sort program has two abnormal exits. Both of these exits occur in the read/write drivers for the tape controller. For the purposes of this program it is assumed that an operating system is present, and that this operating system will display error messages at an appropriate device, should an anomaly be detected.

```
;EQUATES FOR SORT ROUTINE

TAPE$COMMAND$PORT         EQU   20H        ;ARBITRARY #'S. TYPICALLY
TAPE$STATUS$PORT          EQU   20H        ;THESE #'S WOULD BE LISTED
TAPE$DATA$PORT            EQU   22H        ;IN THE SPECIFICATION.

READ$TAPE$COMMAND         EQU   01H        ;FROM SPECIFICATION
WRITE$TAPE$COMMAND        EQU   02H

OPERATION$COMPLETE$FLAG   EQU   04H
TAPE$ERROR$STATUS         EQU   080H

TAPE$ERROR$FLAG           EQU   044H       ;USED BY SYSTEM

;EXTERNAL REFERENCES

EXTRN SYSTEM:             FAR
EXTRN SYSTEM$ERROR:       FAR
```

```
DATA SEGMENT
;RAM LOCATIONS FOR SORT PROGRAM

RECORD$TEMP         DB    2
KEY$TEMP            DB    10

INDEX              DW    1
INTERVAL           DW    1
SUBSORT$COUNTER    DW    1
RECORD$COUNT       DW    1

TAPE$BUFFER        DB    140 DUP(?)
SORT$AREA          DB    4000 DUP (12 DUP(0))
DATA ENDS
```

```
CODE SEGMENT
ASSUME CS: CODE, DS: DATA, ES: DATA
MAIN:
                    MOV   AX,DATA              ;LOAD SEGMENT REGISTERS
                    MOV   DS,AX
                    MOV   ES,AX
                    MOV   RECORD$COUNT,0       ;SET # OF RECORDS TO 0
                    MOV   DI,OFFSET SORT$AREA  ;POINT DI AT SORT AREA
```

```
; READ THE TAPE MODULE OPERATES BY
; 1.   READING A TAPE RECORD
; 2.   CHECKING FOR DONE
; 3.   MOVING 6 WORDS FROM THE TAPE BUFFER TO THE SORT AREA
; 4.   UPDATING THE # OF RECORDS
;
;

READ$THE$TAPE:      CALL  READ$TAPE$BUFFER       ;READ 128 BYTES
                    MOV   SI,OFFSET TAPE$BUFFER  ;TEST FOR EOF RECORD
                    CMP   [SI],OFFFFH            ;GO SORT IF EOF
                    JZ    SORT                   ;NOT EOF, MOVE RECORD #
                    MOV   CX,12                  ;AND KEY
                    REP   MOVS TAPE$BUFFER,      ;INCREMENT # OF RECORDS
                          SORT$AREA
                    INC   RECORD$COUNT           ;GET ANOTHER BYTE
                    JMP   READ$THE$TAPE
```

The OFFSET operator in the statement

```
        MOV     SI,OFFSET TAPE$BUFFER        ;TEST FOR EOF RECORD
```

is used to generate object code that will load the address of TAPE$BUFFER into the SI register as immediate data. Note that the statement

```
        MOV     SI,TAPE$BUFFER
```

would generate object code that will load the contents of TAPE$BUFFER into the SI register. The OFFSET operator is a feature of the standard Intel 8086 assembler; it is not a characteristic of the 8086 microprocessor.

Note that moving an even number of bytes is easier than moving an odd number of bytes. To move an odd number of bytes, two approaches are possible. One approach is:

```
        MOV     CX, ODD$NUMBER              ;LOAD # OF BYTES
        REP     MOVSB                       ;TO MOVE
```

This approach uses the same number of object code bytes as is used moving an even number of bytes; but it takes twice as long to execute. Another method is:

```
        MOV     CX, ODD$NUMBER              ;LOAD # OF WORDS TO MOVE
        SHR     CX,1
        REP     MOVSW
        MOVSB                               ;MOVE LAST BYTE
```

This method requires one additional byte of object code, but it executes in the same amount of time as a routine to move an even number of bytes.

```
:   THE SORT MODULE IS A STRAIGHTFORWARD RENDITION OF THE ALGORITHM
;   PRESENTED IN CHAPTER 3.

SORT:                       MOV     AX,RECORD$COUNT         ;INITIALIZE INTERVAL TO
                            MOV     INTERVAL,AX             ;RECORD COUNT

NEW$INTERVAL:               SHR     INTERVAL,1              ;DIVIDE INTERVAL BY 2
                            JZ      WRITE$TO$TAPE

                            MOV     AX,RECORD$COUNT         ;SUBSORT CTR=RECORD$
                                                            COUNT- INTERVAL
                            SUB     AX,INTERVAL
                            MOV     SUBSORT$COUNTER,AX

NEXT$SUBSORT$COUNTER:       INC     SUBSORT$COUNTER
                            MOV     AX,SUBSORT$COUNTER
                            CMP     AX,RECORD$COUNT         ;TEST FOR NEW INTERVAL

                            JG      NEW$INTERVAL
                            CALL    MOVE$SUBSORT$ TO$TEMP   ;SAVE CURRENT RECORD

                            MOV     AX,SUBSORT$COUNTER      :INDEX=SUBSORT CTR-INTERVAL
                            SUB     AX,INTERVAL
TEST$KEYS:                  MOV     INDEX,AX
                            CALL    COMPARE$KEYS
                            JGE     FOUND$THIS$RECORDS $SPOT

                            MOV     AX,INDEX
                            CALL    COMPUTE$POINTER
                            MOV     SI,AX
                            CALL    MOVE$RECORD

                            MOV     AX,INTERVAL             ;INDEX-INTERVAL=INDEX
                            SUB     INDEX,AX

                            JGE     TEST$KEYS

FOUND$THIS$RECORDS$SPOT:    MOV     SI,OFFSET RECORD$TEMP
                            CALL    MOVE$RECORD
                            JMP     NEXT$SUBSORT$COUNTER
```

Note that the instruction

```
        SHR     INTERVAL,1
```

is more efficient than the sequence

```
        MOV     AX,INTERVAL
        SHR     AX,1
        MOV     INTERVAL,AX
```

in both memory usage and time consumption. In all cases, it is more efficient to operate on a memory location directly, rather than bringing information into a register, manipulating the information, and then returning the result to a memory location.

```
;   WRITE TAPE OPERATES BY
;   1.  INITIALIZING PTRS TO THE TAPE BUFFER AND SORT AREA
;   2.  MOVING 12 BYTES AT A TIME UNTIL EITHER
;
;
;      128 BYTES HAVE BEEN MOVED
;      END OF FILE IS REACHED
;
;   3.  IF 128 BYTES, WRITE A TAPE RECORD
;   4.  IF END OF FILE, APPEND AN EOF RECORD, THEN WRITE
;   THE LAST TAPE RECORD.
;
WRITE$TO$TAPE:          MOV   SI,OFFSET SORT$AREA
NEXT$TAPE$BUFFER:       MOV   DI,OFFSET TAPE$BUFFER
MOVE$NEXT$RECORD:       MOV   CX,12                      ;GET READY TO MOVE 12 BYTES
                        REP   MOVS  TAPE$BUFFER,$SORT$AREA

                        CMP   DI,OFFSET TAPE$BUFFER + 128
                        JL    UPDATE$RECORD$COUNT         ;TEST FOR MOVED FULL BUFFER

                        PUSH  SI                          ;SAVE POINTERS
                        PUSH  DI
                        CALL  WRITE$TAPE$BUFFER           ;WRITE 128 BYTES TO TAPE

                        POP   DI                          ;RESTORE POINTERS
                        POP   SI
                        MOV   AX,OFFSET TAPE$BUFFER + 128 ;ANY EXTRAS IN END OF TAPE
                        SUB   DI,AX                       ;BUFFER
;   NOTE: TO FILL 128 BYTES REQUIRES MOVING 11 RECORDS OR 11 X 12 =
;   132 BYTES INTO TAPE BUFFER
                        MOV   CX,DI                       ;CX GETS COUNT
                        MOV   DI,OFFSET TAPE$BUFFER
                        JZ    UPDATE$RECORD$COUNT         ;JUMP IF NO EXTRAS
                        PUSH  SI                          ;SAVE POINTER INTO SORT AREA
                        MOV   SI,AX

                        REP   MOVS TAPE$BUFFER,TAPE$BUFFER ;MOVE EXTRAS DOWN TO START
                        POP      SI                        ;OF TAPE BUFFER
UPDATE$RECORD$COUNT:    DEC   RECORD$COUNT
                        JNZ   MOVE$NEXT$RECORD
                        CMP   DI,OFFSET TAPE$BUFFER        ;TEST IF ONE MORE RECORD
                        JZ    WRITE$EOF                    ;MUST BE WRITTEN BEFORE EOF
                        MOV   CX, OFFSET TAPE$BUFFER + 128
                        SUB   CX,DI                        ;ZERO OUT THE REST OF
                        XOR   AL,AL                        ;THE TAPE BUFFER
                        REP   STOS TAPE$BUFFER
                        CALL  WRITE$TAPE$BUFFER            ;WRITE LAST TAPE RECORD.
WRITE$EOF:             MOV   TAPE$BUFFER,0FFFFH           ;MOVE IN END OF FILE RECORD
                        CALL  WRITE$TAPE$BUFFER            ;WRITE EOF RECORD, A
                        JMP   SYSTEM                       ;RECORD WITH FFFF IN
                                                          ;THE FIRST TWO BYTES
                                                          ;END OF PROGRAM
                                                          ;RETURN TO SYSTEM
```

```
;PROCEDURES CALLED BY MAIN PROGRAM

COMPUTE$POINTER        PROC   NEAR
;   AX HAS INDEX
;   RETURN ADDR IS IN AX
;   DX IS NOW 0
                       MOV    CX,12
                       MUL    CX
                       ADD    AX,OFFSET SORT$AREA        ;ADD ADDRESS, NOT DATA

                       RET
COMPUTE$POINTER        ENDP
```

This module's speed can be increased by replacing

```
                       MOV    CX,12
                       MUL    CX
```

with

```
                       SHL    AX,1
                       SHL    AX,1
                       MOV    CX,AX
                       SHL    AX,1
                       ADD    AX,CX
```

The MOV/MUL sequence requires 126 cycles to execute. The second sequence requires 11 cycles to execute and does not destroy the DX register. The MOV/MUL sequence, however, requires only 5 bytes of program memory, whereas the second sequence requires 10 bytes.

```
;   WRITE TAPE BUFFER OPERATES BY
;   1.   POINTING AT THE TAPE BUFFER
;   2.   INITIALIZING THE TAPE CONTROLLER FOR A WRITE
;   3.   CHECKING FOR STATUS ERRORS
;   4.   CHECKING FOR OPERATION DONE
;   5.   WRITING TO THE TAPE DATA PORT

WRITE$TAPE$BUFFER      PROC   NEAR
                       MOV    SI,OFFSET TAPE$BUFFER            ;GET ADDRESS OF TAPE BUFFER
                       MOV    AL,WRITE$TAPE$COMMAND            ;START TAPE WRITE
                       OUT    TAPE$COMMAND$PORT,AL

GET$TAPE$STATUS:       IN     AL,TAPE$STATUS$PORT             ;CHECK FOR ERRORS
                       TEST   AL,TAPE$ERROR$STATUS

                       JNZ    OUTPUT$TAPE$ERROR

                       TEST   AL,OPERATION$COMPLETE$FLAG  ;TEST FOR DONE

                       JNZ    WRITE$COMPLETE

                       LODSB                                  ;GET A BYTE
                       OUT    TAPE$DATA$PORT,AL               ;SHIP IT OUT
                       JMP    GET$TAPE$STATUS
OUTPUT$TAPE$ERROR:     MOV    AH,TAPE$ERROR$FLAG
                       JMP    SYSTEM$ERROR

WRITE$COMPLETE:        RET
WRITE$TAPE$BUFFER      ENDP
```

The TEST operation

```
TEST    AL,TAPE$ERROR$STATUS
```

is used instead of an AND operation so that the status byte in AL will be preserved for a subsequent operation. Since the contents of the AL register are not significant after the test for operaton completed, the

```
TEST    AL,OPERATION$COMPLETE$FLAG
```

operation could be replaced by

```
AND     AL,OPERATION$COMPLETE$FLAG
```

```
;   READ TAPE BUFFER OPERATES BY
;   1. INITIALIZING TAPE CONTROLLER TO READ
;   2. CHECKING FOR TAPE ERRORS
;   3. CHECKING FOR COMPLETION
;   4. READING DATA FROM TAPE DATA PORT
;
;   THIS ROUTINE USES SI AND AL
;
;   IF AN ERROR OCCURS, THIS ROUTINE BRANCHES TO THE SYSTEM
;
;
;
;
READ$TAPE$BUFFER    PROC    NEAR
                    MOV     SI,OFFSET TAPE$BUFFER       ;POINT AT TAPE BUFFER
                    MOV     AL,READ$TAPE$COMMAND        ;TELL TAPE TO READ
                    OUT     TAPE$COMMAND$PORT,AL
GET$STATUS:         IN      AL,TAPE$STATUS$PORT
                    TEST    AL,TAPE$ERROR$STATUS        ;CHECK FOR TAPE ERRORS
                    JNZ     TAPE$ERROR

                    TEST    AL,OPERATION$COMPLETE$FLAG  ;CHECK FOR DONE
                    JNZ     READ$COMPLETE

                    IN      AL,TAPE$DATA$PORT           ;GET DATA
                    MOV     [SI],AL                     ;SAVE DATA
                    INC     SI
                    JMP     GET$STATUS

TAPE$ERROR:         MOV     AH,TAPE$ERROR$FLAG          ;CALL SYSTEM
                    JMP     SYSTEM$ERROR                ;ERROR PROCESSOR
READ$COMPLETE:      RET
READ$TAPE$BUFFER    ENDP
```

Note the similarities between this routine and the WRITE$TAPE$BUFFER routine. There are two differences between the read and write routines.

```
WRITE$TAPE$BUFFER:   MOV     AL,WRITE$TAPE$COMMAND
```

is replaced by

```
READ$TAPE$BUFFER:    MOV     AL,READ$TAPE$COMMAND
```

and

```
                    LODSB
                    OUT     AL,TAPE$DATA$PORT
```

is replaced by

```
                    IN      AL,TAPE$DATA$PORT
                    MOV     [SI],AL
                    INC     SI
```

As an exercise for the reader, meld these two routines together so that the read and write tape buffer routines share common code.

Note that it would be more effective to use the DI register as a pointer into the tape buffer, e.g.,

```
MOV    [SI],AL
INC    SI
```

could be replaced by

```
STOSB
```

However, the DI register is used in the main line of code by the READTHETAPE module.

```
;   COMPARE KEYS OPERATES BY COMPARING KEY (INDEX) WITH KEYTEMP
;   1. CALCULATE INDEX
;   2. COMPARE KEYS UNTIL
;      •  DIFFERENCE IS FOUND
;      •  10 BYTES HAVE BEEN COMPARED
COMPARE$KEYS    PROC    NEAR
                MOV     AX,INDEX                    ;GET INDEX
                CALL    COMPUTE$POINTER

                INC     AX                          ;POINT PAST RECORD #
                INC     AX
                MOV     DI,AX                       ;MOVE TO DI FOR COMPARE
                MOV     SI,OFFSET KEY$TEMP

                MOV     CX,0010                     ;10 BYTES TO COMPARE
                CMPS    KEY$TEMP, SORT$AREA
                                                    ;COMPARE 5 WORDS
                RET
COMPARE$KEYS    ENDP
```

The instruction

```
MOV    SI,OFFSET KEY$TEMP
```

loads the address of KEY$TEMP, not the value at KEY$TEMP, into the SI register.

```
;   MOVE RECORD OPERATES BY MOVING WHATEVER SI POINTS AT TO THE LOCATIONS
;   POINTED TO BY INDEX INTERVAL
;   1.   CALCULATE PTR. FOR INDEX + INTERVAL
;   2.   MOVE 12 BYTES
MOVE$RECORD     PROC    NEAR
                MOV     AX,INDEX
                ADD     AX,INTERVAL                 ;CALC INDEX + INCREMENT

                CALL    COMPUTE$POINTER
                MOV     DI,AX
                REP     MOVS SORT$AREA,SORT$AREA     ;COMPUTER POINTER
                                                     RETURNS CX=12
                RET
MOVE$RECORD     ENDP
```

If it is necessary to save time as opposed to memory space, the sequence

```
MOV      DI,AX
REP      MOVSB
RET
```

can be replaced by

```
MOV      DI,AX
SHR      CX,1
REP      MOVSW
RET
```

Replacing MOVSB with MOVSW saves $6 \times 17 = 102$ clock periods. Subtract the time required for the shift instruction, 2 cycles, and a net savings of 100 cycles is realized.

Note that, for some assemblers, specifying the operands determines byte or word operations from the operand types. For our example

```
MOVS     SORT$AREA,    SORT$AREA
```

is a byte operation since SORT$AREA is a buffer of bytes. The MOVSB and MOVSW forms of MOVS tell the assembler what to do, ignoring operand specification and type checking. For concise and readable code, the former technique is often preferred, while the latter allows overrides for efficiency as in the above example.

```
;   MOVE SUBSORT TO TEMP OPERATES BY:
;   1.   CALCULATING SUBSORT PTR.
;   2.   LOADING POINTER TO RECORD TEMP.
;   3.   MOVING BYTES

MOVE$SUBSORT$TO$TEMP    PROC     NEAR
                        MOV      AX,SUBSORT$COUNTER
                        CALL     COMPUTE$POINTER
                        MOV      SI,AX
                        MOV      DI,OFFSET RECORD$TEMP
                        REP      MOVSB                  ;COMPUTE POINTER RETURNS
                                                        ;CX = 12
                        RET
MOVE$SUBSORT$TO$TEMP    ENDP
```

As with the previous module, the time required to execute this code can be decreased by replacing the sequence

```
REP      MOVSB
```

with

```
SHR      CX,1
REP      MOVSW
```

I/O DRIVER

The coding of the I/O driver program poses two basic problems:

- How should these routines be called by external routines wishing to use them?

- How will the parameters be passed to these routines?

These routines can be called in one of three basic ways:

- Call the operating system, which will pass the request on to the appropriate module

- Call a command handler for the entire driver, which will screen parameters and then pass control to the appropriate module

- Call each of the routines directly, using an address present in the calling routine's code.

In this example we will assume that the routines are called directly; the calling program knows the entry address for each routine. This does not preclude the use of the first two methods; if either of these methods is preferable, a simple dispatch table that points to each of the modules would allow the operating system or command handler to distribute the command to the appropriate module.

As mentioned in Chapter 2, these are the three methods used to pass parameters:

- In the registers

- In a task block

- On the stack.

In this example, the parameters will be passed in the registers, except in the case of multiple character input and output routines. For these functions task blocks will be defined. Multiple character input uses the following task block:

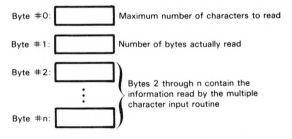

Multiple character output uses the following task block:

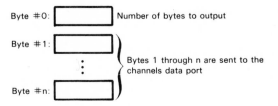

```
CONTROL$PORT                          EQU    12H
STATUS$PORT                           EQU    12H
DATA$PORT                             EQU    10H
;   IF BIT 0 OF THE AH REGISTER IS 1, THE USER HAS LOADED SI WITH A
;   POINTER TO THE STRING TO BE SENT TO THE CONTROL PORT. IF BIT 0 IS A 0, A
;   STANDARD INITIALIZATION STRING WILL BE SENT
;
USER$INITIALIZATION$BIT               EQU    01H
TIMEOUT$VALUE                         EQU    0F000H
;   BITS 3, 4, AND 5 OF THE SIO STATUS BYTE ARE ERROR BITS
SIO$ERRORS                            EQU    38H
;   BIT 1 INDICATES WHETHER OR NOT THE RECEIVER IS READY
;   BIT 0 INDICATES WHETHER OR NOT THE TRANSMITTER IS READY
SIO$RECEIVER$READY                    EQU    02H
SIO$TRANNY$READY                      EQU    01H
TIMEOUT$ERROR$FLAG                    EQU    0FFH
;   CARRIAGE RETURN IS TERMINATION CHARACTER FOR READ
CARRIAGE$RETURN                       EQU    0DH
;   '$' IS TERMINATION CHARACTER FOR WRITE
TERMINATION$CHARACTER                 EQU    24H
EXTRN SYSTEM$ERROR:                   FAR
```

```
CODE SEGMENT
   ASSUME CS: CODE
;   THE INITIALIZATION OPERATES BY:
;   1.   TESTING FOR USER SPECIFIED OR
;        SYSTEM INITIALIZATION STRING
;   2.   SENDING THE STRING TO THE CONTROL PORT,
;        TERMINATING WHEN A 0 IS DETECTED
;
;   THIS ROUTINE USES AX AND SI

INITIALIZATION          PROC   NEAR
                        AND    AH,USER$INITIALIZATION$BIT              ;TEST FOR USER INIT
                        JNZ    SI$LOADED$BY$USER
                        MOV    SI,OFFSET PORT$INITIALIZATION$STRING ;LOAD STANDARD STRING
SI$LOADED$BY$USER:      LODSB
                        OR     AL,AL                                   ;SET FLAGS TO TEST FOR 0
                        JZ     DO$A$RETURN                             ;EXIT IF 0
                        OUT    CONTROL$PORT,AL
                        JMP    SI$LOADED$BY$USER

PORT$INITIALIZATION$STRING DB       0CEH,40H,0CEH,37H,00H
DO$A$RETURN:               RET
INITIALIZATION             ENDP
```

A four-byte initialization string is necessary to allow for the fact that the 8251 is not in a known state when this routine is called. If, for example, a two-byte sequence

$$\begin{array}{ll} CE_{16} & \text{Mode} \\ 37_{16} & \text{Command} \end{array}$$

were sent to the 8251, the 8251 would not be correctly initialized, since it could have been waiting for a Command Control Input. If a three-byte sequence

$$\begin{array}{ll} 40_{16} & \text{Command (Reset)} \\ CF_{16} & \text{Mode} \\ 37_{16} & \text{Command} \end{array}$$

were sent, the 8251 would not be correctly initialized if it happened to be waiting for a Mode Control Input. The four-byte sequence, however, will correctly initialize the 8251 regardless of its prior state.

```
;   SINGLE CHARACTER INPUT OPERATES BY:
;   1.   LOADING TIMEOUT VALUE
;   2.   READING THE STATUS PORT AND TESTING FOR SIO ERRORS
;   3.   CHECKING FOR TIMEOUT ERRORS
;   4.   READING THE DATA
;
;   THIS ROUTINE USES AX AND CX
;
;   IF ZFLAG IS 1 ON RETURN - ERROR CONDITION
;   IF ZFLAG IS 0 ON RETURN - NORMAL OPERATION
;   ERROR CONDITIONS RETURNED IN AH

SINGLE$CHARACTER$INPUT      PROC      NEAR
                            MOV       CX,TIMEOUT$VALUE

TEST$STATUS:                IN        AL,STATUS$PORT           ;READ STATUS
                            TEST      AL,SIO$ERRORS            ;CHECK FOR ERRORS

                            JNZ       INPUT$ERROR$RETURN
                            DEC       CX                       ;CHECK FOR TIMEOUT
                            JZ        INPUT$TIMEOUT$ERROR$RETURN
                            AND       AL,SIO$RECEIVER$READY    ;RECEIVER READY?
                            JZ        TEST$STATUS

                            IN        AL,DATA$PORT             ;GET VALUE
                            RET

INPUT$ERROR$RETURN:         MOV       AH,AL                    ;SAVE STATUS
                            XOR       AL,AL                    ;SET ZERO FLAG
                            RET

INPUT$TIMEOUT$ERROR$        MOV       AH,TIMEOUT$ERROR$FLAG    ;FF IS TIMEOUT ERROR
  RETURN:                   RET
SINGLE$CHARACTER$INPUT      ENDP
```

The sequence

```
                            DEC       CX
                            JZ        INPUT$TIMEOUT$ERROR$RETURN
                            AND       AL,SIO$RECEIVER$READY
```

could be replaced by

```
                            LOOP      NO$TIMEOUT
                            MOV       AH,0FFH                  ;TIMEOUT ERROR
                            RET
    NO$TIMEOUT:             AND       AL,SIO$RECEIVER$READY
```

This would result in shorter and faster object code. However, it would sacrifice source code clarity.

```
;  SINGLE CHARACTER OUTPUT OPERATES BY:
;  1.   LOADING TIMEOUT VALUE
;  2.   READING STATUS PORT
;  3.   CHECKING FOR TIMEOUT ERROR
;  4.   SENDING DATA TO OUTPUT PORT IF TRANSMITTER IS READY
;
;  IF ZFLAG IS 1 ON RETURN - ERROR
;  IF ZFLAG IS 0 ON RETURN - NORMAL
;
;  THIS ROUTINE USES AX, CX, AND DH

SINGLE$CHARACTER$OUTPUT    PROC    NEAR
                           MOV     CX,TIMEOUT$VALUE
                           MOV     DH,AL
TRANNY$READY:              IN      AL,STATUS$PORT
                           TEST    AL,SIO$ERRORS
                           JNZ     OUTPUT$ERROR$RETURN
                           DEC     CX                       ;TEST FOR TIMEOUT
                           JZ      OUTPUT$TIMEOUT$ERROR$RETURN
                           AND     AL,SIO$TRANNY$READY    ;CHECK FOR TRANSMITTER READY
                           JZ      TRANNY$READY

                           MOV     AL,DH              GET DATA FROM DH
                           OUT     DATA$PORT,AL
                           RET
OUTPUT$TIMEOUT$ERROR$      MOV     AH,TIMEOUT$ERROR$FLAG
 RETURN:                   RET
OUTPUT$ERROR$RETURN:       MOV     AH,AL
                           XOR     AL,AL
                           RET
SINGLE$CHARACTER$OUTPUT    ENDP
```

As with the previous module, the timeout error return could be included in the mainline code. This would be accomplished by replacing

```
                           DEC     CX
                           JZ      OUTPUT$TIMEOUT$ERROR$RETURN
                           AND     AL,SIO$TRANNY$READY
```

with

```
                           LOOP    NO$TIMEOUT
                           MOV     AH,0FFH
                           RET
     NO$TIMEOUT:           AND     AL,SIO$TRANNY$READY
```

and deleting the last three lines of the source code.

| CHECK$CHANNEL$STATUS | PROC
IN
RET | NEAR
AL,STATUS$PORT | ;READ |
| CHECK$CHANNEL$STATUS | ENDP | | |

| SEND$CONTROL$INFORMATION | PROC
OUT
RET | NEAR
AL,CONTROL$PORT | ;WRITE |
| SEND$CONTROL$INFORMATION | ENDP | | |

```
;   MULTIPLE CHARACTER INPUT OPERATES BY:
;   1.  GETTING # OF BYTES TO READ
;   2.  CALLING SINGLE CHARACTER INPUT UNTIL
;     •  ERROR FROM SINGLE CHAR
;     •  THE MAXIMUM # OF CHARACTERS HAVE BEEN ENTERED
;     •  A TERMINATION CHARACTER (CARRIAGE RETURN) IS ENTERED
;   THIS ROUTINE IS CALLED WITH SI POINTING AT THE TASK BLOCK
;
;THIS ROUTINE USES SI, DI, AX, CX
```

MULTIPLE$CHARACTER$INPUT	PROC LODSB OR JZ MOV MOV INC	NEAR AL,AL ZERO$COUNT$THEN$RETURN DL,AL DI,SI DI	 ;LOAD MAX # OF BYTES TO READ ;SAVE MAX # IN DL ;POINT AT BUFFER
GETACHARACTER:	CALL JZ STOSB INC CMP JZ CMP JNZ	SINGLE$CHARACTER$INPUT INPUT$ERROR BYTE PRT [SI] DL,[SI] ZERO$COUNT$THEN$RETURN AL,CARRIAGE$RETURN GETACHARACTER	;GET CHARACTER ;INCREMENT # READ ;TEST FOR READ MAXIMUM #
ZERO$COUNT$THEN$RETURN:	RET		
INPUT$ERROR:	JMP	SYSTEM$ERROR	
MULTIPLE$CHARACTER$INPUT	ENDP		

The sequence

```
        OR      AL,AL
        JZ      ZERO$COUNT$THEN$RETURN
```

checks for a zero number of bytes to be read.

DI is used as the pointer into the input buffer because of the string primitive, STOSB, which saves the data and increments the pointer in one instruction. This assumes that the Direction Flag is set correctly.

```
;   MULTIPLE CHARACTER OUTPUT OPERATES BY:
;   1.   GETTING THE NUMBER OF CHARACTERS TO WRITE
;   2.   CALLING SINGLE CHARACTER OUTPUT UNTIL
;        •   ERROR FROM SINGLE CHARACTER OUTPUT
;        •   THE MAXIMUM # OF CHARACTERS HAVE BEEN WRITTEN
;
;   THIS ROUTINE IS CALLED WITH SI POINTING AT THE TASK BLOCK
;
;   THIS ROUTINE USES AX, SI, DX, AND CX

MULTIPLE$CHARACTER$OUTPUT  PROC      NEAR
                           LODSB
                           OR        AL,AL
                           JZ        DO$RETURN
                           MOV       DL,AL                          ;SAVE # OF BYTES TO
                                                                     OUTPUT
OUTPUT$A$CHARACTER:        LODSB
                           CMP       AL,TERMINATION$CHARACTER
                           JZ        DO$RETURN                      ;TEST FOR TERMINATION
                                                                     CHARACTER
                           CALL      SINGLE$CHARACTER$OUTPUT
                           JZ        OUTPUT$ERROR
                           DEC       DL
                           JNZ       OUTPUT$A$CHARACTER
DO$RETURN:                 RET

OUTPUT$ERROR:              JMP       SYSTEM$ERROR
MULTIPLE$CHARACTER$OUTPUT  ENDP
```

7

8086 Microprocessor Description

This is the first chapter devoted to methods of interfacing the 8086 with external logic. Therefore this chapter will examine the signals that the 8086 produces and receives, and will look, in overview, at 8086 system concepts.

This chapter and those that follow deal exclusively with the timing of the 5 MHz standard 8086. The equations provided may also be applied to the 8 and 10 MHz versions by appropriate substitution in the A.C. parameters.

8086 CPU PINS AND SIGNALS

8086 CPU pins and signals are illustrated in Figure 7-1. With the exception of those signals that are specifically labelled, all inputs and outputs are TTL-level compatible.

All microprocessors produce or receive the following kinds of signals:

- Address Lines
- Data Lines
- Control and Status Lines
- Power and Timing Lines

The 8086's 40-pin package has all four types of signals. Some pins carry more than one type of information. For example, the data and address lines are multiplexed. Other pins have their functions defined by the level present at the $MN/\overline{MX}$ pin.

The discussion that follows will describe the function of each pin when $MN/\overline{MX}$ is high or low.

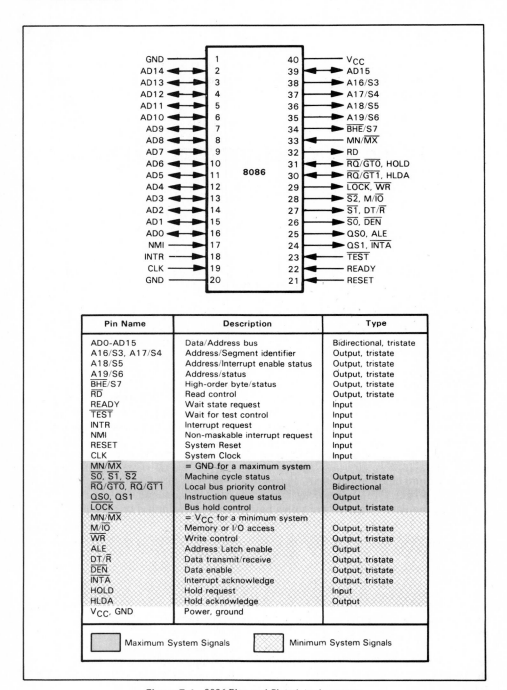

Figure 7-1. 8086 Pins and Signal Assignments

Pin Name	Description	Type
AD0-AD15	Data/Address bus	Bidirectional, tristate
A16/S3, A17/S4	Address/Segment identifier	Output, tristate
A18/S5	Address/Interrupt enable status	Output, tristate
A19/S6	Address/status	Output, tristate
$\overline{BHE}$/S7	High-order byte/status	Output, tristate
$\overline{RD}$	Read control	Output, tristate
READY	Wait state request	Input
$\overline{TEST}$	Wait for test control	Input
INTR	Interrupt request	Input
NMI	Non-maskable interrupt request	Input
RESET	System Reset	Input
CLK	System Clock	Input
MN/$\overline{MX}$	= GND for a maximum system	
$\overline{S0}$, $\overline{S1}$, $\overline{S2}$	Machine cycle status	Output, tristate
$\overline{RQ}/\overline{GT0}$, $\overline{RQ}/\overline{GT1}$	Local bus priority control	Bidirectional
QS0, QS1	Instruction queue status	Output
$\overline{LOCK}$	Bus hold control	Output, tristate
MN/$\overline{MX}$	= V$_{CC}$ for a minimum system	
M/$\overline{IO}$	Memory or I/O access	Output, tristate
$\overline{WR}$	Write control	Output, tristate
ALE	Address Latch enable	Output
DT/$\overline{R}$	Data transmit/receive	Output, tristate
$\overline{DEN}$	Data enable	Output, tristate
$\overline{INTA}$	Interrupt acknowledge	Output, tristate
HOLD	Hold request	Input
HLDA	Hold acknowledge	Output
V$_{CC}$, GND	Power, ground	

Maximum System Signals   Minimum System Signals

ADDRESS AND DATA LINES

The 8086 CPU can directly address one million (1M) bytes of memory — which means that 20 bits of address information are necessary.

The 8086 CPU accesses data in 16-bit units, treated as a low-order byte and a high-order byte.

To allow for a 20-bit address bus and a 16-bit data bus on a 40-pin package, the data bus is multiplexed with the least significant 16 bits of the address bus. The four additional address lines are multiplexed with status information. The address/data and address/status signals are:

> AD0-AD15
> A16/S3
> A17/S4
> A18/S5
> A19/S6
> BHE/S7

Let us examine these lines in detail.

AD0-AD15. These 16 lines are the multiplexed address bus/data bus lines. During the first clock period of a bus cycle, these lines contain the low-order 16 address bits. During all other clock cycles, these lines are used as the data bus. These lines are put into the high impedance state when the 8086 is performing an interrupt acknowledge cycle or a "hold acknowledge" cycle.

A16/S3. During the first clock period of an instruction's execution, this line serves as address line 16. If an I/O instruction is performed, this line is low during the first clock period. During all other clock periods, this line is used in conjunction with line A17/S4 to provide status information.

A17/S4. During the first clock period of an instruction's execution, this line serves as address line 17. If an I/O instruction is performed, this line is low during the first clock period. During other cycles, this line is used in conjunction with line A16/S3 to provide status information.

During all clock periods but the first, A16/S3 and A17/S4 provide information that specifies which segment register is producing the segment portion of the 8086 address, as follows:

A17/S4	A16/S3	Meaning
0	0	Extra Segment
0	1	Stack segment
1	0	Code segment or no segment
1	1	Data segment

This information can be used by external logic to expand the 8086 memory space so that each segment register addresses its own unique 1M byte of memory, but it would then be impossible to overlap memory addresses computed in different segments.

A18/S5. During the first clock period of an instruction's execution, this line serves as address line 18. If an I/O instruction is executed, this line is low during the first clock period. During all other clock periods, this line reflects the state of the 8086's Interrupt Enable flag.

A19/S6. During the first clock period of an instruction's execution, this line serves as address line 19. If an I/O instruction is performed, this line is low during the first clock period. During all other cycles, the 8086 holds this line low if it is controlling the system bus. During a "hold acknowledge" clock period, the 8086 will float this line, allowing another bus master to take control of the system bus.

$\overline{\text{BHE}}$/S7. During the first clock period of an instruction's execution, this line is used as $\overline{\text{BHE}}$. $\overline{\text{BHE}}$ is held low during read, write, and interrupt acknowledge sequences in which data is to be transferred on the high-order eight bits of the data bus. This signal is used in conjunction with the AD0 line to generate select logic for memory banks. A more extensive discussion of 8086 memory selection is present in the next section. During the second and subsequent clock periods $\overline{\text{BHE}}$/S7 maintains its first clock period output level.

CONTROL AND STATUS LINES

8086 control and status lines can be divided into two categories: those which are not affected by the level at the MN/$\overline{\text{MX}}$ pin and those whose function depends on the value at the MN/$\overline{\text{MX}}$ pin. Those which are not affected include:

$\overline{\text{RD}}$
READY
$\overline{\text{TEST}}$
INTR
NMI
RESET

$\overline{\text{RD}}$ is output low when the CPU is reading data from a memory location or an I/O device. The $\overline{\text{S2}}$-(M/$\overline{\text{IO}}$) pin specifies whether a memory or I/O access is requested.

READY is used by a selected memory or I/O device to indicate that it is ready to accomplish the data transfer operation. A signal ($\overline{\text{RDY1}}$ or $\overline{\text{RDY2}}$) is input to the 8284 Clock Generator, which then synchronizes the READY input with the clock. If READY is input low at the appropriate time, then the 8086 will execute "Wait" states until READY is raised high.

$\overline{\text{TEST}}$ is an input that is only used by the 8086 WAIT instruction. When the WAIT instruction is executed, the 8086 will pause until $\overline{\text{TEST}}$ is input low.

INTR is an interrupt request input. This signal is sampled by the 8086 during the final clock period of each instruction's execution. If the interrupt enable bit is a 1 and INTR is high, then the 8086 will execute an interrupt acknowledge sequence and transfer control to the appropriate interrupt service routine. Otherwise the next instruction will be executed. INTR is a level triggered input.

NMI is a non-maskable interrupt request input. NMI is an edge triggered input. Should NMI go from low to high, the 8086 will complete execution of the current instruction, and then transfer control to a non-maskable interrupt service routine. The address of the non-maskable interrupt service routine is present at memory location 00008_{16}. Software may not disable this interrupt.

RESET is a system reset signal; it must be input high to the 8284 Clock Generator for at least four CLK clock periods, except on power-up, when RESET must last at least 50μs. The 8284 synchronizes RESET and re-transmits it to the 8086. When the RESET returns to low, the following events occur:

1. The Flags register is set to 0000_{16}. This has the effect of disabling interrupts and single stepping mode
2. The DS, SS, ES and PC registers are reset to 0000_{16}
3. The CS register is set to $FFFF_{16}$

Execution will continue from memory location $FFFF_{16}$.
The signals that are affected by the MN/$\overline{MX}$ pin include:

```
Max    Min
S̄0-(D̄ĒN)
S̄1-(DT/R̄)
S̄2-(M/ĪŌ)
R̄Q̄/ḠT̄0-(HOLD)
R̄Q̄/ḠT̄1-(HLDA)
QS0-(ALE)
QS1-(ĪNT̄Ā)
L̄ŌCK̄-(W̄R̄)
```

When MN/$\overline{MX}$ is grounded, the 8086 is said to be in "maximum mode." When MN/$\overline{MX}$ is high the 8086 is said to be in "minimum mode."

S̄0-(D̄ĒN). If the MN/$\overline{MX}$ pin is grounded, this pin functions as $\overline{S0}$. $\overline{S0}$ is used with $\overline{S1}$-(DT/$\overline{R}$) and the $\overline{S2}$-(M/$\overline{IO}$) to provide status information. This status information is discussed following the description of $\overline{S2}$-(M/$\overline{IO}$). If the MN/$\overline{MX}$ pin level is high, this pin functions as $\overline{DEN}$. $\overline{DEN}$ is used to control the 8286/8287 buffers by enabling the buffers' data transceivers onto the system or local bus (as determined by DT/$\overline{R}$).

S̄1-(DT/R̄). If the MN/$\overline{MX}$ pin is grounded, this pin functions as $\overline{S1}$. $\overline{S1}$ is used with $\overline{S0}$-($\overline{DEN}$) and the $\overline{S2}$-(M/$\overline{IO}$) to provide status information. This information is discussed following the description of $\overline{S2}$-(M/$\overline{IO}$). If the MN/$\overline{MX}$ pin level is high, this pin functions as DT/$\overline{R}$. DT/$\overline{R}$ is used to control the 8286/8287 buffers, signalling the direction of the data transfer. If DT/$\overline{R}$ is high, the transceivers place data on the system bus; if DT/$\overline{R}$ is low, the transceivers take data off the system bus. The 8288 Bus Controller also generates DEN and DT/$\overline{R}$ outputs. If the Bus Controller is present, its DEN and DT/$\overline{R}$ outputs are used instead of 8086 $\overline{DEN}$ and DT/$\overline{R}$ outputs. We describe these different configurations later.

S̄2-(M/ĪŌ). If the MN/$\overline{MX}$ pin is grounded, this pin functions as $\overline{S2}$. $\overline{S2}$ is used with $\overline{S0}$-($\overline{DEN}$) and $\overline{S1}$-(DT/$\overline{R}$) pin to provide the status information described below. If the MN/$\overline{MX}$ pin level is high, this pin functions as M/$\overline{IO}$. During a memory or I/O access M/$\overline{IO}$ is high for a memory access and low for an I/O access.

If the MN/$\overline{\text{MX}}$ pin is grounded, status is provided to the 8288 Bus Controller via $\overline{\text{S0}}$, $\overline{\text{S1}}$, and $\overline{\text{S2}}$ as follows:

$\overline{\text{S2}}$	$\overline{\text{S1}}$	$\overline{\text{S0}}$	
0	0	0	Interrupt Acknowledge
0	0	1	I/O Read
0	1	0	I/O Write
0	1	1	Halt
1	0	0	Instruction Fetch
1	0	1	Memory Read
1	1	0	Memory Write
1	1	1	Inactive

This information is used by the 8288 Bus Controller to generate memory and I/O control signals for a maximum mode system.

QS0-(ALE). If the MN/$\overline{\text{MX}}$ pin is grounded, this pin functions as QS0. QS0 is used with the QS1-($\overline{\text{INTA}}$) pin to provide 8086 instruction queue status. The instruction queue, which we describe later in detail, is a six-byte space within the 8086 microprocessor; it is used to hold object code bytes awaiting execution. If the MN/$\overline{\text{MX}}$ pin level is high, QS0-(ALE) functions as ALE. A high ALE pulse is output while a valid memory address is present on the address/data bus. In a maximum mode system, ALE is provided by the 8288 Bus Controller.

QS1-($\overline{\text{INTA}}$). If the MN/$\overline{\text{MX}}$ pin is grounded, this pin functions as QS1. QS1 is used with QS0-(ALE) to provide 8086 instruction queue status, as described below. If the MN/$\overline{\text{MX}}$ pin level is high, this pin functions as $\overline{\text{INTA}}$. $\overline{\text{INTA}}$ is output low while the 8086 is executing an interrupt acknowledge sequence. In a maximum system $\overline{\text{INTA}}$ is provided by the 8288 Bus Controller.

If the MN/$\overline{\text{MX}}$ pin is grounded, 8086's instruction queue status is provided by QS0 and QS1 as follows:

QS0	QS1	
0	0	No operation
0	1	The first byte of an instruction is being executed
1	0	The queue is being emptied
1	1	A subsequent instruction byte is being taken from the queue

QS0 and QS1 are valid during the clock period that follows any queue operation.

$\overline{\text{RQ}}$/$\overline{\text{GT0}}$-(HOLD). If the MN/$\overline{\text{MX}}$ pin is grounded, this pin functions as $\overline{\text{RQ}}$/$\overline{\text{GT0}}$. $\overline{\text{RQ}}$/$\overline{\text{GT0}}$ is a request/grant line. Other bus masters may force the 8086 to enter a HOLD state by inputting a low pulse at this pin. The 8086 will acknowledge that it is entering a HOLD state by outputting a low pulse via $\overline{\text{RQ}}$/$\overline{\text{GT0}}$ to the requesting bus master. The 8086 will then relinquish control of the system bus and three-state outputs. When the new bus master subsequently relinquishes control of the system bus, it does so by sending another low $\overline{\text{RQ}}$/$\overline{\text{GT0}}$ pulse. The 8086 then reasserts bus control. Request/grant sequences are described in detail in Chapter 8. If the MN/$\overline{\text{MX}}$ pin level is high, $\overline{\text{RQ}}$/$\overline{\text{GT0}}$-(HOLD) functions as HOLD. HOLD is used as a HOLD request line by external logic. When external logic sets the HOLD level high, the 8086 will enter a HOLD state upon completing the current bus cycle. The 8086 acknowledges that it has entered the HOLD state by outputting HLDA high.

RQ/GT1-(HLDA). If the MN/$\overline{\text{MX}}$ pin is grounded, this pin functions as $\overline{\text{RQ}/\text{GT1}}$. $\overline{\text{RQ}/\text{GT1}}$ is functionally identical to $\overline{\text{RQ}/\text{GT0}}$, except that $\overline{\text{RQ}/\text{GT1}}$ has lower priority than $\overline{\text{RQ}/\text{GT0}}$. If an $\overline{\text{RQ}/\text{GT0}}$ request/grant sequence is not in progress, then the 8086 can begin an $\overline{\text{RQ}/\text{GT1}}$ request/grant sequence. Request grant sequences are covered in detail in Chapter 8. If the MN/$\overline{\text{MX}}$ pin level is high, $\overline{\text{RQ}/\text{GT1}}$-(HLDA) functions as HLDA. HLDA is the HOLD Acknowledge signal. HLDA is output high to acknowledge a Hold request made via HOLD. When the HLDA signal is raised high, the 8086 CPU also floats its three-state output signals. Thus it floats the system bus.

LOCK-($\overline{\text{WR}}$). If the MN/$\overline{\text{MX}}$ pin is grounded, this pin functions as the $\overline{\text{LOCK}}$ pin. $\overline{\text{LOCK}}$ is output low to prevent the 8086 from losing system bus control while executing an instruction. While $\overline{\text{LOCK}}$ is low, external hardware should guarantee that other bus masters do not gain control of the system bus. When the 8086 executes a $\overline{\text{LOCK}}$ instruction the $\overline{\text{LOCK}}$ signal is output low for the duration of the next instruction's execution. If the MN/$\overline{\text{MX}}$ pin level is high, LOCK-($\overline{\text{WR}}$) functions as the $\overline{\text{WR}}$ pin. $\overline{\text{WR}}$ is pulsed low during a memory or I/O write. The trailing edge of the pulse occurs while the data being output is stable on the address/data bus.

POWER AND TIMING LINES

CLK is the clock signal used to synchronize all 8086 logic. This signal is typically output by the 8284 Clock Generator.

Vcc is the power supply pin. The 8086 requires +5 V ± 10% be present on this pin.

There are two **GND** pins. These are both ground pins.

Three-state Lines and Signals

The following 8086 signals are three-state signals:

```
AD0-AD15
A16/S3
A17/S4
A18/S5
A19/S6
BHE/S7
RD
S0-(DEN)
S1-(DT/R)
S2-(M/IO)
LOCK-(WR)
INTA
```

All of these signals are in the high impedance state while the 8086 is in a HOLD state. The $\overline{\text{S0}}$-($\overline{\text{DEN}}$), $\overline{\text{S1}}$-(DT/$\overline{\text{R}}$), and $\overline{\text{S2}}$-(M/$\overline{\text{IO}}$) signals are floated just prior to 8086 issuing a hold acknowledge.

During an interrupt acknowledge, the AD0-AD15, A16/S3, A17/S4, A18/S5, A19/S6 lines are floated.

8086 OVERVIEW AND BASIC SYSTEM CONCEPTS

This section discusses basic 8086 system concepts, including bus cycles, the address/data bus, the system data bus, the Execution Unit, the Bus Interface Unit, and the instruction queue.

8086 BUS CYCLE DEFINITION

The 8086 communicates with external logic via its system bus. The 8086 executes "bus cycles" to transfer data or fetch instructions. A "bus cycle" is shown in Figure 7-2.

The minimum bus cycle consists of four CPU clock periods called T States. During the first T state (T1), the 8086 outputs an address on the 20-bit multiplexed address/data/status bus. The address on the bus is considered valid when the ALE signal makes the transition from high to low. In a minimum system, this signal is produced by the 8086. In a maximum system, this sgnal is produced by the 8288 Bus Controller. The $\overline{S2}$-(M/$\overline{IO}$) signal indicates whether a memory or an I/O access is being performed.

During the second T State (T2), the 8086 removes the address from the address bus. For a read bus cycle the data bus lines are floated in preparation for a read cycle. For a write bus cycle data is output on the data bus lines.

Data bus transceivers are enabled in either T1 or T2, depending on the 8086 system configuration, and the direction of the transfer (into or out of the 8086). Read, write, or interrupt acknowledge control signals are always enabled in T2.

During T2, bus cycle status (S3, S4, S5, S6) is output on the upper four address/status bus lines. The status information below is available for the rest of the bus cycle.

S4	S3	
0	0	Extra (Relative to the ES segment)
0	1	Stack (Relative to the SS segment)
1	0	Code/None (Relative to the CS segment or a default zero)
1	1	Data (Relative to the DS segment)

S5 = IF (Interrupt enable flag)
S6 = 0 (Indicates the 8086 is on the bus)

The 8086 continues to provide status information on the upper four address/status bus lines during T3. Also, the 8086 continues to output data during a write bus cycle. For a read bus cycle, the 8086 samples input data at the end of T3. If the selected device is not capable of transferring data at the required transfer rate, the device must signal "not ready" by inputting READY low. This causes the 8086 to insert additional clock cycles after T3. These additional clock cycles are designated as Tw states (wait states). The "not ready" indication must be presented to the CPU before the start of T3. Bus activity during Tw is the same as T3. When the selected device has had sufficient time to complete the transfer, it raises READY high. After Tw clock periods end, T4, the last clock period of the bus cycle, is executed.

During T4, memory and I/O control lines are disabled and the selected external device disconnects itself from the system bus.

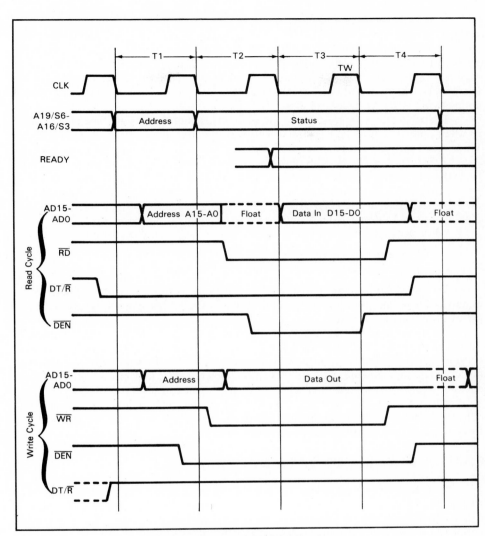

Figure 7-2. Basic 8086 Bus Cycles

A bus cycle appears to devices on the system bus as an asynchronous event, consisting of an address to select the device, and a register or memory location within the device, plus a read strobe, or a write strobe with accompanying data. The selected device accepts bus data during a write cycle; the selected device must place data on the bus during a read cycle. At the end of the bus cycle, the device latches written data or disables its bus drivers. The only way a device can modify a bus cycle is by inserting wait state clock periods via the READY control input.

The 8086 only executes a bus cycle when instruction fetches are being performed or when operands must be transferred between the 8086 and memory or I/O devices. When not executing a bus cycle, 8086 bus interface logic executes idle clock periods (labeled TI). During idle clock periods the 8086 continues to output status information from the previous bus cycle on the four upper address lines. If the previous bus cycle was a write, the CPU continues to output data onto the 16 data bus lines until the start of the next bus cycle. If the 8086 executes idle clock periods following a read cycle, the 8086 floats the 16 data bus lines until the start of the next bus cycle.

When accessing memory, the 8086 performs two types of operations:

- An instruction fetch
- A memory access to read or write operands required by the instruction

The normally simple sequential relationship between instruction fetch and memory access bus cycles is modified in the 8086 by the presence of a 6-byte instruction object code queue.

If the 8086 bus interface logic would otherwise be idle, instead it executes instruction fetch bus cycles during which it fetches the next sequential object code bytes from program memory, until the instruction queue is full. If more than one instruction's object code is in the queue, then an instruction fetch bus cycle may be separated from its operand memory access bus cycles by additional instruction fetch bus cycles.

When a jump or call instruction is executed, the next sequential instruction's object code bytes, currently in the instruction queue, are no longer needed. Queue contents are therefore discarded with no adverse effects.

8086 ADDRESS AND DATA BUS CONCEPTS

Since most memory devices and peripherals that interface to the 8086 require a stable address for an entire bus cycle, the address present on the multiplexed address/ data bus during T1 should be latched. This latched address is used to select the desired peripheral or memory location. To demultiplex the address/data bus, the 8086 provides an Address Latch Enable signal (ALE), which can be used to capture the address either in 8282 or in 8283 8-bit bistable latches.

These latches are either inverting (8283) or non-inverting (8282) and have outputs driven by tristate buffers that supply 32 mA drive capability and can switch a 300 pF capacitive load in 22 ns (inverting) or 30 ns (non-inverting). The 8282/8283 latches propagate the address through to the outputs while ALE is high and latch the address on the following edge of ALE. But this delays address access and chip select decoding by the propagation delay of the latch.

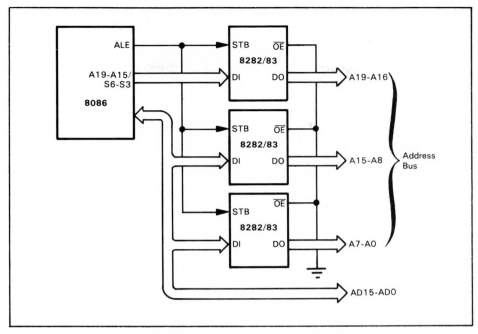

Figure 7-3. Demultiplexing the Address/Data Bus

The latch outputs are enabled by the low active $\overline{OE}$ input. Demultiplexing of the multiplexed address/data bus (latchings of the address from the multiplexed bus) can be handled locally at appropriate points in the system or at the CPU, with a separate address bus distributing the address throughout the system.

For optimum system performance and compatibility with multiprocessor and Multibus configurations, local demultiplexing, illustrated in Figure 7-4, is strongly recommended over distributed demultiplexing, as illustrated in Figure 7-5. The remainder of this chapter will assume the bus is demultiplexed at the CPU, as illustrated in Figure 7-4.

The 8086 memory address space can be viewed as a sequence of one million bytes in which any byte may contain an 8-bit data element and any two consecutive bytes may contain a 16-bit data element. There is no constraint on byte or word address boundaries. The address space is physically connected to a 16-bit data bus by dividing the address space into two 8-bit banks of up to 512K bytes each.

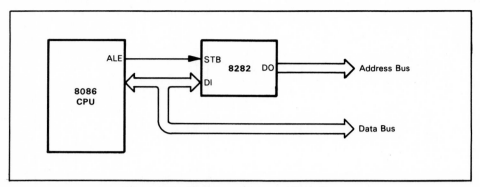

Figure 7-4. Separate Address and Data Busses

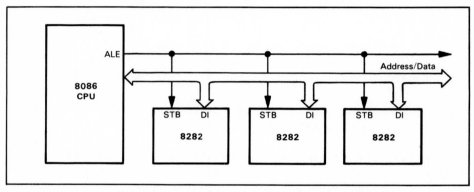

Figure 7-5. Multiplexed Bus with Local Address Demultiplexing

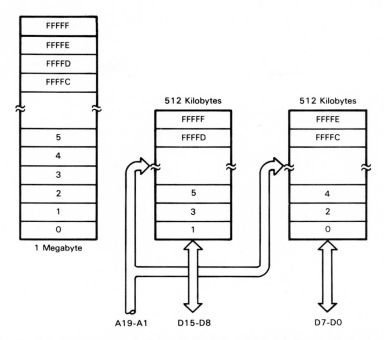

One bank is connected to the lower half of the 16-bit data bus (D7-0) and contains even address bytes (A0=0). The other bank is connected to the upper half of the data bus (D15-8) and contains odd address bytes (A0=1). A specific byte within each bank is selected by address lines A19-A1. Data bytes are transferred to even addresses over the lower half of the data bus (D7-0).

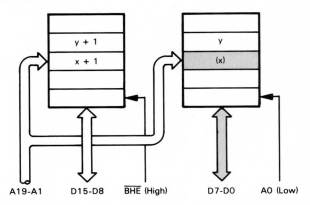

A0, when low, selects the memory bank connected to the lower half of the data bus; Bus High Enable ($\overline{\text{BHE}}$) is output high to disable the memory bank on the upper half of the data bus. This disabling process is necessary to prevent a write operation to the lower memory bank from destroying data in the upper bank. Since $\overline{\text{BHE}}$ is a multiplexed signal, with timing identical to the A19-A16 address lines, it also must be latched by ALE to provide a stable signal for the entire bus cycle.

During T2 through T4, the $\overline{\text{BHE}}$ output is available on status line S7. (The meaning of status line S7 has not yet been defined.)

When accessing memory bytes with odd addresses, information is transferred over the upper half of the data bus (D15-D8). $\overline{\text{BHE}}$ is output low to enable the upper memory bank. A0 is output high to disable the lower memory bank. This may be illustrated as follows:

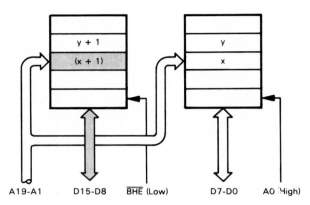

The 8086 transfers data via the correct half of the data bus and outputs $\overline{\text{BHE}}$ and A0 with the required signal levels.

As an example, consider loading a byte of data into the CL register (lower half of the CX register) from a memory location with an odd address. This data will be accessed via the upper half of the 16-bit data bus. Although this data is transferred into the 8086 over the upper eight data bus lines, the 8086 automatically redirects the data to the lower half of its internal 16-bit data path and hence to the CL register. This capability allows byte I/O transfers via the AL register to access I/O devices connected to either the upper or lower half of the 16-bit data bus.

16-bit words that are located at even addresses (two consecutive bytes with the least significant byte at an even byte address) are accessed in a single bus cycle. A19-A1 select the appropriate byte within each bank; A0 low and $\overline{\text{BHE}}$ low enable both banks simultaneously.

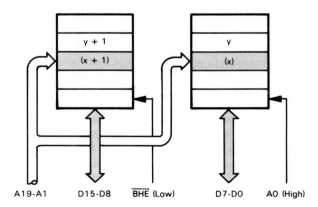

16-bit words located at odd addresses (two consecutive bytes with the least significant byte at an odd byte address) are accessed using two bus cycles. During the first bus cycle the lower byte (with the odd byte address) is accessed. During the second bus cycle, the upper byte (with the even byte address) is accessed. During the first bus cycle, A19-A1 specifies the address. A0 is 1 (for an odd address) and $\overline{BHE}$ is low. Therefore the lower memory bank is disabled and the upper memory bank is enabled. During the second bus cycle, the address is incremented. Therefore A0 is 0. $\overline{BHE}$ is high, however, so the lower memory bank is enabled, and the upper memory bank is disabled. This may be illustrated as follows:

First Bus Cycle

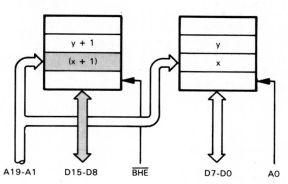

Second Bus Cycle

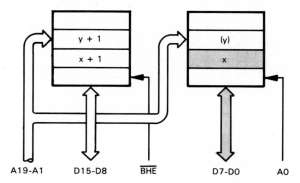

The sequence illustrated above is automatically executed by the 8086 whenever a word transfer specifies an odd address. The 8086 automatically connects the upper and lower bytes of the 8086's internal 16-bit registers with the appropriate halves of the data bus. Note, however, that accessing a word on an odd address boundary requires an extra bus cycle; this degrades system performance.

During a byte read, the CPU floats the entire 16-bit data bus during clock period T2, even though data is expected on the upper or lower half of the data bus but not on both halves. This simplifies the chip select decoding requirements for read only devices (ROM, EPROM). (We describe chip select logic later.) During a byte write operation, the 8086 will drive the entire 16-bit data bus. The information on the half of the data bus not transferring data is indeterminate. These concepts also apply to the I/O address space.

SYSTEM DATA BUS CONCEPTS

When referring to the system data bus, two implementation alternatives must be considered; (a) a multiplexed address/data bus, as illustrated in Figure 7-6, or (b) a data bus buffered from the multiplexed bus by transceivers, as illustrated in Figure 7-7.

When using the multiplexed data bus, a designer must guarantee that memory or I/O devices that are connected directly to the multiplexed bus do not corrupt the address on the bus during T1. To avoid this situation, device output drivers should not be enabled by the device chip select but should have an output enable controlled by the system read signal, as illustrated in Figure 7-8.

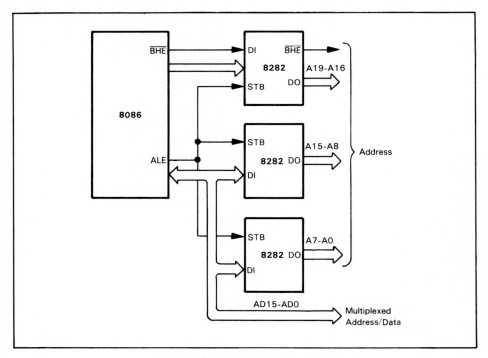

Figure 7-6. Multiplexed Data Bus

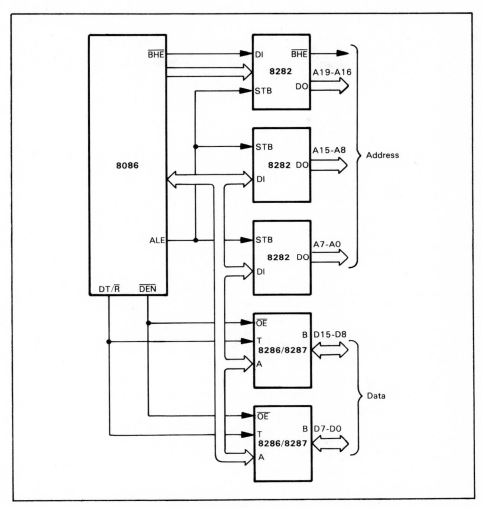

Figure 7-7. Buffered Data Bus

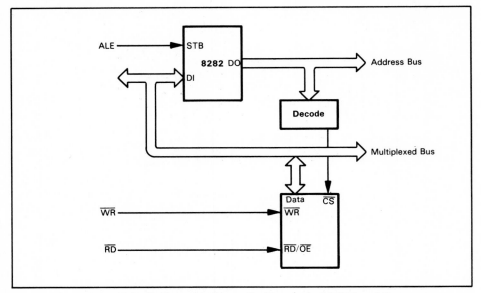

Figure 7-8. Devices with Output Enables on the Multiplexed Bus

8086 timing guarantees that read is not valid until after the address is latched by ALE and the multiplexed address/data bus is floated.

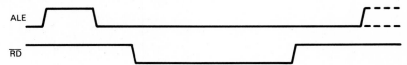

(All Intel Peripherals, EPROM Products and RAMs, if they are intended for microprocessors, provide output enable or read inputs that let them connect to the multiplexed bus in the manner illustrated in Figure 7-8.)

Several techniques exist for interfacing devices to the multiplexed bus when they do not have output enables. But each introduces restrictions or limitations if the device chip select is externally gated with a command as follows:

Consider Figure 7-8, which has chip select gated with read and write. If external gating is used, as illustrated above, this presents two problems. First the chip select access time is reduced to the read access time, which may force the use of an otherwise unnecessarily fast support device, assuming that maximum system performance (no wait states) is to be achieved. This is illustrated in Figure 7-9.

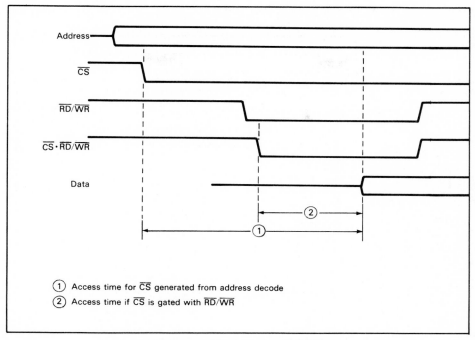

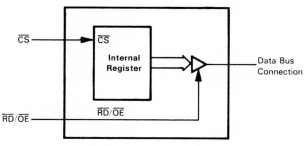

Figure 7-9. $\overline{CS}$ Gated with $\overline{RD/WR}$

In Figure 7-8, for a device which provides separate $\overline{CS}$ and $\overline{RD/OE}$ inputs, the access actually starts from $\overline{CS}$ internally; but the output drivers onto the bus are not enabled until $\overline{RD/OE}$. Thus the access time is not from $\overline{RD/OE}$. This may be illustrated as follows:

The designer must also verify that chip select to write set-up and hold times for the device are not violated, when chip select is gated externally. This is illustrated in Figure 7-10.

Alternative device select techniques are available, but they also impose special restrictions. It is therefore recommended that you connect devices having output enables to a multiplexed data bus.

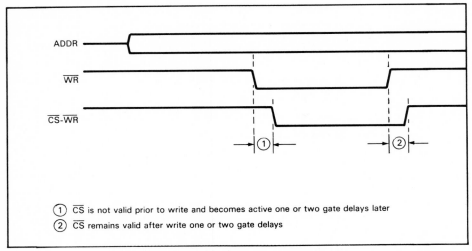

① $\overline{CS}$ is not valid prior to write and becomes active one or two gate delays later

② $\overline{CS}$ remains valid after write one or two gate delays

Figure 7-10. $\overline{CS}$ to $\overline{WR}$ Set-up and Hold

Another limitation on the multiplexed data bus illustrated in Figure 7-6 is the 8086's drive capability of 2.0 mA, and its capacitive loading of 100 pf, to guarantee the specified AC characteristics. Assuming capacitive loads of 20 pf per I/O device, 12 pf per address latch and 5-12 pf per memory device, a system mix of three peripherals and two to four memory devices (per bus line) is very close to the loading limit.

To satisfy the capacitive loading and drive requirements of larger systems, the data bus must be buffered as illustrated in Figure 7-11. The 8286 non-inverting and 8287 inverting octal transceivers are offered as part of the 8086 family to satisfy this requirement. They have tristate output buffers that drive 32 mA on the bus interface and 10 mA on the component interface; also, they can switch capacitive loads of 300 pf at the bus interface and 100 pf on the component interface in 22 ns (8287) or 30 ns (8286). The 8086 system provides Data ENable ($\overline{DEN}$) and Data Transmit/Receive (DT/$\overline{R}$) signals to enable the 8286 and 8287 transceivers and to control their direction, as illustrated in Figure 7-12.

These signals provide the appropriate timing to guarantee isolation of the multiplexed bus from the system during T1 and to eliminate bus contention with the CPU during read and write bus cycles.

Although the memory and peripheral devices are isolated from the CPU, bus contention may still exist in the system if the memory/peripheral devices do not have an output enable control in addition to the chip select. This configuration is illustrated in Figure 7-13. As an example, bus contention may exist during the transition from one chip select to another; the newly selected device may begin driving the bus before the previously selected device disables its drivers. A more severe problem can occur during a write bus cycle. A device whose outputs are controlled only by chip select will drive the bus from chip select to write active, simultaneously with data output being written through the transceivers by the CPU. This condition is illustrated in Figure 7-14.

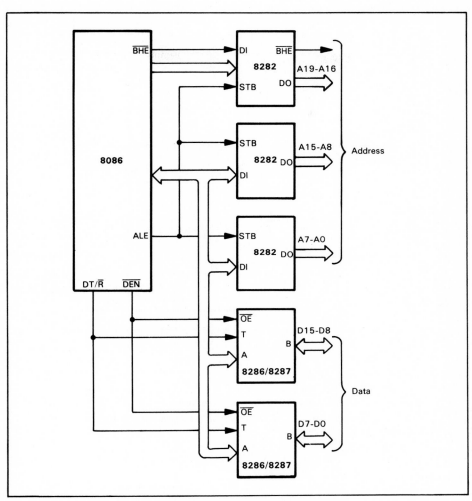

Figure 7-11. Buffered Data Bus

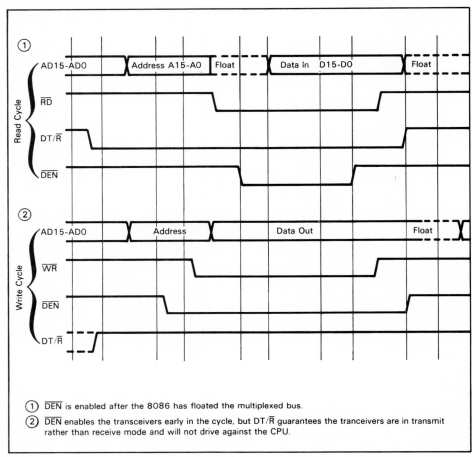

1. DEN is enabled after the 8086 has floated the multiplexed bus.
2. DEN enables the transceivers early in the cycle, but DT/R̄ guarantees the tranceivers are in transmit rather than receive mode and will not drive against the CPU.

Figure 7-12. Bus Transceiver Control

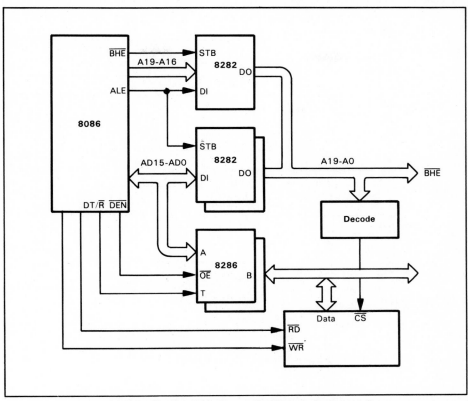

Figure 7-13. Devices with Output Enables on the System Bus

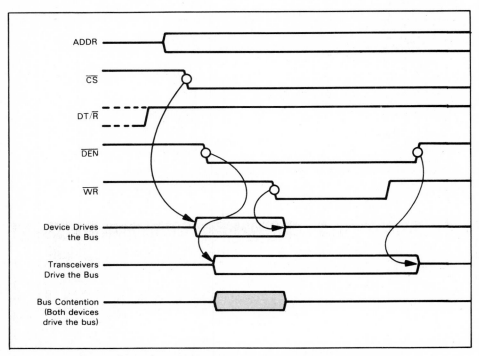

Figure 7-14. Bus Contention on the System Bus During Write for
Devices Without Output Enables

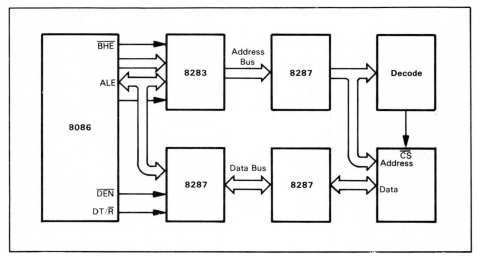

Figure 7-15. Fully Buffered System

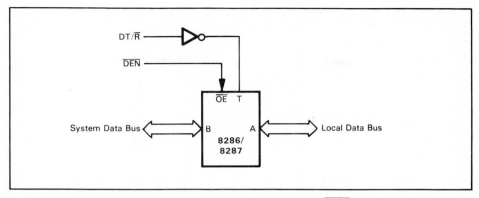

Figure 7-16. Controlling System Transceivers with $\overline{\text{DEN}}$ and DT/$\overline{\text{R}}$

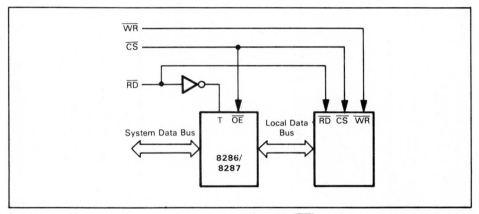

Figure 7-17. Devices with $\overline{\text{OE}}$

The same technique given for circumventing select timing problems on the multiplexed bus can be applied here but with the same limitations.

A second level of buffering can reduce the total load seen by devices on the system bus. This is illustrated in Figure 7-15.

Typically, double buffering is used in multiboard systems to isolate memory arrays. Double buffering, however, introduces additional access delays, and more important, you must pay attention to control of the second transceiver in relationship to the system bus and the device being interfaced to the system bus. Several techniques for controlling the second transceiver are available.

This first technique, shown in Figure 7-16, simply distributes $\overline{\text{DEN}}$ and DT/$\overline{\text{R}}$ throughout the system. DT/$\overline{\text{R}}$ is inverted to provide proper direction control for the second level transceivers.

The second technique, shown in Figure 7-17, provides control for devices with output enables.

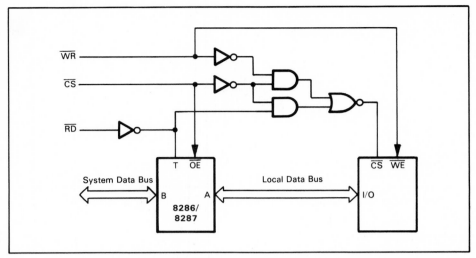

Figure 7-18. Devices without $\overline{\text{OE}}$. Common or Separate Input/Output Limited Read Access. Limited $\overline{\text{CS}}$ to $\overline{\text{WE}}$ Hold and Set-Up

$\overline{\text{RD}}$ is normally used to direct data from the peripheral to the system bus. In Figure 7-17 the buffer is selected whenever a device on the local bus is selected. Bus contention is possible on the device's local bus during a read, as the read simultaneously enables the device output and changes the transceiver direction. The contention may also occur while the read is terminating.

For devices without output enables, the technique illustrated in Figure 7-17 can be applied if the chip select to the device is conditioned by read or write. This is illustrated in Figure 7-18.

Controlling the chip select with read/write prevents the device from driving against the second transceiver prior to the command being received. The limitations of this technique are:

1. Access limited to read/write time, as discussed previously, and
2. Chip select limited to write set-up and hold times.

An alternate technique applicable to devices with and without output enables is shown in Figure 7-19.

$\overline{\text{RD}}$ again controls the direction of the second transceiver, but it is not enabled until a command and chip select are active. The possibility for bus contention still exists but is reduced to variations in output enable versus direction change time for the transceiver. Full access time from chip select is now available. However, data will not be valid prior to write and will only be held valid after write by the amount of delay required to disable a transceiver.

One last technique is given for devices with separate inputs and outputs. See Figure 7-20.

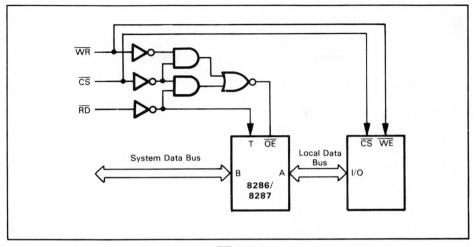

Figure 7-19. Devices without $\overline{\text{OE}}$. Common or Separate Input/Output
Full Read Access. Limited Write Data Set-Up and Hold

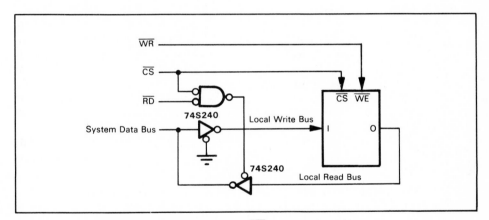

Figure 7-20. Devices without $\overline{\text{OE}}$. Separate Input/Output

Separate bus receivers and drivers are provided, rather than the single transceiver illustrated thus far. The receiver is always enabled, while the bus driver is controlled by $\overline{\text{RD}}$ and chip select. The only possibility for bus contention in this system occurs when multiple devices on each line of the read bus are enabled and disabled during chip selection changes.

Throughout this section on interfacing the 8086, the multiplexed bus will be considered the "local" CPU bus, and the demultiplex address and buffered data bus will be the "system bus."

8086 EXECUTION UNIT AND BUS INTERFACE UNIT

The most important concept to understand when looking at 8086 instruction execution timing is the fact that 8086 bus control logic has been separated from the 8086 instruction execution logic. That is to say, the 8086 has an Execution Unit (EU) and a Bus Interface Unit (BIU).

The Execution Unit (EU) contains data and address registers, the Arithmetic and Logic Unit, plus the Control Unit. The Bus Interface Unit (BIU) contains bus interface logic, segment registers, memory addressing logic, and a six-byte instruction object code queue. This may be illustrated as follows:

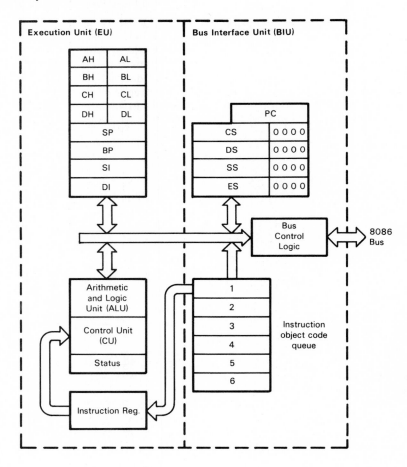

The Execution Unit (EU) and the Bus Interface Unit (BIU) operate asynchronously. Whenever the Execution Unit is ready to execute a new instruction, it fetches the instruction object code from the front of the Bus Interface Unit instruction queue, then it executes the instruction in some number of clock periods that have nothing to do with bus cycles. If the instruction object code queue is empty, then the Bus Interface Unit (BIU) executes an instruction fetch machine cycle — and the CPU waits for the instruction object code to be fetched. But the queue will rarely be empty, for reasons that will soon become apparent. Therefore, the EU will usually not have to wait while an instruction fetch is executed.

If memory or an I/O device must be accessed in the course of executing an instruction, then the EU informs the BIU of its needs. The BIU executes an appropriate external access machine cycle in response to the EU demand.

The Bus Interface Unit (BIU), for its part, is independent of the Execution Unit (EU) and attempts to keep the six-byte queue filled with instruction object codes. If two or more of these six bytes are empty, then the Bus Interface Unit (BIU) executes instruction fetch machine cycles — provided the EU does not have an active request for bus access pending. If the EU issues a request for bus access while the BIU is in the middle of an instruction fetch machine cycle, then the BIU will complete the instruction fetch machine cycle before honoring the EU bus access request.

8086 INSTRUCTION QUEUE

Consider what happens when an instruction is executed. Beginning with the simplest case, the instruction object code queue within the Bus Interface Unit will be empty. Therefore, when the EU requests an instruction, the BIU will execute a bus cycle to fetch the first byte of the instruction.

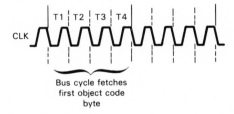

Let us assume that this particular instruction requires two bytes of object code. Keeping things simple, we will illustrate another bus cycle executed immediately to fetch the next instruction byte:

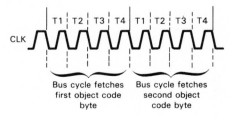

Let us suppose that this instruction reads a word of data from memory, then performs an arithmetic operation using this data. The instruction is going to require some number of clock periods to compute the effective address for the data memory location to be accessed (we will assume seven clock periods are needed). Some additional number of clock periods will also be needed to perform the arithmetic operation (we will assume nine clock periods). In a normal microprocessor, this instruction might be executed as the following sequence of machine cycles:

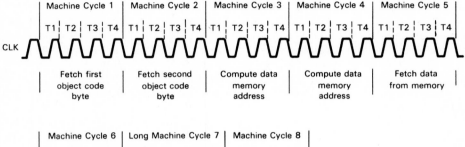

But the 8086, having asynchronous CPU and Bus Control Unit logic, will use clock periods to execute the instruction illustrated above as follows:

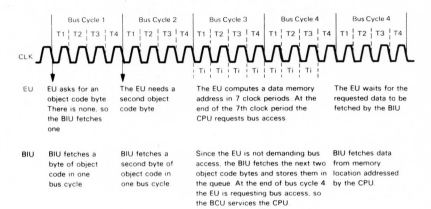

	Bus Cycle 1	Bus Cycle 2	Bus Cycle 3	Bus Cycle 4
EU	EU asks for an object code byte. There is none, so the BIU fetches one	The EU needs a second object code byte	The EU computes a data memory address in 7 clock periods. At the end of the 7th clock period the CPU requests bus access.	The EU waits for the requested data to be fetched by the BIU
BIU	BIU fetches a byte of object code in one bus cycle.	BIU fetches a second byte of object code in one bus cycle	Since the EU is not demanding bus access, the BIU fetches the next two object code bytes and stores them in the queue. At the end of bus cycle 4 the EU is requesting bus access, so the BCU services the CPU	BIU fetches data from memory location addressed by the CPU.

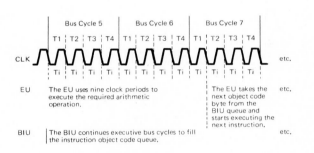

	Bus Cycle 5	Bus Cycle 6	Bus Cycle 7	
EU	The EU uses nine clock periods to execute the required arithmetic operation.		The EU takes the next object code byte from the BIU queue and starts executing the next instruction.	etc.
BIU	The BIU continues executive bus cycles to fill the instruction object code queue.			etc.

Now, the illustration above is not accurate because, you will recall, the 8086 fetches data in 16-bit increments, provided the data address lies on an even-byte boundary. Also, the BIU fetches instruction bytes and loads them into the queue only when there are at least two free bytes in the queue. Let us assume that all data does lie on even-byte boundaries. This is how our timing will now look:

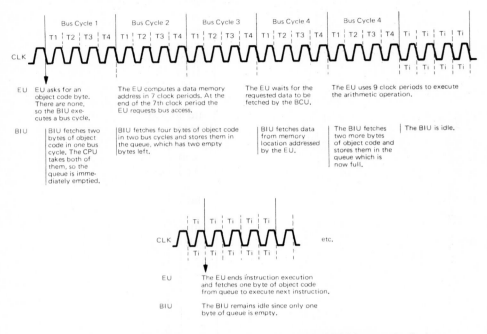

There are some important points to note regarding 8086 bus cycle timing.

Bus cycles are a Bus Interface Unit (BIU) phenomenon.

So far as the EU logic is concerned, bus cycles do not exist. The EU experiences periods of activity while executing instructions and periods of inactivity while waiting for instruction object codes or data that the BIU must process via bus cycles. Periods of EU activity are timed by a sequence of clock periods. The EU makes no attempt to group clock periods into machine cycles, nor do EU clock periods have to occur in any special numeric combinations.

So far as the BIU is concerned, clock periods are grouped into bus cycles only when data must be transferred to or from the 8086. First priority is given to a bus access request coming from the EU. If the EU is not requesting bus access, then the BIU executes instruction fetch bus cycles until the queue is full. These are the prerequisites for the BIU to execute an instruction fetch bus cycle:

1. The clock period that initiates the bus cycle would otherwise be an idle clock period.
2. The EU does not have an active bus access request pending.
3. There are at least two bytes empty in the queue.

If the queue is full, then the BIU ceases to execute bus cycles; as illustrated above, a sequence of idle clock periods occurs.

Note that the CPU may have to wait for bus access. In the illustrations above, the CPU requires seven clock periods in order to compute a data memory address. At the end of the seventh clock period, the EU issues a bus access request to the BIU. But at this time the BIU is part way through executing an instruction fetch bus cycle. The BIU completes the instruction fetch bus cycle, then honors the EU bus access request.

In the final illustration above, no bus cycle accompanies the beginning of a new instruction's execution. We are assuming that the next instruction executed has one byte of object code. This object code byte is fetched from the front of the queue — which then has just one empty byte. No bus cycle is executed to fetch the instruction object code, since it is taken out of the queue. Subsequently, the BIU does not execute an instruction fetch bus cycle since there is only one empty byte. There must be at least two empty bytes in the queue before the BIU will execute an instruction fetch bus cycle.

Based on the foregoing discussion of 8086 instruction fetch queuing, we can see that the 8086 has essentially eliminated instruction fetch time. The only time the EU will have to wait while the BIU fetches instruction object codes is when a Branch-on-Condition instruction causes execution to branch out of the queue sequence or when (for any reason) the memory accesses accompanying an instruction's execution are so dense that the BIU has insufficient idle clock periods within which to insert instruction fetch bus cycles.

For additional information regarding queue effects on system design, see page 8-28, the last paragraph of the section on Ready Implementation and Timing.

Basic 8086 Design Single CPU

OPERATING MODES

The 8086 is easily configured to operate in a variety of markedly different applications. The MN/$\overline{\text{MX}}$ input, which we described in Chapter 7, is a strapping option that allows the 8086 to function with two different sets of outputs, identified as "minimum mode" and "maximum mode". We will now examine these two modes in more detail.

MINIMUM MODE

The minimum mode 8086 has the MN/$\overline{\text{MX}}$ pin connected to V_{CC}. Minimum mode should be used in one or two board single CPU systems. Figure 8-1 illustrates a minimum mode 8086.

In minimum mode the 8086 addresses a full megabyte memory space and 64K byte I/O space. The data bus is 16 bits wide. The 8086 directly provides bus controls (DT/$\overline{\text{R}}$, $\overline{\text{DEN}}$, ALE, M/$\overline{\text{IO}}$, $\overline{\text{RD}}$, $\overline{\text{WR}}$, $\overline{\text{INTA}}$). A simple CPU preemption mechanism, compatible with existing DMA controllers, is enabled via the HOLD and HLDA signals.

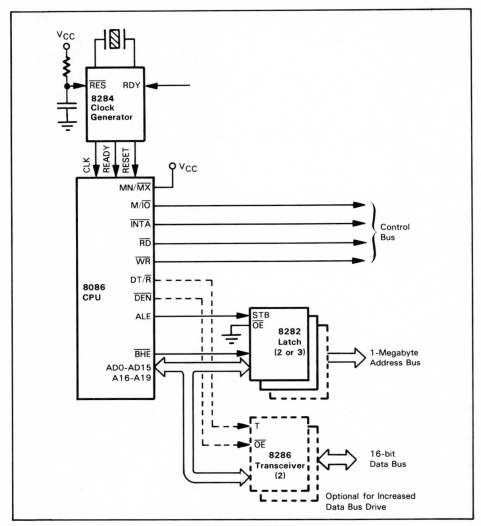

Figure 8-1. Minimum Mode 8086

MAXIMUM MODE

The maximum mode, illustrated in Figure 8-2, has the MN/$\overline{\text{MX}}$ pin connected to ground. Maximum mode is used in multiprocessor and co-processor configurations.

In maximum mode, an 8288 Bus Controller receives control signals, as inputs, from the 8086. These inputs are decoded by the 8288 to generate Control output signals. Other 8086 Control outputs are also modified to provide external logic with more information. Specifically, 8086 output signals are redefined as follows:

1. Queue status is output at QS0 and QS1. This allows external devices, e.g., an ICE/86 or special instruction set extension co-processors, to track the CPU instruction execution.

2. System control and configuration options are expanded via the bus cycle status outputs $\overline{\text{S0}}$, $\overline{\text{S1}}$, and $\overline{\text{S2}}$. These outputs are used by the 8288 bus controller, 8289 bus arbiter, and similar external devices.

3. Access control to shared resources in multiprocessor systems is supported by a bus lock mechanism.

4. Two prioritized levels of processor preemption ($\overline{\text{RQ/GT0}}$, $\overline{\text{RQ/GT1}}$) allow multiple processors to reside on the 8086's local bus sharing a system bus interface.

We will now examine how these expanded capabilities may be used.

The queue status indicates what information is being removed from the internal queue and when the queue is being reset due to a transfer of control. Table 8-1 summarizes Queue Status interpretation.

Using logic akin to that illustrated in Figure 8-3, you can track 8086 queue status. When $\overline{\text{S0}}$, $\overline{\text{S1}}$, and $\overline{\text{S2}}$ are 1, 0, and 0, respectively, an instruction fetch is being performed. QS0 and QS1 indicate whether the instruction is being fetched from the 8086 queue or from external memory. For an external memory access, A0 and $\overline{\text{BHE}}$ indicate a word or byte access. This logic can be used in a number of ways; consider the following examples.

The ICE/86 can track execution of an instruction stored in a specific memory location. Figure 8-3 gives an example of a circuit used by the ICE/86 to track the queue.

Table 8-1. Queue Status Outputs

QS1	QS0	Interpretation
0	0	No Operation
0	1	First Byte of Op-code from Queue
1	0	Empty the Queue
1	1	Subsequent Byte from Queue

The queue status is valid during the CLK cycle after which the queue operation is performed.

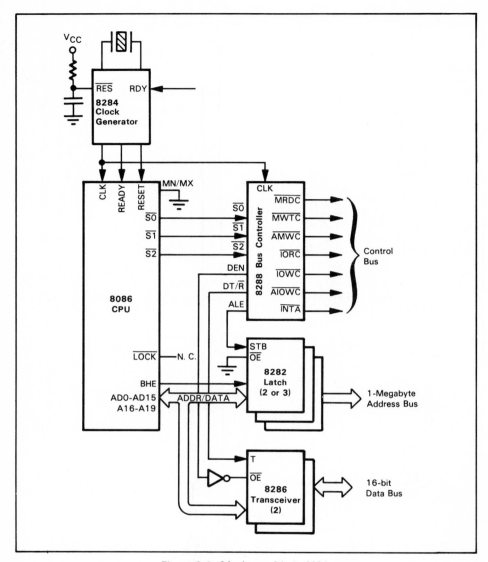

Figure 8-2. Maximum Mode 8086

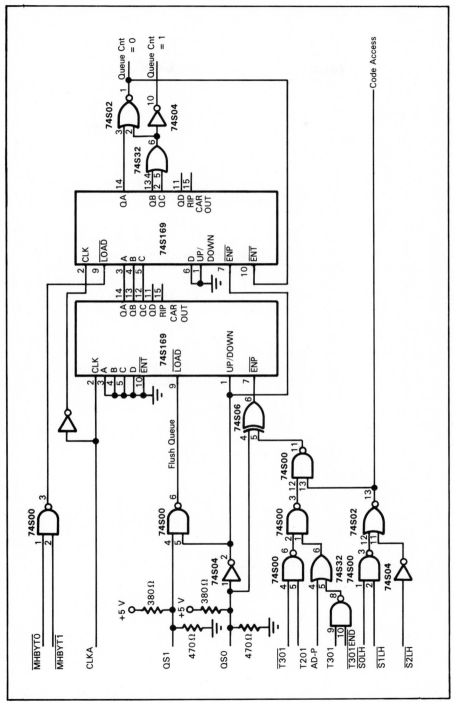

Figure 8-3. Circuit to Track the 8086 Queue

The first up-down counter tracks the depth of the queue, while a second up-down counter captures the queue depth on a match. The second counter decrements on further fetches from the queue until the queue is flushed, or the count goes to zero, indicating execution of the match address. The first counter decrements on a fetch from the queue (QS0 = 1) and increments when an object code byte is stored into the queue. Note that a normal instruction fetch from external memory will transfer two bytes into the queue so two clock increments are given to the counter (T201 and T301). When a single byte is loaded over the upper half of the bus (A0 is high and $\overline{BHE}$ is low), the counter is incremented once. Since the EU is not synchronized to the BIU, a fetch from the queue can occur simultaneously with a transfer into the queue. The exclusive-OR gate driving the ENP input of the first counter allows these simultaneous operations to cancel each other and not modify the queue depth.

The 8086 queue might be tracked by a co-processor to detect execution of an ESCAPE instruction. The ESCAPE instruction will direct the co-processor to perform some specific task.

Table 8-2 defines interpretations of status lines $\overline{S0}$, $\overline{S1}$, and $\overline{S2}$. These status lines, you will recall, tell the 8288 when to initiate a bus cycle, what type of command to issue, and when to terminate the bus cycle. The 8288 samples the status lines at the beginning of each CPU clock period. At the start of a bus cycle, the CPU drives the status lines from the passive state (the $\overline{S0}$, $\overline{S1}$, $\overline{S2}$ lines are all high) to one of the seven possible active states.

For each new bus cycle the 8086 will alter the state of $\overline{S0}$, $\overline{S1}$, and $\overline{S2}$ on the rising edge of the T4 clock during the previous bus cycle, or during a TI idle cycle, if there is no current bus activity. The 8288 detects a status change by sampling the status lines on the high-to-low transition of each clock period. The 8288 starts a bus cycle by generating a high ALE pulse, accompanied by appropriate buffer direction controls; this occurs during the clock period immediately following detection of the status change. The bus transceivers and the selected operation are enabled during the next clock period. When the status returns to the passive state, the 8288 will terminate the operation. Timing is illustrated in Figure 8-4.

Table 8-2. Status Line Outputs

$\overline{S2}$	$\overline{S1}$	$\overline{S0}$	Interpretation
0	0	0	Interrupt Acknowledge
0	0	1	Read I/O Port
0	1	0	Write I/O Port
0	1	1	Halt
1	0	0	Code Access
1	0	1	Read Memory
1	1	0	Write Memory
1	1	1	Passive

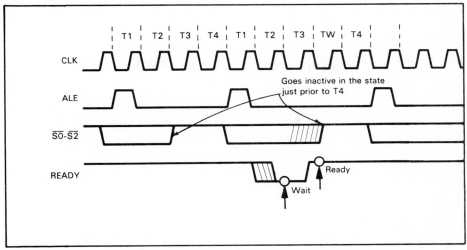

Figure 8-4. Status Line Activation and Termination

The 8086 maintains $\overline{S0}$, $\overline{S1}$, and $\overline{S2}$ levels during Wait states. A Wait state, you will recall, is induced by external logic inputting a low RDY signal to the 8284 Clock Generator. The Clock Generator outputs a high READY signal, which is synchronized with CLK and transmitted to the 8086. Since the 8086 maintains $\overline{S0}$, $\overline{S1}$ and $\overline{S2}$ levels during Wait states, the 8288 will maintain active bus control for a Wait state extending over any number of clock periods. The status lines may also be used by any other processors on the 8086's local bus to monitor bus activity and control the 8288 if those other processors gain control of the local bus.

The 8288 provides bus control signals DEN, DT/$\overline{R}$, ALE, and control signals $\overline{INTA}$, $\overline{MRDC}$, $\overline{IORC}$, $\overline{MWTC}$, $\overline{AMWC}$, $\overline{IOWC}$, $\overline{AIOWC}$. The control signals separate read and write operations for memory and I/O, to be compatible with the Intel MULTIBUS.

The advanced write control signals are enabled one clock period earlier than normal write control signals to accommodate the wider write pulse widths often required by peripherals and static RAMs. The normal write control signal allows data to be set in advance of the write pulse, to accommodate dynamic RAM memories and I/O devices that strobe data on the leading edge of the write control pulse. The advanced write control signals do not guarantee that data is valid prior to the leading edge of the control signal.

The DEN signal in the maximum mode is inverted, as compared to the minimum mode. This makes it easier to logically gate DEN with other signals, particularly interrupt controls. Figure 8-5 compares the timing of the minimum and maximum mode bus transfer control signals.

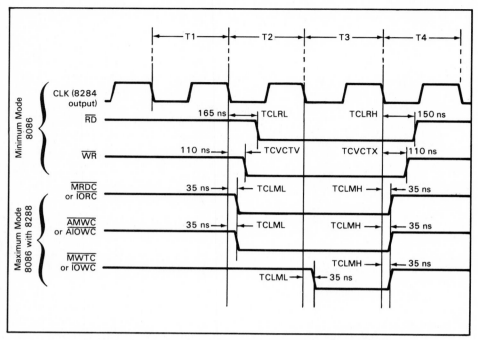

Figure 8-5. Minimum and Maximum Bus Transfer Timing

Maximum mode is designed for multiprocessing configurations, and for large single CPU designs (either Multibus systems or systems that contain two or more PC boards). The 8288 is a bipolar device; therefore, its 32 ma output drive for the Control signals and tolerances on timing parameters and worse case delays provide better large system performance than the minimum mode 8086.

In addition to assuming the functions removed from the 8086, the 8288 provides additional strapping options and controls to support multiprocessor configurations and peripheral devices on an 8086 local bus. These capabilities allow resources, including memory or I/O, to be assigned as either shared or local. Shared resources are available on the Multibus system bus. Local resources are accessible only by this 8086 on its local bus. This technique reduces contention for access to the Multibus system bus, and improves multi-CPU system performance. Specific configurations are described in a later chapter.

The 8086 maximum mode $\overline{\text{LOCK}}$ output helps control access to shared resources. The $\overline{\text{LOCK}}$ output is activated when the 8086 executes the LOCK prefix instruction. The $\overline{\text{LOCK}}$ output goes low during the first clock period following execution of the LOCK prefix; it remains low through the last instruction execution clock period for the instruction following the LOCK prefix, and during the first clock period of the next instruction's execution. The LOCK signal must be part of every microprocessor's system bus arbitration logic.

During normal multiprocessor system operations, priority for shared system bus access is determined by arbitration circuitry on a cycle by cycle basis. When an 8086 needs to transfer data via the system bus, it requests bus access. When the 8086 gains priority, as determined by any system bus arbitration scheme selected, it takes control of the system bus, executes its bus cycle, then either maintains system bus control, voluntarily releases the system bus or is forced off the system bus by the loss of priority. The lock mechanism prevents an 8086 from losing system bus control, either voluntarily or involuntarily. This guarantees an 8086 the ability to execute multiple bus cycle instructions without intervention and possible corruption of the data by another CPU. The activity of the LOCK output is shown in Figure 8-6.

Note that the LOCK output will go inactive between separate locked instructions. Also, the LOCK prefix adds two clock periods to execution time.

Since queue status reflects the queue operation in the previous clock period, the LOCK output actually goes active coincident with the start of the next (locked) instruction and remains active for one clock period following the locked instruction's execution.

If the instruction following the LOCK prefix does not have its object code in the queue, the LOCK output goes low as shown while the instruction object code is being fetched from external memory.

The Bus Interface Unit (BIU) will still perform instruction fetch cycles during execution of a locked instruction. The LOCK merely guarantees that one 8086 will maintain system bus control for the duration of an instruction's execution; it in no way restricts the type of bus activity that this CPU can perform during this locked time.

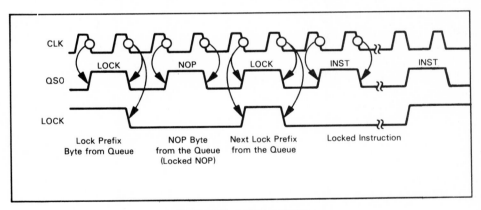

Figure 8-6. LOCK Activity

The lock mechanism is commonly used during a TEST and SET handshaking sequence. During this sequence an 8086 reads from a shared memory location and returns data to the location. No other CPU can be allowed to reference this memory location between the TEST, which is a read operation, and the SET, which is a write operation. The 8086 accomplishes this with a locked Exchange instruction, as follows:

```
LOCK  XCHG      reg,memory      ;reg is any of the 8086
                                ;registers, memory is the
                                ;address of the semaphore
```

Another interesting use of the LOCK in multiprocessor systems is a locked block move, which allows high speed message transfer from one CPU's message buffer to another.

During the locked instruction, a request for processor preemption is recorded, occurring via a RQ/GT line but not acknowledged until completion of the locked instruction.

The LOCK prefix does not have any direct effect on interrupts. In general, prefix bytes are considered extensions of the instructions they precede. Therefore, interrupts that occur during execution of a prefix are not acknowledged (assuming interrupts are enabled) until completion of the instruction following the prefixes. Note that multiple prefix bytes may precede an instruction; the repetition prefix (REP) is interruptible after each execution of the following instruction. This is true even if the REP is combined with the LOCK prefix, so that interrupts are not locked out during a block move, or other repeated string operation. Further information on the operation and string operation with multiple prefixes is presented later in this chapter in the section dealing with the 8086 interrupt structure.

Additional levels of prioritized processor preemption are discussed in greater detail later in this chapter.

CLOCK GENERATION

The 8086 requires a clock signal with fast rise and fall times (10 ns max) between low and high voltages of −0.5 to +0.6 low and +3.9 to VCC+1.0 high. Maximum clock frequency of the 8086 is 5 MHz. Since the design of the 8086 incorporates dynamic cells, a minimum frequency of 2 MHz is required. Due to the minimum frequency requirement, single stepping or cycling of the CPU may not be accomplished by disabling the clock. Timing and voltage requirements of the CPU clock are illustrated in Figure 8-7.

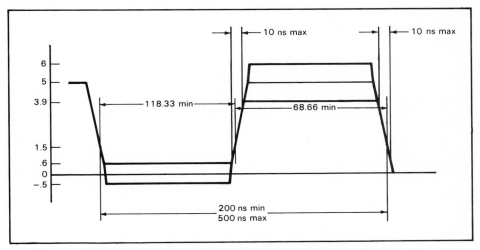

Figure 8-7. Timing and Voltage Requirements for the 8086 CPU

In general, for frequency below the maximum, the CPU clock need not satisfy the frequency dependent pulse width limitations stated in the 8086 data sheets. The values specified only reflect the minimum values that must be satisfied, and they are stated in terms of the maximum clock frequency. As the clock frequency approaches the maximum frequency of the CPU, the clock must conform to a 33% duty cycle to satisfy the CPU minimum clock low and high time specifications.

An optimum 33% duty cycle clock with the required voltage levels and transition times can be obtained with the 8284 clock generator, as illustrated in Figure 8-8.

Either an external frequency source or a series resonant crystal may drive the 8284. The selected source must oscillate at three times (3X) the desired CPU frequency. To select the crystal inputs of the 8284 as the frequency source for clock generation, the F/$\overline{C}$ input to the 8284 must be strapped to ground. The strapping option allows either the crystal or the external frequency input to be selected as the clock generator source. Although the 8284 provides an input for a tank circuit to accommodate overtone mode crystals, fundamental mode crystals are recommended for more accurate (and stable) frequency generation. When selecting a crystal for use with the 8284, series resistance should be as low as possible. Since other circuit components will tend to shift the operating frequency from resonance, the operating impedance will typically be higher than the specified series resistance. If the attenuation of the oscillator's feedback circuit reduces

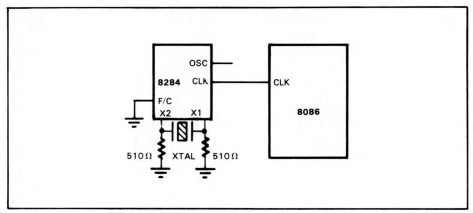

Figure 8-8. Using the 8284 to Provide CLK

the loop gain to less than one, the oscillator will fail.

To provide maximum oscillator stability over voltage and temperature variations, a 510Ω resistor to ground is recommended on the X1 and X2 crystal connections.

Two of the many vendors who supply crystals for Intel microprocessors are listed in Table 8-3, along with crystal part numbers for various frequencies that may be of interest.

If a high accuracy frequency source, externally variable frequency source or a common source for driving 8284s is desired, the External Frequency Input (EFI) of the 8284 can be selected by strapping the F/$\overline{C}$ input to +5 volts through 1K ohms as illustrated in Figure 8-9.

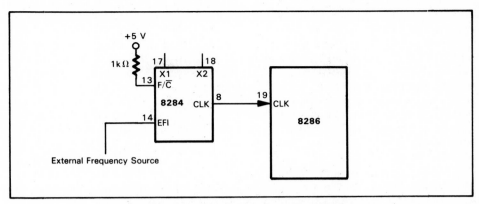

Figure 8-9. Using an External Frequency Source

Table 8-3. Crystal Vendors

f	Parallel/ Series	Crystek[1] Corp.	CTS Knight,[2] Inc.
3.6 MHz	P	**	**
5.185 MHz	S	CY8A	**
6.0 MHz	P	**	MP060
6.144 MHz	P	**	MP061
6.25 MHz	P	**	MP062
10.0 MHz	P	**	MP10A
15.0 MHz	S	CY15A	MP150
18.432	S	CY19B*	MP184*
24.0 MHz	S	**	MP240
25.0 MHz	S	**	MP250
27.0 MHz	S (overtone)	CY27A	MP270

*Intel also supplies a crystal numbered 8801 for this applicaton.

**Contact vendor with the appropriate specifications.

Notes: 1. Address: 1000 Crystal Drive, Fort Meyers, Florida 33901
2. Address: 400 Reimann Ave., Sandwich, Illinois

The external frequency source should be TTL compatible, have a 50% duty cycle and oscillate at three times the desired CPU operation frequency. The maximum EFI frequency the 8284 can accept is slighty above 24 MHz, with minimum clock low and high times of 13 ns. Although no minimum EFI frequency is specified, it should not violate the CPU minimum clock rate. If a common frequency is used to drive 8284s distributed throught the system, each 8284 should be driven by its own line from the source. To minimize noise in the system, each line should be a twisted pair, driven by a buffer such as the 74LS04, with the ground of the twisted pair connecting the grounds of the source and receiver. To minimize clock skew, the lines to all 8284s should be of equal length. A simple technique for generating a master frequency source for additional 8284s is shown in Figure 8-10.

In Figure 8-10 one 8284, with a crystal, is used to generate the desired frequency. The oscillator output of the 8284 (OSC) equals the crystal frequency, and is used to drive the external frequency to all other 8284s in the system.

The oscillator output (OSC) is inverted, becoming the complement of the oscillator signal used to drive the CPU clock generator circuit. Therefore the oscillator output of one 8284 should not drive the EFI input of a second 8284 if both are driving clock inputs of separate CPUs that are to be synchronized. The variation on EFI to CLK delay over a range of 8284s may approach 35 to 45 ns. If, however, all 8284s are of the same package type, have the same relative supply voltage and operate in the same temperature environment, the variation will be reduced to between 15 and 25 ns.

There are three frequency outputs in the 8284: the oscillator (OSC) mentioned above, the system clock (CLK) that drives the CPU, and a peripheral clock (PCLK) that runs at one half the CPU clock frequency. OSC is only driven by the crystal, and is not affected by the $F/\overline{C}$ strapping option. If a crystal is not connected to the 8284 when the external frequency input is used, OSC is indeterminate. CLK is derived from the selected frequency source by an internal divide by three counter. The counter generates the 33% duty cycle clock, which is optimum for the CPU at maximum frequency. PCLK has a 50% duty cycle and runs at one half the frequency of CLK.

Since the state of the 8284 divide by three counter is indeterminate at system initialization (power on), an external synchronization signal to the counter (CSYNC) is provided to allow synchronization of the CPU clock to an external event. When CSYNC is brought high, the CLK and PCLK outputs are forced high. When CSYNC returns low, the next positive clock from the frequency source starts clock generation. CSYNC must be active for a minimum of two periods of the frequency source. If CSYNC is asynchronous with the frequency source, the circuit in Figure 8-11 should be used for synchronization.

The two latches minimize the probability of a meta-stable state in the latch driving CSYNC. The latches are clocked with the inverse of the frequency source to guarantee the 8284 set up and hold time of CSYNC to the frequency source, as shown in Figure 8-12.

If a single 8284 is to be synchronized to an external event, and an external frequency source is not used, the oscillator output of the 8284 may be used to synchronize CSYNC, as illustrated in Figure 8-13.

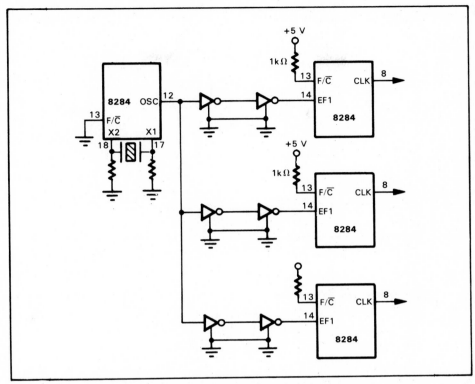

Figure 8-10. Generating a Master Frequency Source

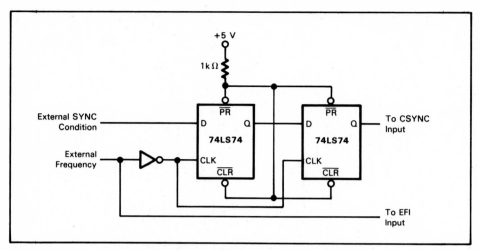

Figure 8-11. Synchronizing CSYNC

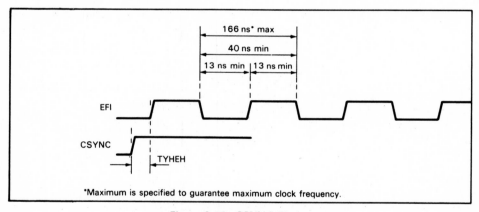

*Maximum is specified to guarantee maximum clock frequency.

Figure 8-12. CSYNC Timing

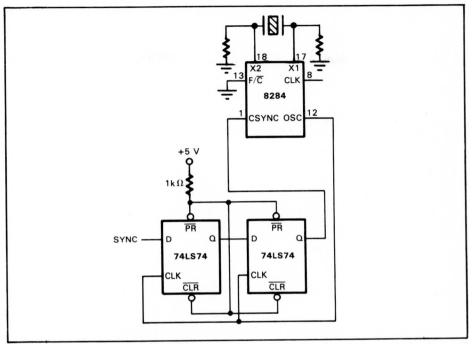

Figure 8-13. Synchronizing CSYNC using OSC

Since the oscillator output is inverted with respect to the internal oscillator signal, the inverter in the previous example is not required. If multiple 8284s are to be synchronized, an external frequency source must drive all 8284s, and a single CSYNC synchronization circuit must drive the CSYNC input of all 8284s as illustrated in Figure 8-14.

Since the 8086 minimum clock low time may not be met when CSYNC is activated, it should be enabled only during a reset, or while the CPU clock is high. CSYNC must also be disabled for a minimum of four clock periods before the end of reset to guarantee proper CPU reset.

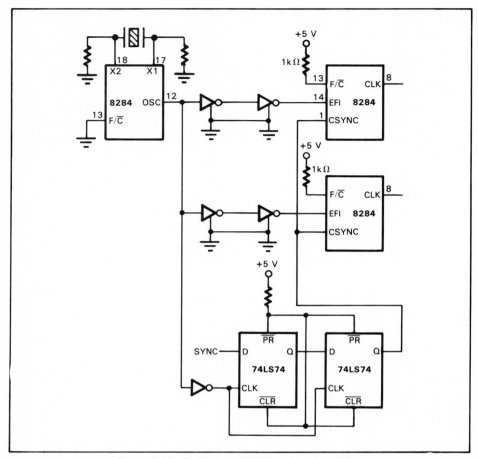

Figure 8-14. Delivering CSYNC to Multiple 8284s

Due to the fast transitions and high drive (5 mA) of the 8284 CLK output, it may be necessary to put a 100 ohm resistor in series with the clock line to eliminate ringing. If multiple sources of CLK are needed with minimum skew, CLK can be buffered by a high drive device (74S241) with outputs tied to five volts through 100 ohms to guarantee VCH=3.9 min (8086 minimum input high voltage).

A single 8284 should not be used to generate the CLK for multiple CPUs since the 8284 synchronizes READY to the CPU and can only accommodate READY for a single CPU.

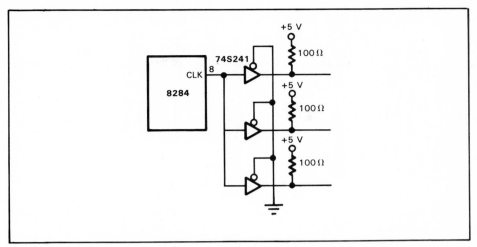

Figure 8-15. Buffering CLK with a High-Drive Device

RESET

The 8086 requires an active high reset with minimum pulse width of four CPU clock periods, except after power on, which requires a 50 μs reset pulse. Since the CPU internally synchronizes reset with a clock, the reset is internally active for up to one clock period after the external reset goes low. A Non-Maskable Interrupt (NMI), a minimum mode hold request, or a maximum mode RQ pulse that occurs during the internal reset, will not be acknowledged. A minimum mode hold request or a maximum mode RQ pulse active immediately after the internal reset will be honored before the first instruction fetch.

After the 8086 recognizes the reset, the CPU will condition the bus as shown in Table 8-4.

Table 8-4. 8086 Bus Signals during Reset

Signals	Condition
AD0-AD15	Tristate
A16-A19/S3-S6	Indeterminant
$\overline{BHE}$/S7	Indeterminant
S2/(M/$\overline{IO}$)	
S1/(DT/$\overline{R}$)	
S0/($\overline{DEN}$)	Driven to "1" then Tristate
$\overline{LOCK}$/$\overline{WR}$	
$\overline{RD}$	
$\overline{INTA}$	
ALE	0
HLDA	0
$\overline{RQ}$/$\overline{GT0}$	1
$\overline{RQ}$/$\overline{GT1}$	1
QS0	0
QS1	0

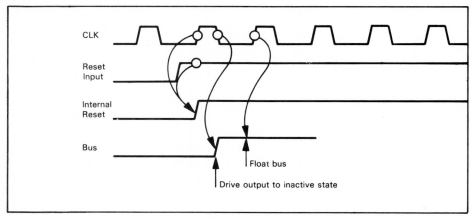

CLK

Reset
Input

Internal
Reset

Bus

Float bus

Drive output to inactive state

Figure 8-16. 8086 Bus Condition on Reset

The multiplexed bus signal connections are floated by the CPU when it detects a reset. Other signals which can be floated are driven to the inactive state for one low state of CLK prior to entering tristate. This is illustrated in Figure 8-16.

In minimum mode, ALE and HLDA are driven inactive but are not floated. In the maximum mode, RQ/GT lines are held inactive and the queue status outputs (Q0 and Q1) indicate no activity. The queue status will not indicate a queue reset, so any user defined external circuits monitoring the queue should also be reset by the system reset. 22K ohm pull-up resistors should be connected to the CPU command and bus control lines; this will guarantee the inactive state of these lines in systems where leakage currents (or bus capacitance) may cause the voltage levels to settle below the minimum high voltage of devices in the system. In maximum mode systems, the 8288 contains internal pull-ups on the $\overline{S0}$-$\overline{S2}$ inputs; this maintains the inactive state for these lines when the CPU floats its bus. The high state of the status lines during a reset causes the 8288 to treat the reset sequence as a passive state. The condition of the 8288 outputs for the passive state are shown in Table 8-5.

Table 8-5. 8288 Outputs
during Passive State

ALE	0
DEN	0
DT/$\overline{R}$	1
MCE/$\overline{PDEN}$	0/1
Commands	1

If a reset occurs during a bus cycle, the status lines will return to the passive state, ぃ. e bus cycle will end, and the command lines will become inactive. Note that the 8288 does not float the command outputs based on the passive state of the status lines. If the designer needs to disconnect the CPU from the bus during reset in a single-CPU system, the reset signal should also be connected to the 8288's AEN input, and the output enable of the address latches, as illustrated in Figure 8-17.

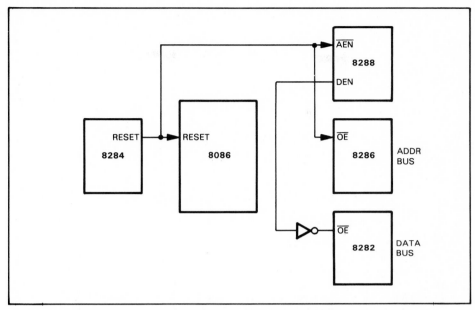

Figure 8-17. Reset Disable for Maximum Mode 8086 Bus Interface

This technique forces the command and address bus interface to float while the inactive state of DEN from the 8288 floats the transceivers on the data bus.

In multiple processor systems using arbitration to establish microprocessor-shared bus connections, the system reset should be connected to the INIT input of the 8289 Bus Arbiter in addition to the 8284 reset input, as shown in Figure 8-18.

The active low INIT input forces all 8289 outputs to their inactive state. The inactive state of the 8289 AEN output will force the 8288 to float the command outputs; also, the address latches will float the address bus interface. For multi-microprocessor systems where more than one microprocessor can function as the master, the reset should be common to all CPUs, 8289s, and 8284s; this reset must satisfy the maximum of either the CPU reset requirements, or three 8289 bus clock period times (TBLBL) plus three 8086 clock period times. This will satisfy 8289 reset requirements.

The 8288 command outputs are floated during reset, the command lines should be pulled up to V_{CC} through 2.2K ohm resistors.

The reset signal to the 8086 can be derived from the 8284. The 8284 has a Schmitt trigger input for generating reset from an active low external reset. The hysterisis specified in the 8284 data sheet implies that at least 0.25 volts will separate the 0 and 1 switching point of the 8284 reset input. Inputs without hysterisis will switch from low to high and high to low at approximately the same voltage threshold. The inputs are guaranteed to switch at specified low and high voltages (VIL and VIH), but the actual switching point is anywhere in between. Since VIL_{min} is specified at 0.8 volts, the hysterisis guarantees that the reset will be active until the input reaches at least 1.05 volts. A reset will not be recognized until the input drops at least 0.25 volts below the reset input's VIH of 2.6 volts.

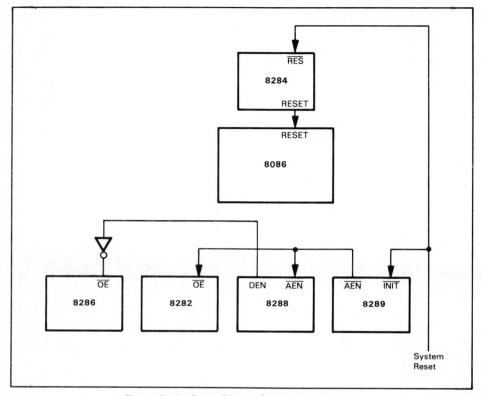

Figure 8-18. Reset Disable for Maximum Mode
8086 Bus Interface in Multi-CPU System

To guarantee reset from powerup, the reset input must remain below 1.05 volts for 50 microseconds after V_{CC} has reached the minimum supply voltage of 4.5 volts. The hysterisis allows the reset input to be driven by a simple RC circuit as shown in Figure 8-19.

The calculated RC value does not include time for the power supply to reach 4.5 volts, or the charge accumulated during this interval. Without the hysterisis, the reset output might oscillate as the input voltage passes through the switching voltage of the input. The calculated RC value provides the minimum required reset period of 50 microseconds for 8284s that switch at the 1.05 volt level, and a reset period of approximately 162 microseconds for 8284s that switch at the 2.6 volt level. If tighter tolerance between the minimum and maximum reset times is necessary, the reset circuit shown in Figure 8-20 might be used, rather than the simple RC circuit.

The circuit illustrated in Figure 8-20 provides a constant current source and linear charge rate on the capacitor, rather than the inverse exponential charge rate of the RC circuit. The maximum reset period for this implementation is 124 microseconds.

The 8284 synchronizes the reset input with the CPU clock to generate the reset signal to the CPU, as illustrated in Figure 8-21.

The output is also available as a general reset to the entire system. The reset has no effect on any clock circuits in the 8284.

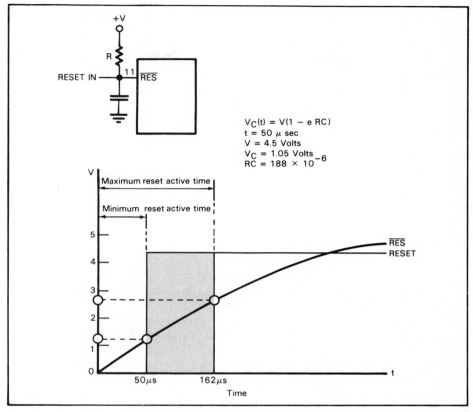

$$V_C(t) = V(1 - e\ RC)$$
$$t = 50\ \mu\ sec$$
$$V = 4.5\ Volts$$
$$V_C = 1.05\ Volts$$
$$RC = 188 \times 10^{-6}$$

Figure 8-19. 8284 Reset Circuit

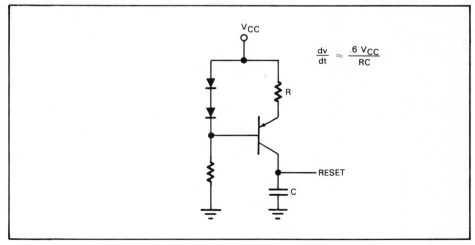

$$\frac{dv}{dt} \approx \frac{.6\ V_{CC}}{RC}$$

Figure 8-20. Constant Current Power-On Reset Circuit

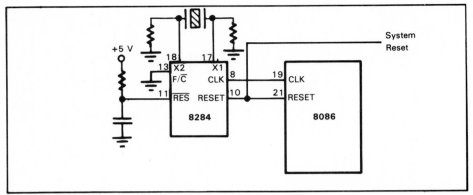

Figure 8-21. 8086 Reset

READY IMPLEMENTATION AND TIMING

The 8086 uses the READY signal to accommodate memory and I/O devices that cannot transfer information at the maximum CPU bus band width. READY is also used in multi-microprocessor systems to force the 8086 to wait for access to the system bus. To insert a wait state in a bus cycle, the READY signal to the CPU must be inactive (low) by the end of T2. To avoid insertion of a wait state, READY must be active (high) within a specified setup time prior to the positive transition during T3. Depending on the size and characteristics of the system, READY logic may take one of two approaches:

(1) The system is normally not ready. When the selected memory or I/O device is ready to perform the data transfer, it inputs a high READY signal.

(2) The system may normally be ready. If the selected memory or I/O device is not able to perform the data transfer at the maximum CPU transfer rate, it must then input a low READY signal.

The "classical" READY implementation keeps the system "normally not ready." When the selected device receives a read, write, or interrupt acknowledge command, if it has had sufficient time to respond to this command, it inputs READY high to the 8086; this allows the 8086 to advance the bus cycle. This implementation is characteristic of large multi-microprocessor, multibus systems, or systems where propagation delays, bus access delays, and device characteristics inherently slow down the system. Using this technique, devices that can run with no wait states must return READY high within the previously described limit for maximum system performance. Failure of a fast device to respond in time will cause wait clock periods to be inserted in the bus cycle.

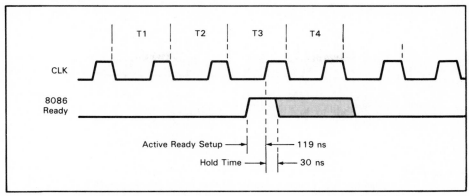

Figure 8-22. Normally Not Ready System Avoiding a Wait State

An alternate technique is to have the system "normally ready." All devices are assumed to operate at the maximum CPU bus band width. Devices that do not meet the requirement must input READY low by the end of T2 to ensure that wait state clock periods will be inserted. This implementation is typically applied to small, single CPU systems; it reduces the logic required to control the READY signal. Since the failure of the device requiring wait states to disable READY by the end of T2 will result in premature termination of the bus cycle, system timing must be carefully analyzed when using this approach.

It will be shown in Chapter 10 that the 8086 system allows the designer to combine the two READY techniques described above in a single system in order to optimize system performance.

The 8086 has two different timing requirements for READY, depending on the system implementation. For a "normally not ready" system, to avoid wait states, READY must be high within 119 ns (TRYHCH) of the positive clock transition during T3. This is illustrated in Figure 8-22.

A "normally ready" system inserts a wait state by inputting READY low within 8 ns (TRYLCL) after the end of T2 (start of T3), as illustrated in Figure 8-23.

To guarantee proper operation of the 8086, the READY input must not change from high to low during the clock low time of T3. In both cases READY must satisfy a hold time of 30 ns (TCHRYX) from the T3 positive clock transition.

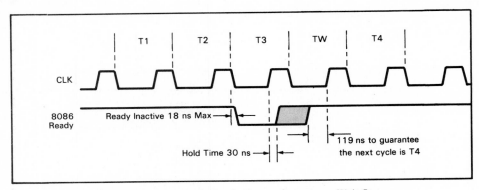

Figure 8-23. Normally Ready System Inserting a Wait State

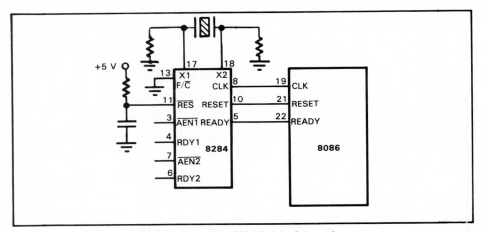

Figure 8-24. 8284-8086 Ready Connection

To generate a stable READY signal that satisfies the previous setup and hold times, the 8284 provides two separate system ready inputs (RDY1, RDY2) and a single synchronized ready output (READY). The RDY inputs are gated with separate access enables ($\overline{\text{AEN1}}$, $\overline{\text{AEN2}}$); this allows one of the two READY signals to be selected, as illustrated in Figure 8-24. The gated RDY signals are logically ORed by the 8284, and sampled at the beginning of each CLK cycle to generate READY to the CPU. This timing is illustrated in Figure 8-25.

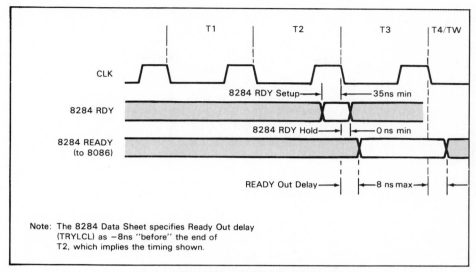

Figure 8-25. 8284 with 8086 Ready Timing

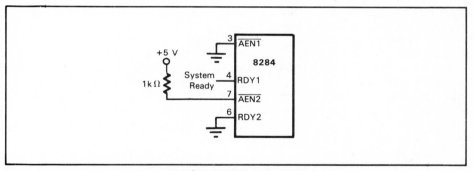

Figure 8-26. 8284 Using One RDY Input

The sampled READY signal is valid within 8 ns (TRYLCL) after CLK to satisfy the CPU timing requirements on "not ready" and "ready." Since READY cannot change until the next CLK, the hold time requirements are also satisfied. The system ready inputs to the 8284 (RDY1, RDY2) must be valid 35 ns (TRIVCL) before T3, and AEN must be valid 60 ns before T3. For a system using only one RDY input, the associated AEN is tied to ground while the other AEN is connected to five volts through 1K ohms, as illustrated in Figure 8-26.

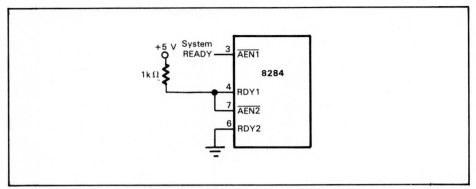

Figure 8-27. 8284 with SYSTEM READY Driving Access Enable

If the system generates a low active ready signal, it can be connected to the 8284 $\overline{\text{AEN}}$ input, providing the additional setup time required by the 8284 $\overline{\text{AEN}}$ input is satisfied. In this case, the associated RDY input would be tied high, as illustrated in Figure 8-27.

The majority of memory and peripheral devices that operate at less than the maximum CPU frequency typically do not require more than one wait state. The circuit given in Figure 8-28 generates a single wait state.

The system ready line in Figure 8-28 is driven low whenever a device requiring one wait state is selected. The flip-flop is cleared by ALE, enabling RDY to the 8284. If no wait states are required, the flip-flop does not change. If the system ready is driven low, the flip-flop toggles on the low-to-high clock transition of T2, to force one wait state. The next low-to-high transition of CLK toggles the flip-flop again, to indicate ready and allow completion of the bus cycle. Further changes in the state of the flip-flop will not affect the bus cycle. The circuit allows approximately 100 ns for chip select to system ready, as illustrated in Figure 8-29.

If the system is ''normally not ready'' programs should not assign executable code to the last six bytes of physical memory. Since the 8086 prefetches instructions, the CPU may attempt to access non-existent memory when executing code at the end of physical memory. If the access to non-existent memory fails to enable READY, the system will be caught in an indefinite wait.

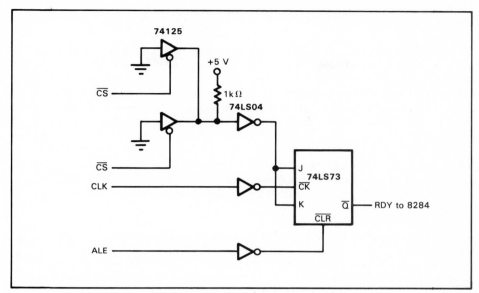

Figure 8-28. Single Wait State Generator

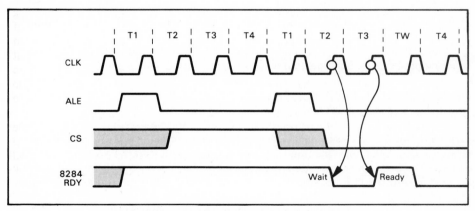

Figure 8-29. Timing for Single Wait State Generator

INTERRUPT STRUCTURE

The 8086 interrupt structure is based on a table of interrupt vectors stored in memory locations 0_{16} through $003FF_{16}$, as illustrated in Figure 8-30. Each vector has four bytes; the first two bytes hold a new program counter address, the next two bytes hold a new Code Segment register address. These two addresses combine to form the 20-bit execution address of an interrupt service routine. This 20-bit address is computed using normal 8086 segmented program memory addressing. The interrupt vector table may contain up to 256 interrupt vectors, specifying starting addresses for interrupt service routines residing anywhere in the one megabyte address space of the 8086. If a particular configuration uses fewer than 256 interrupts, then you need only allocate memory for those interrupt vectors that are used. But when a system is being debugged, you should assign all undefined interrupts to a trap routine as a means of detecting erroneous interrupts.

Each interrupt vector has an associated interrupt number. The interrupt number identifies the interrupt vector within the interrupt vector table. The interrupt number, multiplied by four, gives the absolute address for the first byte of the interrupt vector's entry within the interrupt vector table. For example, interrupt number five points to the sixth entry in the interrupt vector table; the first byte of this vector has the address 20_{10} ($= 14_{16}$). This is illustrated in Figure 8-30.

The 8086 interrupt structure thus allows you to specify the starting memory address for every interrupt service routine.

The 8086 has three types of interrupts: predefined interrupts that are requested by specific functions within the 8086, user defined hardware interrupts, and software interrupts.

Predefined interrupts can be requested by hardware and/or software. Let us examine predefined interrupts in detail.

PREDEFINED INTERRUPTS

''Predefined'' interrupts are so named because they have assigned interrupt numbers and automatic vectoring logic. Therefore, when a predefined interrupt is acknowledged, 8086 logic automatically vectors to the interrupt's assigned vector table entries. However, you must initialize these vector table entries with program counter and code segment addresses, and you must provide each interrupt with its interrupt service routine.

There are predefined hardware interrupts, which are requested by external logic, and there are predefined software interrupts, which are requested in consequence of an instruction's execution.

Interrupt numbers 0 through 31 have been assigned to predefined interrupts. If you do not use a predefined interrupt, you can use the interrupt number for some other interrupt. But this is not recommended, since it may result in your system being incompatible with future 8086 hardware and software products.

We will now describe predefined interrupts, one at a time.

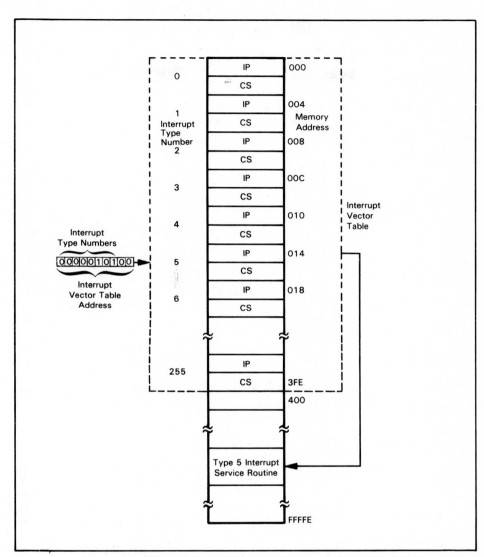

Figure 8-30. Obtaining the Interrupt Service Routine Address
from the Interrupt Vector Table

Interrupt 0 — Divide by Zero

This interrupt is automatically requested if, following execution of the division instruction, the quotient exceeds the maximum value that the division instruction allows. The interrupt is non-maskable. It is requested as a part of standard divide instruction execution logic. If interrupts are not reenabled by the divide by zero interrupt service routine, then this service routine's execution time should be included when computing the "worst-case" divide instruction time. This becomes the longest execution time for the divide instruction.

Interrupt 1 — Single Step

This interrupt occurs one instruction after TF (the Trap Flag) is set in the Program Status Word. This interrupt is used to execute programs one instruction at a time. After each program instruction is executed, an interrupt is requested. Following the interrupt request, various diagnostic capabilities might be provided by an interrupt service routine, at the conclusion of which the next program instruction is executed — and another single stepping interrupt request occurs.

To initiate single stepping, push the Program Status Word contents onto the stack; then set the Trap Flag bit within the saved Program Status Word at the top of the stack and pop the stack back to the Program Status Word. A single stepping interrupt will be requested following the next instruction's execution.

When a single stepping interrupt request is acknowledged the TF flag is reset in the Program Status Word to prevent the single stepping interrupt service routine itself from being interrupted by a single step interrupt request. TF remains set in the flags saved in the stack.

You should use the IRET instruction to return from a single step interrupt service routine. This return will restore the flags (including TF) and allow another TF interrupt to occur on completion of the next instruction.

Interrupt 2 — NMI (Non-Maskable Interrupt)

This is the highest priority hardware interrupt. As its name would imply, it is non-maskable. The NMI interrupt request input is edge triggered by a low-to-high NMI input transition, and is internally synchronized with a low-to-high transition of the CPU clock signal CLK. NMI must then remain high for at least two clock periods to guarantee recognition. Since any low-to-high transition of the NMI input can generate an interrupt request, spurious transitions must be suppressed.

If NMI is normally high, it must be low for two CPU clock periods before making its active low-to-high transition in order to guarantee recognition. This input is typically reserved for catastrophic interrupt requests, for example, following a power failure, or if a system watchdog timer times out.

Interrupt 3 — One Byte Interrupt

This is a software interrupt. It is generated by executing a special interrupt request instruction that occupies a single byte of object code. This interrupt instruction is used to set breakpoints in software debug programs. Since the smallest 8086 instruction object code is one byte, the one byte interrupt can replace any 8086 instruction as a means of setting breakpoints.

The one byte interrupt is not maskable.

Interrupt 4 — Interrupt On Overflow

This interrupt request occurs if the Overflow Flag (OF) is set in the Program Status Word, and the INTO instruction is executed. The INTO instruction allows the 8086 to trap to an overflow error service routine. Interrupt on overflow is non-maskable.

USER-DEFINED SOFTWARE INTERRUPTS

You can generate a software interrupt by executing the two byte interrupt INT nn instruction. The first object code byte is the INT op-code; the second object code byte (nn) contains the number of the interrupt to be executed. The INT instruction is not maskable.

This instruction is frequently used to call dynamically relocatable programs; the called program's location in memory is not known by the calling program. However, when the called program is loaded into memory, its execution address is loaded into its interrupt vector. The called program must return with an interrupt return (IRET) instruction.

USER-DEFINED HARDWARE INTERRUPTS

Maskable hardware interrupts are requested via the INTR pin of the 8086; these interrupts can be masked by the IF bit (Interrupt Flag) of the Program Status Word. During the last clock period of each instruction's execution, the state of the INTR pin is sampled. There are two exceptions to this rule:

1. When the instruction is a MOV to a segment register or a POP to a segment register.

2. During execution of an instruction prefix, which is treated as part of the instruction it precedes.

These two exceptions will be discussed following a description of the "general case" interrupt acknowledge execution sequence.

THE INTERRUPT ACKNOWLEDGE SEQUENCE

We will describe the interrupt acknowledge sequence, taking the user defined hardware interrupt as the "general case."

If the INTR signal is high when sampled, and the IF bit in the Program Status Word is 0, then a user defined interrupt has been requested; these interrupts are enabled, so the 8086 executes an interrupt acknowledge sequence. To guarantee the interrupt has been acknowledged, the INTR input must be held high until the 8086 returns an interrupt acknowledge, via $\overline{INTA}$ in a minimum system, or via $\overline{S0}$, $\overline{S1}$, and $\overline{S2}$ in a maximum system.

If the BIU is running a bus cycle when an interrupt condition is detected, the request must be valid at INTR two clock cycles prior to T4 of the bus cycle. If the two clock cycle setup is not satisfied, another bus cycle will be executed (if one is pending) before the interrupt is acknowledged.

If a hold request is pending, as might occur if an interrupt and hold are requested while a locked instruction is executing, then hold is serviced first, and the interrupt is acknowledged after the hold has been serviced.

Only user defined hardware interrupt requests occurring at the INTR pin receive a specific hardware acknowledge. This acknowledge takes the form of two interrupt acknowledge bus cycles, separated by two idle clock periods, as illustrated in Figure 8-31. Software interrupts and non-maskable interrupts do not receive the acknowledge sequence illustrated in Figure 8-31.

The complete interrupt acknowledge sequence, as illustrated in Figure 8-30, consists of two $\overline{INTA}$ bus cycles, separated by two idle clock periods. During the two bus cycles, $\overline{INTA}$ is output low (in minimum mode) to acknowledge the interrupt. The address/data bus (including $\overline{BHE}$), and the associated status (S3-S7) is floated during both bus cycles; however, a high ALE pulse is output, so address latches will be loaded with indeterminate information. Therefore devices should always use READ ($\overline{RD}$) low as a qualifier before driving their outputs.

During the $\overline{INTA}$ bus cycles, DT/$\overline{R}$ and $\overline{DEN}$ are active; this allows the 8086 to receive a one-byte interrupt number from the device requesting the interrupt.

The first $\overline{INTA}$ bus cycle signals that an interrupt acknowledge is in progress; this allows the interrupting device time to ready its interrupt number for transmittal during the next $\overline{INTA}$ bus cycle. The interrupt number must be transferred to the 8086 on the lower half of the 16-bit data bus during the second $\overline{INTA}$ bus cycle. Therefore devices that supply interrupt vectors must connect to the lower half of the 16-bit data bus.

Timing for $\overline{INTA}$ bus cycles (with the exception of address timing) is the same as read bus cycle timing.

Note that the 8086 interrupt acknowledge sequence deviates from the 8080 and the 8085 in that no instruction is read by the CPU during the interrupt acknowledge sequence. The 8080 and 8085 require either a restart or a call instruction to be issued by the interrupting device to the CPU as part of the acknowledge sequence.

In the minimum mode system, the M/$\overline{IO}$ signal will be low during interrupt acknowledge bus cycles.

The 8086 prevents the BIU from honoring a hold request occurring between the two INTA cycles.

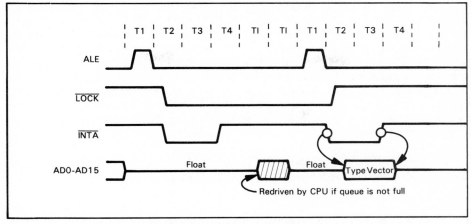

Figure 8-31. Interrupt Acknowledge Sequence in Minimum Mode

In a maximum mode system, status lines $\overline{S0}$-$\overline{S2}$ will cause the 8288 Bus Controller to output $\overline{INTA}$ low during each interrupt acknowledge bus cycle. The $\overline{LOCK}$ output of the 8086 will be active from T2 of the first interrupt acknowledge bus cycle until T2 of the second interrupt acknowledge bus cycle to prevent the 8086 from honoring a hold request on either $\overline{RQ}/\overline{GT}$ input, and to prevent bus arbitration logic from relinquishing the bus between the two interrupt acknowledge bus cycles in multimaster systems. READY logic functions identically in interrupt acknowledge, read or write bus cyles.

The 8086 will not sample INTR after a MOV to a segment register or POP to a segment register; this allows a 32-bit pointer to be loaded into the Stack Pointer SS and SP registers without the possibility of an interrupt separating the two loads.

Here is an example of an uninterruptable instruction sequence:

```
MOV     SS,     NEW$STACK$SEGMENT
MOV     SP,     NEW$STACK$POINTER
```

The 8086 will not sample INTR after executing an instruction prefix, since prefixes are treated as part of the instruction they precede. The one exception to this rule occurs when a string primitive is preceded by the Repeat (REP) prefix. The repeated string operation will sample INTR after completing each repeated string primitive's execution. This includes repeat string operations having a LOCK prefix. If multiple prefixes precede a repeated string operation, and the instruction is interrupted, only the prefix immediately preceding the string primitive is restored following a return from the interrupt routine. To allow correct resumption of program execution you should use the following programming technique:

```
LOCKED$BLOCK$MOVE =     LOCK
                        REP
                        MOVS    DEST,CS: SOURCE
                        AND     CX,CX
                        JNZ     LOCKED$BLOCK$MOVE
```

The object code bytes generated for the MOVS instruction are (in descending order) LOCK prefix, REP prefix, Segment Override prefix, and MOVS. Upon return from the interrupt, the segment override prefix is restored to guarantee that one additional transfer will occur between the correct memory locations. The instructions following the move test the repetition count value to determine if the move was completed; a return to the block move instruction occurs if the move was not completed.

The 8086 reads the interrupt number from the bus for hardware interrupts and from the instruction stream for software interrupts. The interrupt number is multiplied by four to generate the address of the corresponding interrupt vector in the interrupt vector table. The four bytes of the interrupt vector are:

Least significant byte for the program counter.

Most significant byte for the program counter.

Least significant byte for the Code Segment register.

Most significant byte for the Code Segment register.

Next the 8086 pushes the Program Status Word contents onto the stack, resets the trap and interrupt flags, then pushes the current Code Segment register and the program counter contents onto the stack. The new Code Segment register and program counter contents are loaded from the interrupt vector table; read bus cycles are executed for this to occur.

No segment registers are used when referencing the interrupt vector table during the interrupt acknowledge sequence. The vector displacement is added to zero to form the 20-bit address; S4 is 1 and S3 is 0, indicating no segment register selection.

This is the actual bus sequence executed when a user defined, maskable interrupt is acknowledged:

1. Two interrupt acknowledge bus cycles are executed, separated by two idle clock periods. As illustrated in Figure 8-30, the acknowledged device returns an interrupt number, as a byte of data, during the second interrupt acknowledge bus cycle. This data byte, shifted left two bit positions, becomes the interrupt vector starting address.

2. A read bus cycle is executed, during which new CS register contents are read from the first two interrupt vector bytes.

3. A read bus cycle is executed, during which new program counter contents are read from the third and fourth interrupt vector bytes.

4. A write bus cycle is executed, during which the Program Status Word contents is pushed onto the stack.

5. The Interrupt (I) and Test (TF) flags in the Program Status Word are reset to 0. This disables maskable or single step interrupts.

6. A write bus cycle is executed, during which the CS register contents is pushed onto the stack.

7. A write bus cycle is executed, during which program counter contents are pushed onto the Stack.

Program execution now branches to the interrupt service routine — whose address has been fetched from the interrupt vector.

When a non-maskable interrupt, a software interrupt, or a single step interrupt is acknowledged, steps 2 through 7 above are executed; step 1 is not needed since the interrupt number is known.

62 clock periods separate the end of the instruction during which a user defined maskable interrupt is requested, and the start of interrupt service routine execution.

The same sequence of bus cycles is executed for software generated interrupts, except that no interrupt acknowledge bus cycles are executed. In consequence, the delay to execution of the interrupt service routine is 51 clock periods for INT nn and single step, 52 clock periods for INT3, and 53 clock periods for INTO.

If wait states are inserted in any bus cycle, the number of interrupt acknowledge clock periods given above will, of course, increase accordingly.

Let us now examine multiple interrupts and interrupt priorities.

Only external interrupts requested via INTR can be disabled. In consequence, these interrupts have lowest priority. Any other interrupt's acknowledge sequence resets the IF flag in the Program Status Word. An interrupt requested via INTR, therefore, cannot be acknowledged until other interrupt service routines are completed or interrupts are reenabled (IF flag is set).

A program being debugged using single stepping could be modified to acknowledge external, user defined interrupts only within the single step interrupt service routine. This will allow the external interrupts to be serviced quickly in spite of single stepping. To do this requires that the single step interrupt service routine reset the IF flag for the interrupted program, which will be in the Program Status Word stored in two words from the top of the stack, and enable interrupts during the single step routine. This may be illustrated as follows:

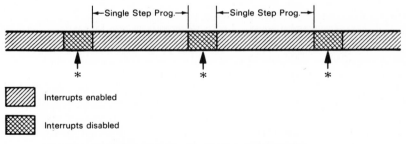

```
                |←Single Step Prog.→|   |←Single Step Prog.→|
```

```
              ↑                   ↑                   ↑
              *                   *                   *
```

▨ Interrupts enabled

▧ Interrupts disabled

*   Execution of single instruction of program being single stepped

On the other hand, you may wish to single step the interrupted program only — or the external, user defined interrupt's service routine only. If the TF flag in the Program Status Word is set to 1 by the interrupted program, then the interrupted program will be subject to single stepping; otherwise it will not. In either case, a user defined interrupt's service routine will begin execution with TF reset to 0, and single stepping consequently disabled. Program logic within the interrupt service routine must therefore enable single stepping for the duration of the interrupt service routine's execution.

You can, if you wish, disable INTR within single stepping traps. This requires that the single stepping interrupt service routine keep the IF flag reset to 0 within the Program Status Word. Bus disabling INTR, for what could become a long time, might disrupt your program logic.

We will now examine non-maskable interrupt priorities. We have described three such interrupts: NMI, single stepping, and software traps. All have priority over user defined external interrupts requested via INTR. Among themselves, when two of the three non-maskable interrupts occur simultaneously, single stepping has highest priority, followed by NMI, with software traps having lowest priority. But when all three non-maskable interrupts are requested simultaneously, NMI has highest priority, followed by software traps, with single stepping acquiring lowest priority.

Since single stepping may have higher priority than NMI, or lower priority, the single stepping interrupt service routine will have to examine whether its execution does or does not follow an NMI interrupt. If it does follow an NMI interrupt and you wish to immediately service the NMI, the single stepping interrupt service routine must contain logic to disable itself. This program logic will examine the return address at the top of the stack, and upon detecting an NMI interrupt service routine address, it need only return, allowing the NMI routine to execute. The NMI routine will return to the program being single stepped and single stepping is automatically reenabled by restoring the flags during the return. The net affect is: if the NMI is detected, single stepping is bypassed for one instruction of the program being single stepped. Since single stepping is disabled during the interrupt acknowledge process, the NMI interrupt service routine need only keep the TF flag reset to 0 within its Program Status Word in order to disable single stepping for the duration of its execution.

SYSTEM INTERRUPT CONFIGURATIONS

The 8259A Priority Interrupt Controller can handle multiple, external user defined interrupts requested via INTR. This device will operate in 8080A/8085 or 8086 systems. The 8259A is cascadable; in master/slave configurations it will handle up to 64 interrupts within a single system.

Figures 8-32 and 8-33 illustrate 8259As in minimum and maximum mode 8086 systems.

The minimum mode configuration illustrated in Figure 8-32a shows an 8259A connected to an 8086 multiplexed bus. The configuration shown in Figure 8-32b illustrates an 8259A connected to a demultiplexed bus system. These interconnections are also applicable to maximum mode systems. The configuration given for a maximum mode system shows a master 8259A on the 8086 multiplexed bus, with additional slave 8259As out on the buffered system bus. This configuration demonstrates several unique characteristics of the maximum mode system interface. If the master 8259A receives interrupts from a mix of slave 8259As and regular interrupting devices, the slaves must provide the interrupt numbers for devices connected to them, while the master must provide the interrupt numbers for devices directly attached to its interrupt inputs. The master 8259A can determine if an interrupt is being received directly from the requesting device or from a slave 8259A. The master 8259A uses this information to enable or disable data bus transceivers (via the NAND function of DEN and EN). If the master 8259A must provide the interrupt number, it will disable the data bus transceivers. If a slave 8259A must provide the type number, the 8086 will enable the data bus transceivers. The EN output is normally high, allowing the 8086/8288 to control the bus transceivers. To select the proper slave when servicing a slave interrupt, the master must provide a cascade address (CAS) to the slave. If the 8288 is not strapped in the I/O bus mode (the 8288 IOB input connected to ground), the MCE/$\overline{\text{PDEN}}$ output becomes an MCE or Master Cascade Enable output (use of the I/O bus mode is explained in

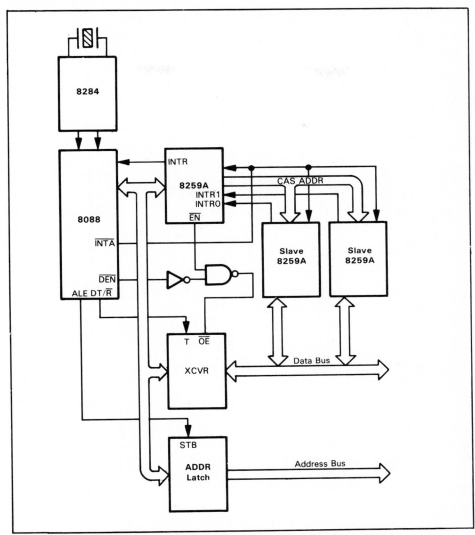

Figure 8-32a. 8259s Connected to a Minimum Mode 8086
— Multiplexed Bus

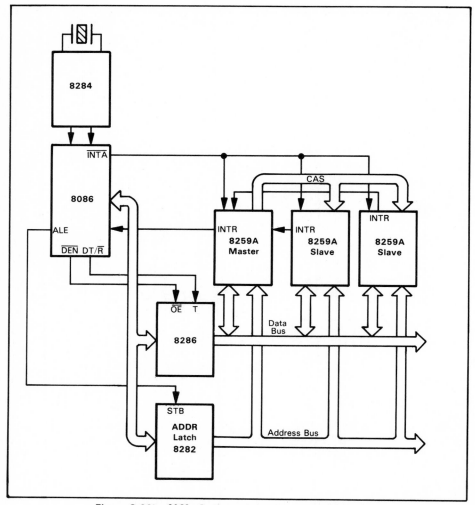

Figure 8-32b. 8259s Connected to a Minimum Mode 8086
— Demultiplexed Bus

Chapter 10). MCE is active only during $\overline{\text{INTA}}$ cycles, as shown in Figure 8-34. MCE enables the master 8259A's cascade address onto the 8086's local bus during ALE.

This allows the address latches to capture the cascade address with ALE, with the system address bus being used to select the proper slave 8259A. MCE is gated with $\overline{\text{LOCK}}$ to minimize local bus contention between the 8086 floating its bus output, and the cascade address (CAS) being enabled onto the bus. The first $\overline{\text{INTA}}$ bus cycle allows the master 8259A to resolve internal priorities and output of the cascade address (CAS), which is transmitted to the slaves during the second $\overline{\text{INTA}}$ bus cycle. For additional information on the 8259A, refer to Intel Application Note AP59, or *An Introduction to Microcomputers — Volume 2, Some Real Microprocessors*, by A. Osborne.

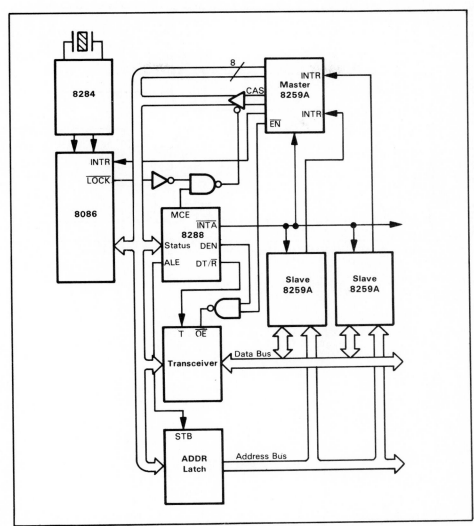

Figure 8-33. 8259s Connected to a Maximum Mode 8086

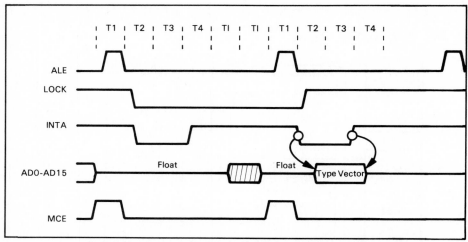

Figure 8-34. Timing to Gate 8259A CAS Address onto the 8086 Local Bus

INTERPRETING THE 8086 BUS TIMING DIAGRAMS

8086 minimum and maximum mode bus timing diagrams are shown in the data sheets at the back of this book. These timing diagrams may be divided into six sections as follows:

1. Address and ALE timing

2. Read cycle timing

3. Write cycle timing

4. Interrupt acknowledge timing

5. Ready timing

6. Bus control transfer timing

Since the A.C. characteristics of the signal are specified relative to the CPU clock, the relationship between the majority of signals can be deduced by simply determining the clock periods that separate the clock edges to which the signals are relative, then adding or subtracting the appropriate minimum/maximum parameter values. One aspect of system timing not compensated for in this approach is the "worst case" relationship between minimum and maximum parameter values (also known as tracking relationships). For example, consider a signal that has specified minimum and maximum turn on and turn off delays. Depending on device characteristics, it may not be possible for a component to simultaneously demonstrate a maximum turn-on and minimum turn-off delay, even though worst case analysis might imply this possibility. This argument is characteristic of MOS devices and is therefore applicable to the 8086 A.C. characteristics. The message is: worst case analysis mixing/minimum and maximum delay parameters will typically exceed the worst case obtainable. Therefore they should not be subjectively degraded further, to obtain worse-worst case values. We will now examine guidelines for specific areas of 8086 timing that are sensitive to tracking relationships.

MINIMUM MODE BUS TIMING

ADDRESS AND ALE

The address/ALE timing relationship is important since it determines a device's ability to capture a valid address from the multiplexed bus. Since the 8282 and 8283 latches capture the address on the trailing edge of ALE, the critical timing involves the state of the address lines when ALE terminates. The parameter $TAVAL = TCLCH - 60$ ns guarantees that addresses are valid at the CPU 58 ns before the trailing edge of ALE. This satisfies the zero data setup time to end of strobe required by the 8282/8283 and assures that a valid address is captured. The address is guaranteed to remain valid beyond the end of ALE by the TLLAZ parameter. This specification overrides the relationship between TCHLL and TCLAX, which might seem to imply that the address may not be valid by the latest possible ALE. TLLAZ timing applies to the entire address bus, even though only shown for A19-A16 in the timing diagram. The TCLAX min specification on the address indicates the earliest possible time the bus will float if not restrained by a slow ALE. TCLAX only applies to the multiplexed address/data lines AD15-0 during read cycles. During write cycles, the multiplexed Address/Data Bus switches directly from address to write data. Address hold time to ALE is again guaranteed by the TLLAZ specification, with the absolute minimum (for the case of an early ALE termination) specified by TCLAX. For both the read and write case, the A19-A16 lines switch directly from address to status with the same timing as the multiplexed address/data bus for the write case. The minimum ALE pulse width is guaranteed by TLHLL min, which takes precedence over the value obtained by relating TCLLH max and TCHLl min.

To determine the worst delay to valid address on a demultiplexed address bus, two paths must be considered:

1. Delay of valid address

2. Delay of ALE

Since the 8282 and 8283 are flow through latches, a valid address is not transmitted to the address bus until ALE is active. A comparison of address valid delay TCLAV max, with ALE active delay TCLLH max indicates TCLAV max is the worst case. Subtracting the latch propagation delay gives the worst case address bus valid delay from the start of the bus cycle.

READ CYCLE TIMING

Read cycle timing consists of three parts:

1.   Conditioning the bus

2.   Activating the Read Control signal

3.   Establishing the data transceiver enable and direction controls

If the memory or I/O devices are connected directly to the multiplexed address/ data bus, the TAZRL parameter guarantees that the 8086 will float the bus before activating the read control and allowing the selected device to drive the bus. At the end of the bus cycle, the TRHAV parameter specifies the bus float delay the device being deselected must satisfy if it is to avoid contention with the 8086 driving the address for the next bus cycle. The next bus cycle may start during the CLK period following T4 or any number of CLK periods later.

The minimum delay from read active to valid data at the CPU is 2TCLCL − TCLRL max − TDVCL = 205 ns. The minimum pulse width is 2TRLRH which gives a minimum pulse width of 325 ns.

DT/$\overline{\text{R}}$ is established early in the bus cycle and requires no further consideration.

During a read, the $\overline{\text{DEN}}$ signal must allow the transceivers to propagate data to the CPU with the appropriate data set up time, and continue to do so for the required hold time. The $\overline{\text{DEN}}$ turn on delay allows TCLCL + TCHCL min − TCVCTV max − TDVCL = 127 ns transceiver enable time prior to valid data required by the 8086. Since the 8086 data hold time TCLDZ min and the minimum $\overline{\text{DEN}}$ turn off delay TCVCTX min are both 10 ns relative to the same clock edge, the hold time is guaranteed. Additionally, $\overline{\text{DEN}}$ must disable the transceivers prior to the 8086 driving the bus with the address for the next bus cycle. The maximum $\overline{\text{DEN}}$ turn off delay (TCVCTX max), compared with the minimum delay for the addresses out of the 8086 (TCLRH min), indicates the transceivers are disabled at least 55 ns before the CPU drives the address onto the multiplexed bus.

WRITE CYCLE TIMING

The write cycle consists of three major functions:

1. Providing write data to the system

2. Generating the write command

3. Controlling data bus transceivers

The Write Data and Write command are both enabled from the leading edge of T2. Comparing minimum WR active delay TCVCTV min with the maximum write data delay TCLDV indicates that write data may not be valid until 100 ns after write is active. Therefore, devices in the system should capture data on the trailing edge of the Write command rather than the leading edge to guarantee valid data. The 8086 floats the bus after write only if forced off the bus by a HOLD or RQ/GT input, otherwise the 8086 simply switches the output drivers from data to address at the beginning of the next bus cycle. As with the read cycle, the next bus cycle may start in the clock period following T4 or any later clock period.

Data from the 8086 is valid a minimum of 2TCLCL − TCLDV max + TCVCTX min = 300 ns before the trailing edge of WRITE. The minimum WRITE pulse width is TWLWH = 340 ns. The CPU maintains valid write data TWHDX ns after write. The TWHDZ specification overrides the result derived by relating TCLCH min and TCHDZ min, which implies write data may only be valid 18 ns after WR. The TCHDZ minimum bus float time takes effect only if TCVCTX + TWHDZ < TCLCH + TCHDZ.

The transceiver direction control signal DT/$\overline{\text{R}}$ is conditioned to transmit at the end of each read cycle; it does not change during a write cycle. This allows the transceiver enable signal $\overline{\text{DEN}}$ to be active early in the cycle, while addresses are valid, without corrupting the address on the multiplexed bus. $\overline{\text{DEN}}$ is disabled a minimum of TCLCH min + TCVCTX min − TCVCTX max = 18 ns after write, to guarantee data hold time to the selected device. Since we are again evaluating a minimum TCVTCX with a maximum TCVTCX, the real delay from the end of write to transceiver disable is approximately 60 ns.

INTERRUPT ACKNOWLEDGE TIMING

The interrupt acknowledge sequence consists of two interrupt acknowledge bus cycles. Timing of each cycle is identical to read cycle timing, with two exceptions: control signal timing and address/data bus timing.

The $\overline{INTA}$ control signal has the same timing as the $\overline{WR}$ Control signal. $\overline{INTA}$ is active within 110 ns of the start of T2, providing 260 ns of access time from control to data valid at the 8086. The $\overline{INTA}$ control is active following the leading edge of T4 for a minimum of TCVCTX min = 10 ns, to satisfy the data hold time of the 8086. This insures that the minimum $\overline{INTA}$ pulse width is 300 ns; however, taking signal delay tracking into consideration (TCVCTX min = 50 if TCVCTX max = 110), gives a minimum pulse width of 340 ns. Since the maximum inactive delay of $\overline{INTA}$ is TCVCTX max = 110 ns, and the 8086 will not drive the bus until 15 ns (TCLAV min) into the next clock cycle, 105 ns are available for interrupt devices on the local bus to float their outputs. If the data bus is buffered, $\overline{DEN}$ provides the same amount of time for local bus transceivers to float their outputs.

The multiplexed address/data bus is floated from T1 at the beginning of the $\overline{INTA}$ cycle, within TCLAZ ns. The upper four multiplexed address/status lines do not float. The address value on A19-A16 is indeterminate, but the status information will be valid (S3=0, S4=0, S5=IF, S6=0, S7=$\overline{BHE}$=0). The multiplexed address/data lines will remain floating until the clock period following T4 of the $\overline{INTA}$ bus cycle. This sequence occurs for both of the $\overline{INTA}$ bus cycles. The interrupt number read by the 8086 on the second $\overline{INTA}$ bus cycle must satisfy the data setup and hold times of a read cycle.

The $\overline{DEN}$ and DT/$\overline{R}$ signals are enabled for each $\overline{INTA}$ cycle; they do not remain active between the two cycles. Timing for these two signals is identical in $\overline{INTA}$ and Read bus cycles.

READY TIMING

The detailed timing requirements of the 8086 READY signal and the system Ready signal (RDY) input into the 8284 were given earlier in this chapter. The system Ready signal (RDY) is typically generated from either the address decode of the selected device or the address and control signals $\overline{RD}$, $\overline{WR}$, $\overline{INTA}$.

If RDY is enabled by the address decode, there are two cases to consider. For a system which is normally not ready, the time to generate ready from a valid address and not insert a wait state is 2TCLCL − TCLAV max − TRIVCL max = 255 ns. This time is available for buffer delays and address decoding to determine if the selected device does not require a wait state and drive the RDY line high. If wait clock periods are required, user hardware must provide the appropriate ready delay. Since the address will not change until the next ALE, RDY will remain valid throughout the bus cycle. For a system which is normally ready, selected devices requiring wait states also have 255 ns to disable the RDY lines. User hardware must delay reenabling RDY by the appropriate number of wait state clock periods.

If RDY is enabled by the $\overline{RD}$ control, TCLCL − TCLRL max − TRIVCL max = 15 ns are available for external logic. If the $\overline{WR}$ control is used, TCLCL − TCVCTV max − TRIVCL max = 55 ns are available.

Comparison of RDY generated by an address or control signal indicates that address decoding provides the best timing. If the system is normally not ready, address decoding alone could be used to provide RDY for devices not requiring wait states, while devices requiring wait states may use a combination of address decode and control signals to activate a wait state generator. If the system is normally ready, devices not requiring wait states do nothing to RDY, while devices needing wait states should disable RDY via the address decode, and use a combination of address decode and control signals to activate a delay until RDY is reenabled.

If the system requires no wait states for memory, and a fixed number of wait states for $\overline{RD}$ and $\overline{WR}$ to all I/O devices, the $M/\overline{IO}$ signal can be used as an early indication that wait state clock periods are needed. This allows a common circuit to control ready timing for the entire system, without feedback of address decodes.

BUS CONTROL TRANSFER TIMING

Detailed HOLD/HLDA timing is covered later in this chapter.

The $\overline{TEST}$ input is sampled by the 8086 only during execution of the WAIT instruction. The $\overline{TEST}$ signal should be active for a minimum of six clock periods during the WAIT instruction to guarantee detection.

MAXIMUM MODE BUS TIMING

The maximum mode 8086 bus operations are logically equivalent to the minimum mode operation. Detailed timing analysis now involves signals generated by the 8086 CPU and the 8288 Bus Controller.

In addition to supplying signals provided by a minimum mode 8086, the 8288 provides additional control signals that expand the flexibility of the system. In the following discussion, when calculating signal relationships, be sure to use the proper maximum mode values, rather than equivalent minimum mode values.

ADDRESS AND ALE

In maximum mode, address information continues to come from the 8086, but the ALE strobe is generated by the 8288 Bus Controller. To determine the worst case relationships between ALE and a valid address, activation of the 8288 ALE relative to the $\overline{S0}$-$\overline{S2}$ status from the 8086 must be analyzed.

The maximum mode timing diagram specifies two possible delay paths to generate ALE. The first is TCHSV + TSVLH, measured from the rising edge of the clock period preceding T1. The second path is TCLLH, measured from the start of T1. Since the 8288 initiates a bus cycle from the status lines leaving the passive state ($\overline{S0}, \overline{S1}, \overline{S2} = 1,1,1$), if the 8086 is late in issuing the status (TCHSV max) while the clock high time is a minimum (TCHCL min), the status will not have changed by the start of T1, and ALE is issued TSVLH ns after the status changes. If the status changes prior to the beginning of T1, the 8288 will not issue the ALE until TCLLH ns after the start of T1. The resulting worst case delay to enable ALE (relative to start of T1) is TCHSV max + TSVLH max − TCHCL min = 58 ns.

The trailing edge of ALE is triggered in the 8288 by the positive clock edge in T1, regardless of the delay to enable ALE. The resulting minimum ALE pulse width is TCLCH max − 58 ns = 75 ns assuming TCHLL = 0. TCLCH max must be used, since TCHCL min was assumed to derive the 58 ns ALE enable delay. The address is guaranteed to be valid TCLCH min + TCHLL min − TCLAV max = 8 ns prior to the trailing edge of ALE to capture the address in the 8288 or 8283 latches. Again we have assumed a very conservative TCHLL = 0. Note that since the address and ALE are driven by separate devices, no tracking of A.C. characteristics can be assumed.

The address hold time to the latches is guaranteed by the address remaining valid until the end of T1, while ALE is disabled a maximum of 15 ns from the positive clock transition in T1 (TCHCL min − TCHLL max = 52 ns address hold time). The multiplexed bus transitions from address to status and write data, or tristate (for read) are identical to minimum mode timing. Also, since the address valid delay (TCLAV) remains the critical path in establishing a valid address, the address access times to Valid Data and Ready are the same as the minimum mode system.

READ CYCLE TIMING

The maximum mode system offers two read signals, generated separately by the 8086 and the 8288. The 8086 $\overline{RD}$ output signal timing is identical to the minimum mode system, but the A.C. characteristics of the Read Control signal generated by the 8288 are significantly better. Devices on a demultiplexed buffered system bus should therefore use the 8288 Read Control signal. The 8086 $\overline{RD}$ signal is available for devices that reside directly on the multiplexed bus.

The following evaluation only considers the 8288 Read Control signal timing.

The 8288 outputs separate Memory and I/O Read Control signals ($\overline{IORC}$ and $\overline{MRDC}$); both have the same A.C. characteristics. These control signals are issued TCLML ns after the start of T2; they terminate TCLMH ns after the start of T4. The minimum control pulse length is 2TCLCL − TCLML max + TCLML min = 375 ns. The access time to valid data at the 8086 is 2TCLCL − TCLML max − TDVCL max = 335 ns. Since the 8288 was designed for systems with buffered data busses, control signals $\overline{IORC}$ and $\overline{MRDC}$ are enabled before the 8086 has floated the multiplexed bus; therefore control signals $\overline{IORC}$ and $\overline{MRDC}$ should not be used by devices that connect directly to the multiplexed bus, otherwise bus contention could result during 8086 bus float and device turn on.

The direction control for data bus transceivers is established in T1. Transceivers are enabled by DEN until the positive clock transition of T2. This provides TCLCH + TCVNV min = 123 ns for 8086 bus float delay, and TCHCL min + TCVNV max − TDVCL max = 187 ns of transceiver active to data valid at the 8086. Since both DEN and control signals are valid a minimum of 10 ns into T4, the 8086 data hold time TCLDZ is guaranteed. A maximum DEN disable of 45 ns (TCVNX max) guarantees the transceivers are disabled by the start of the next 8086 bus cycle (215 ns minimum from the same clock edge). On a positive clock transition of T4, DT/$\overline{R}$ is returned to transmit, in preparation for a possible write operation on the next bus cycle. Since the system memory and I/O devices reside on a buffered system bus, they must float their outputs before the device for the next bus cycle is selected (approximately 2TCLCL), or the transceivers drive write data onto the bus (approximately 2TCLCL).

WRITE CYCLE TIMING

In the maximum mode, the 8288 provides normal and advanced write control signals for memory and I/O ($\overline{MWTC}$, $\overline{AMWC}$, $\overline{IOWC}$, $\overline{AIOWC}$). The advanced write control signals are active a full clock period ahead of the normal write control signals. The timing for advanced write control signals is identical to the timing for the read control signals. The advanced Write pulse width is 2TCLCL − TCLML max + TCLMH min = 375 ns, while a normal write pulse width is TCLCL − TCLML max + TCLMH min = 175 ns. Write data set up time to the selected device is a function of either the data valid delay from the 8086 (TCLDV), or the transceiver enable delay (TCVNV). The worst case delay to valid write data is TCLDV = 110 ns, minus transceiver propagation delays. This implies that data may not be valid until 100 ns after the leading edge of the advanced write control signal, but will be valid approximately TCLCL − TCLDV max + TCLML min = 100 ns prior to the leading edge of the normal write control signal. Data will be valid 2TCLCL − TCLDV max + TCLMH min = 300 ns before the trailing edge of either write control signal. The data and control signal overlap for the advanced write control is 300 ns, while the overlap with a normal write control is 175 ns. The transceivers are disabled a minimum of TCLCH min − TCLMH max + TCVNX min = 85 ns after write control, while the 8086 provides valid data a minimum of TCLCH min − TCLMH max + TCHDZ min = 85 ns. This guarantees write data hold of 85 ns after the write control. The transceivers are disabled TCLCL − TCVNX max + TCHDTL min = 155 ns (assuming TCHDTL = 0) prior to transceiver direction change for a subsequent read bus cycle.

INTERRUPT ACKNOWLEDGE TIMING

The maximum mode $\overline{INTA}$ sequence is logically identical to the minimum mode sequence. The transceiver control (DEN and DT/$\overline{R}$) and $\overline{INTA}$ control timing of both of the interrupt acknowledge cycles are identical to the transceiver control timing of the read cycle. As in the minimum mode system, the multiplexed address/data bus will float from the leading edge of T1 for each $\overline{INTA}$ bus cycle and will not be driven by the 8086 until after T4 of each $\overline{INTA}$ cycle. The setup and hold times on the vector returned by external hardware during the second $\overline{INTA}$ cycle are the same as data setup and hold for the read bus cycle. If the device providing the interrupt vector is connected to the local bus, TCLCL − TCLAZ max + TCLML min = 130 ns are available from the 8086 bus float to $\overline{INTA}$ command active. The selected device on the local bus must disable the system data bus transceivers, since DEN is still generated by the 8288.

If the 8288 is not in the IOB (I/O Bus) mode, the 8288 MCE/$\overline{\text{PDEN}}$ output becomes the MCE output. This output is active during each $\overline{\text{INTA}}$ cycle and overlaps the ALE signal during T1. The MCE is available for gating cascade addresses from a master 8259A onto three of the upper AD15-AD8 lines; also MCE allows ALE to latch the cascade address into the address latches. The address lines may then be used to provide CAS address selection to slave 8259As located on the system bus. (Refer to Figure 8-32 for a description of this technique.) MCE is active within 15 ns of status or the start of T1 for each $\overline{\text{INTA}}$ cycle. MCE should not enable the CAS lines onto the mutliplexed bus during the first cycle, since the 8086 does not guarantee to float the bus until 80 ns into the first $\overline{\text{INTA}}$ cycle. The first MCE can be inhibited by gating MCE with $\overline{\text{LOCK}}$. The 8086 $\overline{\text{LOCK}}$ output is activated during T2 of the first $\overline{\text{INTA}}$ cycle; it is disabled during T2 of the second $\overline{\text{INTA}}$ cycle. The overlap of $\overline{\text{LOCK}}$ with MCE allows the first MCE to be masked and the second MCE to gate the cascade address onto the local bus. Since the 8259A will not provide a cascade address until the second $\overline{\text{INTA}}$ bus cycle, no information is lost. As with ALE, MCE is guaranteed valid within 58 ns of the start of T1 to allow 75 ns CAS address set up of the trailing edge of ALE. MCE remains active TCHCL min − TCHLL max + TCLMCL min = 52 ns after ALE to provide data hold time to the latches.

If the 8288 is strapped in the IOB mode, the MCE output becomes $\overline{\text{PDEN}}$ and all I/O references are assumed to be devices on the local bus rather than on the demultiplexed system bus. Since $\overline{\text{INTA}}$ cycles are considered I/O cycles, all interrupts are assumed to come from the local system bus, and cascade addresses are not gated onto the system address bus. Additionally, the DEN signal is not enabled since no I/O transfers occur on the system bus. If the local I/O bus is also buffered by transceivers, the $\overline{\text{PDEN}}$ signal is used to enable those transceivers. $\overline{\text{PDEN}}$ A.C. characteristics are identical to DEN, with $\overline{\text{PDEN}}$ enabled for I/O references and DEN enabled for instruction or data memory references. The system implications of the various modes are discussed in a later chapter.

READY TIMING

Ready timing, when based on the address valid timing, is the same for maximum and minimum mode systems. The delay from 8288 control valid to RDY valid at the 8284 is TCLCL − TCLML max − TRIVCL min = 130 ns. This time can be used by external circuits to determine whether wait state clock periods need to be inserted; external circuits must disable RDY to insert a wait state, or enable RDY to avoid a wait state. $\overline{\text{INTA}}$, all read controls, and advanced write controls provide this timing. The normal write control is not valid until after RDY must be valid. Since both normal and advanced write controls are generated by the 8288 for all write bus cycles, the advanced write control may be used to generate a RDY indication, even though the selected device uses the normal write control.

OTHER CONSIDERATIONS

$\overline{RQ}/\overline{GT}$ timing is covered later in this chapter.

The only signals to be considered in the maximum mode are the queue status lines QS0 and QS1. These signals change on the leading edge of each clock period (high-to-low transition), including idle and wait clock periods. The queue status indicates Execution Unit status, independent of the BIU activity. External logic may sample the lines on the low-to-high transition of each clock pulse. When sampled, the QS0 and QS1 signals identify queue activity in the previous clock period, and therefore lag the CPU's activity by one clock period.

The $\overline{TEST}$ input requirements are identical to those stated for minimum mode.

BUS CONTROL TRANSFER
(HOLD/HLDA AND RQ/GT)

The 8086 has protocol signals that are used to transfer local bus control between the 8086 itself and other devices capable of acting as bus masters. The minimum mode configuration offers a single level handshake, identical to 8080A and 8085 systems. The maximum mode configuration has an enhanced pulse sequence protocol which makes more efficient use of CPU pins, while extending system configurations to two levels of alternate bus masters, with two levels of priority. These protocol signals arbitrate control of the 8086 local bus; they should not be confused with arbitration on a system bus.

MINIMUM MODE

The minimum mode 8086 system uses a hold request input (HOLD) to the CPU and a hold acknowledge output (HLDA) from the CPU. To gain control of the local bus, a device must assert HOLD to the CPU and wait for the HLDA before driving the bus. When the 8086 can relinquish the bus, it floats the $\overline{RD}$, $\overline{WR}$, $\overline{INTA}$, and M/$\overline{IO}$ control lines, the $\overline{DEN}$ and DT/$\overline{R}$ bus control lines, and the multiplexed address/data/status lines. The ALE signal is not floated. The CPU acknowledges the request for the local bus with HLDA; this allows the requesting device to take control of the local bus. The requesting device must maintain the HOLD request active until it no longer requires the local bus. The HOLD request to the 8086 directly affects the bus interface unit; it indirectly affects the Execution Unit. The Execution Unit will continue to execute from its internal queue until either more instructions are needed, or an operand transfer is required. This allows a small degree of overlap between CPU and auxiliary bus master operations. When the requesting master drops the HOLD signal, the 8086 will respond by dropping HLDA. The 8086 will not redrive the bus and control signals; these signals will continue to float until the 8086 needs to perform a bus transfer. Since the 8086 may still be executing from its internal queue when HOLD drops, there may exist a period of time during which no device is driving the bus. To prevent the control lines from drifting below the minimum VIH level during a transition of bus control, 22K ohm pull-up resistors should be connected to the bus control lines. The timing diagram in Figure 8-35 shows the bus control handshake sequence in the 8086 timing to sample HOLD, float the bus, and enable/disable HLDA relative to the CPU clock.

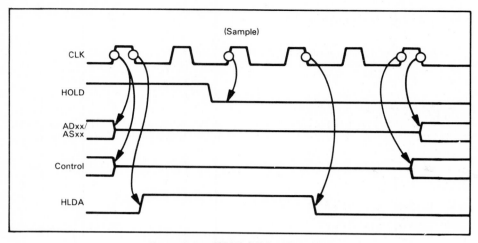

Figure 8-35. HOLD/HLDA Sequence

To guarantee valid system operation, the designer must ensure that the requesting device does not assert control of the bus prior to the 8086 relinquishing control — also, that the device relinquishes control of the bus prior to the 8086 driving the bus. The maximum delay between HLDA and the 8086 floating the bus is TCHDZ max — TCHCL min − TCLHAV min = 10 ns. If the system cannot tolerate the 10 ns overlap, HLDA active from the 8086 should be delayed to the device. The minimum delay from HOLD inactive until the 8086 drives control signals on the local bus is THVCH min + 3TCLCL = 635 ns; to drive a multiplexed bus, this delay is THVCH min + 3TCLCL + TCHCL = 70l ns. If the device does not release the local bus within the specified time, HOLD inactive to the 8086 should be delayed. The delay from HLDA inactive to driving the busses is TCLCL + TCLCH min − TCLHAV max = 158 ns for control signals on the local bus, and TCLCL − TCLHAV max = 240 ns for the local data bus.

Latency of HLDA to HOLD

The decision to respond to a HOLD REQUEST is made by the bus interface unit. The major factors that influence the decision are current bus activity, the state of the $\overline{LOCK}$ signal internal to the CPU (activated by the software LOCK prefix), and pending interrupts.

If the $\overline{LOCK}$ is not active, no interrupt acknowledge cycle is in progress, and the BIU (Bus Interface Unit) is executing a T4 or TI clock period when the HOLD request is received, the minimum latency to HLDA is:

35 ns	THVCH min (Hold setup)
65 ns	TCHCL min
200 ns	TCLCL (Bus float delay)
10 ns	TCLHAV min (HLDA delay)
310 ns	@ 5 MHz

The maximum latency to HLDA under the above conditions is:

34 ns	(Just missed set up time)
200 ns	Delay to next sample
82 ns	TCHCL max
200 ns	TCLCL (Bus float delay)
160 ns	TCLHAV max (HLDA)
677 ns	@ 5 MHz

If the BIU just initiated a bus cycle when the Hold Request was received, the worst case response time is:

34 ns	THVCH (Just missed)
82 ns	TCHCL max
7*200	Bus cycle execution
N*200	N wait states/bus cycle
160 ns	TCLHAV max (HLDA delay)
1.676 μs	@ 5 MHz, no wait states

Note that 200 ns for missing the Hold Request is included in the delay for bus cycle execution. If the operand transfer is a word transfer to an odd byte boundary, two bus cycles are executed to perform the transfer. The BIU will not acknowledge a Hold Request between the two bus cycles. This type of transfer would extend the above maximum latency by four additional clock periods, plus N additional wait states. With no wait states in the bus cycle, the maximum would be 2.476 microseconds.

Although the minimum mode 8086 does not have a hardware $\overline{LOCK}$ output, the software LOCK prefix may still be included in the instruction stream. The CPU internally reacts to the LOCK prefix in the same manner that the maximum mode 8086 would. Therefore LOCK does not allow a Hold Request to be honored until completion of the instruction following a prefix. In consequence, instructions which perform more than one memory reference, such as ADD (BX), CX, which adds CX to (BX) then stores the result in (BX), can execute without another bus master gaining control of the bus between memory references. Since the $\overline{LOCK}$ signal is active for one clock period more than instruction execution, the maximum latency to HLDA is:

34 ns	THVCH (Just missed)
200 ns	Delay to next sample
82 ns	TCHCL max
(M + 1)*200 ns	LOCK instruction execution
200 ns	Set up HLDA (Internal)
160 ns	TCLHAV max (HLDA delay)
(M*200 ns) + 876 ns	@ 5 MHz
	m is the number of clocks to execute
	the locked instructions

If the Hold Request is made at the beginning of an interrupt acknowledge sequence, the maximum latency to HLDA is:

34 ns	THVCH (Just missed)
82 ns	TCHCL max
2600 ns	13 clock cycles for INTA
160 ns	TCLHAV max
2.876 μs	@ 5 MHz

Minimum Mode DMA Configuration

A typical use of the minimum mode HOLD/HLDA signals is to exchange bus control with DMA controller devices such as the Intel 8257-5 or 8237 DMA controllers. Figure 8-36 functionally illustrates this type of configuration, using the 8257-5.

The DMA controller resides on the upper half of the 8086's local multiplexed address data bus; it shares the A15-A8 demultiplexing address latch with the 8086. 8257-5 registers must be accessed over the upper half of the bus. Therefore, odd addressed registers (A0=1) are accessed with byte transfers to an odd I/O address, while even addressed registers are accessed via word I/O, with the expected data transferred in the upper byte. The 8086 read and write control signals must be demultiplexed to provide separate I/O and memory controls that are compatible with 8257-5 requirements. The AEN control from the 8257-5 must disable the 8086 control signals and the lower (A7-A0) and upper (A19-A16) address bus latches. Also, AEN must select the 8257-5 address strobe (ADSTB) for the A15-A8 address latch. If the data bus is buffered, a pull-up resistor on the $\overline{DEN}$ line will keep the buffers disabled. The DMA controller will only transfer bytes between memory and I/O; the DMA controller requires that the I/O devices reside on an 8-bit bus derived from the 16-bit to 8-bit bus multiplex circuit shown below. Address lines A7-A0 are driven directly by the 8257 and $\overline{BHE}$ is generated by inverting A0. If A19-A16 are used, they must be provided by an additional port with either a fixed value or a value that is initialized by software; this additional port must be enabled onto the address bus by AEN.

Figure 8-37 illustrates the 8257 connected to the system bus.

By using a separate latch to hold the upper address from the 8257-5, while outputs are connected to the address bus as shown, 16-bit DMA transfers are provided. In this configuration, AEN simultaneously enables A0 and $\overline{BHE}$ to allow word transfers. AEN still disables the CPU interface to the control and address busses.

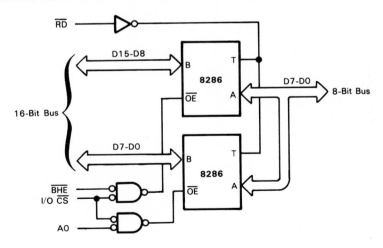

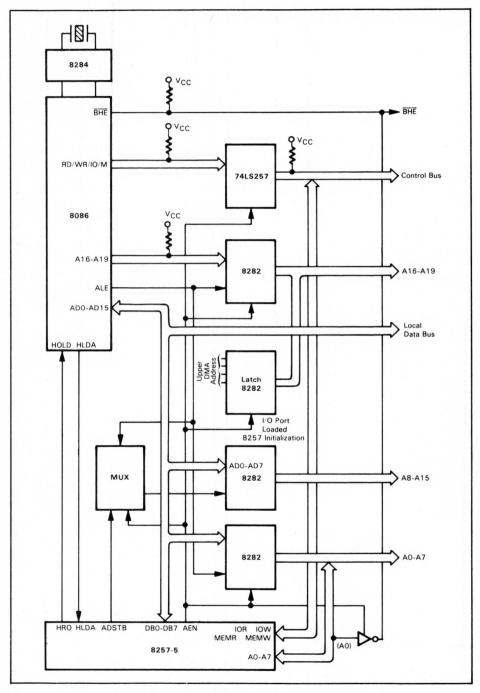

Figure 8-36. DMA Using Minimum Mode

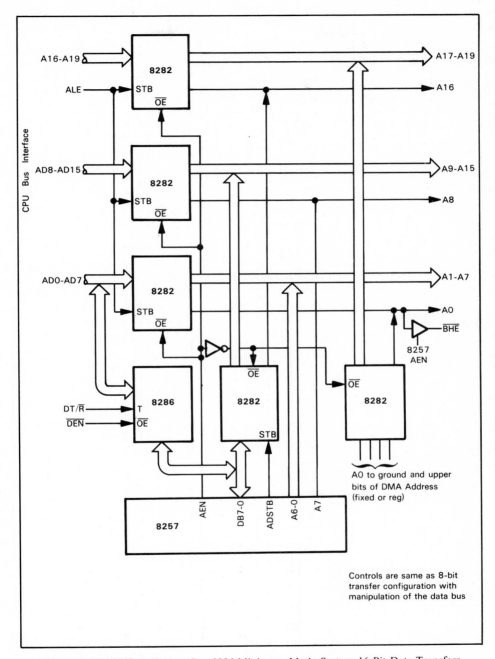

Figure 8-37. 8257 on System Bus 8086 Minimum Mode System 16-Bit Data Transfers

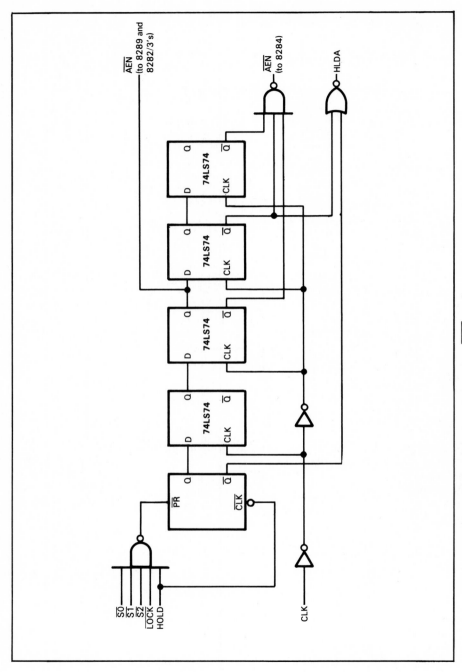

Figure 8-38. Translating HOLD into $\overline{AEN}$ Disable for Maximum Mode 8086

MAXIMUM MODE (RQ/GT)

The maximum mode 8086 configuration supports a significantly different bus control transfer protocol.

Shared System Bus (RQ/GT Alternative)

The maximum mode $\overline{RQ}/\overline{GT}$ sequence is used to transfer control of the local bus between the 8086 and alternative bus masters, such as DMA controllers, which reside totally on the local bus and share the complete CPU interface to the system bus. The complete CPU interface to the system bus includes the address latches, data transceivers, 8288 bus controller and 8289 multimaster bus arbiter. If the alternate bus masters in the system do not reside directly on the 8086 local bus, then system bus arbitration is required, and local bus arbitration will not do. Multimaster system bus arbitration requires the 8289 bus arbiter; $\overline{RQ}/\overline{GT}$ logic cannot be used.

If a device with a simple HOLD/HLDA protocol is to gain control of a system bus with just one connected CPU, the circuit in Figure 8-38 could be used.

This circuit is, in effect, a simple bus arbiter that isolates the CPU from the system bus when an alternate bus master issues a Hold Request. The output of the circuit, $\overline{AEN}$ (Access ENable) disables the 8288 and 8284 when the 8086 indicates idle status ($\overline{S0}$, $\overline{S1}$, $\overline{S2}$ = 1), $\overline{LOCK}$ is inactive and a Hold Request is active. With $\overline{AEN}$ inactive, the 8288 floats the control outputs and disables DEN, which floats the data bus transceivers. $\overline{AEN}$ must also float the address latch (8282 or 8283) outputs. These actions remove the 8086 from the system bus and allow the requesting device to drive the system bus. The $\overline{AEN}$ signal to the 8284 disables the READY input and forces the bus cycle initiated by the 8086 to wait until the 8086 regains control of the system bus. The CPU may actively drive its local bus during this interval.

The requesting device will not gain control of the system bus during an 8086-initiated bus cycle, a locked instruction's execution or an interrupt acknowledge cycle. The $\overline{LOCK}$ signal from the 8086 is active between $\overline{INTA}$ cycles to guarantee that the 8086 maintains control of the bus. Unlike the minimum mode 8086 HLDA response, the requesting master can gain control of the bus between consecutive bus cycles that transfer a word operand on an odd address boundary. Depending on the characteristics of the requesting device, one of the other 74LS74 outputs could be used to generate a HLDA to the device. This would be useful when interfacing to a device that requires some delay before it uses the bus.

Upon completion of its system bus operations, the alternate bus master must relinquish control of the system bus and drop the HOLD request. After $\overline{\text{AEN}}$ goes active, the address latches and data transceivers are enabled, but if an 8086 initiated bus cycle is pending, the 8288 will not drive the control lines until a minimum delay of 105 ns or a maximum delay of 275 ns has elapsed. If the system is normally not ready, the 8284 $\overline{\text{AEN}}$ input may be enabled immediately, with READY returning to the 8086 when the selected device completes the transfer. If the system is normally ready, the 8284 $\overline{\text{AEN}}$ input must be delayed long enough to provide access time equivalent to a normal bus cycle. The 74LS74 latches in the design provide a minimum of TCLCH ns for the alternate devices to float the system bus after releasing HOLD. They also provide 2TCLCL ns address access and 2TCLCL − TAEVCH max ns (8288 command enable delay) control access prior to enabling 8284 READY detection. If HLDA is generated as shown in Figure 8-38, TCLCL ns are available for the 8086 to release the bus prior to issuing HLDA, while HLDA is dropped almost immediately upon loss of HOLD.

The circuit configuration for an 8257-5 using this technique to interface to the maximum mode 8086 can be derived from Figure 8-37. The 8257-5 has its own address latch to buffer the address lines A15-A8; the 8257-5 uses its AEN output to enable the latch onto the address bus. The maximum latency from HOLD to HLDA for this circuit is dependent on the state of the system when the HOLD is issued. For an idle system, the maximum latency is the propagation delay through the NAND gate and R/S flip-flop (TD1) + 2TCLCL + TCLCH max + the propagation delay of the 74LS74 and 74LS02 (TD2). For a locked instruction it becomes TD1 + TD2 + (M + 2) * TCLCL + TCLCH max where M is the number of clocks required for execution of the locked instruction. For the interrupt acknowledge cycle the latency is TD1 + TD2 + 9 * TCLCL + TCLCH max.

Shared Local Bus (RQ/GT Usage)

The $\overline{RQ}/\overline{GT}$ protocol was developed to allow one or two other instruction set extension processors (co-processors) or special function processors to connect directly with the 8086 local bus. Each 8086 $\overline{RQ}/\overline{GT}$ pin supports the full protocol for exchange of bus control.

The bus control exchange sequence consists of a request from the alternate bus master to gain control of the local bus, a grant from the 8086 to indicate that the local bus has been relinquished, and a release pulse from the alternate bus master when done. The two $\overline{RQ}/\overline{GT}$ pins ($\overline{RQ}/\overline{GT0}$ and $\overline{RQ}/\overline{GT1}$) are prioritized, with $\overline{RQ}/\overline{GT0}$ having the higher priority. Priorities are meaningful only when requests are received on both pins, before a response has been given to either. For example, if a request is received on $\overline{RQ}/\overline{GT1}$, followed by a request on $\overline{RQ}/\overline{GT0}$ prior to a grant on $\overline{RQ}/\overline{GT1}$, then $\overline{RQ}/\overline{GT0}$ will gain priority over $\overline{RQ}/\overline{GT1}$. If, however, $\overline{RQ}/\overline{GT1}$ had already been granted priority, a request on $\overline{RQ}/\overline{GT0}$ must wait until a release pulse is received on $\overline{RQ}/\overline{GT1}$.

The request/grant interaction sequence with a bus interface unit is similar to HOLD/HLDA. The 8086 continues to execute instructions taken from its internal queue until it requests a bus cycle, to fetch an instruction, or to process an operand. But if the release pulse is received before the 8086 needs the bus, it will not drive the bus until a bus cycle is required.

Upon receipt of a request pulse, the 8086 floats the multiplexed address/data bus, the $\overline{S0}$, $\overline{S1}$, and $\overline{S2}$ status lines, the $\overline{LOCK}$ pin and $\overline{RD}$. This action does not disable the 8288 control outputs nor does it disable the address latches, which continue to drive the address bus. The 8288 contains internal pull-up resistors on the $\overline{S0}$, $\overline{S1}$, and $\overline{S2}$ status lines to maintain the passive state while the 8086 outputs are floated. The passive state prevents the 8288 from initiating any control outputs or activating DEN to enable the transceivers buffering the data bus. If the device issuing the $\overline{RQ}$ does not use the 8288, it must disable the 8288 control outputs by disabling the 8288 $\overline{AEN}$ input. Also, address latches not used by the requesting device must be disabled by the requesting device.

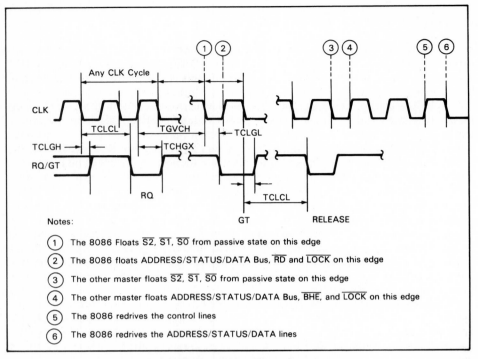

Notes:

① The 8086 Floats $\overline{S2}$, $\overline{S1}$, $\overline{S0}$ from passive state on this edge

② The 8086 floats ADDRESS/STATUS/DATA Bus, $\overline{RD}$ and $\overline{LOCK}$ on this edge

③ The other master floats $\overline{S2}$, $\overline{S1}$, $\overline{S0}$ from passive state on this edge

④ The other master floats ADDRESS/STATUS/DATA Bus, $\overline{BHE}$, and $\overline{LOCK}$ on this edge

⑤ The 8086 redrives the control lines

⑥ The 8086 redrives the ADDRESS/STATUS/DATA lines

Figure 8-39. Request/Grant Sequence

$\overline{\text{RQ}}/\overline{\text{GT}}$ Operation

Detailed timing of the $\overline{\text{RQ}}/\overline{\text{GT}}$ sequence is given in Figure 8-39.

To request a transfer of bus control via the $\overline{\text{RQ}}/\overline{\text{GT}}$ lines, a device must drive the line low for no more than one CPU clock period. This constitutes a request pulse. The request pulse must be synchronized with the CPU clock to guarantee appropriate set-up and hold times, relative to the 8086 clock edge which samples the $\overline{\text{RQ}}/\overline{\text{GT}}$ lines. After issuing a request pulse, the device must begin sampling for a grant pulse, beginning with the next low-to-high clock edge. Since the 8086 can respond with a grant pulse in the clock period immediately following a request, the $\overline{\text{RQ}}/\overline{\text{GT}}$ line may not return to the positive level between the request and grant pulses. Therefore, edge trigger logic cannot capture a grant pulse. It is also necessary that the circuitry which generates the request pulse guarantee that the request is removed in time to detect a grant from the CPU. After receiving the grant pulse, the requesting device may drive the local bus. The 8086 does not float the address or data bus, $\overline{\text{LOCK}}$ or $\overline{\text{RD}}$ until the clock edge, which the requesting master uses to start looking for a grant. Therefore the requesting master should wait the float delay time of the 8086 (TCLAZ address float or TCHDZ data float) before driving the local bus. This precaution prevents bus contention while the requesting master gains local bus access.

To return local bus control to the 8086, the alternate bus master issues a release pulse on the same $\overline{\text{RQ}}/\overline{\text{GT}}$ line. The 8086 may drive the $\overline{\text{S0}}$-$\overline{\text{S2}}$ status lines three clock cycles after detecting the release pulse. The 8086 may drive the address/data bus TCHCL ns (clock high time) after the status lines are driven. The alternate bus master must be floated off the local bus and must reenable other interface circuits, such as the 8288 and address latches, by the time the 8086 regains control of the bus. The requesting device may not issue a release pulse until at least one clock cycle after receiving the grant pulse, and must not issue a new request until at least one clock cycle after a previous release pulse.

$\overline{\text{RQ}}/\overline{\text{GT}}$ Latency

The $\overline{\text{RQ}}$ to $\overline{\text{GT}}$ delay for a single $\overline{\text{RQ}}/\overline{\text{GT}}$ line is similar to the HOLD to HLDA delay. The cases given for a minimum mode 8086 also apply to the maximum mode. In each case, the delay from $\overline{\text{RQ}}$ detection by the 8086 to $\overline{\text{GT}}$ detection by the requesting master is: (HOLD to HLDA delay) $-$ (THVCH + TCHCL + TCLHAV). This gives a clock period maximum delay for an idle bus interface. In all other cases, the delay is equal to the minimum mode result minus 476 ns. If the 8086 has previously issued a grant on one of the $\overline{\text{RQ}}/\overline{\text{GT}}$ lines, a request on the other $\overline{\text{RQ}}/\overline{\text{GT}}$ line will not receive a grant until the first device releases the interface with a release pulse on its $\overline{\text{RQ}}/\overline{\text{GT}}$ lines. The delay from release on one $\overline{\text{RQ}}/\overline{\text{GT}}$ line to a grant on the other is typically one clock period as shown in Figure 8-40.

Occasionally, the delay from a release on $\overline{\text{RQ}/\text{GT1}}$ to a grant on $\overline{\text{RQ}/\text{GT0}}$ will take two clock periods, and is a function of any pending request for transfer of control from the 8086 execution unit. The delay from request to grant when the interface is under control of a bus master on the other $\overline{\text{RQ}}/\overline{\text{GT}}$ line is a function of the other bus master. The protocol embodies no mechanism whereby the 8086 can force an alternate bus master off the bus. To ensure that an errant alternate bus master does not "hang" the system, a watchdog timer should be employed.

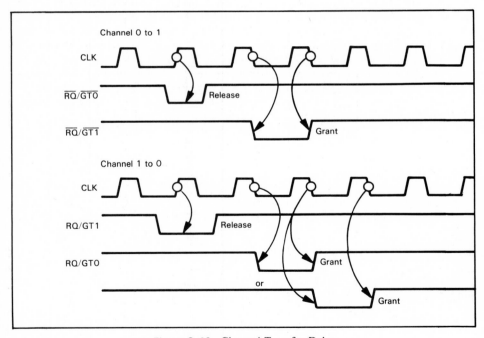

Figure 8-40. Channel Transfer Delay

$\overline{\text{RQ}/\text{GT}}$ to HOLD/HLDA Conversion

A circuit that translates a HOLD/HLDA handshake sequence into a $\overline{\text{RQ}/\text{GT}}$ pulse sequence is given in Figure 8-41.

After receiving the grant pulse, the HLDA is enabled TCHCL (min) ns before the 8086 disconnects itself from the local bus. If the requesting circuit drives the bus within 20 ns of HLDA, it may be desirable to delay the acknowledge pulse by one clock period. The HLDA is dropped no later than one clock period after HOLD is disabled. The HLDA also drops at the beginning of the release pulse to provide 2TCLCL + TCLCH for the requesting master to relinquish control of the status lines, and 3TCLCL to float through remaining signals.

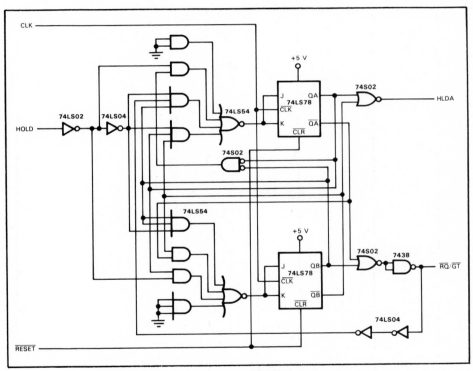

Figure 8-41. HOLD/HLDA to $\overline{\text{RQ}/\text{GT}}$ Conversion Circuit

9

The Multibus

The Multibus is a general purpose multiprocessing system bus. This standard bus has mechanical, electrical, and form specifications. The Multibus is used in Intel iSBC single board microcomputer products. Multibus-compatible products are also offered by other manufacturers. Anyone designing multiprocessing systems should consider building his or her systems around the Multibus for two important reasons:

1. To save the time and costs associated with developing a new system;

2. To gain compatibility with a wide variety of products available for the Multibus.

When the 8086 is configured in the maximum mode, the 8288 bus controller and 8289 bus arbiter provide a bus access and control interface that is fully compatible with the electrical and A.C. characteristics of the Multibus system bus. When configured in the minimum mode, the 8086 can operate easily on the Multibus (albeit with some external logic to encode appropriate signals), unless a multiprocessor system is desired. In all multiprocessor systems, the 8086 should be configured in the maximum mode.

The Multibus provides a versatile communications channel that can be used to coordinate a wide variety of computing modules. Modules in the system are either masters or slaves. Masters obtain use of the bus and initiate data transfers, while slaves merely perform data transfers. The bus allows both 8-bit and 16-bit masters and slaves to be intermixed in the system. The bus supports 16 data lines, 20 address lines, 8 interrupt lines, plus control and bus arbitration lines. Other lines contain power busses, power backup, and power sense signals for switching memories to battery backup systems. A complete listing of pin assignments on the Multibus is given in Tables 9-1 and 9-2. A functional description of the signals follows.

Table 9-1. Pin Assignment of Bus Signals on Multibus Board P1 Connector

	Pin	(Component Side) Mnemonic*	(Component Side) Description	Pin	(Circuit Side) Mnemonic	(Circuit Side) Description
Power Supplies	1	GND	Signal GND	2	GND	Signal GND
	3	+5 V	+5 Vdc	4	+5 V	+5 Vdc
	5	+5	+5 Vdc	6	+5	+5 Vdc
	7	+12 V	+12 Vdc	8	+12 V	+12 Vdc
	9	−5 V	−5 Vdc	10	−5 V	−5 Vdc
	11	GND	Signal GND	12	GND	Signal GND
Bus Controls	13	BCLK/	Bus Clock	14	INIT/	Initialize
	15	BPRN/	Bus Priority In	16	BPRO/	Bus Priority Out
	17	BUSY/	Bus Busy	18	BREQ/	Bus Request
	19	MRDC/	Memory Read Command	20	MWTC/	Memory Write Command
	21	IORC/	I/O Read Command	22	IOWC/	I/O Write Command
	23	XACK/	Transfer Acknowledge	24	INH1/	Inhibit 1 disable RAM
Bus Controls and Address	25		Reserved	26	INH2/	Inhibit 2 disable PROM or ROM
	27	BHEN/	Byte High Enable	28	AD10/	
	29	CBRQ/	Common Bus Request	30	AD11/	Address Bus
	31	CCLK/	Constant Clock	32	AD12/	
	33	INTA/	Interrupt Acknowledge	34	AD13/	
Interrupts	35	INT6/		36	INT7/	
	37	INT4/	Parallel Interrupt Requests	38	INT5/	Parallel Interrupt Requests
	39	INT2/		40	INT3/	
	41	INT0/		42	INT1/	
Address	43	ADRE/		44	ADRF/	
	45	ADRC/		46	ADRD/	
	47	ADRA/		48	ADRB/	
	49	ADR8/	Address Bus	50	ADR9/	Address Bus
	51	ADR6/		52	ADR7/	
	53	ADR4/		54	ADR5/	
	55	ADR2/		56	ADR3/	
	57	ADR0/		58	ADR1/	
Data	59	DATE/		60	DATF/	
	61	DATC/		62	DATD/	
	63	DATA/		64	DATB/	
	65	DAT8/	Data Bus	66	DAT9/	Data Bus
	67	DAT6/		68	DAT7/	
	69	DAT4/		70	DAT5/	
	71	DAT2/		72	DAT3/	
	73	DAT0/		74	DAT1/	
Power Supplies	75	GND	Signal GND	76	GND	Signal GND
	77		Reserved	78		Reserved
	79	−12 V	−12 Vdc	80	−12 V	−12 Vdc
	81	+5 V	+5 Vdc	82	+5 V	+5 Vdc
	83	+5 V	+5 Vdc	84	+5 V	+5 Vdc
	85	GND	Signal GND	86	GND	Signal GND

All Mnemonics © Intel Corporation 1978

*Two notations for negative true (active low) signals are used in this book:
a bar over the signal name, or a slash after the signal name (e.g., $\overline{\text{BUSY}}$ = BUSY/).

Table 9-2. P2 Connector Pin Assignment of Optional Bus Signals

Pin	(Component Side) Mnemonic	(Component Side) Description	Pin	(Circuit Side) Mnemonic	(Circuit Side) Description
1	GND	Signal GND	2	GND	Signal GND
3	V_{CCB}	+5 V Battery	4	V_{CCB}	+5 V Battery
5		Reserved	6	V_{CCPP}	+5 V Pulsed Power
7	V_{BBB}	−5 V Battery	8	V_{BBB}	−5 V Battery
9		Reserved	10	Reserved	+
11	V_{DDB}	+12 V Battery	12	V_{DDB}	+12 V Battery
13	PFSR/	Power Fail Sense Reset	14	Reserved	+
15	V_{AAB}	−12 V Battery	16	V_{AAB}	−12 V Battery
17	PFSN/	Power Fail Sense	18	ACLO	AC Low
19	PFIN/	Power Fail Interrupt	20	MPRO/	Memory Protect
21	GND	Signal GND	22	GND	Signal GND
23	+15 V	+15 V	24	+15 V	+15 V
25	−15 V	−15 V	26	−15 V	−15 V
27	PAR1/	Parity 1	28	HALT/	Bus Master HALT
29	PAR2/	Parity 2	30	WAIT/	Bus Master WAIT STATE
31			32	ALE	Bus Master ALE
33			34	Reserved	
35			36	Reserved	
37			38	AUX RESET/	Reset switch
39			40		
41			42		
43	Reserved		44		
45			46		
47			48	Reserved	
49			50		
51			52		
55			56		
57			58		
59			60		

Notes:

1. PFIN, on slave modules, if possible, should have the option of connecting to INTO/ on P1.
2. All undefined pins are reserved for future use.

All Mnemonics © Intel Corporation 1978

INITIALIZATION SIGNAL LINE

$\overline{\text{INIT}}$

The Initialization signal resets the entire system to a predetermined state. $\overline{\text{INIT}}$ may be supplied by one of the bus masters or by external logic.

ADDRESS AND INHIBIT LINES

$\overline{\text{ADR0}}\text{-}\overline{\text{ADR13}}$

The 20 address lines are used to transmit the address of the memory location or I/O port to be accessed. $\overline{\text{ADR13}}$ is the most significant bit, while $\overline{\text{ADR0}}$ is the least significant bit. 8-bit bus masters use 16 address lines ($\overline{\text{ADR0}}\text{-}\overline{\text{ADRF}}$) to address memory, and 8 address lines ($\overline{ADR0}$-$\overline{ADR7}$) to select I/O ports. 16-bit bus masters address memory via all 20 address lines and select I/O ports via the low-order 12 address lines ($\overline{ADR0}$-$\overline{ADRB}$). The 8088 however can use all 20 address lines even though considered an 8-bit bus CPU.

$\overline{INH1}$

The Inhibit RAM signal prevents RAM memory devices from responding to the address on the address bus. $\overline{INH1}$ allows ROM memory devices to override RAM devices when ROM and RAM memory are assigned the same memory space.

$\overline{INH2}$

The Inhibit ROM signal prevents ROM memory devices from responding to the address on the Address Bus. $\overline{INH2}$ allows auxiliary ROM to override ROM devices when ROM and auxiliary ROM memory are assigned the same memory space.

$\overline{INH1}$ and $\overline{INH2}$ may also be used to allow memory mapped I/O devices to override RAM and ROM devices respectively.

$\overline{BHEN}$

$\overline{BHEN}$ is used to specify that data will be transferred on the high-order 8 data lines of the Multibus. This signal is used in systems that utilize 16-bit memory or I/O modules.

DATA LINES

$\overline{DAT0}$-$\overline{DATF}$

The 16 bidirectional data lines are used to exchange information with a memory location or I/O port. $\overline{DATF}$ is the most significant bit, although in 8-bit systems only lines $\overline{DAT0}$-$\overline{DAT7}$ are used, and $\overline{DAT7}$ becomes the most significant bit. $\overline{DAT0}$ is always the least significant bit.

BUS CONTENTION RESOLUTION LINES

$\overline{BCLK}$

The negative edge of the Bus Clock is used to synchronize bus contention. $\overline{BCLK}$ is asynchronous with the CPU clock. $\overline{BCLK}$ may be slowed, stopped, or single-stepped during debugging.

$\overline{CCLK}$

The Constant Clock provides a clock signal of constant unspecified frequency.

BPRN

The Bus Priority In signal tells a bus master that no higher priority device is requesting use of the system bus. $\overline{\text{BPRN}}$ is synchronized with $\overline{\text{BCLK}}$. This signal is "daisy chained" if you use serial priority arbitration. When using parallel priority arbitration, a bus arbiter generates $\overline{\text{BPRN}}$.

BPRO

This is a Bus Priority Out signal. Like $\overline{\text{BPRN}}$, $\overline{\text{BPRO}}$ is "daisy-chained" when serial priority arbitration is used; $\overline{\text{BPRO}}$ is fed to the $\overline{\text{BPRN}}$ input of the next lower priority module. When using parallel priority arbitration, a bus arbiter must provide this signal. $\overline{\text{BPRO}}$ is synchronized with $\overline{\text{BCLK}}$.

BUSY

The Bus Busy signal is supplied by the current bus master to indicate that the system bus is in use. $\overline{\text{BUSY}}$ is used by other devices to determine whether or not they may acquire control of the system bus. $\overline{\text{BUSY}}$ is synchronized with $\overline{\text{BCLK}}$.

BREQ

The Bus Request signal is used by devices to indicate that they wish to become bus master. $\overline{\text{BREQ}}$ is synchronized with $\overline{\text{BCLK}}$; it is not bussed on the motherboard.

CBRQ

$\overline{\text{CBRQ}}$ is used by all potential bus masters to inform the current bus master that another master wishes to use the bus. If $\overline{\text{CBRQ}}$ is high, the current bus master knows that no other device is requesting the bus and therefore the present bus master is to retain the bus.

INFORMATION TRANSFER PROTOCOL LINES

A bus master that has control of the system bus generates all data transfer control signals. All address signals (and data signals when a write is to occur) must be stable at least 50 ns prior to the transfer control signal pulse and must remain valid for at least 50 ns after the control signal pulse is removed.

Information transfer protocol lines are not synchronous with $\overline{\text{BCLK}}$.

MRDC

The Memory Read Control indicates that the address of a memory location has been placed on the address lines, and that the contents of the address location are to be placed on the data lines.

$\overline{\text{MWTC}}$

The Memory Write Control indicates that the address of a memory location has been placed on the address lines and that data has been placed on the system data lines; the data is to be written into the addressed memory location.

$\overline{\text{IORC}}$

The I/O Read Control indicates that the address of an input port has been placed on the system address lines, and that the data at that input port is to be placed on the data lines.

$\overline{\text{IOWC}}$

The I/O Write Control indicates that the address of an output port has been placed on the system address lines and that the data has been placed on the system data lines; the data is to be output to the addressed port.

$\overline{\text{XACK}}$

All exchanges involve handshaking. Therefore the selected bus slave must provide the bus master with an acknowledge signal in response to the transfer control signal. The Transfer Acknowledge signal is the required response that indicates that the specified operation has been completed.

$\overline{\text{AACK}}$

The Advanced Acknowledge signal is used by 8080A microprocessors. $\overline{\text{AACK}}$ is an advance acknowledge that allows the CPU to complete a specified operation without entering a Wait state. Bus slaves that provide $\overline{\text{AACK}}$ must also provide $\overline{\text{XACK}}$. This requirement must be met since not all bus masters will respond to the $\overline{\text{AACK}}$ signal.

ASYNCHRONOUS INTERRUPT LINES

$\overline{\text{INT0}}$-$\overline{\text{INT7}}$

These eight priority interrupt request lines are used with parallel interrupt resolution circuitry. $\overline{\text{INT7}}$ has the lowest priority, $\overline{\text{INT0}}$ the highest priority.

$\overline{\text{INTA}}$

$\overline{\text{INTA}}$ is used by a bus master to request that external logic place interrupt vector information on the Multibus data lines.

POWER SUPPLY LINES

Various regulated power supply lines are provided on the bus. Each module must provide both bulk decoupling and high frequency decoupling local to the resident logic devices.

RESERVED LINES

Reserved lines should not be used; they must be left available for future Intel definition.

The Multibus is logically similar to the 8086 demultiplexed bus. An address is provided on address lines $\overline{ADR0}$ through $\overline{ADR13}$. (The address line number is now a hex number.)

The Multibus requires a delay from valid address of 50 ns before a Read Control signal can be transmitted to a selected device. The read control pulse must be at least 100 ns wide, and the address must remain stable at least 50 ns after the Read Control signal terminates. If the selected device requires more than the 100 ns read signal or the 150 ns minimum specified address access time, then the device may extend the read cycle by using the $\overline{XACK}$ (transfer acknowledge) signal. This signal is equivalent to the Ready signal connected to the 8284 RDY input. $\overline{XACK}$ is normally "not ready"; it is driven active to tell the CPU that the device is ready to receive or transmit data and to allow termination of the bus cycle. The Multibus specifies data setup and hold times relative to the $\overline{XACK}$ signal, rather than the Read or Write Control signal, to allow autonomous operation of the selected device in a multiple - processor system with mixed CPU types.

The write bus cycle is similar to the read bus cycle. Written data must be valid a minimum of 50 ns prior to the Write Control signal and must be held valid a minimum of 50 ns following the Write Control signal.

Master modules attached to the Multibus must not violate the minimum setup and hold times or control pulse widths. Many designs provide better than minimum margins when running at their maximum band width. Slave modules must be able to tolerate the minimum setup and hold times but may extend the access times if they delay return of $\overline{XACK}$ by an appropriate amount.

The Multibus provides two basic interrupt handling methods. These are:

1. A method whereby interrupt vectors are not transferred on the bus. Rather they are generated by the bus master's interrupt controller. The slave that requests the interrupt must be part of the same module as the bus master. If the interrupting slave is part of another module, then the slave will use the Multibus interrupt request lines ($\overline{INT0\text{-}INT7}$) to request an interrupt; this interrupt will be processed by the bus master's interrupt controller.

2. A method where the interrupt vector is transferred on the bus. When a slave device requests an interrupt, interrupt control logic interrupts the processor. The processor acknowledges the interrupt by lowering the $\overline{INTA}$ line and locking the system bus. This allows an interrupt vector to be transferred. Following the initial $\overline{INTA}$ cycle, interrupt control logic determines the address of the highest priority slave currently requesting an interrupt. This address is placed on the address bus. The addressed slave responds by transmitting an interrupt vector address back to the master.

In addition to providing a standard asynchronous data transfer protocol and timing specifications for designing master and slave modules, the Multibus provides a standard protocol which multiple masters use to exchange bus control. To allow asynchronous masters to share the bus, the Multibus maintains its own clock signal independent of clock signals local to modules that might connect to the Multibus. The Multibus clock signed $\overline{BCLK}$ synchronizes asynchronous requests for bus access. This allows arbitration logic to resolve priorities and grant access to one master at a time. This bus arbitration technique allows masters operating at various speeds to compete equitably for use of the system bus. When a master gains control of the system bus, however, transfer speeds depend only on the capabilities of the master and its associated slave modules, not on $\overline{BCLK}$, the Multibus clock signal. The maximum bus band width is 5 MHz, taking into account minimum address setup and hold times and minimum control pulse width. When one considers the additional overhead of bus arbitration and typical memory response times, the actual transfer speeds are often on the order of 2 MHz.

The Multibus allows serial or parallel priority arbitration among bus masters. Serial priority technique is illustrated in Figure 9-1.

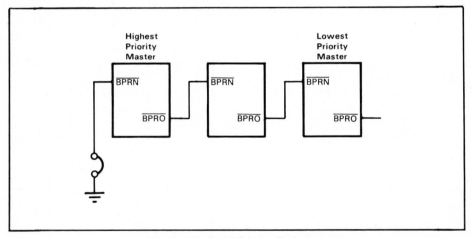

Figure 9-1. Serial Priority Technique

The highest priority master has $\overline{BPRN}$ grounded. The priority enable output $\overline{BPRO}$ from each master is connected to the priority input $\overline{BPRN}$ of the next lowest priority master. If that master does not need the bus, it propagates its $\overline{BPRN}$ to $\overline{BPRO}$. This propagates upstream priority to downstream masters. A master that needs the bus will output $\overline{BPRO}$ high; this denies priority to lower level masters. This logic daisy chains the priority enable from the highest priority master in the system to the lowest. Since a higher priority master must wait until the current bus master has completed any bus cycles already in progress, another signal must be included to indicate an idle or "not busy" status of the Multibus. The $\overline{BUSY}$ line, which serves this function, is a signal common to all bus masters. Each master using the Multibus clocks $\overline{BUSY}$ to determine its ability to gain access to the bus.

When sampled on a high-to-low transition of $\overline{\text{BCLK}}$, if $\overline{\text{BPRN}}$ is low (active) and $\overline{\text{BUSY}}$ is high (inactive), indicating an idle bus, then the current master must drive $\overline{\text{BUSY}}$ low prior to the next high-to-low transition of $\overline{\text{BCLK}}$ to prevent a higher priority master from gaining control of the bus before the current master completes its transfer.

If a current master loses priority, it must release $\overline{\text{BUSY}}$ after completing its transfer and float its connection to the Multibus.

If another master wishes to request the bus, it must disable lower priority masters before the high-to-low transition of $\overline{\text{BCLK}}$. Otherwise race conditions will occur in priority resolution circuits and lower priority masters. Also, since the priority disable from a higher priority master must propagate through the daisy chain to the lowest priority master, the total propagation delay from highest to lowest priority master must not exceed one $\overline{\text{BCLK}}$ clock period. This places an upper bound on the number of masters the serial priority arbitration can accommodate.

The parallel priority arbitration is similar to serial priority arbitration, except that each master issues a bus request, $\overline{\text{BREQ}}$, on the high-to-low transition of $\overline{\text{BCLK}}$, and an external user-defined circuit resolves priorities. The priority resolving circuit must resolve and return stable priority inputs, $\overline{\text{BPRN}}$'s, back to each master within one period of $\overline{\text{BCLK}}$. A parallel resolving circuit and an example of bus exchange timing are given in Figure 9-2.

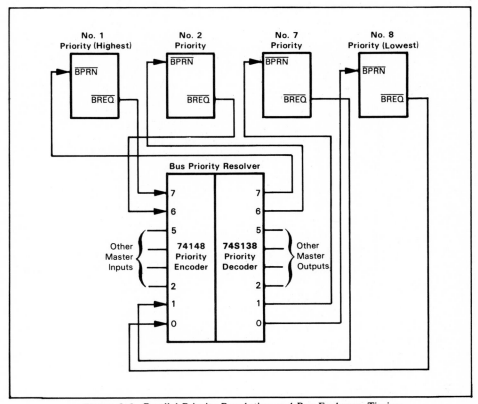

Figure 9-2. Parallel Priority Resolution and Bus Exchange Timing

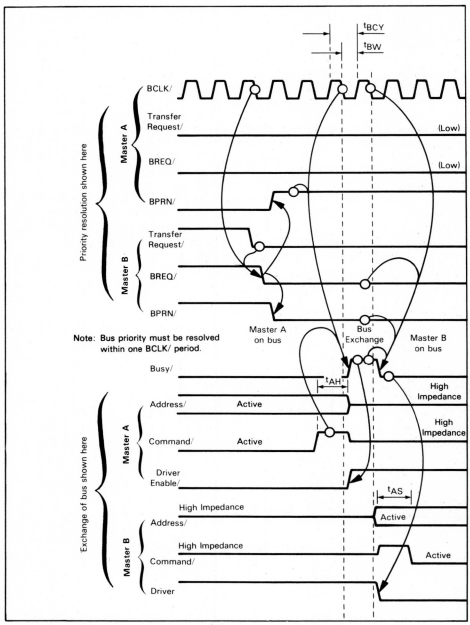

Figure 9-2. Parallel Priority Resolution and Bus Exchange Timing (Continued)

MULTIBUS ARCHITECTURAL CONCEPTS

The Multibus architecture provides a well-defined bus structure for multiprocessor systems. The bus serves as a means of sharing resources between multiprocessors and communicating between the processors in the system. There are two elementary forms of multiprocessor systems. They are:

1. A tightly coupled system. In a tightly coupled system, multiple processors communicate with each other by passing information through a common memory space.

2. A loosely coupled system. In a loosely coupled system, multiple processors communicate with each other by passing information via the I/O structure. Typically, a serial communications link is used. However, in some cases information is passed via a mass storage device such as a high-speed disk.

The Multibus is designed to satisfy the requirements of tightly coupled systems, while still allowing multi-CPU processing systems to be loosely coupled via standard I/O communication protocols like Bisync or HDLC. The mechanisms for sharing the bus consist of a combination of the Multibus protocol and user-defined priority resolution circuitry. The Multibus provides the basic controls for each processor to request the bus, to receive an acknowledgement when the processor has bus priority, and to indicate bus availability. The user must select the priority resolution technique most applicable to any task. Be cautious when selecting a priority system, otherwise the Multibus may become a system bottleneck, degrading overall system performance. To ensure an equitable utilization of the bus, the MULTIBUS supports a common bus request, $\overline{CBRQ}$. This signal allows low priority devices to request the bus from a higher priority bus master or to indicate a pending lower priority request. This allows the current bus master to maintain control of the bus until the higher priority master forces the current master off the bus (via the loss of priority) or a lower priority master requests the bus (via common bus request). The response by the current master to a common bus request is user-definable. It may cause the master to release the bus at the end of the current transfer or immediately if there is no bus activity, or the master may simply ignore the request and only relinquish bus control to higher priority masters. The common bus request gives the designer another level of control when defining the utilization of the system bus. In consequence the current master is not forced to release and re-request the bus for every transfer. This minimizes the overhead associated with bus access and transfer.

The Multibus $\overline{BUSY}$ signal allows the current master to maintain bus control even though a higher priority master has forced it to lose priority (forced its $\overline{BPRN}$ signal inactive). This is necessary for operations requiring multiple bus cycles, where the current master's bus cycles cannot be separated by bus cycles executed for another bus master. If the current bus master has control of the bus, it may continue to control the bus by not releasing $\overline{BUSY}$ to indicate that the bus is available. This capability is required for multiple bus cycle interrupt acknowledge sequences and for test and set operations. It is a function of the master module to interpret those conditions for which it must not relinquish control of the bus. When these conditions arise, the master must ignore the loss of $\overline{BPRN}$ until the required operation is complete.

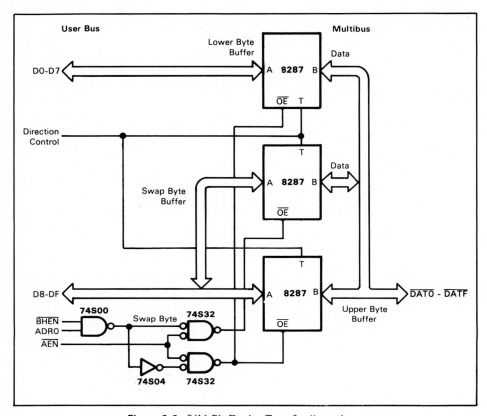

Figure 9-3. 8/16-Bit Device Transfer Operations

The Multibus is a demultiplexed system bus with separate address and data lines. The system maintains a one megabyte address space via 20 address lines, and there is a 16-bit data bus. For compatibility with existing Multibus-compatible modules, which only maintain an 8-bit data bus, all 8-bit transfers are performed over the least significant half of the data bus regardless of the address. Only 16-bit transfers use the full 16 data lines. This departs from the standard 8086 procedure of high and low byte transfers on the upper and lower halves of the data bus. As a result, byte transfers to existing 8-bit interface slave modules are independent of the CPU. Slave modules supporting 16-bit interfaces are accessible, a byte at a time, by master modules that only interface to an 8-bit data bus, yet slaves can be accessed a word at a time or a byte at a time by masters that support the full 16-bit data bus. The Multibus signal $\overline{\text{BHEN}}$ provides the additional information required to determine whether a byte or a word transfer is being performed. Figure 9-3 shows how $\overline{\text{BHEN}}$ controls the gating of byte and word information to and from the Multibus system bus.

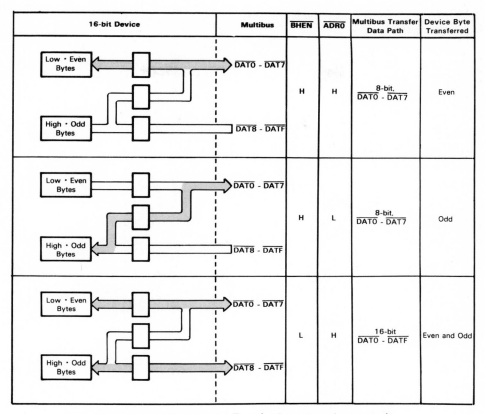

Figure 9-3. 8/16-Bit Device Transfer Operations (Continued)

10

Multiprocessor Configurations for the 8086

The 8086 family of components was devised to provide a system architecture that would allow for both single processor and multiprocessor configurations. This chapter will describe how maximum mode is used in a multiprocessor system; we will also examine various configurations supported by the 8086 family of components.

The multiprocessing capabilities of the 8086 family are based on these two separate and distinct features:

1. Special function processors which reside on the local bus and enhance the basic architecture of the 8086 CPU.

2. Multiple CPUs sharing a common system bus.

A special function processor is dedicated to one CPU; it executes extensions to the CPU's instruction set and processes in parallel with this CPU. Special function processors are therefore referred to as co-processors. A multiple microprocessor system, in contrast, more closely resembles the classical multi-CPU environment where the interaction of CPUs is user defined. Note that a system may combine the two capabilities, i.e., each CPU in a multiprocessor system may have its own unique dedicated co-processors. Multi-CPU, multiprocessor systems' needs are met by the Multibus defined in Chapter 9.

CO-PROCESSOR

The 8086 has hardware and software characteristics aimed at enabling co-processing. The hardware support includes the queue status signals (QS0, QS1), a $\overline{\text{TEST}}$ input, and a mechanism for sharing the CPU's local bus ($\overline{\text{RQ}/\text{GT}}$). The software support consists of a special class of instructions called ESCAPE instructions which activate the co-processor, and a WAIT instruction which samples the $\overline{\text{TEST}}$ input (used for software synchronization between the CPU and the co-processors).

The co-processor interfaces directly to the CPU's local bus. The CPU's local bus includes the multiplexed address/status and address/data lines, the S0, S1, and S2 status lines, the QS0 and QS1 queue status lines, $\overline{\text{TEST}}$, READY, RESET, one of the $\overline{\text{RQ}/\text{GT}}$ lines and, perhaps, the $\overline{\text{LOCK}}$ line. The need for the $\overline{\text{LOCK}}$ signal varies, depending on the co-processor. The co-processor is allowed to reside on a local bus for two reasons:

1. The co-processor is able to monitor the CPU's activity.

2. The co-processor has full access to the CPU's resources.

The co-processor requests control of the local bus via one of the $\overline{\text{RQ}/\text{GT}}$ lines. After the CPU has relinquished bus control to the co-processor, the co-processor may run local bus cycles exactly as the CPU would. When the co-processor is done with the local bus, control is returned to the CPU via the same $\overline{\text{RQ}/\text{GT}}$ line that was used to gain control of the bus. An example of this interface is shown in Figure 10-1.

The co-processor is activated via the following sequence; while the CPU is fetching and executing instructions, the co-processor monitors the instruction stream looking for an ESCAPE instruction. Information that is transferred from memory into the CPU's instruction queue (as opposed to memory data used as an operand by an instruction) is selected by decoding the status lines (S0, S1, S2) which identify an instruction fetch. A0 and $\overline{\text{BHE}}$ are decoded to determine whether a single or double byte instruction fetch is performed. Information coming out of the queue is identified as the first instruction byte, or a subsequent instruction byte, via the queue status lines (QS0, QS1). The queue status lines also indicate that no byte was fetched, or that the queue is empty. If the information coming out of the co-processor's queue (it tracks the CPU's queue) indicates an ESCAPE instruction, and the queue status identifies it as the first byte of an instruction's object code, then the co-processor is activated. The ESCAPE instruction object code is:

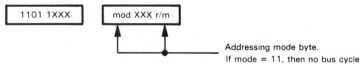

Addressing mode byte.
If mode = 11, then no bus cycle

The Xs are "don't care" bits to the CPU, but they can represent 64 possible instructions to the co-processor. In response to the ESCAPE instruction, the CPU uses the mod and r/m fields as a normal addressing mode specification; it executes a bus cycle to read data from the specified address. The co-processor can capture both the address and the data present at the selected memory location. This mechanism allows a programmer to treat the ESCAPE instructions defined for the co-processor as normal CPU instructions, with the full range of memory addressing modes. It allows an address to be passed to the co-processor along with one parameter. If the co-processor needs to transfer additional data to or from memory, it may request control of the CPU's bus.

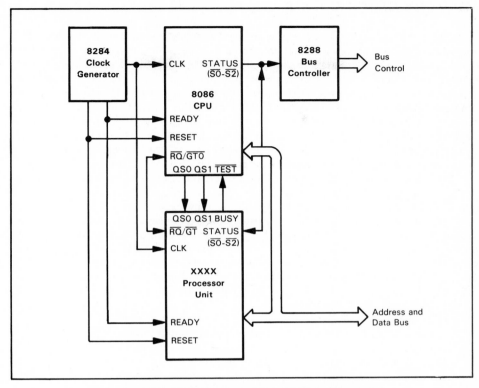

Figure 10-1. 8086 Maximum Mode Multiple Processors

Note that all information used by the co-processor must reside in memory, since the co-processor does not have access to the CPU's registers. The CPU does not capture data read during the ESCAPE instruction, and except for the read bus cycle treats the instruction as a null operation. After execution of the ESCAPE instruction, both the CPU and co-processor are free to continue executing their specific tasks in parallel. While executing an instruction, the co-processor will typically hold the $\overline{\text{TEST}}$ line high to indicate that it is busy. If a program cannot guarantee the co-processor is not busy, before executing another ESCAPE instruction, the program should either read the status of the co-processor (if possible) or insert a WAIT instruction before each ESCAPE instruction. The WAIT instruction will force the CPU to wait until the co-processor is not busy before it executes the ESCAPE instruction. During the WAIT instruction, the CPU does not require the bus, except possibly to fill the instruction queue. The CPU will, however, respond to interrupts (if enabled) during a WAIT cycle. Note that the co-processor may continue to monitor the CPU's instruction stream while executing an ESCAPE instruction. Although Intel has only announced the 8087 co-processor, the general purpose nature of the interface makes it applicable to a wide range of higher level commands for numerics, language support, etc.

MULTIPROCESSING ON A SHARED SYSTEM BUS

With the increasing complexity of microprocessor applications and the declining cost/performance ratio of the microprocessor, it is becoming more cost effective to design systems with more than one microprocessor. Multiprocessor systems are implemented by partitioning the design into functional subsystems that are easily identifiable and have a clean communications interface to other systems. After partitioning the design and defining both the hardware interface and the software interface, each subsystem may be designed and developed in parallel by individual teams as a means of reducing total end product design time. Although this approach requires a high degree of cooperation and coordination among all design teams, benefits such as modularity, extensibility, and ease of maintenance are provided.

When partitioning a system into a multiprocessor distributed intelligence system, the requirements of the functional subsystems will dictate the need for loosely coupled, tightly coupled, or both loosely and tightly coupled processors.

In the discussion that follows, loosely coupled processors communicate via a shared I/O mechanism; tightly coupled processors communicate through shared memory. For those processors that are loosely coupled, each CPU communicates with other CPUs through an I/O interface, which the CPU treats as it would any other I/O device attached to it. There are a wide variety of standard protocols for this type of interface, e.g., SDLC, ASYNC, GPIB. These interfaces require that the subsystem hardware provide an I/O interface, plus software to control the interface and interpret the message protocol.

Loosely coupled subsystems typically require neither frequent nor high-speed communications; they may be physically distant from each other, even miles apart.

If multiple processors are tightly coupled, a technique must be provided for sharing memory among the processors. The 8086 family shares memory by connecting it to the shared system bus. The memory and I/O devices accessible over this bus may be utilized by all CPUs capable of being bus master.

Shared memory and I/O devices provide the desired interprocessor communications mechanisms.

The basic CPU interface to the multimaster system bus is shown in Figure 10-2.

Figure 10-3 shows the basic interface for an 8086 system. The 8289 Bus Arbiter has the priority arbitration and protocol logic needed to transfer bus control. This logic was described in Chapter 9 for the Multibus. The 8288 bus controller provides system bus control signals for the CPU; it also takes care of the CPU's address and data bus interface with the system bus. The 8283s and 8287s implement this CPU's interface to the shared system bus. The 8288 and 8289 also let you direct bus transfers to shared resources on the system bus, or to private resources on the CPU's local bus.

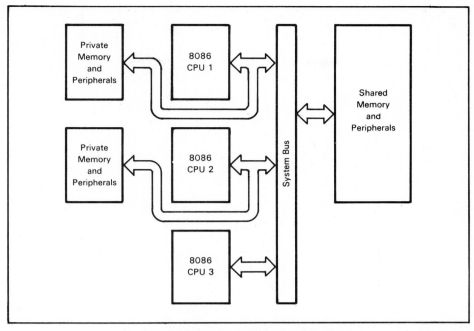

Figure 10-2. Multiprocessor Configuration

In Figure 10-3, all resources, and hence all bus transfers, are directed over the system bus. To initiate a bus cycle the 8086 drives the status lines from the passive state (S2, S1, S0 = 1,1,1) to one of the active states. The 8288 and 8289 and the CPU operate synchronously via the common clock, CLK, and detect a bus cycle request by monitoring the status lines. The 8288 will issue ALE to strobe the address from the local multiplexed bus into the 8283s. If the 8289 does not have control of the system bus (is not driving BUSY low), it will issue a bus request ($\overline{\text{BREQ}}$) and common bus request ($\overline{\text{CBRQ}}$) to gain control. This protocol is identical to that described for the Multibus system bus. The 8289 will maintain $\overline{\text{AEN}}$ in an inactive (high) state until gaining bus control. This action prevents the 8283s from driving the address onto the system bus and prevents the 8288 from driving the bus command or enabling the data transceivers (via DEN). Note that the 8283s will capture the address during ALE, regardless of the state of its $\overline{\text{OE}}$ input. The inactive state of $\overline{\text{AEN}}$ is also used to disable the 8284 RDY input from the system. Disabling the RDY input forces the CPU to wait (by inserting wait states) until this interface gains control of the bus and completes the bus cycle. Once the 8289 has gained bus priority and the bus is not busy, it enables $\overline{\text{AEN}}$ and asserts $\overline{\text{BUSY}}$ to other bus masters. $\overline{\text{AEN}}$ immediately enables the address onto the bus and allows the 8288 to enable the data bus transceiver (8287s). The 8288 will not enable the command until 105 to 275 ns later, to allow address setup and chip select decode time in the system. To prevent the 8284 and CPU from detecting Ready immediately after $\overline{\text{AEN}}$ is enabled and terminating the bus cycle prematurely, the RDY input from the system should normally be inactive and be disabled until a command is issued by the 8288. To satisfy this, the system device selected to participate in the transfer will typically not return RDY ($\overline{\text{XACK}}$ for Multibus system bus definition) until it has com-

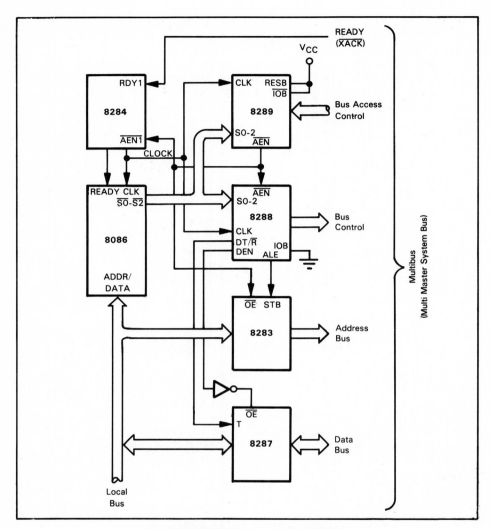

Figure 10-3. CPU with no Local Resources

completed the transfer. Since the time to complete the transfer is device dependent, each device provides an appropriate delay from selection of command to RDY (or $\overline{\text{XACK}}$). After detecting Ready, the CPU returns the status lines to the passive state. This action allows the 8288 to terminate the bus cycle, which the 8288 does by dropping the command and disabling the transceivers. If a higher priority bus master tries to force this bus master off the bus during a bus cycle (via the loss of bus priority ($\overline{\text{BPRN}}$), the 8289 will maintain bus control by holding $\overline{\text{BUSY}}$ active (low) until the status (S2, S1, S0) returns to the passive state. If the 8289 has control of the bus, it maintains $\overline{\text{AEN}}$ active, allowing bus cycles initiated by the CPU to be performed immediately. The timing and signal sequence under these conditions are identical to a single-CPU maximum mode system. The full complement of bus surrender conditions supported by the 8289 are discussed later in this chapter.

The previous discussion represented a single CPU with all memory and I/O connecting to the multimaster system bus. If you consider how many clock cycles are available for bus cycles, assuming four clocks per bus cycle, and count the number of bus cycles executed, you will discover that a single 8086 CPU can utilize between 50% and 80% of the available bus band width, depending on whether the application is compute bound. If two 8086s are attached to a shared bus, with all memory and I/O for both processors connecting to this shared bus, then the throughput for each CPU may degrade by up to 37%:

$$\frac{80 - 50}{80} = 37\%$$

This degradation is a direct consequence of contention for access to the shared bus. This calculation assumes that each CPU could use 80% of the total available bus cycles, but only receives 50% of the available bus cycles, since it is sharing a single bus with the other CPU. As more CPUs are added to the system, more degradation occurs for all CPUs. To gain appreciable benefits from multiprocessor systems, there must be a high degree of concurrent processing. Therefore, delays due to contention for access to the shared bus must be minimized.

As a solution to this problem, the 8086 family allows local and shared resources to be defined for each CPU. Local resources may include memory and/or I/O, which connect to the CPU's local or resident bus and can only be accessed by the CPU to which they are assigned. Shared resources, in contrast, consist of memory and I/O which connect directly to the multimaster system bus and are accessible by more than one master.

Two primary techniques for partitioning resources are supported by the 8288 and 8289: address mapping and memory versus I/O. Figures 10-4a through 10-4c demonstrate the variations derivable from these techniques. The common elements in all of these examples are the inclusion of a second set of address latches and use of both 8284 RDY inputs. The major differences in the configurations presented in Figures 10-4a through 10-4c are the number of additional components required to support the local resources, and the types of local resources supported.

Figure 10-4a allows ROM or EPROM on the CPU's local bus, and only requires additional address latches and possible address decode latches. The 8289 is strapped into the resident bus mode (RESB to V_{CC}), which tells the 8289 that this CPU supports resident memory. Strapping options on the 8288 do not differ from the configuration shown in Figure 10-3. During a bus cycle, the 8288 issues ALE, latching the address into both the 8283s and 8282s. The address space assigned to the resident memory is decoded and used to determine whether this bus cycle will use resident or system resources. If the bus cycle is to utilize the system bus, then the decode result must be high to indicate SYSB to the 8289, CEN to the 8288, and to disable the local bus RDY via the associated $\overline{\text{AEN}}$. When the 8289 is in the RESB mode, the SYSB/$\overline{\text{RESB}}$ input to the 8289 determines whether the 8289 will request or release the system bus. If SYSB/$\overline{\text{RESB}}$ is high, the 8289 will request the system bus; if SYSB/$\overline{\text{RESB}}$ is low, the 8289 will release the bus. The CEN input of the 8288 prevents the control outputs from being driven to their active state during resident bus accesses. This input is necessary to prevent a control signal from being issued to the system if the 8289 has control of the bus. The input does not cause the 8288 to float the control outputs, since the 8288 must maintain them in an inactive state as long as the 8289 has control of the bus. Note that the 8282s are always enabled ($\overline{\text{OE}}$ strapped low); this allows each bus cycle address to quickly decode into the appropriate system bus or resident bus select.

The stable address latched in the 8282s also provides chip select and addresses to the local ROM or EPROM. The read signal from the 8086 ($\overline{\text{RD}}$) is used to enable the selected local device to drive data onto the local multiplexed bus. When local resources are selected, the 8284 $\overline{\text{AEN2}}$ input is enabled to allow a local RDY2 to generate Ready to the CPU. Since the 8288 will not drive control signals on the system bus, RDY1 (or $\overline{\text{XACK}}$) should not be received, even if the 8289 has bus control and $\overline{\text{AEN1}}$ is active. If the local resources require buffering from the local multiplexed bus, the local chip select and $\overline{\text{RD}}$ should be used to enable the buffers. If the I/O address space overlaps the local memory address space, S2 should be latched and included in the local address decode to prevent an I/O address from decoding into a resident bus access.

This technique only works for local ROM and EPROM in the memory space, since no I/O commands or write commands are available for the local bus. Note, however, that object code accesses typically utilize 50% to 70% of the bus cycles. Therefore, if the majority of the object code executed by the CPU is in local ROM or EPROM, the system bus utilization per CPU can be reduced to less than 30%. All RAM and I/O must reside on the shared system bus and therefore will be subject to contention.

Figure 10-4b adds local I/O to the previous configuration shown in Figure 10-4a. This is achieved by strapping both the 8288 and 8289 to operate in the IOB (I/O Bus) mode. In this mode, all I/O is assumed to reside on the local bus; thus I/O does not require access to the system bus. But when the IOB option is used, the CPU cannot access I/O on the system bus unless it is memory mapped. For each I/O bus transfer, the 8289 will not attempt to gain bus control and may release the bus if it currently has control. The 8288 will drive the I/O control outputs, regardless of the state of the $\overline{\text{AEN}}$ input. In this mode, the 8288 I/O control outputs must not be connected to the system bus I/O control lines. They should only be used to provide control to the local I/O devices. No additional circuitry is required to support this extension to Figure 10-4a. The $\overline{\text{AEN2}}$ input to the 8284 is now enabled by a chip select to either the local memory or local I/O. The 8288 CEN input must be high during I/O cycles to allow the I/O control output to be driven low (active). If the data lines to/from the I/O devices must be buffered from the local multiplexed bus, the DT/$\overline{\text{R}}$ signal from the 8288 can be used as a direction control signal for the buffers. To enable the buffers, the 8288 can be used as a direction control signal for the buffers. To enable the buffers, the 8288 provides a separate peripheral data enable control ($\overline{\text{PDEN}}$). This signal is only available when the 8288 is strapped in the I/O Bus (IOB) mode. $\overline{\text{PDEN}}$ is enabled for I/O transfers, while DEN is enabled only for data transfers over the system bus.

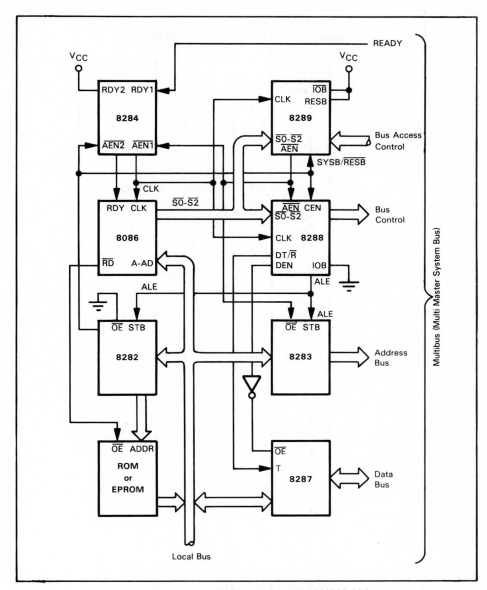

Figure 10-4a. 8086 with Local ROM/EPROM

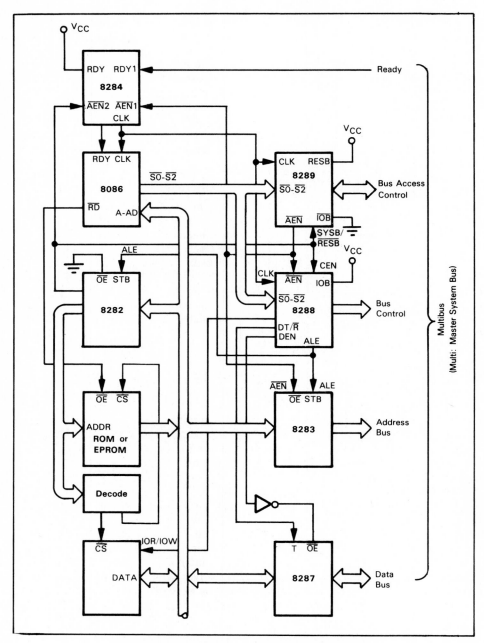

Figure 10-4b. 8086 with Local ROM/EPROM and I/O

The next extension to the configuration alternatives is shown in Figure 10-4c. For this case, we have added a second 8288 and data bus transceivers. This configuration is the most flexible since it is totally based on address mapping, and allows access to both shared and local ROM/EPROM, RAM and I/O. The IOB mode is not used on either 8288. Since the local bus is not a multimaster bus, a second 8289 is not required. The PROM or decoder sources in the address map are for both memory and I/O references. The resulting SYSB/$\overline{\text{RESB}}$ signal is inverted to provide the proper enable polarity for the resident bus 8288 CEN input. The 8288 provides address latching and full data bus transceiver control for the resident data bus, and a complete set of read and write controls for memory and I/O. The multimaster system bus interface functions as described for configuration 10-4a.

The configuration in Figure 10-4c allows the CPU to support resident ROM/EPROM for fixed program and constants, resident RAM for stacks and local variables, and resident I/O which only this CPU need access. The result is modular self-contained processing modules which communicate control and data via shared memory or shared I/O. This allows a high degree of concurrent processing within the system with a typical system bus usage per CPU reduced to less than 25%.

A final extension to the concept of multiple busses per CPU is to implement a second multimaster bus, rather than a resident bus. This is useful in fault tolerant systems; also, it allows performance enhancements based on multiple interprocessor communication channels. In this case, a CPU wishing to access the system bus would first attempt to utilize the primary bus; if this is not available, the secondary bus would be accessed.

BUS ACCESS AND RELEASE OPTIONS FOR THE 8289

In addition to the RESB and IOB modes, the 8289 has several other options that optimize multi-master system bus use. These additional capabilities affect the bus release rather than its request. With respect to bus request operations, one additional comment needs to be made. With the exception of the RESB mode, the 8289 will issue a bus request on the second high-to-low clock transition (BCLK) following the low-to-high CPU clock transition of T2. The one-CPU clock delay for the RESB mode provides address decode time for generating a stable SYSB/$\overline{\text{RESB}}$ signal.

The 8289 provides $\overline{\text{LOCK}}$, ANYRQST, and $\overline{\text{CRQLCK}}$ inputs for additional control over bus control release. In general, the 8289 will relinquish control of the bus either at the end of the current cycle or immediately (if no bus cycle is in progress) when it loses priority ($\overline{\text{BPRN}}$ goes high). An exception arises if the $\overline{\text{LOCK}}$ input is active. The $\overline{\text{LOCK}}$ allows the 8289 to maintain bus control (continue to drive $\overline{\text{BUSY}}$ low) regardless of bus priority. The 8289 $\overline{\text{LOCK}}$ input should be driven by the CPU $\overline{\text{LOCK}}$ output to guarantee the CPU will maintain bus control during execution of the instruction preceded by the $\overline{\text{LOCK}}$ prefix and during interrupt acknowledge sequences. The $\overline{\text{LOCK}}$ signal allows operations like locked exchanges to serve as primitives for basic semaphore control of non-reentrant shared resources (also known as critical code sections).

ANYRQST is a strapping option which forces the 8289 to release the bus either at the end of the current bus cycle or immediately (if no bus cycle is in progress) if Common Bus Request ($\overline{\text{CBRQ}}$) is active. Assertion of ANYRQST forces the 8289 to release the bus to a lower priority bus master. Releasing the bus for this case requires the 8289

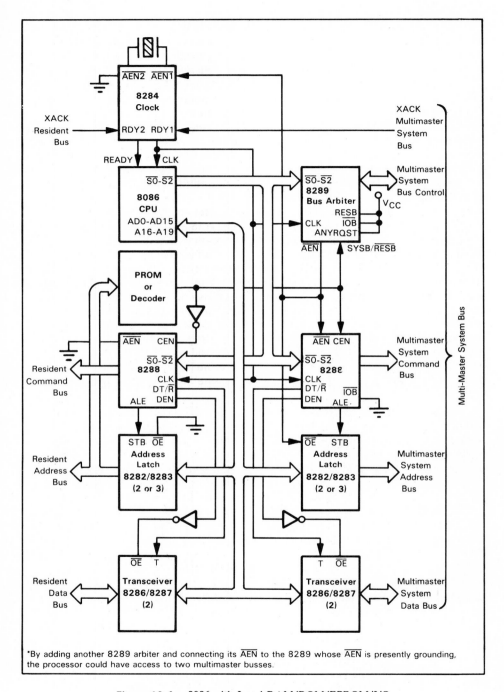

Figure 10-4c. 8086 with Local RAM/ROM/EPROM/I/O

to drop its bus request ($\overline{\text{BREQ}}$ returns high) and enable $\overline{\text{BPRO}}$ (Bus Priority Out). (Note that $\overline{\text{BREQ}}$ is used for parallel priority resolving circuits, while $\overline{\text{BPRO}}$ is provided to support a serial priority arbitration scheme via daisy chaining $\overline{\text{BPRO}}$ to the next lower priority $\overline{\text{BPRN}}$. Only one of the two techniques is applicable within a single system). The 8289 will then release the bus one bus clock period later by releasing BUSY. The 8289 must release its $\overline{\text{BREQ}}$ and $\overline{\text{BPRO}}$ to allow the lower priority 8289 to receive $\overline{\text{BPRN}}$. For the normal case of a higher priority master forcing another 8289 off the bus, the higher priority master receives $\overline{\text{BPRN}}$ from the priority scheme and does not require the lower priority master to release its $\overline{\text{BPRO}}$ or $\overline{\text{BREQ}}$.

If ANYRQST is strapped high and $\overline{\text{CBRQ}}$ is tied low, the 8289 will release the bus at the completion of each bus cycle. This may impose a high overhead on bus transfer logic, but it may be useful for masters which infrequently use the system bus, or use it at a very low band width.

If ANYRQST is not tied high, the 8289 will release the bus to a lower priority device on $\overline{\text{CBRQ}}$ only when the CPU local bus is idle (S2, S1, S0 = 1,1,1). To override $\overline{\text{CBRQ}}$ and never release the bus to a lower priority master, $\overline{\text{CRQLCK}}$ (Common Bus Request Lock) is provided. Strapping this input low effectively disables the $\overline{\text{CBRQ}}$ as an input. Although the same effect can be attained by tying $\overline{\text{CBRQ}}$ high, the strapping option allows it to be a programmable option rather than a static function.

Note: $\overline{\text{CBRQ}}$ is bidirectional — an 8289 will drive it low to get the bus and monitor it when it has the bus. The CRQLCK therefore allows an 8289 to ignore $\overline{\text{CBRQ}}$ while it has the bus yet use $\overline{\text{CBRQ}}$ to get the bus.

Other special conditions which cause the 8289 to release the bus are: an I/O cycle with the 8289 strapped for I/O Bus (IOB) mode, a resident bus cycle where the 8289 is in the RESB mode, and whenever the CPU enters the halt state by executing a HALT instruction. Entering the halt state is indicated to the 8289 via the halt status on the status lines (S2, S1, S0 = 0, 1, 1).

A

The 8086 Instruction Set Listed Alphabetically

Instruction		Object Code	Bytes	Clock Periods
AAA		37	1	4
AAD		D5 0A	2	60
AAM		D4 0A	2	83
AAS		3F	1	4
ADC	ac,data	0001010w kk [jj]	2 or 3	4
ADC	mem/reg$_1$,data	100000sw mod 010 r/m [DISP] [DISP] kk [jj]	3, 4, 5 or 6	reg: 4 mem: 17 + EA
ADC	mem/reg$_1$,mem/reg$_2$	000100dw mod rrr r/m [DISP] [DISP]	2, 3 or 4	reg to reg: 3 mem to reg: 9 + EA reg to mem: 16 + EA
ADD	ac,data	0000010w kk [jj]	2 or 3	4
ADD	mem/reg,data	100000sw mod 000 r/m [DISP] [DISP] kk [jj]	3, 4, 5 or 6	reg: 4 mem: 17 + EA
ADD	mem/reg$_1$,mem/reg$_2$	000000dw mod rrr r/m [DISP] [DISP]	2, 3 or 4	reg to reg: 3 mem to reg: 9 + EA reg to mem: 16 + EA
AND	ac,data	0010010w kk [jj]	2 or 3	4
AND	mem/reg,data	1000000w mod 100 r/m [DISP] [DISP] kk [jj]	3, 4, 5 or 6	reg: 4 mem:17 + EA
AND	mem/reg$_1$,mem/reg$_2$	001000dw mod rrr r/m [DISP] [DISP]	2, 3 or 4	reg to reg: 3 mem to reg: 9 + EA reg to mem: 16 + EA
CALL	addr	9A kk jj hh gg	5	28
CALL	disp16	E8 kk jj	3	19
CALL	mem	FF mod 011 r/m [DISP] [DISP]	2, 3 or 4	32-bit mem pointer: 37 + EA
CALL	mem/reg	FF mod 010 r/m [DISP] [DISP]	2, 3, or 4	16-bit reg pointer: 16 16-bit mem pointer: 21 + EA

Instruction		Object Code	Bytes	Clock Periods
CBW		98	1	2
CLC		F8	1	2
CLD		FC	1	2
CLI		FA	1	2
CMC		F5	1	2
CMP	ac,data	0011110w kk [jj]	2 or 3	4
CMP	mem/reg,data	100000sw mod 111 r/m [DISP] [DISP] kk [jj]	3, 4, 5 or 6	reg: 4 mem: 10 + EA
CMP	mem/reg₁,mem/reg₂	001110dw mod rrr r/m [DISP] [DISP]	2, 3 or 4	reg to reg: 3 mem to reg: 9 + EA reg to mem: 9 + EA
CMPS		1010011w	1	22 9 + 22/repetition*
CWD		99	1	5
DAA		27	1	4
DAS		2F	1	4
DEC	mem/reg	1111111w mod 001 r/m [DISP] [DISP]	2, 3 or 4	reg: 3 mem: 15 + EA
DEC	16-bit reg	01001rrr	1	2
DIV	mem/reg	1111011w mod 110 r/m [DISP] [DISP]	2, 3 or 4	8-bit reg: 80 → 90 16-bit reg: 144 → 162 8-bit mem: (86 → 96) + EA 16-bit mem: (150 → 168) + EA
ESC	mem/reg	11011xxx mod xxx r/m [DISP] [DISP]	2, 3 or 4	mem: 8 + EA reg: 2
HLT		F4	1	2
IDIV	mem/reg	1111011w mod 111 r/m [DISP] [DISP]	2, 3 or 4	8-bit reg: 101 → 112 16-bit reg: 165 → 184 8-bit mem: (107 → 118) + EA 16-bit mem: (171 → 190) + EA
IMUL	mem/reg	1111011w mod 101 r/m [DISP] [DISP]	2, 3 or 4	8-bit reg: 80 → 98 16-bit reg: 128 → 154 8-bit mem: (86 → 104) + EA 16-bit mem: (134 → 160) + EA
IN	ac, DX	1110110w	1	8
IN	ac, port	1110010w	2	10

* When preceded by REP prefix

Instruction		Object Code	Bytes	Clock Periods
INC	mem/reg	1111111w mod 000 r/m [DISP] [DISP]	2, 3 or 4	reg: 3 mem: 15 + EA
INC	16-bit reg	01000rrr	1	2
INT		11001100*	1	52
		11001101 type	2	51
INTO		CE	1	interrupt: 53 no interrupt: 4
IRET		CF	1	32
JA JNBE	disp	77 disp	2	4/No Branch 16/Branch
JAE JNB	disp	73 disp	2	4/No Branch 16/Branch
JB JNAE	disp	72 disp	2	4/No Branch 8/Branch
JBE JNA	disp	76 disp	2	4/No Branch 16/Branch
JCXZ	disp	E3 disp	2	6/No Branch 18/Branch
JE JZ	disp	74 disp	2	4/No Branch 16/Branch
JG JNLE	disp	7F disp	2	4/No Branch 16/Branch
JGE JNL	disp	7D disp	2	4/No Branch 16/Branch
JL JNGE	disp	7C disp	2	4/No Branch 16/Branch
JLE JNG	disp	7E disp	2	4/No Branch 16/Branch
JMP	addr	EA kk jj hh gg	5	15
JMP	disp	EB disp	2	15
JMP	disp16	E9 kk jj	3	15
JMP	mem	FF mod 101 r/m [DISP] [DISP]	2, 3 or 4	mem ptr 32: 24 + EA
JMP	mem/reg	FF mod 100 rr/m [DISP] [DISP]	2, 3 or 4	reg ptr 16: 11 mem ptr 16: 16 + EA
JNE JNZ	disp	75 disp	2	4/No Branch 16/Branch
JNO	disp	71 disp	2	4/No Branch 16/Branch
JNP JPO	disp	7B disp	2	4/No Branch 16/Branch
JNS	disp	79 disp	2	4/No Branch 16/Branch
JO	disp	70 disp	2	4/No Branch 16/Branch

* Implied type = 3

Instruction		Object Code	Bytes	Clock Periods
JP	disp	7A	2	4/No Branch
JPE		disp		16/Branch
JS	disp	78	2	4/No Branch
		disp		16/Branch
LAHF		9F	1	4
LDS	reg,mem	C5	2, 3 or 4	16 + EA
		mod rrr r/m		
		[DISP]		
		[DISP]		
LEA	reg,mem	8D	2, 3 or 4	2 + EA
		mod rrr r/m		
		[DISP]		
		[DISP]		
LES	reg,mem	C4	2, 3 or 4	16 + EA
		mod rrr r/m		
		[DISP]		
		[DISP]		
LOCK		F0	1	2
LODS		1010110w	1	12
				9 + 13/repetition*
LOOP	disp	E2	2	5/No Branch
		disp		17/Branch
LOOPE	disp	E1	2	6/No Branch
LOOPZ		disp		18/Branch
LOOPNE	disp	E0	2	5/No Branch
LOOPNZ		disp		19/Branch
MOV	mem/reg$_1$,mem/reg$_2$	100010dw	2, 3 or 4	reg to reg: 2
		mod rrr r/m		reg to mem: 8 + EA
		[DISP]		mem to reg: 9 + EA
		[DISP]		
MOV	reg,data	1011wrrr	2 or 3	4
		kk		
		[jj]		
MOV	ac,mem	1010000w	3	10
		kk		
		jj		
MOV	mem,ac	1010001w	3	10
		kk		
		jj		
MOV	segreg,mem/reg	8E	2, 3 or 4	reg to reg: 2
		mod 0rr r/m		mem to reg: 8 + EA
		[DISP]		
		[DISP]		
MOV	mem/reg,segreg	8C	2, 3 or 4	reg to reg: 2
		mod 0rr r/m		reg to mem: 9 + EA
		[DISP]		
		[DISP]		
MOV	mem/reg,data	1100011w	3, 4, 5 or	reg/mem: 10 + EA
		mod 000 r/m	6	
		[DISP]		
		[DISP]		
		kk		
		[jj]		
MOVS		1010010w	1	18
				9 + 17/repetition*

* When preceded by REP prefix

Instruction		Object Code	Bytes	Clock Periods
MUL	mem/reg	1111011w mod 100 r/m [DISP] [DISP]	2, 3 or 4	8-bit reg: 70 → 77 16-bit reg: 118 → 133 8-bit mem: (76 → 83) + EA 16-bit mem: (124 → 139) + EA
NEG	mem/reg	1111011w mod 011 r/m [DISP] [DISP]	2, 3 or 4	reg: 3 mem: 16 + EA
NOP		90	1	3
NOT	mem/reg	1111011w mod 010 r/m [DISP] [DISP]	2, 3 or 4	reg: 3 mem: 16 + EA
OR	ac,data	0000110w kk [jj]	2 or 3	4
OR	mem/reg,data	1000000w mod 001 r/m [DISP] [DISP] kk [jj]	3, 4, 5 or 6	reg: 4 mem: 17 + EA
OR	mem/reg$_1$,mem/reg$_2$	000010dw mod rrr r/m [DISP] [DISP] kk [jj]	3, 4, 5 or 6	reg to reg: 3 mem to reg: 9 + EA reg to mem: 16 + EA
OUT	DX,ac	1110111w	1	8
OUT	port,ac	1110011w yy	2	10
POP	mem/reg	8F mod 000 r/m [DISP] [DISP]	2, 3 or 4	reg: 8 mem: 17 + EA
POP	reg	01011rrr	1	8
POP	segreg	000ss111	1	8
POPF		9D	1	8
PUSH	mem/reg	FF mod 110 r/m [DISP] [DISP]	2, 3 or 4	reg: 11 mem: 16 + EA
PUSH	reg	01010rrr	1	10
PUSH	segreg	000ss110	1	10
PUSHF		9C	1	10
RCL	mem/reg,count	110100cw mod 010 r/m [DISP] [DISP]	2, 3 or 4	count = 1 reg: 2 mem:15 + EA count = [CL] reg: 8 + (4 * N) mem: 20 + EA + (4 * N)

N = count value in CL

Instruction		Object Code	Bytes	Clock Periods
RCR	mem/reg,count	110100cw mod 011 r/m [DISP] [DISP]	2, 3 or 4	count = 1 reg: 2 mem:15 + EA count = [CL] reg: 8 + (4 * N) mem: 20 + EA + (4 * N)
REP	/REPE/REPNE	1111001z	1	2
RET	(Inter-segment)	CB	1	24
RET	(Intra-segment)	C3	1	16
RET	disp16(Inter-segment)	CA kk jj	3	23
RET	disp16(Intra-segment)	C2 kk jj	3	20
ROL	mem/reg,count	110100cw mod 000 r/m [DISP] [DISP]	2, 3 or 4	count = 1 reg: 2 mem:15 + EA count = [CL] reg: 8 + (4 * N) mem: 20 + EA + (4 * N)
ROR	mem/reg,count	110100cw mod 001 r/m [DISP] [DISP]	2, 3 or 4	count = 1 reg: 2 mem:15 + EA count = [CL] reg: 8 + (4 * N) mem: 20 + EA + (4 * N)
SAHF		9E	1	4
SAR	mem/reg,count	110100cw mod 111 r/m [DISP] [DISP]	2, 3 or 4	count = 1 reg: 2 mem:15 + EA count = [CL] reg: 8 + (4 * N) mem: 20 + EA + (4 * N)
SBB	ac,data	0001110w kk [jj]	2 or 3	4
SBB	mem/reg,data	100000sw mod 011 r/m [DISP] [DISP] kk [jj]	3, 4, 5 or 6	reg: 4 mem: 17 + EA
SBB	mem/reg₁,mem/reg₂	000110dw mod rrr r/m [DISP] [DISP]	2, 3 or 4	reg from reg: 3 mem from reg: 9 + EA reg from mem: 16 + EA
SCAS		1010111w	1	15 9 + 15/repetition*
SEG	segreg	001ss110	1	2
SHL SAL	mem/reg,count	110100cw mod 100 r/m [DISP] [DISP]	2, 3 or 4	count = 1 reg: 2 mem:15 + EA count = [CL] reg: 8 + (4 * N) mem: 20 + EA + (4 * N)

* When preceded by REP prefix

N = count value in CL

Instruction		Object Code	Bytes	Clock Periods
SHR	mem/reg,count	110100cw mod 101 r/m [DISP] [DISP]	2, 3 or 4	count = 1 reg: 2 mem:15 + EA count = [CL] reg: 8 + (4 * N) mem: 20 + EA + (4 * N)
STC		F9	1	2
STD		FD	1	2
STI		FB	1	2
STOS		1010101w	1	11 9 + 10/repetition*
SUB	ac,data	0010110w kk [jj]	2 or 3	4
SUB	mem/reg,data	100000sw mod 101 r/m [DISP] [DISP] kk [jj]	3, 4, 5 or 6	reg: 4 mem: 17 + EA
SUB	mem/reg₁,mem/reg₂	001010dw mod rrr r/m [DISP] [DISP]	2, 3 or 4	reg from reg: 3 mem from reg: 9 + EA reg from mem: 16 + EA
TEST	ac,data	1010100w kk [jj]	2 or 3	4
TEST	mem/reg,data	1111011w mod 000 r/m [DISP] [DISP] kk [jj]	3, 4, 5 or 6	reg: 5 mem: 11 + EA
TEST	reg,mem/reg	1000010w mod rrr r/m [DISP] [DISP]	2, 3 or 4	reg with reg: 3 reg with mem: 9 + EA
WAIT		9B	1	3(min.) + 5n
XCHG	reg,ac	10010rrr	1	3
XCHG	reg,mem/reg	1000011w mod rrr r/m [DISP] [DISP]	2, 3 or 4	reg with reg: 4 reg with mem: 17 + EA
XLAT		D7	1	11
XOR	ac,data	0011010w kk [jj]	2 or 3	4
XOR	mem/reg,data	1000000w mod 110 r/m [DISP] [DISP] kk [jj]	3, 4, 5 or 6	reg: 4 mem: 17 + EA
XOR	mem/reg₁,mem/reg₂	001100dw mod rrr r/m [DISP] [DISP]	2, 3 or 4	reg with reg: 3 mem with reg: 9 + EA reg with mem: 16 + EA

*When preceded by REP prefix

n = clocks per sample of the $\overline{\text{TEST}}$ input

B

The 8086 Instruction Set
Object Codes in
Ascending Numeric Sequence

Object Code			Mnemonic
Byte # 0	Byte # 1	Succeeding Bytes	
00	mod reg r/m	[disp][disp]	ADD mem/reg,reg (byte)
01	mod reg r/m	[disp][disp]	ADD mem/reg,reg (word)
02	mod reg r/m	[disp][disp]	ADD reg, mem/reg (byte)
03	mod reg r/m	[disp][disp]	ADD reg, mem/reg (word)
04	kk		ADD AL,kk
05	kk	jj	ADD AX, jjkk
06			PUSH ES
07			POP ES
08	mod reg r/m	[disp][disp]	OR mem/reg,reg (byte)
09	mod reg r/m	[disp][disp]	OR mem/reg,reg (word)
0A	mod reg r/m	[disp][disp]	OR reg,mem/reg (byte)
0B	mod reg r/m	[disp][disp]	OR reg,mem/reg (word)
0C	kk		OR AL,kk
0D	kk	jj	OR AL,jjkk
0E			PUSH CS
0F			Not used
10	mod reg r/m	[disp][disp]	ADC mem/reg,reg (byte)
11	mod reg r/m	[disp][disp]	ADC mem/reg,reg (word)
12	mod reg r/m	[disp][disp]	ADC reg,mem/reg (byte)
13	mod reg r/m	[disp][disp]	ADC reg,mem/reg (word)
14	kk		ADC AL,kk
15	kk	jj	ADC AX,jjkk
16			PUSH SS
17			POP SS
18	mod reg r/m	[disp][disp]	SBB mem/reg,reg (byte)
19	mod reg r/m	[disp][disp]	SBB mem/reg,reg (word)
1A	mod reg r/m	[disp][disp]	SBB reg,mem/reg (byte)
1B	mod reg r/m	[disp][disp]	SBB reg,mem/reg (word)
1C	kk		SBB AL,kk
1D	kk	jj	SBB AX,jjkk
1E			PUSH DS
1F			POP DS
20	mod reg r/m	[disp][disp]	AND mem/reg,reg (byte)
21	mod reg r/m	[disp][disp]	AND mem/reg,reg (word)
22	mod reg r/m	[disp][disp]	AND reg,mem/reg (byte)
23	mod reg r/m	[disp][disp]	AND reg,mem/reg (word)
24	kk		AND AL,kk
25	kk	jj	AND AX,jjkk
26			SEG ES
27			DAA
28	mod reg r/m	[disp][disp]	SUB mem/reg,reg (byte)
29	mod reg r/m	[disp][disp]	SUB mem/reg,reg (word)
2A	mod reg r/m	[disp][disp]	SUB reg,mem/reg (byte)
2B	mod reg r/m	[disp][disp]	SUB reg,mem/reg (word)
2C	kk		SUB AL,kk
2D	kk	jj	SUB AX,jjkk
2E			SEG CS
2F			DAS

Object Code			Mnemonic
Byte ≠ 0	Byte # 1	Succeeding Bytes	
30	mod reg r/m	[disp][disp]	XOR mem/reg,reg (byte)
31	mod reg r/m	[disp][disp]	XOR mem/reg,reg (word)
32	mod reg r/m	[disp][disp]	XOR reg,mem/reg (byte)
33	mod reg r/m	[disp][disp]	XOR reg,mem/reg (word)
34	kk		XOR AL,kk
35	kk	jj	XOR AX,jjkk
36			SEG SS
37			AAA
38	mod reg r/m	[disp][disp]	CMP mem/reg,reg (byte)
39	mod reg r/m	[disp][disp]	CMP mem/reg,reg (word)
3A	mod reg r/m	[disp][disp]	CMP reg,mem/reg (byte)
3B	mod reg r/m	[disp][disp]	CMP reg,mem/reg (word)
3C	kk		CMP AL,kk
3D	kk	jj	CMP AX,jjkk
3E			SEG DS
3F			AAS
40			INC AX
41			INC CX
42			INC DX
43			INC BX
44			INC SP
45			INC BP
46			INC SI
47			INC DI
48			DEC AX
49			DEC CX
4A			DEC DX
4B			DEC BX
4C			DEC SP
4D			DEC BP
4E			DEC SI
4F			DEC DI
50			PUSH AX
51			PUSH CX
52			PUSH DX
53			PUSH BX
54			PUSH SP
55			PUSH BP
56			PUSH SI
57			PUSH DI
58			POP AX
59			POP CX
5A			POP DX
5B			POP BX
5C			POP SP
5D			POP BP
5E			POP SI
5F			POP DI
60-6F			Not Used

Object Code			Mnemonic
Byte # 0	Byte # 1	Succeeding Bytes	
70	disp		JO disp
71	disp		JNO disp
72	disp		JB or JNAE or JC disp
73	disp		JNB or JAE or JNC disp
74	disp		JE or JZ disp
75	disp		JNE or JNZ disp
76	disp		JBE or JNA disp
77	disp		JNBE or JA disp
78	disp		JS disp
79	disp		JNS disp
7A	disp		JP or JPE disp
7B	disp		JNP or JPO disp
7C	disp		JL or JNGE disp
7D	disp		JNL or JGE disp
7E	disp		JLE or JNG disp
7F	disp		JNLE or JG disp
80	mod 000 r/m	[disp][disp] kk	ADD mem/reg,kk
80	mod 001 r/m	[disp][disp] kk	OR mem/reg,kk
80	mod 010 r/m	[disp][disp] kk	ADC mem/reg,kk
80	mod 011 r/m	[disp][disp] kk	SBB mem/reg,kk
80	mod 100 r/m	[disp][disp] kk	AND mem/reg,kk
80	mod 101 r/m	[disp][disp] kk	SUB mem/reg,kk
80	mod 110 r/m	[disp][disp] kk	XOR mem/reg, kk
80	mod 111 r/m	[disp][disp] kk	CMP mem/reg,kk
81	mod 000 r/m	[disp][disp] kkjj	ADD mem/reg,jjkk
81	mod 001 r/m	[disp][disp] kkjj	OR mem/reg,jjkk
81	mod 010 r/m	[disp][disp] kkjj	ADC mem/reg,jjkk
81	mod 011 r/m	[disp][disp] kkjj	SBB mem/reg,jjkk
81	mod 100 r/m	[disp][disp] kkjj	AND mem/reg,jjkk
81	mod 101 r/m	[disp][disp] kkjj	SUB mem/reg,jjkk
81	mod 110 r/m	[disp][disp] kkjj	XOR mem/reg,jjkk
81	mod 111 r/m	[disp][disp] kkjj	CMP mem/reg,jjkk
82	mod 000 r/m	[disp][disp] kk	ADD mem/reg,kk (byte)
82	xx 001 xxx		Not used
82	mod 010 r/m	[disp][disp] kk	ADC mem/reg,kk (byte)
82	mod 011 r/m	[disp][disp] kk	SBB mem/reg,kk (byte)
82	xx 100 xxx		Not used
82	mod 101 r/m	[disp][disp] kk	SUB mem/reg,kk (byte)
82	xx 110 xxx		Not used
82	mod 111 r/m	[disp][disp] kk	CMP mem/reg,kk (byte)
83	mod 000 r/m	[disp][disp] kk	ADD mem/reg,jjkk (word-sign extended)
83	xx 001 xxx		Not used
83	mod 010 r/m	[disp][disp] kk	ADC mem/reg,jjkk (word-sign extended)
83	mod 011 r/m	[disp][disp] kk	SBB mem/reg,jjkk (word-sign extended)
83	xx 100 r/m		Not used
83	mod 101 r/m	[disp][disp] kk	SUB mem/reg,jjkk (word-sign extended)
83	xx 110 xxx		Not used
83	mod 111 r/m	[disp][disp] kk	CMP mem/reg,jjkk (word-sign extended)
84	mod reg r/m	[disp][disp]	TEST mem/reg,reg (byte)
85	mod reg r/m	[disp][disp]	TEST mem/reg,reg (word)
86	mod reg r/m	[disp][disp]	XCHG reg,mem/reg (byte)
87	mod reg r/m	[disp][disp]	XCHG reg,mem/reg (word)
88	mod reg r/m	[disp][disp]	MOV mem/reg,reg (byte)
89	mod reg r/m	[disp][disp]	MOV mem/reg,reg (word)

Object Code			Mnemonic
Byte # 0	Byte # 1	Succeeding Bytes	
8A	mod reg r/m	[disp][disp]	MOV reg,mem/reg (byte)
8B	mod reg r/m	[disp][disp]	MOV reg,mem/reg (word)
8C	mod 0ss r/m	[disp][disp]	MOV mem/reg,segreg
8C	xx 1xxxxx		Not used
8D	mod reg r/m	[disp][disp]	LEA reg,addr
8E	mod 0ss r/m	[disp][disp]	MOV segreg, mem/reg
8E	xx 1xxxxx		Not used
8F	mod 000 r/m	[disp][disp]	POP mem/reg
8F	xx 001 xxx		Not used
8F	xx 010 xxx		Not used
8F	xx 011 xxx		Not used
8F	xx 100 xxx		Not used
8F	xx 101 xxx		Not used
8F	xx 110 xxx		Not used
8F	xx 111 xxx		Not used
			Not used
90			NOP
91			XCHG AX,CX
92			XCHG AX,DX
93			XCHG AX,BX
94			XCHG AX,SP
95			XCHG AX,BP
96			XCHG AX,SI
97			XCHG AX,DI
98			CBW
99			CWD
9A	kk	jj hh gg	CALL addr
9B			WAIT
9C			PUSHF
9D			POPF
9E			SAHF
9F			LAHF
A0	qq	pp	MOV AL,addr
A1	qq	pp	MOV AX,addr
A2	qq	pp	MOV addr,AL
A3	qq	pp	MOV addr,AX
A4			MOVS BYTE
A5			MOVS WORD
A6			CMPS BYTE
A7			CMPS WORD
A8	kk		TEST, AL,kk
A9	kk	jj	TEST AX,jjkk
AA			STOS BYTE
AB			STOS WORD
AC			LODS BYTE
AD			LODS WORD
AE			SCAS BYTE
AF			SCAS WORD

Object Code			Mnemonic
Byte # 0	Byte # 1	Succeeding Bytes	
B0	kk		MOV AL,kk
B1	kk		MOV CL,kk
B2	kk		MOV DL,kk
B3	kk		MOV BL,kk
B4	kk		MOV AH,kk
B5	kk		MOV CH,kk
B6	kk		MOV DH,kk
B7	kk		MOV BH,kk
B8	kk	jj	MOV AX,jjkk
B9	kk	jj	MOV CX,jjkk
BA	kk	jj	MOV DX,jjkk
BB	kk	jj	MOV BX,jjkk
BC	kk	jj	MOV SP,jjkk
BD	kk	jj	MOV BP,jjkk
BE	kk	jj	MOV SI,jjkk
BF	kk	jj	MOV DI,jjkk
C0			Not used
C1			Not used
C2	kk	jj	RET jjkk
C3			RET
C4	mod reg r/m	[disp][disp]	LES reg,addr
C5	mod reg r/m	[disp][disp]	LDS reg,addr
C6	mod 000 r/m	[disp][disp] kk	MOV mem,kk
C6	xx 001 xxx		Not used
C6	xx 010 xxx		Not used
C6	xx 011 xxx		Not used
C6	xx 100 xxx		Not used
C6	xx 101 xxx		Not used
C6	xx 110 xxx		Not used
C6	xx 111 xxx		Not used
C7	mod 000 r/m	[disp][disp] kkjj	MOV mem,jjkk
C7	xx 001 xxx		Not used
C7	xx 010 xxx		Not used
C7	xx 011 xxx		Not used
C7	xx 100 xxx		Not used
C7	xx 101 xxx		Not used
C7	xx 110 xxx		Not used
C7	xx 111 xxx		Not used
C8			Not used
C9			Not used
CA	kk	jj	RET jjkk
CB			RET
CC			INT 3
CD	type		INT Type
CE			INTO
CF			IRET

Object Code			Mnemonic
Byte # 0	Byte # 1	Succeeding Bytes	
D0	mod 000 r/m	[disp][disp]	ROL mem/reg,1 (byte)
D0	mod 001 r/m	[disp][disp]	ROR mem/reg,1 (byte)
D0	mod 010 r/m	[disp][disp]	RCL mem/reg,1 (byte)
D0	mod 011 r/m	[disp][disp]	RCR mem/reg,1 (byte)
D0	mod 100 r/m	[disp][disp]	SAL or SHL mem/reg,1 (byte)
D0	mod 101 r/m	[disp][disp]	SHR mem/reg,1 (byte)
D0	xx 110 xxx		Not used
D0	mod 111 r/m	[disp][disp]	SAR mem/reg,1 (byte)
D1	mod 000 r/m	[disp][disp]	ROL mem/reg,1 (word)
D1	mod 001 r/m	[disp][disp]	ROR mem/reg,1 (word)
D1	mod 010 r/m	[disp][disp]	RCL mem/reg,1 (word)
D1	mod 011 r/m	[disp][disp]	RCR mem/reg,1 (word)
D1	mod 100 r/m	[disp][disp]	SAL or SHL mem/reg,1 (word)
D1	mod 101 r/m	[disp][disp]	SHR mem/reg,1 (word)
D1	xx 110 xxx		Not used
D1	mod 111 r/m	[disp][disp]	SAR mem/reg,1 (word)
D2	mod 000 r/m	[disp][disp]	ROL mem/reg,CL (byte)
D2	mod 001 r/m	[disp][disp]	ROR mem/reg,CL (byte)
D2	mod 010 r/m	[disp][disp]	RCL mem/reg,CL (byte)
D2	mod 011 r/m	[disp][disp]	RCR mem/reg,CL (byte)
D2	mod 100 r/m	[disp][disp]	SAL or SHL mem/reg,CL (byte)
D2	mod 101 r/m	[disp][disp]	SHR mem/reg,CL (byte)
D2	xx 110 xxx		Not used
D2	mod 111 r/m	[disp][disp]	SAR mem/reg,CL (byte)
D3	mod 000 r/m	[disp][disp]	ROL mem/reg,CL (word)
D3	mod 001 r/m	[disp][disp]	ROR mem/reg,CL (word)
D3	mod 010 r/m	[disp][disp]	RCL mem/reg,CL (word)
D3	mod 011 r/m	[disp][disp]	RCR mem/reg,CL (word)
D3	mod 100 r/m	[disp][disp]	SAL or SHL mem/reg,CL (word)
D3	mod 101 r/m	[disp][disp]	SHR mem/reg,CL (word)
D3	xx 110 xxx		Not used
D3	mod 111 r/m	[disp][disp]	SAR mem/reg,CL (word)
D4	0A		AAM
D5	0A		AAD
D6			Not used
D7			XLAT
D8	mod xxx r/m	[disp][disp]	ESC mem/reg
D9	mod xxx r/m	[disp][disp]	ESC mem/reg
DA	mod xxx r/m	[disp][disp]	ESC mem/reg
DB	mod xxx r/m	[disp][disp]	ESC mem/reg
DC	mod xxx r/m	[disp][disp]	ESC mem/reg
DD	mod xxx r/m	[disp][disp]	ESC mem/reg
DE	mod xxx r/m	[disp][disp]	ESC mem/reg
DF	mod xxx r/m	[disp][disp]	ESC mem/reg
E0	disp		LOOPNE/LOOPNZ disp
E1	disp		LOOPE/LOOPZ disp
E2	disp		LOOP disp
E3	disp		JCXZ disp
E4	kk		IN AL,kk
E5	kk		IN AX,kk
E6	kk		OUT kk,AL
E7	kk		OUT kk,AX
E8	disp	disp	CALL disp16
E9	disp	disp	JMP disp16

Object Code			Mnemonic
Byte # 0	**Byte # 1**	**Succeeding Bytes**	
EA	kk	jj hh gg	JMP addr
EB	disp		JMP disp
EC			IN AL,DX
ED			IN AX,DX
EE			OUT DX,AL
EF			OUT DX,AX
FO			LOCK
F1			Not used
F2			REPNE or REPNZ
F3			REP or REPE or REPZ
F4			HLT
F5			CMC
F6	mod 000 r/m	[disp][disp] kk	TEST mem/reg,kk
F6	xx 001 xxx		Not used
F6	mod 010 r/m	[disp][disp]	NOT mem/reg (byte)
F6	mod 011 r/m	[disp][disp]	NEG mem/reg (byte)
F6	mod 100 r/m	[disp][disp]	MUL mem/reg (byte)
F6	mod 101 r/m	[disp][disp]	IMUL mem/reg (byte)
F6	mod 110 r/m	[disp][disp]	DIV mem/reg (byte)
F6	mod 111 r/m	[disp][disp]	IDIV mem/reg (byte)
F7	mod 000 r/m	[disp][disp] kkjj	TEST mem/reg,jjkk
F7	xx 001 xxx		Not used
F7	mod 010 r/m	[disp][disp]	NOT mem/reg (word)
F7	mod 011 r/m	[disp][disp]	NEG mem/reg (word)
F7	mod 100 r/m	[disp][disp]	MUL mem/reg (word)
F7	mod 101 r/m	[disp][disp]	IMUL mem/reg (word)
F7	mod 110 r/m	[disp][disp]	DIV mem/reg (word)
F7	mod 111 r/m	[disp][disp]	IDIV mem/reg (word)
F8			CLC
F9			STC
FA			CLI
FB			STI
FC			CLD
FD			STD
FE	mod 000 r/m	[disp][disp]	INC mem/reg (byte)
FE	mod 001 r/m	[disp][disp]	DEC mem/reg (byte)
FE	xx 010 xxx		Not used
FE	xx 011 xxx		Not used
FE	xx 100 xxx		Not used
FE	xx 101 xxx		Not used
FE	xx 110 xxx		Not used
FE	xx 111 xxx		Not used
FF	mod 000 r/m	[disp][disp]	INC mem/reg (word)
FF	mod 001 r/m	[disp][disp]	DEC mem/reg (word)
FF	mod 010 r/m	[disp][disp]	CALL mem/reg
FF	mod 011 r/m	[disp][disp]	CALL mem
FF	mod 100 r/m	[disp][disp]	JMP mem/reg
FF	mod 101 r/m	[disp][disp]	JMP mem
FF	mod 110 r/m	[disp][disp]	PUSH mem
FF	xx 111 xxx		Not used

The 8086 and 8088 Family
AC and DC Characteristics
and Signal Waveforms

This section contains specific electrical and timing data for the following devices:

- · 8086 CPU
- · 8086-1 CPU
- · 8088 CPU
- · 8282/8283 Octal Latch
- · 8284 Clock Generator
- · 8284A Clock Generator
- · 8286/8287 Octal Bus Transceiver
- · 8288 Bus Controller

8086/8086-2/8086-4

PRELIMINARY

8086 MAX MODE SYSTEM (USING 8288 BUS CONTROLLER)
TIMING REQUIREMENTS

Symbol	Parameter	8086/8086-4 Min.	8086/8086-4 Max.	8086-2 Min.	8086-2 Max.	Units	Test Conditions
TCLCL	CLK Cycle Period — 8086 — 8086-4	200 250	500 500	125	500	ns	
TCLCH	CLK Low Time	(⅔ TCLCL) – 15		(⅔ TCLCL) – 15		ns	
TCHCL	CLK High Time	(⅓ TCLCL) + 2		(⅓ TCLCL) + 2		ns	
TCH1CH2	CLK Rise Time		10		10	ns	From 1.0V to 3.5V
TCL2CL1	CLK Fall Time		10		10	ns	From 3.5V to 1.0V
TDVCL	Data In Setup Time	30		20		ns	
TCLDX	Data In Hold Time	10		10		ns	
TR1VCL	RDY Setup Time into 8284 (See Notes 1, 2)	35		35		ns	
TCLR1X	RDY Hold Time into 8284 (See Notes 1, 2)	0		0		ns	
TRYHCH	READY Setup Time into 8086	(⅔ TCLCL) – 15		(⅔ TCLCL) – 15		ns	
TCHRYX	READY Hold Time into 8086	30		20		ns	
TRYLCL	READY Inactive to CLK (See Note 4)	– 8		– 8		ns	
TINVCH	Setup Time for Recognition (INTR, NMI, TEST) (See Note 2)	30		15		ns	
TGVCH	RQ/GT Setup Time	30		15		ns	
TCHGX	RQ Hold Time into 8086	40		30		ns	

TIMING RESPONSES

Symbol	Parameter	8086/8086-4 Min.	8086/8086-4 Max.	8086-2 Min.	8086-2 Max.	Units	Test Conditions
TCLML	Command Active Delay (See Note 1)	10	35	10	35	ns	
TCLMH	Command Inactive Delay (See Note 1)	10	35	10	35	ns	
TRYHSH	READY Active to Status Passive (See Note 3)		110		65	ns	
TCHSV	Status Active Delay	10	110	10	60	ns	
TCLSH	Status Inactive Delay	10	130	10	70	ns	
TCLAV	Address Valid Delay	10	110	10	60	ns	
TCLAX	Address Hold Time	10		10		ns	
TCLAZ	Address Float Delay	TCLAX	80	TCLAX	50	ns	
TSVLH	Status Valid to ALE High (See Note 1)		15		15	ns	
TSVMCH	Status Valid to MCE High (See Note 1)		15		15	ns	
TCLLH	CLK Low to ALE Valid (See Note 1)		15		15	ns	
TCLMCH	CLK Low to MCE High (See Note 1)		15		15	ns	
TCHLL	ALE Inactive Delay (See Note 1)		15		15	ns	
TCLMCL	MCE Inactive Delay (See Note 1)		15		15	ns	
TCLDV	Data Valid Delay	10	110	10	60	ns	C_L = 20-100 pF for all 8086 Outputs (In addition to 8086 self-load)
TCHDX	Data Hold Time	10		10		ns	
TCVNV	Control Active Delay (See Note 1)	5	45	5	45	ns	
TCVNX	Control Inactive Delay (See Note 1)	10	45	10	45	ns	
TAZRL	Address Float to Read Active	0		0		ns	
TCLRL	RD Active Delay	10	165	10	100	ns	
TCLRH	RD Inactive Delay	10	150	10	80	ns	
TRHAV	RD Inactive to Next Address Active	TCLCL–45		TCLCL–40		ns	
TCHDTL	Direction Control Active Delay (See Note 1)		50		50	ns	
TCHDTH	Direction Control Inactive Delay (See Note 1)		30		30	ns	
TCLGL	GT Active Delay	0	85	0	50	ns	
TCLGH	GT Inactive Delay	0	85	0	50	ns	
TRLRH	RD Width	2TCLCL–75		2TCLCL–50		ns	

NOTES: 1. Signal at 8284 or 8288 shown for reference only.
2. Setup requirement for asynchronous signal only to guarantee recognition at next CLK.
3. Applies only to T3 and wait states.
4. Applies only to T2 state (8 ns into T3).

8086/8086-2/8086-4   PRELIMINARY

ABSOLUTE MAXIMUM RATINGS*

Ambient Temperature Under Bias . . . . 0 °C to 70 °C
Storage Temperature . . . . − 65 °C to + 150 °C
Voltage on Any Pin with
   Respect to Ground . . . . − 1.0 to + 7V
Power Dissipation . . . . 2.5 Watt

*COMMENT: Stresses above those listed under "Absolute Maximum Ratings" may cause permanent damage to the device. This is a stress rating only and functional operation of the device at these or any other conditions above those indicated in the operational sections of this specification is not implied. Exposure to absolute maximum rating conditions for extended periods may affect device reliability.

D.C. CHARACTERISTICS

       8086: $T_A = 0\,°C$ to 70 °C, $V_{CC} = 5V \pm 10\%$
8086-2/8086-4: $T_A = 0\,°C$ to 70 °C, $V_{CC} = 5V \pm 5\%$

Symbol	Parameter	Min.	Max.	Units	Test Conditions
V_{IL}	Input Low Voltage	− 0.5	+ 0.8	V	
V_{IH}	Input High Voltage	2.0	$V_{CC} + 0.5$	V	
V_{OL}	Output Low Voltage		0.45	V	$I_{OL} = 2.0$ mA
V_{OH}	Output High Voltage	2.4		V	$I_{OH} = -400\,\mu A$
I_{CC}	Power Supply Current 8086/8086-4 8086-2		340 350	mA mA	$T_A = 25\,°C$
I_{LI}	Input Leakage Current		± 10	μA	$0V < V_{IN} < V_{CC}$
I_{LO}	Output Leakage Current		± 10	μA	$0.45V \leqslant V_{OUT} \leqslant V_{CC}$
V_{CL}	Clock Input Low Voltage	− 0.5	+ 0.6	V	
V_{CH}	Clock Input High Voltage	3.9	$V_{CC} + 1.0$	V	
C_{IN}	Capacitance of Input Buffer (All input except $AD_0 - AD_{15}$, $\overline{RQ/GT}$)		10	pF	fc = 1 MHz
C_{IO}	Capacitance of I/O Buffer ($AD_0 - AD_{15}$, $\overline{RQ/GT}$)		20	pF	fc = 1 MHz

8086/8086-2/8086-4

PRELIMINARY

A.C. CHARACTERISTICS

8086: $T_A = 0°C$ to $70°C$, $V_{CC} = 5V \pm 10\%$
8086-2/8086-4: $T_A = 0°C$ to $70°C$, $V_{CC} = 5V \pm 5\%$

8086 MINIMUM COMPLEXITY SYSTEM (Figures 8, 9, 12, 15)
TIMING REQUIREMENTS

Symbol	Parameter	8086/8086-4 Min.	8086/8086-4 Max.	8086-2 Min.	8086-2 Max.	Units	Test Conditions
TCLCL	CLK Cycle Period — 8086	200	500	125	500	ns	
	-- 8086-4	250	500				
TCLCH	CLK Low Time	(⅔ TCLCL) − 15		(⅔ TCLCL) − 15		ns	
TCHCL	CLK High Time	(⅓ TCLCL) + 2		(⅓ TCLCL) + 2		ns	
TCH1CH2	CLK Rise Time		10		10	ns	From 1.0V to 3.5V
TCL2CL1	CLK Fall Time		10		10	ns	From 3.5V to 1.0V
TDVCL	Data In Setup Time	30		20		ns	
TCLDX	Data In Hold Time	10		10		ns	
TR1VCL	RDY Setup Time into 8284 (See Notes 1, 2)	35		35		ns	
TCLR1X	RDY Hold Time into 8284 (See Notes 1, 2)	0		0		ns	
TRYHCH	READY Setup Time into 8086	(⅔ TCLCL) − 15		(⅔ TCLCL) − 15		ns	
TCHRYX	READY Hold Time into 8086	30		20		ns	
TRYLCL	READY Inactive to CLK (See Note 3)	− 8		− 8		ns	
THVCH	HOLD Setup Time	35		20		ns	
TINVCH	INTR, NMI, TEST Setup Time (See Note 2)	30		15		ns	

TIMING RESPONSES

Symbol	Parameter	8086/8086-4 Min.	8086/8086-4 Max.	8086-2 Min.	8086-2 Max.	Units	Test Conditions
TCLAV	Address Valid Delay	10	110	10	60	ns	
TCLAX	Address Hold Time	10		10		ns	
TCLAZ	Address Float Delay	TCLAX	80	TCLAX	50	ns	
TLHLL	ALE Width	TCLCH−20		TCLCH−10		ns	
TCLLH	ALE Active Delay		80		50	ns	
TCHLL	ALE Inactive Delay		85		55	ns	
TLLAX	Address Hold Time to ALE Inactive	TCHCL−10		TCHCL−10		ns	
TCLDV	Data Valid Delay	10	110	10	60	ns	
TCHDX	Data Hold Time	10		10		ns	
TWHDX	Data Hold Time After WR	TCLCH−30		TCLCH−30		ns	C_L = 20-100 pF for all 8086 Outputs (In addition to 8086 self-load)
TCVCTV	Control Active Delay 1	10	110	10	70	ns	
TCHCTV	Control Active Delay 2	10	110	10	60	ns	
TCVCTX	Control Inactive Delay	10	110	10	70	ns	
TAZRL	Address Float to READ Active	0		0		ns	
TCLRL	RD Active Delay	10	165	10	100	ns	
TCLRH	RD Inactive Delay	10	150	10	80	ns	
TRHAV	RD Inactive to Next Address Active	TCLCL−45		TCLCL −40		ns	
TCLHAV	HLDA Valid Delay	10	160	10	100	ns	
TRLRH	RD Width	2TCLCL−75		2TCLCL−50		ns	
TWLWH	WR Width	2TCLCL−60		2TCLCL−40		ns	
TAVAL	Address Valid to ALE Low	TCLCH−60		TCLCH−40		ns	

NOTES: 1. Signal at 8284 shown for reference only.
2. Setup requirement for asynchronous signal only to guarantee recognition at next CLK.
3. Applies only to T2 state. (8 ns into T3)

8086/8086-2/8086-4 PRELIMINARY

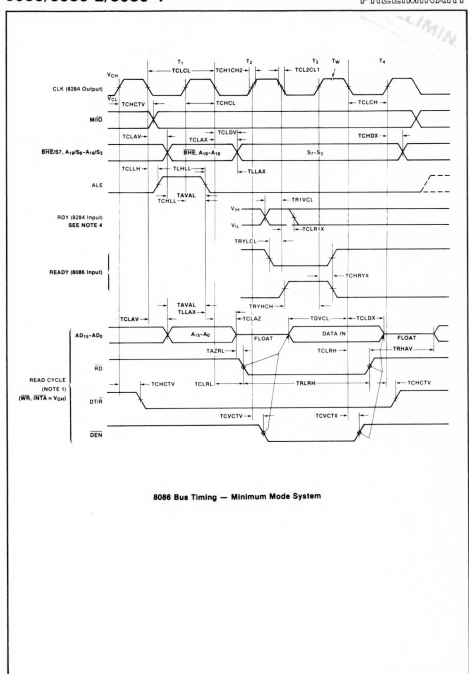

8086 Bus Timing — Minimum Mode System

8086/8086-2/8086-4 PRELIMINARY

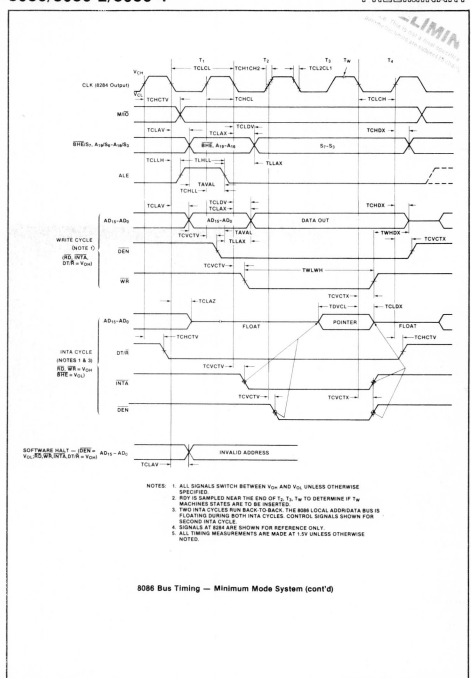

8086 Bus Timing — Minimum Mode System (cont'd)

8086/8086-2/8086-4

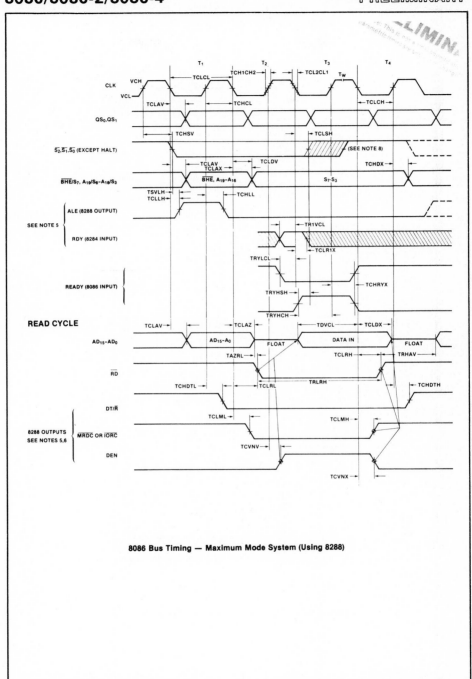

8086 Bus Timing — Maximum Mode System (Using 8288)

8086/8086-2/8086-4

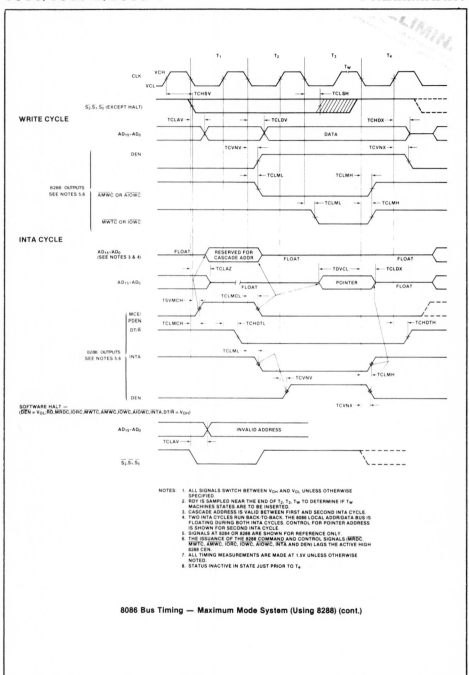

8086 Bus Timing — Maximum Mode System (Using 8288) (cont.)

8086/8086-2/8086-4

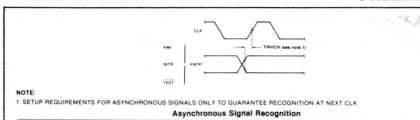

NOTE:

1. SETUP REQUIREMENTS FOR ASYNCHRONOUS SIGNALS ONLY TO GUARANTEE RECOGNITION AT NEXT CLK

Asynchronous Signal Recognition

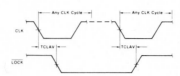

Bus Lock Signal Timing (Maximum Mode Only)

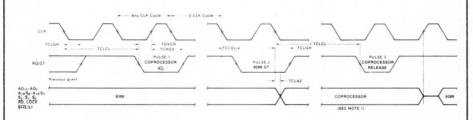

NOTES: 1 THE COPROCESSOR MAY NOT DRIVE THE BUSES OUTSIDE THE REGION
SHOWN WITHOUT RISKING CONTENTION.

Request/Grant Sequence Timing (Maximum Mode Only)

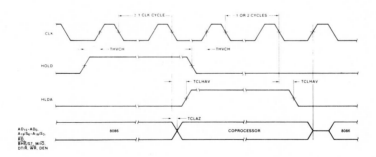

Hold/Hold Acknowledge Timing (Minimum Mode Only)

8086-1

ABSOLUTE MAXIMUM RATINGS*

Ambient Temperature Under Bias . . . . 0 °C to 70 °C
Storage Temperature . . . . − 65 °C to + 150 °C
Voltage on Any Pin with
   Respect to Ground . . . . − 1.0 to + 7V
Power Dissipation . . . . 2.5 Watt

*NOTICE: Stresses above those listed under "Absolute Maximum Ratings" may cause permanent damage to the device. This is a stress rating only and functional operation of the device at these or any other conditions above those indicated in the operational sections of this specification is not implied. Exposure to absolute maximum rating conditions for extended periods may affect device reliability.

D.C. CHARACTERISTICS

8086-1: $T_A = 0$ °C to 70 °C, $V_{CC} = 5V \pm 5\%$

Symbol	Parameter	Min.	Max.	Units	Test Conditions
V_{IL}	Input Low Voltage	− 0.5	+ 0.8	V	
V_{IH}	Input High Voltage	2.0	$V_{CC} + 0.5$	V	
V_{OL}	Output Low Voltage		0.45	V	$I_{OL} = 2.0$ mA
V_{OH}	Output High Voltage	2.4		V	$I_{OH} = − 400 \mu A$
I_{CC}	Power Supply Current 8086-1		360	mA	$T_A = 25$ °C
I_{LI}	Input Leakage Current		± 10	μA	$0V < V_{IN} < V_{CC}$
I_{LO}	Output Leakage Current		± 10	μA	$0.45V \leqslant V_{OUT} \leqslant V_{CC}$
V_{CL}	Clock Input Low Voltage	− 0.5	+ 0.6	V	
V_{CH}	Clock Input High Voltage	3.9	$V_{CC} + 1.0$	V	
C_{IN}	Capacitance of Input Buffer (All input except $AD_0 - AD_{15}$, $\overline{RQ/GT}$)		15	pF	fc = 1 MHz
C_{IO}	Capacitance of I/O Buffer ($AD_0 - AD_{15}$, $\overline{RQ/GT}$)		15	pF	fc = 1 MHz

8086-1

A.C. CHARACTERISTICS

8086-1: $T_A = 0°C$ to $70°C$, $V_{CC} = 5V \pm 5\%$

8086 MINIMUM COMPLEXITY SYSTEM (Figures 3, 4, 7, 10)
TIMING REQUIREMENTS

Symbol	Parameter	8086-1 Min.	8086-1 Max.	Units	Test Conditions
TCLCL	CLK Cycle Period — 8086	100	500	ns	
TCLCH	CLK Low Time	$(2/3 \text{ TCLCL}) - 14$		ns	
TCHCL	CLK High Time	$(1/3 \text{ TCLCL}) + 6$		ns	
TCH1CH2	CLK Rise Time		10	ns	From 1.0V to 3.5V
TCL2CL1	CLK Fall Time		10	ns	From 3.5V to 1.0V
TDVCL	Data In Setup Time	5		ns	
TCLDX	Data In Hold Time	10		ns	
TR1VCL	RDY Setup Time into 8284A (See Notes 1, 2)	35		ns	
TCLR1X	RDY Hold Time into 8284A (See Notes 1, 2)	0		ns	
TRYHCH	READY Setup Time into 8086	53		ns	
TCHRYX	READY Hold Time into 8086	20		ns	
TRYLCL	READY Inactive to CLK (See Note 3)	– 10		ns	
THVCH	HOLD Setup Time	20		ns	
TINVCH	INTR, NMI, $\overline{\text{TEST}}$ Setup Time (See Note 2)	15		ns	

TIMING RESPONSES

Symbol	Parameter	8086-1 Min.	8086-1 Max.	Units	Test Conditions
TCLAV	Address Valid Delay	10	50	ns	
TCLAX	Address Hold Time	10		ns	
TCLAZ	Address Float Delay	10	40	ns	
TLHLL	ALE Width	TCLCH-10		ns	
TCLLH	ALE Active Delay		40	ns	
TCHLL	ALE Inactive Delay		45	ns	
TLLAX	Address Hold Time to ALE Inactive	TCHCL-10		ns	
TCLDV	Data Valid Delay	10	50	ns	C_L = 20-100 pF for
TCHDX	Data Hold Time	10		ns	all 8086-1 Outputs
TWHDX	Data Hold Time After WR	TCLCH-25		ns	(In addition to 8086-1
TCVCTV	Control Active Delay 1	10	50	ns	self-load)
TCHCTV	Control Active Delay 2	10	45	ns	
TCVCTX	Control Inactive Delay	10	50	ns	
TAZRL	Address Float to READ Active	0		ns	
TCLRL	$\overline{\text{RD}}$ Active Delay	10	70	ns	
TCLRH	$\overline{\text{RD}}$ Inactive Delay	10	60	ns	
TRHAV	$\overline{\text{RD}}$ Inactive to Next Address Active	TCLCL-35		ns	
TCLHAV	HLDA Valid Delay	10	60	ns	
TRLRH	$\overline{\text{RD}}$ Width	2TCLCL-40		ns	
TWLWH	$\overline{\text{WR}}$ Width	2TCLCL-35		ns	
TAVAL	Address Valid to ALE Low	TCLCH-35		ns	

NOTES: 1. Signal at 8284A shown for reference only.
2. Setup requirement for asynchronous signal only to guarantee recognition at next CLK.
3. Applies only to T2 state. (8 ns into T3)

8086-1

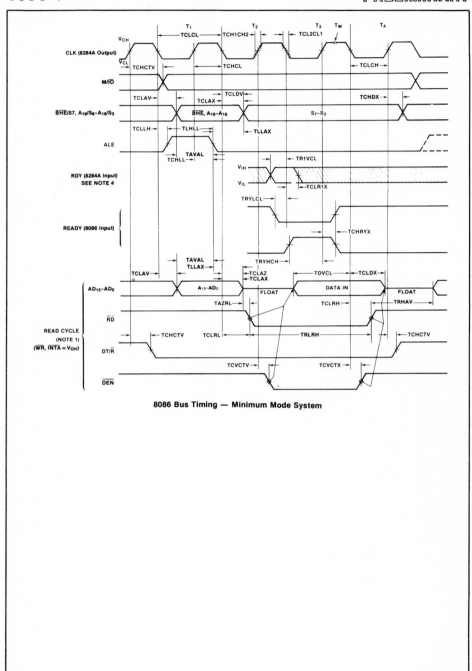

8086 Bus Timing — Minimum Mode System

8086-1

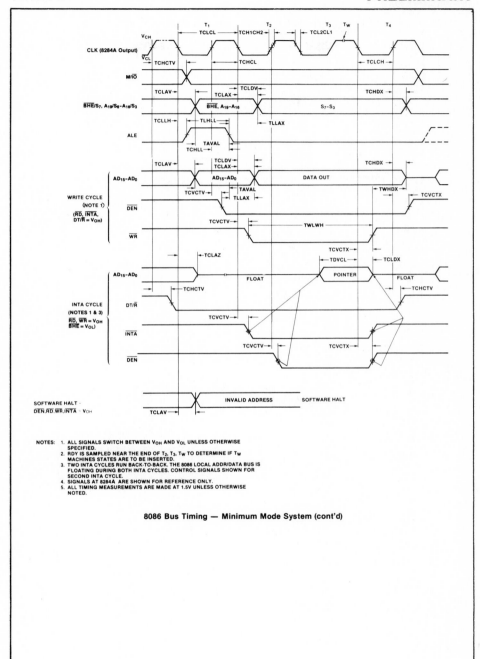

8086 Bus Timing — Minimum Mode System (cont'd)

NOTES:
1. ALL SIGNALS SWITCH BETWEEN V_{OH} AND V_{OL} UNLESS OTHERWISE SPECIFIED.
2. RDY IS SAMPLED NEAR THE END OF T_2, T_3, T_W TO DETERMINE IF T_W MACHINES STATES ARE TO BE INSERTED.
3. TWO INTA CYCLES RUN BACK-TO-BACK. THE 8086 LOCAL ADDR/DATA BUS IS FLOATING DURING BOTH INTA CYCLES. CONTROL SIGNALS SHOWN FOR SECOND INTA CYCLE.
4. SIGNALS AT 8284A ARE SHOWN FOR REFERENCE ONLY.
5. ALL TIMING MEASUREMENTS ARE MADE AT 1.5V UNLESS OTHERWISE NOTED.

8086-1

8086 MAX MODE SYSTEM (USING 8288 BUS CONTROLLER) (Figures 5 — 9)
TIMING REQUIREMENTS

Symbol	Parameter	8086-1 Min.	8086-1 Max.	Units	Test Conditions
TCLCL	CLK Cycle Period — 8086 — 8086-4	100	500	ns	
TCLCH	CLK Low Time	(⅔ TCLCL) − 14		ns	
TCHCL	CLK High Time	(⅓ TCLCL) + 6		ns	
TCH1CH2	CLK Rise Time		10	ns	From 1.0V to 3.5V
TCL2CL1	CLK Fall Time		10	ns	From 3.5V to 1.0V
TDVCL	Data In Setup Time	5		ns	
TCLDX	Data In Hold Time	10		ns	
TR1VCL	RDY Setup Time into 8284A (See Notes 1, 2)	35		ns	
TCLR1X	RDY Hold Time into 8284A (See Notes 1, 2)	0		ns	
TRYHCH	READY Setup Time into 8086	53		ns	
TCHRYX	READY Hold Time into 8086	20		ns	
TRYLCL	READY Inactive to CLK (See Note 4)	−10		ns	
TINVCH	Setup Time for Recognition (INTR, NMI, TEST) (See Note 2)	15		ns	
TGVCH	RQ/GT Setup Time	12		ns	
TCHGX	RQ Hold Time into 8086	20		ns	

TIMING RESPONSES

Symbol	Parameter	8086-1 Min.	8086-1 Max.	Units	Test Conditions
TCLML	Command Active Delay (See Note 1)	10	35	ns	
TCLMH	Command Inactive Delay (See Note 1)	10	35	ns	
TRYHSH	READY Active to Status Passive (See Note 3)		45	ns	
TCHSV	Status Active Delay	10	45	ns	
TCLSH	Status Inactive Delay	10	55	ns	
TCLAV	Address Valid Delay	10	50	ns	
TCLAX	Address Hold Time	10		ns	
TCLAZ	Address Float Delay	10	40	ns	
TSVLH	Status Valid to ALE High (See Note 1)		15	ns	
TSVMCH	Status Valid to MCE High (See Note 1)		15	ns	
TCLLH	CLK Low to ALE Valid (See Note 1)		15	ns	
TCLMCH	CLK Low to MCE High (See Note 1)		15	ns	
TCHLL	ALE Inactive Delay (See Note 1)		15	ns	C_L = 20-100 pF for
TCLMCL	MCE Inactive Delay (See Note 1)		15	ns	all 8086-1 Outputs
TCLDV	Data Valid Delay	10	50	ns	(In addition to
TCHDX	Data Hold Time	10		ns	8086-1 self-load)
TCVNV	Control Active Delay (See Note 1)	5	45	ns	
TCVNX	Control Inactive Delay (See Note 1)	10	45	ns	
TAZRL	Address Float to Read Active	0		ns	
TCLRL	RD Active Delay	10	70	ns	
TCLRH	RD Inactive Delay	10	60	ns	
TRHAV	RD Inactive to Next Address Active	TCLCL−35		ns	
TCHDTL	Direction Control Active Delay (See Note 1)		50	ns	
TCHDTH	Direction Control Inactive Delay (See Note 1)		30	ns	
TCLGL	GT Active Delay	0	45	ns	
TCLGH	GT Inactive Delay	0	45	ns	
TRLRH	RD Width	2TCLCL−40		ns	

NOTES: 1. Signal at 8284A or 8288 shown for reference only.
2. Setup requirement for asynchronous signal only to guarantee recognition at next CLK.
3. Applies only to T3 and wait states.
4. Applies only to T2 state (8 ns into T3).

8086-1

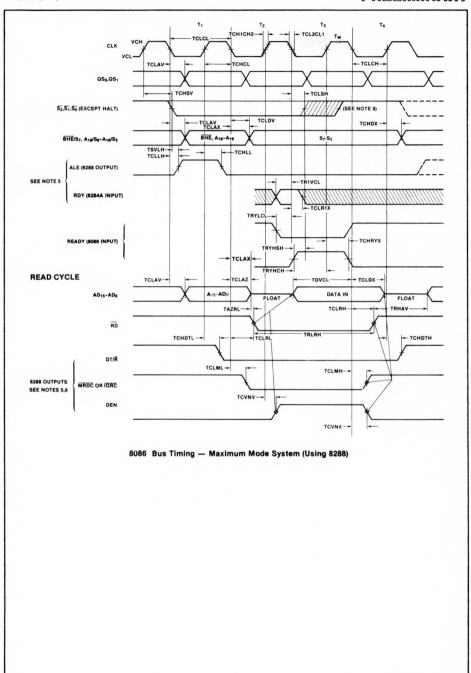

8086 Bus Timing — Maximum Mode System (Using 8288)

8086-1

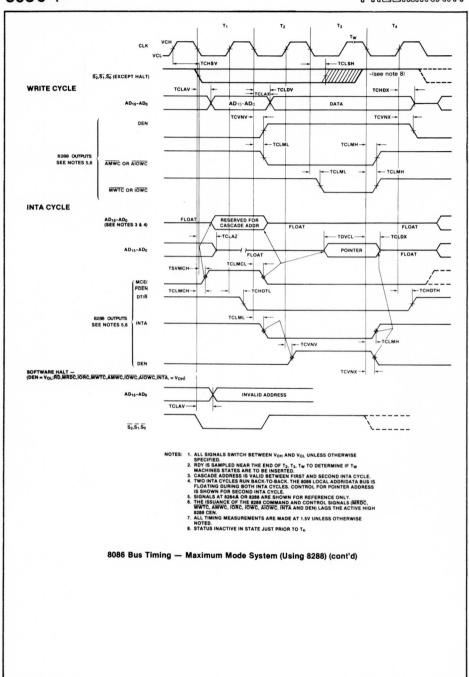

NOTES: 1. ALL SIGNALS SWITCH BETWEEN V_{OH} AND V_{OL} UNLESS OTHERWISE SPECIFIED.
2. RDY IS SAMPLED NEAR THE END OF T_2, T_3, T_W TO DETERMINE IF T_W MACHINES STATES ARE TO BE INSERTED.
3. CASCADE ADDRESS IS VALID BETWEEN FIRST AND SECOND INTA CYCLE.
4. TWO INTA CYCLES RUN BACK-TO-BACK. THE 8086 LOCAL ADDR/DATA BUS IS FLOATING DURING BOTH INTA CYCLES. CONTROL FOR POINTER ADDRESS IS SHOWN FOR SECOND INTA CYCLE.
5. SIGNALS AT 8284A OR 8288 ARE SHOWN FOR REFERENCE ONLY.
6. THE ISSUANCE OF THE 8288 COMMAND AND CONTROL SIGNALS (MRDC, MWTC, AMWC, IORC, IOWC, AIOWC, INTA AND DEN) LAGS THE ACTIVE HIGH 8288 CEN.
7. ALL TIMING MEASUREMENTS ARE MADE AT 1.5V UNLESS OTHERWISE NOTED.
8. STATUS INACTIVE IN STATE JUST PRIOR TO T_4.

8086 Bus Timing — Maximum Mode System (Using 8288) (cont'd)

8086-1   PRELIMINARY

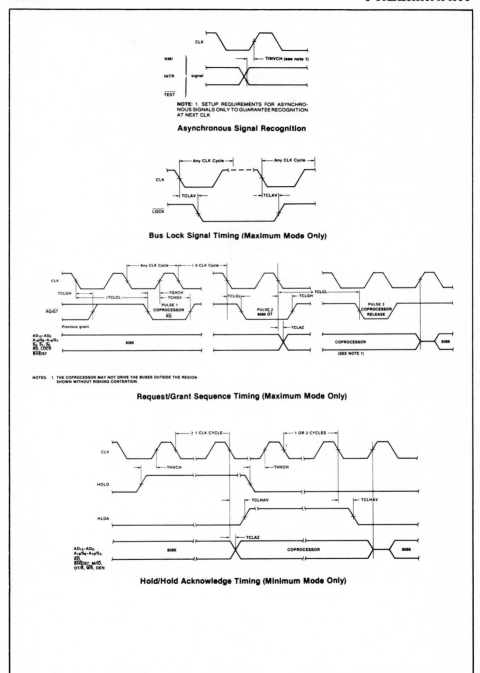

Asynchronous Signal Recognition

Bus Lock Signal Timing (Maximum Mode Only)

Request/Grant Sequence Timing (Maximum Mode Only)

Hold/Hold Acknowledge Timing (Minimum Mode Only)

8088

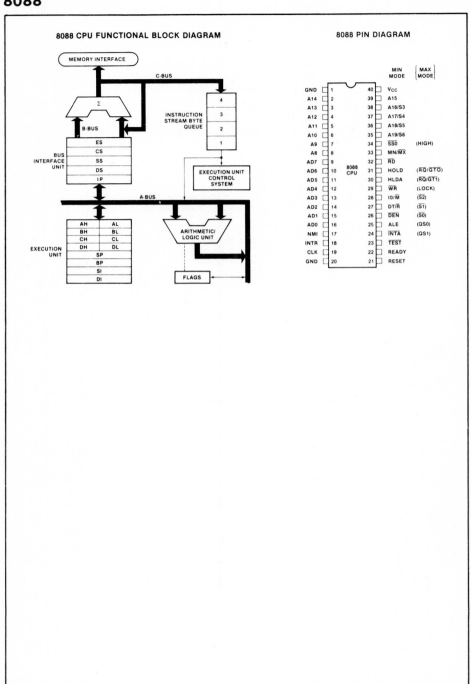

8088 CPU FUNCTIONAL BLOCK DIAGRAM

MEMORY INTERFACE

C-BUS

Σ

B-BUS

INSTRUCTION STREAM BYTE QUEUE

4
3
2
1

BUS INTERFACE UNIT

| ES |
| CS |
| SS |
| DS |
| IP |

EXECUTION UNIT CONTROL SYSTEM

A-BUS

EXECUTION UNIT

AH	AL
BH	BL
CH	CL
DH	DL
SP	
BP	
SI	
DI	

ARITHMETIC/ LOGIC UNIT

FLAGS

8088 PIN DIAGRAM

			MIN MODE	(MAX MODE)
GND	1	40	Vcc	
A14	2	39	A15	
A13	3	38	A16/S3	
A12	4	37	A17/S4	
A11	5	36	A18/S5	
A10	6	35	A19/S6	
A9	7	34	$\overline{SS0}$	(HIGH)
A8	8	33	MN/$\overline{MX}$	
AD7	9	32	$\overline{RD}$	
AD6	10	31	HOLD	($\overline{RQ/GT0}$)
AD5	11	30	HLDA	($\overline{RQ/GT1}$)
AD4	12	29	$\overline{WR}$	($\overline{LOCK}$)
AD3	13	28	IO/$\overline{M}$	($\overline{S2}$)
AD2	14	27	DT/$\overline{R}$	($\overline{S1}$)
AD1	15	26	$\overline{DEN}$	($\overline{S0}$)
AD0	16	25	ALE	(QS0)
NMI	17	24	$\overline{INTA}$	(QS1)
INTR	18	23	$\overline{TEST}$	
CLK	19	22	READY	
GND	20	21	RESET	

8088 CPU

8088

ABSOLUTE MAXIMUM RATINGS*

Ambient Temperature Under Bias . . . . 0°C to 70°C
Storage Temperature . . . . − 65°C to + 150°C
Voltage on Any Pin with
   Respect to Ground . . . . − 0.3 to + 7V
Power Dissipation . . . . 2.5 Watt

*COMMENT: Stresses above those listed under "Absolute Maximum Ratings" may cause permanent damage to the device. This is a stress rating only and functional operation of the device at these or any other conditions above those indicated in the operational sections of this specification is not implied. Exposure to absolute maximum rating conditions for extended periods may affect device reliability.

D.C. CHARACTERISTICS

8088: $T_A = 0°C$ to $70°C$, $V_{CC} = 5V \pm 10\%$

Symbol	Parameter	Min.	Max.	Units	Test Conditions
V_{IL}	Input Low Voltage	− 0.5	+ 0.8	V	
V_{IH}	Input High Voltage	2.0	$V_{CC} + 0.5$	V	
V_{OL}	Output Low Voltage		0.45	V	$I_{OL} = 2.0$ mA
V_{OH}	Output High Voltage	2.4		V	$I_{OH} = 400 \mu A$
I_{CC}	Power Supply Current		340	mA	
I_{LI}	Input Leakage Current		± 10	μA	$V_{IN} = V_{CC}$
I_{LO}	Output Leakage Current		± 10	μA	$0.45V \leqslant V_{OUT} \leqslant V_{CC}$
V_{CL}	Clock Input Low Voltage	− 0.5	+ 0.6	V	
V_{CH}	Clock Input High Voltage	3.9	$V_{CC} + 1.0$	V	
C_{IN}	Capacitance of Input Buffer (All input except AD_0-AD_7 RQ/GT)		10	pF	fc = 1 MHz
C_{IO}	Capacitance of I/O Buffer (AD_0-AD_7 RQ/GT)		20	pF	fc = 1 MHz

8088

A.C. CHARACTERISTICS

8088: $T_A = 0°C$ to $70°C$, $V_{CC} = 5V \pm 10\%$

8088 MINIMUM COMPLEXITY SYSTEM TIMING REQUIREMENTS

Symbol	Parameter	Min.	Max.	Units	Test Conditions
TCLCL	CLK Cycle Period	200	500	ns	
TCLCH	CLK Low Time	(⅔TCLCL)-15		ns	
TCHCL	CLK High Time	(⅓TCLCL) + 2		ns	
TCH1CH2	CLK Rise Time		10	ns	From 1.0V to 3.5V
TCL2CL1	CLK Fall Time		10	ns	From 3.5V to 1.0V
TDVCL	Data In Setup Time	30		ns	
TCLDX	Data In Hold Time	10		ns	
TR1VCL	RDY Setup Time into 8284 (See Notes 1, 2)	35		ns	
TCLR1X	RDY Hold Time into 8284 (See Notes 1, 2)	0		ns	
TRYHCH	READY Setup Time into 8088	(⅔TCLCL)-15		ns	
TCHRYX	READY Hold Time into 8088	30		ns	
TRYLCL	READY Inactive to CLK (See Note 3)	-8		ns	
THVCH	HOLD Setup Time	35		ns	
TINVCH	INTR, NMI, TEST Setup Time (See Note 2)	30		ns	

TIMING RESPONSES

Symbol	Parameter	Min.	Max.	Units	Test Conditions
TCLAV	Address Valid Delay	15	110	ns	
TCLAX	Address Hold Time	10		ns	
TCLAZ	Address Float Delay	TCLAX	80	ns	
TLHLL	ALE Width	TCLCH-20		ns	
TCLLH	ALE Active Delay		80	ns	
TCHLL	ALE Inactive Delay		85	ns	
TLLAX	Address Hold Time to ALE Inactive	TCHCL-10		ns	
TCLDV	Data Valid Delay	10	110	ns	C_L = 20-100 pF for all 8088 Outputs in addition to internal loads
TCHDX	Data Hold Time	10		ns	
TWHDX	Data Hold Time After WR	TCLCH-30		ns	
TCVCTV	Control Active Delay 1	10	110	ns	
TCHCTV	Control Active Delay 2	10	110	ns	
TCVCTX	Control Inactive Delay	10	110	ns	
TAZRL	Address Float to READ Active	0		ns	
TCLRL	RD Active Delay	10	165	ns	
TCLRH	RD Inactive Delay	10	150	ns	
TRHAV	RD Inactive to Next Address Active	TCLCL-45		ns	
TCLHAV	HLDA Valid Delay	10	160	ns	
TRLRH	RD Width	2TCLCL-75		ns	
TWLWH	WR Width	2TCLCL-60		ns	
TAVAL	Address Valid to ALE Low	TCLCH-60		ns	

NOTES: 1. Signal at 8284 shown for reference only.
2. Setup requirement for asynchronous signal only to guarantee recognition at next CLK.
3. Applies only to T2 state (8 ns into T3 state).

8088

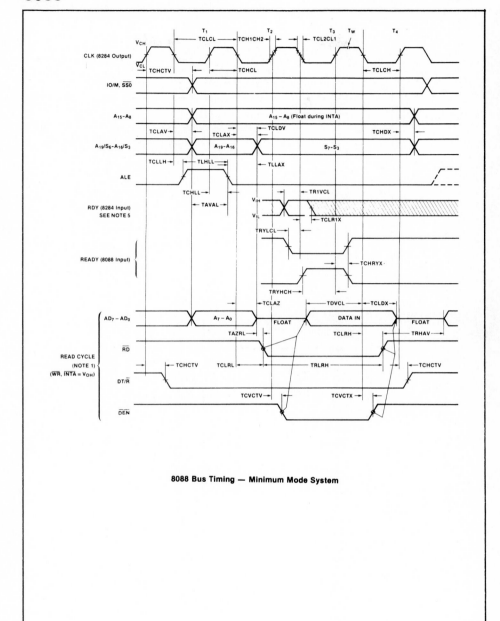

8088 Bus Timing — Minimum Mode System

8088

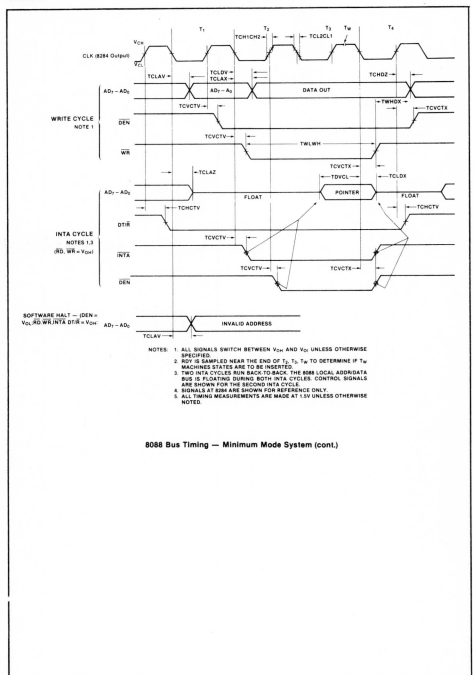

8088 Bus Timing — Minimum Mode System (cont.)

8088

8088 MAX MODE SYSTEM (USING 8288 BUS CONTROLLER)
TIMING REQUIREMENTS

Symbol	Parameter	Min.	Max.	Units	Test Conditions
TCLCL	CLK Cycle Period	200	500	ns	
TCLCH	CLK Low Time	(²⁄₃TCLCL)−15		ns	
TCHCL	CLK High Time	(⅓TCLCL)+2		ns	
TCH1CH2	CLK Rise Time		10	ns	From 1.0V to 3.5V
TCL2CL1	CLK Fall Time		10	ns	From 3.5V to 1.0V
TDVCL	Data In Setup Time	30		ns	
TCLDX	Data In Hold Time	10		ns	
TR1VCL	RDY Setup Time into 8284 (See Notes 1, 2)	35		ns	
TCLR1X	RDY Hold Time into 8284 (See Notes 1, 2)	0		ns	
TRYHCH	READY Setup Time into 8088	(²⁄₃TCLCL)−15		ns	
TCHRYX	READY Hold Time into 8088	30		ns	
TRYLCL	READY Inactive to CLK (See Note 4)	−8		ns	
TINVCH	Setup Time for Recognition (INTR, NMI, TEST) (See Note 2)	30		ns	
TGVCH	RQ/GT Setup Time	30		ns	
TCHGX	RQ Hold Time into 8086	40		ns	

TIMING RESPONSES

Symbol	Parameter	Min.	Max.	Units	Test Conditions
TCLML	Command Active Delay (See Note 1)	10	35	ns	
TCLMH	Command Inactive Delay (See Note 1)	10	35	ns	
TRYHSH	READY Active to Status Passive (See Note 3)		110	ns	
TCHSV	Status Active Delay	10	110	ns	
TCLSH	Status Inactive Delay	10	130	ns	
TCLAV	Address Valid Delay	15	110	ns	
TCLAX	Address Hold Time	10		ns	
TCLAZ	Address Float Delay	TCLAX	80	ns	
TSVLH	Status Valid to ALE High (See Note 1)		15	ns	
TSVMCH	Status Valid to MCE High (See Note 1)		15	ns	
TCLLH	CLK Low to ALE Valid (See Note 1)		15	ns	
TCLMCH	CLK Low to MCE High (See Note 1)		15	ns	
TCHLL	ALE Inactive Delay (See Note 1)		15	ns	
TCLMCL	MCE Inactive Delay (See Note 1)		15	ns	C_L = 20-100 pF for all 8088 Outputs in addition to internal loads
TCLDV	Data Valid Delay	15	110	ns	
TCHDX	Data Hold Time	10		ns	
TCVNV	Control Active Delay (See Note 1)	5	45	ns	
TCVNX	Control Inactive Delay (See Note 1)	10	45	ns	
TAZRL	Address Float to Read Active	0		ns	
TCLRL	RD Active Delay	10	165	ns	
TCLRH	RD Inactive Delay	10	150	ns	
TRHAV	RD inactive to Next Address Active	TCLCL−45		ns	
TCHDTL	Direction Control Active Delay (See Note 1)		50	ns	
TCHDTH	Direction Control Inactive Delay (See Note 1)		30	ns	
TCLGL	GT Active Delay		110	ns	
TCLGH	GT Inactive Delay		85	ns	
TRLRH	RD Width	2TCLCL−75		ns	

NOTES: 1. Signal at 8284 or 8288 shown for reference only.
2. Setup requirement for asynchronous signal only to guarantee recognition at next CLK.
3. Applies only to T3 and wait states.
4. Applies only to T2 state (8 ns into T3 state).

8088 Bus Timing — Minimum Mode System (cont.)

8088

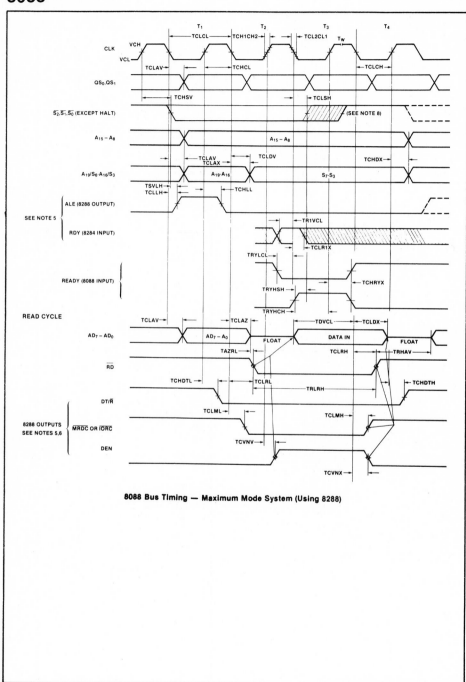

8088 Bus Timing — Maximum Mode System (Using 8288)

8088

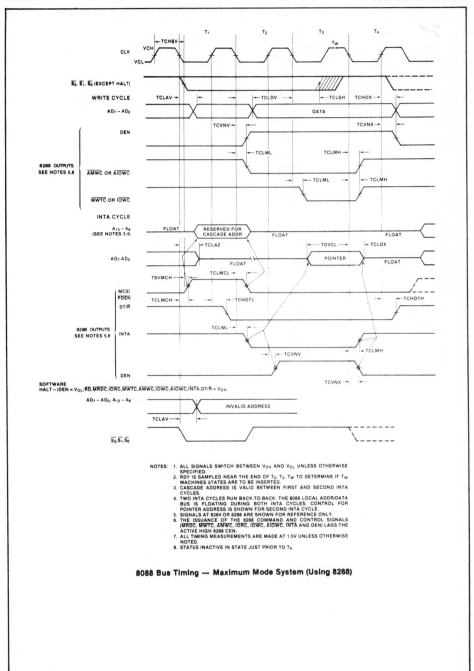

NOTES: 1. ALL SIGNALS SWITCH BETWEEN V$_{OH}$ AND V$_{OL}$ UNLESS OTHERWISE SPECIFIED.
2. RDY IS SAMPLED NEAR THE END OF T$_2$, T$_3$, T$_W$ TO DETERMINE IF T$_W$ MACHINES STATES ARE TO BE INSERTED.
3. CASCADE ADDRESS IS VALID BETWEEN FIRST AND SECOND INTA CYCLES.
4. TWO INTA CYCLES RUN BACK-TO-BACK. THE 8088 LOCAL ADDR/DATA BUS IS FLOATING DURING BOTH INTA CYCLES. CONTROL FOR POINTER ADDRESS IS SHOWN FOR SECOND INTA CYCLE.
5. SIGNALS AT 8284 OR 8288 ARE SHOWN FOR REFERENCE ONLY.
6. THE ISSUANCE OF THE 8288 COMMAND AND CONTROL SIGNALS ($\overline{MRDC}$, $\overline{MWTC}$, $\overline{AMWC}$, $\overline{IORC}$, $\overline{IOWC}$, $\overline{AIOWC}$, $\overline{INTA}$ AND DEN) LAGS THE ACTIVE HIGH 8288 CEN.
7. ALL TIMING MEASUREMENTS ARE MADE AT 1.5V UNLESS OTHERWISE NOTED.
8. STATUS INACTIVE IN STATE JUST PRIOR TO T$_4$.

8088 Bus Timing — Maximum Mode System (Using 8288)

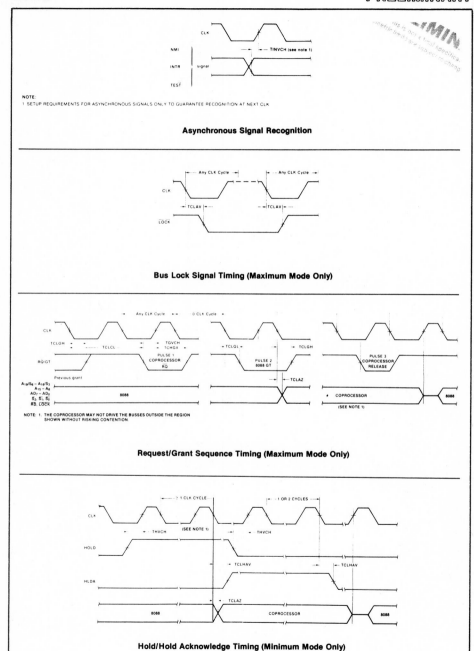

NOTE:
1 SETUP REQUIREMENTS FOR ASYNCHRONOUS SIGNALS ONLY TO GUARANTEE RECOGNITION AT NEXT CLK

Asynchronous Signal Recognition

Bus Lock Signal Timing (Maximum Mode Only)

NOTE: 1. THE COPROCESSOR MAY NOT DRIVE THE BUSSES OUTSIDE THE REGION
SHOWN WITHOUT RISKING CONTENTION.

Request/Grant Sequence Timing (Maximum Mode Only)

Hold/Hold Acknowledge Timing (Minimum Mode Only)

8282/8283

ABSOLUTE MAXIMUM RATINGS*

Temperature Under Bias . . . . 0°C to 70°C
Storage Temperature . . . . − 65°C to + 150°C
All Output and Supply Voltages . . . . − 0.5V to + 7V
All Input Voltages . . . . − 1.0V to + 5.5V
Power Dissipation . . . . 1 Watt

*NOTICE: Stresses above those listed under "Absolute Maximum Ratings" may cause permanent damage to the device. This is a stress rating only and functional operation of the device at these or any other conditions above those indicated in the operational sections of this specification is not implied. Exposure to absolute maximum rating conditions for extended periods may affect device reliability.

D.C. CHARACTERISTICS

Conditions: $V_{CC} = 5V \pm 10\%$, $T_A = 0°C$ to $70°C$

Symbol	Parameter	Min	Max	Units	Test Conditions
V_C	Input Clamp Voltage		− 1	V	$I_C = -5$ mA
I_{CC}	Power Supply Current		160	mA	
I_F	Forward Input Current		− 0.2	mA	$V_F = 0.45V$
I_R	Reverse Input Current		50	μA	$V_R = 5.25V$
V_{OL}	Output Low Voltage		.45	V	$I_{OL} = 32$ mA
V_{OH}	Output High Voltage	2.4		V	$I_{OH} = -5$ mA
I_{OFF}	Output Off Current		± 50	μA	$V_{OFF} = 0.45$ to $5.25V$
V_{IL}	Input Low Voltage		0.8	V	$V_{CC} = 5.0V$ See Note 1
V_{IH}	Input High Voltage	2.0		V	$V_{CC} = 5.0V$ See Note 1
C_{IN}	Input Capacitance		12	pF	$F = 1$ MHz $V_{BIAS} = 2.5V$, $V_{CC} = 5V$ $T_A = 25°C$

NOTE: 1. Output Loading $I_{OL} = 32$ mA, $I_{OH} = -5$ mA, $C_L = 300$ pF.

A.C. CHARACTERISTICS

Conditions: $V_{CC} = 5V \pm 10\%$, $T_A = 0°C$ to $70°C$

Loading: Outputs — $I_{OL} = 32$ mA, $I_{OH} = -5$ mA, $C_L = 300$ pF

Symbol	Parameter	Min	Max	Units	Test Conditions
TIVOV	Input to Output Delay				(See Note 1)
	—Inverting	5	22	ns	
	—Non-Inverting	5	30	ns	
TSHOV	STB to Output Delay				
	—Inverting	10	40	ns	
	—Non-Inverting	10	45	ns	
TEHOZ	Output Disable Time	5	18	ns	
TELOV	Output Enable Time	10	30	ns	
TIVSL	Input to STB Setup Time	0		ns	
TSLIX	Input to STB Hold Time	25		ns	
TSHSL	STB High Time	15		ns	

NOTE: 1. See waveforms and test load circuit on following page.

8282/8283

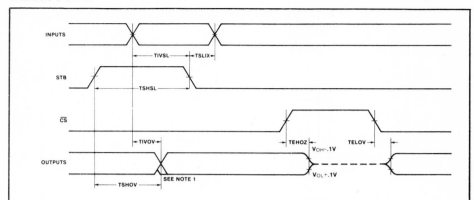

NOTE: 1. 8283 ONLY — OUTPUT MAY BE MOMENTARILY INVALID FOLLOWING THE HIGH GOING STB TRANSITION.
2. ALL TIMING MEASUREMENTS ARE MADE AT 1.5V UNLESS OTHERWISE NOTED.

Timing Diagram

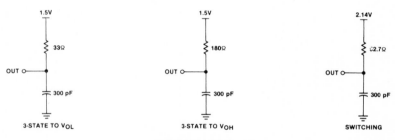

Output Test Load Circuits

8282/8283

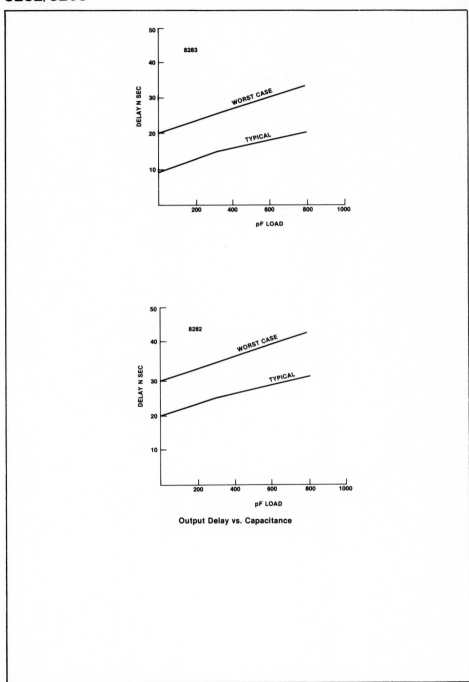

Output Delay vs. Capacitance

8284

D.C. AND OPERATING CHARACTERISTICS

ABSOLUTE MAXIMUM RATINGS*

Temperature Under Bias.................0°C to 70°C
Storage Temperature.............− 65°C to + 150°C
All Output and Supply Voltages........− 0.5V to + 7V
All Input Voltages..................− 1.0V to + 5.5V
Power Dissipation.........................1 Watt

*COMMENT: Stresses above those listed under "Absolute Maximum Ratings" may cause permanent damage to the device. This is a stress rating only and functional operation of the device at these or any other conditions above those indicated in the operational sections of this specification is not implied. Exposure to absolute maximum rating conditions for extended periods may affect device reliability.

8284 PIN CONFIGURATION

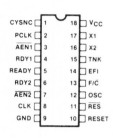

CYSNC	1	18	V$_{CC}$
PCLK	2	17	X1
$\overline{AEN1}$	3	16	X2
RDY1	4	15	TNK
READY	5	14	EFI
RDY2	6	13	F/$\overline{C}$
$\overline{AEN2}$	7	12	OSC
CLK	8	11	$\overline{RES}$
GND	9	10	RESET

8284 BLOCK DIAGRAM

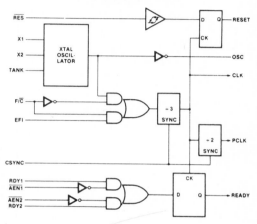

8284 PIN NAMES

X1 X2	CONNECTIONS FOR CRYSTAL
TANK	USED WITH OVERTONE CRYSTAL
F/$\overline{C}$	CLOCK SOURCE SELECT
EFI	EXTERNAL CLOCK INPUT
CSYNC	CLOCK SYNCHRONIZATION INPUT
RDY1 RDY2	READY SIGNAL FROM TWO MULTIBUS™ SYSTEMS
$\overline{AEN1}$ $\overline{AEN2}$	ADDRESS ENABLED QUALIFIERS FOR RDY1,2
$\overline{RES}$	RESET INPUT
RESET	SYNCHRONIZED RESET OUTPUT
OSC	OSCILLATOR OUTPUT
CLK	MOS CLOCK FOR THE PROCESSOR
PCLK	TTL CLOCK FOR PERIPHERALS
READY	SYNCHRONIZED READY OUTPUT
V$_{CC}$	+ 5 VOLTS
GND	0 VOLTS

8284

D.C. CHARACTERISTICS FOR 8284

Conditions: $T_A = 0°C$ to $70°C$; $V_{CC} = 5V \pm 10\%$

Symbol	Parameter	Min	Max	Units	Test Conditions
I_F	Forward Input Current		− 0.5	mA	$V_F = 0.45V$
I_R	Reverse Input Current		50	μA	$V_R = 5.25V$
V_C	Input Forward Clamp Voltage		− 1.0	V	$I_C = -5$ mA
I_{CC}	Power Supply Current		140	mA	
V_{IL}	Input LOW Voltage		0.8	V	$V_{CC} = 5.0V$
V_{IH}	Input HIGH Voltage	2.0		V	$V_{CC} = 5.0V$
V_{IH_R}	Reset Input HIGH Voltage	2.6		V	$V_{CC} = 5.0V$
V_{OL}	Output LOW Voltage		0.45	V	5 mA
V_{OH}	Output HIGH Voltage CLK	4		V	− 1 mA
	Other Outputs	2.4		V	− 1 mA
$V_{IH_R} - V_{IL_R}$	RES Input Hysteresis	0.25		V	$V_{CC} = 5.0V$

A.C. CHARACTERISTICS FOR 8284

Conditions: $T_A = 0°C$ to $70°C$; $V_{CC} = 5V \pm 10\%$

TIMING REQUIREMENTS

Symbol	Parameter	Min	Max	Units	Test Conditions
TEHEL	External Frequency High Time	13		ns	90% - 90% V_{IN}
TELEH	External Frequency Low Time	13		ns	10% - 10% V_{IN}
TELEL	EFI Period	TEHEL + TELEH + δ		ns	(Note 1)
	XTAL Frequency	12	25	MHz	
TR1VCL	RDY1, RDY2 Set-Up to CLK	35		ns	
TCLR1X	RDY1, RDY2 Hold to CLK	0		ns	
TA1VR1V	AEN1, AEN2 Set-Up to RDY1, RDY2	15		ns	
TCLA1X	AEN1, AEN2 Hold to CLK	0		ns	
TYHEH	CSYNC Set-Up to EFI	20		ns	
TEHYL	CSYNC Hold to EFI	20		ns	
TYHYL	CSYNC Width	2 TELEL		ns	
TI1HCL	RES Set-Up to CLK	65		ns	(Note 2)
TCLI1H	RES Hold to CLK	20		ns	(Note 2)

TIMING RESPONSES

Symbol	Parameter	Min	Max	Units	Test Conditions
TCLCL	CLK Cycle Period	125		ns	
TCHCL	CLK High Time	(⅓TCLCL) + 2.0		ns	Fig. 3 & Fig. 4
TCLCH	CLK Low Time	(⅔TCLCL) − 15.0		ns	Fig. 3 & Fig. 4
TCH1CH2 TCL2CL1	CLK Rise or Fall Time		10	ns	1.0V to 3.5V
TPHPL	PCLK High Time	TCLCL − 20		ns	
TPLPH	PCLK Low Time	TCLCL − 20		ns	
TRYLCL	Ready Inactive to CLK (See Note 4)	−8		ns	Fig. 5 & Fig. 6
TRYHCH	Ready Active to CLK (See Note 3)	(⅔TCLCL)−15.0		ns	Fig. 5 & Fig. 6
TCLIL	CLK to Reset Delay	40		ns	
TCLPH	CLK to PCLK High Delay		22	ns	
TCLPL	CLK to PCLK Low Delay		22	ns	
TOLCH	OSC to CLK High Delay	−5	12	ns	
TOLCL	OSC to CLK Low Delay	2	20	ns	

Notes: 1. δ = EFI rise (5 ns max) + EFI fall (5 ns max).
2. Set up and hold only necessary to guarantee recognition at next clock.
3. Applies only to T3 and TW states.
4. Applies only to T2 states.

8284

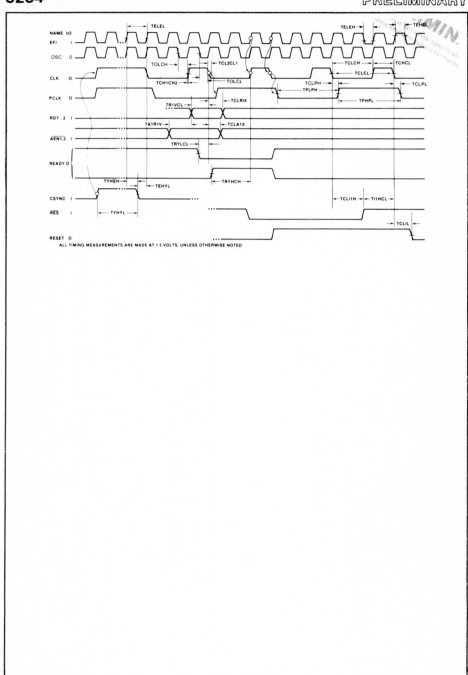

ALL TIMING MEASUREMENTS ARE MADE AT 1.5 VOLTS, UNLESS OTHERWISE NOTED

8284A

ABSOLUTE MAXIMUM RATINGS*

Temperature Under Bias . . . . 0°C to 70°C
Storage Temperature . . . . −65°C to +150°C
All Output and Supply Voltages . . . . −0.5V to +7V
All Input Voltages . . . . −1.0V to +5.5V
Power Dissipation . . . . 1 Watt

NOTICE: Stresses above those listed under "Absolute Maximum Ratings" may cause permanent damage to the device. This is a stress rating only and functional operation of the device at these or any other conditions above those indicated in the operational sections of this specification is not implied. Exposure to absolute maximum rating conditions for extended periods may affect device reliability.

D.C. CHARACTERISTICS ($T_A = 0°C$ to $70°C$; $V_{CC} = 5V \pm 10\%$)

Symbol	Parameter	Min.	Max.	Units	Test Conditions
I_F	Forward Input Current ($\overline{ASYNC}$)		−1.3	mA	$V_F = 0.45V$
	Other Inputs		−0.5	mA	$V_F = 0.45V$
I_R	Reverse Input Current ($\overline{ASYNC}$)		50	µA	$V_R = V_{CC}$
	Other Inputs		50	µA	$V_R = 5.25V$
V_C	Input Forward Clamp Voltage		−1.0	V	$I_C = −5\,mA$
I_{CC}	Power Supply Current		162	mA	
V_{IL}	Input LOW Voltage		0.8	V	
V_{IH}	Input HIGH Voltage	2.0		V	
V_{IHR}	Reset Input HIGH Voltage	2.6		V	
V_{OL}	Output LOW Voltage		0.45	V	5 mA
V_{OH}	Output HIGH Voltage CLK	4		V	−1 mA
	Other Outputs	2.4		V	−1 mA
$V_{IHR} - V_{ILR}$	$\overline{RES}$ Input Hysteresis	0.25		V	

A.C. CHARACTERISTICS ($T_A = 0°C$ to $70°C$; $V_{CC} = 5V \pm 10\%$)

TIMING REQUIREMENTS

Symbol	Parameter	Min.	Max.	Units	Test Conditions
t_{EHEL}	External Frequency HIGH Time	13		ns	90% – 90% V_{IN}
t_{ELEH}	External Frequency LOW Time	13		ns	10% – 10% V_{IN}
t_{ELEL}	EFI Period	$t_{EHEL} + t_{ELEH} + \delta$		ns	(Note 1)
	XTAL Frequency	12	25	MHz	
t_{R1VCL}	RDY1, RDY2 Active Setup to CLK	35		ns	$\overline{ASYNC}$ = HIGH
t_{R1VCH}	RDY1, RDY2 Active Setup to CLK	35		ns	$\overline{ASYNC}$ = LOW
t_{R1VCL}	RDY1, RDY2 Inactive Setup to CLK	35		ns	
t_{CLR1X}	RDY1, RDY2 Hold to CLK	0		ns	
t_{AYVCL}	$\overline{ASYNC}$ Setup to CLK	50		ns	
t_{CLAYX}	$\overline{ASYNC}$ Hold to CLK	0		ns	
t_{A1VR1V}	$\overline{AEN1}$, $\overline{AEN2}$ Setup to RDY1, RDY2	15		ns	
t_{CLA1X}	$\overline{AEN1}$, $\overline{AEN2}$ Hold to CLK	0		ns	
t_{YHEH}	CSYNC Setup to EFI	20		ns	
t_{EHYL}	CSYNC Hold to EFI	20		ns	
t_{YHYL}	CSYNC Width	$2 \cdot t_{ELEL}$		ns	
t_{I1HCL}	$\overline{RES}$ Setup to CLK	65		ns	(Note 2)
t_{CLI1H}	$\overline{RES}$ Hold to CLK	20		ns	(Note 2)

8284A

A.C. CHARACTERISTICS (cont.) ($T_A = 0\,°C$ to $70\,°C$; $V_{CC} = 5V \pm 10\%$)

TIMING RESPONSES†

Symbol	Parameter	Min.	Max.	Units	Test Conditions
t_{CLCL}	CLK Cycle Period	125		ns	
t_{CHCL}	CLK HIGH Time	($\frac{1}{3}\,t_{CLCL}$) + 2.0		ns	Fig. 7 & Fig. 8
t_{CLCH}	CLK LOW Time	($\frac{2}{3}\,t_{CLCL}$) − 15.0		ns	Fig. 7 & Fig. 8
t_{CH1CH2} t_{CL2CL1}	CLK Rise or Fall Time		10	ns	1.0V to 3.5V
t_{PHPL}	PCLK HIGH Time	t_{CLCL} − 20		ns	
t_{PLPH}	PCLK LOW Time	t_{CLCL} − 20		ns	
t_{RYLCL}	Ready Inactive to CLK (See Note 4)	−8		ns	Fig. 9 & Fig. 10
t_{RYHCH}	Ready Active to CLK (See Note 3)	($\frac{2}{3}\,t_{CLCL}$) − 15.0		ns	Fig. 9 & Fig. 10
t_{CLIL}	CLK to Reset Delay		40	ns	
t_{CLPH}	CLK to PCLK HIGH Delay		22	ns	
t_{CLPL}	CLK to PCLK LOW Delay		22	ns	
t_{OLCH}	OSC to CLK HIGH Delay	−5	22	ns	
t_{OLCL}	OSC to CLK LOW Delay	2	35	ns	

Notes:

1. δ = EFI rise (5 ns max) + EFI fall (5 ns max).
2. Setup and hold necessary only to guarantee recognition at next clock.
3. Applies only to T3 and TW states.
4. Applies only to T2 states.

†Figure 11 illustrates test load measurement condition.

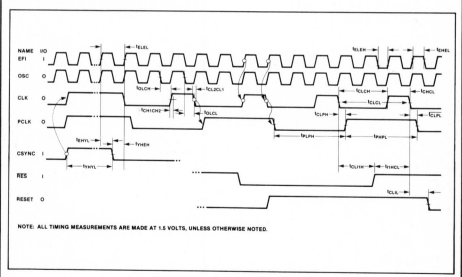

NOTE: ALL TIMING MEASUREMENTS ARE MADE AT 1.5 VOLTS, UNLESS OTHERWISE NOTED.

Waveforms for Clocks and Reset Signals

8284A   PRELIMINARY

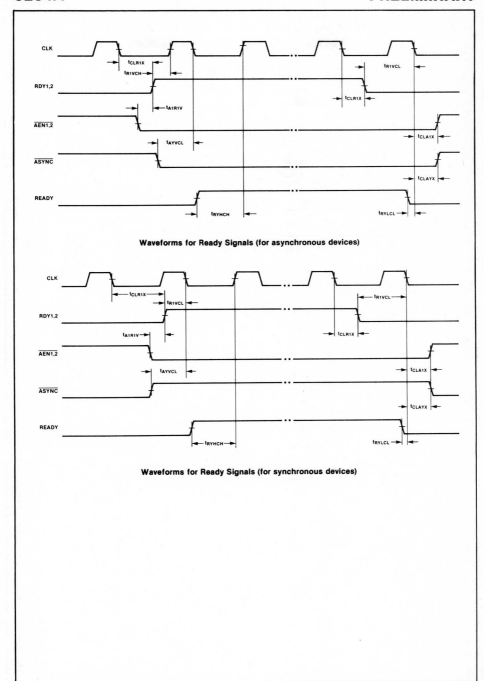

Waveforms for Ready Signals (for asynchronous devices)

Waveforms for Ready Signals (for synchronous devices)

8284A

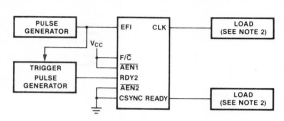

Ready to Clock (using EFI)

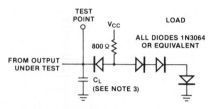

Test Load Measurement Condition

NOTES: 1. $C_L = 100\,pF$
2. $C_L = 30\,pF$
3. C_L INCLUDES PROBE AND JIG CAPACITANCE.

8286/8287

ABSOLUTE MAXIMUM RATINGS*

Temperature Under Bias................0°C to 70°C
Storage Temperature............. − 65°C to + 150°C
All Output and Supply Voltages....... − 0.5V to + 7V
All Input Voltages.................. − 1.0V to + 5.5V
Power Dissipation...........................1 Watt

D.C. CHARACTERISTICS FOR 8286/8287

Conditions: $V_{CC} = 5V \pm 10\%$ $T_A = 0°C$ to $70°C$

Symbol	Parameter	Min	Max	Units	Test Conditions
V_C	Input Clamp Voltage		−1	V	$I_C = -5$ mA
I_{CC}	Power Supply Current—8287 —8286		130 160	mA mA	
I_F	Forward Input Current		−0.2	mA	$V_F = 0.45V$
I_R	Reverse Input Current		50	µA	$V_R = 5.25V$
V_{OL}	Output Low Voltage —B Outputs —A Outputs		.45 .45	V V	$I_{OL} = 32$ mA $I_{OL} = 16$ mA
V_{OH}	Output High Voltage —B Outputs —A Outputs	2.4 2.4		V V	$I_{OH} = -5$ mA $I_{OH} = -1$ mA
I_{OFF} I_{OFF}	Output Off Current Output Off Current		I_F I_R		$V_{OFF} = 0.45V$ $V_{OFF} = 5.25V$
V_{IL}	Input Low Voltage —A Side —B Side		0.8 0.9	V V	$V_{CC} = 5.0V$, See Note 1 $V_{CC} = 5.0V$, See Note 1
V_{IH}	Input High Voltage	2.0		V	$V_{CC} = 5.0V$, See Note 1
C_{IN}	Input Capacitance		12	pF	F = 1 MHz $V_{BIAS} = 2.5V$, $V_{CC} = 5V$ $T_A = 25°C$

NOTE: 1. B Outputs — $I_{OL} = 32$ mA, $I_{OH} = -5$ mA, $C_L = 300$ pF; A Outputs — $I_{OL} = 16$ mA, $I_{OH} = -1$ mA, $C_L = 100$ pF.

A.C. CHARACTERISTICS FOR 8286/8287

Conditions: $V_{CC} = 5V \pm 10\%$, $T_A = 0°C$ to $70°C$

Loading: B Outputs — $I_{OL} = 32$ mA, $I_{OH} = -5$ mA, $C_L = 300$ pF
A Outputs — $I_{OL} = 16$ mA, $I_{OH} = -1$ mA, $C_L = 100$ pF

Symbol	Parameter	Min	Max	Units	Test Conditions
TIVOV	Input to Output Delay Inverting Non-Inverting	5 5	22 30	ns ns	(See Note 1)
TEHTV	Transmit/Receive Hold Time	5		ns	
TTVEL	Transmit/Receive Setup	10		ns	
TEHOZ	Output Disable Time	5	18	ns	
TELOV	Output Enable Time	10	30	ns	

NOTE: 1. See waveforms and test load circuit on following page.

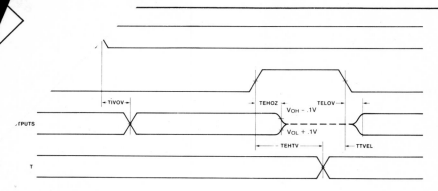

NOTE: 1. All timing measurements are made at 1.5V unless otherwise noted.

8286/8287 Timing

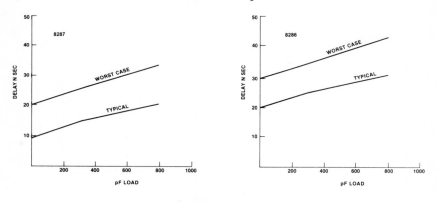

Output Delay vs. Capacitance

8286/8287

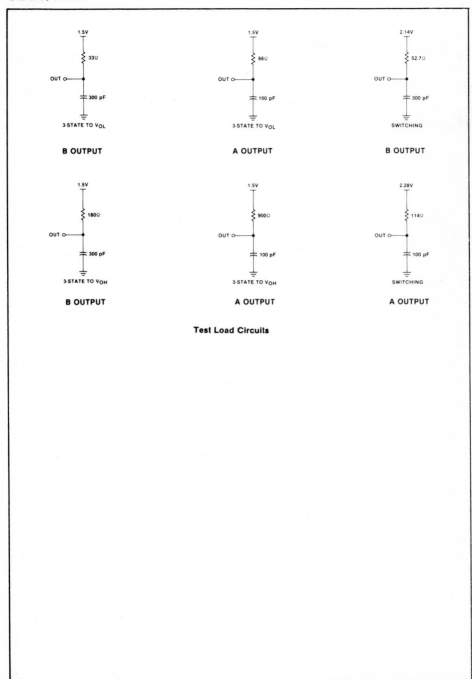

Test Load Circuits

8288

D.C. AND A.C. CHARACTERISTICS

ABSOLUTE MAXIMUM RATINGS*

Temperature Under Bias.............................0°C to 70°C
Storage Temperature......................... − 65°C to + 150°C
All Output and Supply Voltages..................... − 0.5V to + 7V
All Input Voltages................................. − 1.0V to + 5.5V
Power Dissipation.................................... 1.5 Watt

*NOTICE: Stresses above those listed under "Absolute Maximum Ratings" may cause permanent damage to the device. This is a stress rating only and functional operation of the device at these or any other conditions above those indicated in the operational sections of this specification is not implied. Exposure to absolute maximum rating conditions for extended periods may affect device reliability.

D.C. CHARACTERISTICS

Conditions: $V_{CC} = 5V \pm 10\%$, $T_A = 0°C$ to $70°C$

Symbol	Parameter	Min	Max	Unit	Test Conditions
V_C	Input Clamp Voltage		− 1	V	$I_C = − 5$ mA
I_{CC}	Power Supply Current		230	mA	
I_F	Forward Input Current		− 0.7	mA	$V_F = 0.45V$
I_R	Reverse Input Current		50	μA	$V_R = V_{CC}$
V_{OL}	Output Low Voltage—Command Outputs		0.5	V	$I_{OL} = 32$ mA
	Control Outputs		0.5	V	$I_{OL} = 16$ mA
V_{OH}	Output High Voltage— Command Outputs	2.4		V	$I_{OH} = − 5$ mA
	Control Outputs	2.4		V	$I_{OH} = − 1$ mA
V_{IL}	Input Low Voltage		0.8	V	
V_{IH}	Input High Voltage	2.0		V	
I_{OFF}	Output Off Current		100	μA	$V_{OFF} = 0.4$ to $5.25V$

A.C. CHARACTERISTICS

Conditions: $V_{CC} = 5V \pm 10\%$, $T_A = 0°C$ to $70°C$

TIMING REQUIREMENTS

Symbol	Parameter	Min	Max	Unit	Loading
TCLCL	CLK Cycle Period	125		ns	
TCLCH	CLK Low Time	66		ns	
TCHCL	CLK High Time	40		ns	
TSVCH	Status Active Setup Time	35		ns	
TCHSV	Status Active Hold Time	10		ns	
TSHCL	Status Inactive Setup Time	35		ns	
TCLSH	Status Inactive Hold Time	10		ns	

TIMING RESPONSES

Symbol	Parameter	Min	Max	Unit	Loading	
TCVNV	Control Active Delay	5	45	ns		
TCVNX	Control Inactive Delay	10	45	ns		
TCLLH, TCLMCH	ALE MCE Active Delay (from CLK)		20	ns		
TSVLH, TSVMCH	ALE MCE Active Delay (from Status)		20	ns	MRDC	
TCHLL	ALE Inactive Delay	4	15	ns	IORC	
TCLML	Command Active Delay	10	35	ns	MWTC	$I_{OL} = 32$ mA
TCLMH	Command Inactive Delay	10	35	ns	IOWC	$I_{OH} = − 5$ mA
TCHDTL	Direction Control Active Delay		50	ns	INTA	$C_L = 300$ pF
TCHDTH	Direction Control Inactive Delay		30	ns	AMWC	
TAELCH	Command Enable Time		40	ns	AIOWC	
TAEHCZ	Command Disable Time		40	ns		
TAELCV	Enable Delay Time	115	200	ns	Other	$I_{OL} = 16$ mA
TAEVNV	AEN to DEN		20	ns		$I_{OH} = − 1$ mA
TCEVNV	CEN to DEN, PDEN		25	ns		$C_L = 80$ pF
TCELRH	CEN to Command		TCLML	ns		

8288

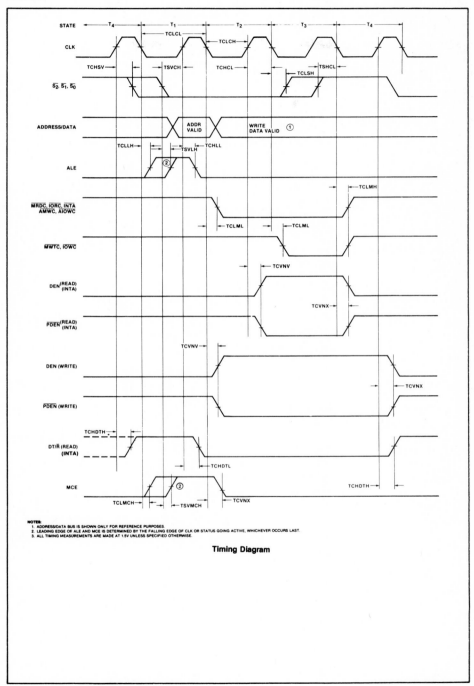

Timing Diagram

NOTES:
1. ADDRESS/DATA BUS IS SHOWN ONLY FOR REFERENCE PURPOSES.
2. LEADING EDGE OF ALE AND MCE IS DETERMINED BY THE FALLING EDGE OF CLK OR STATUS GOING ACTIVE, WHICHEVER OCCURS LAST.
3. ALL TIMING MEASUREMENTS ARE MADE AT 1.5V UNLESS SPECIFIED OTHERWISE.

8288

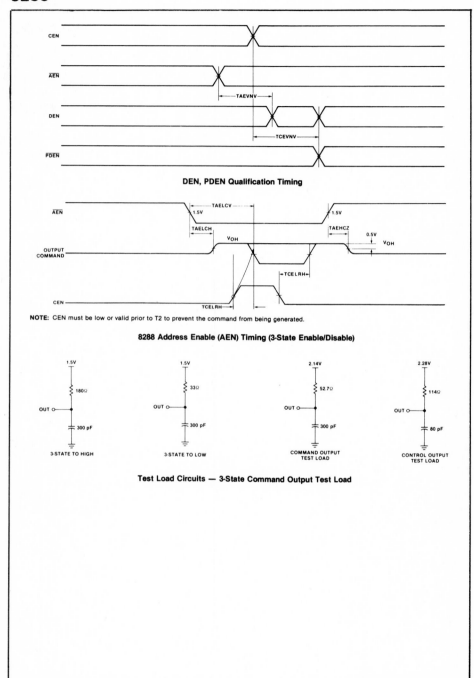

DEN, PDEN Qualification Timing

NOTE: CEN must be low or valid prior to T2 to prevent the command from being generated.

8288 Address Enable (AEN) Timing (3-State Enable/Disable)

Test Load Circuits — 3-State Command Output Test Load

The 8088 CPU

The 8088 is an 8086 microprocessor with an 8-bit data bus. The two parts are otherwise identical. Therefore we will describe differences between the 8088 and the 8086 in the text which follows.

8088 PROGRAMMABLE REGISTERS AND ADDRESSING MODES

8088 programmable registers and addressing modes are identical to the 8086 in every way. Except for execution speed, to the programmer the 8088 is identical to the 8086.

8088 CPU PINS AND SIGNALS

8088 CPU pins and signals are illustrated in Figure D-1. As compared to the 8086 pins and signals illustrated in Figure 10-1, only pin 34 differs (with the exception of pins 2-8 and 39 being address only).

For the 8086, pin 34 outputs $\overline{BHE}$. This signal discriminates between the high-order byte and the low-order byte on the 16-bit 8086 data bus. Since the 8088 has an 8-bit data bus, $\overline{BHE}$ and associated logic is irrelevant. The 8088 outputs maximum mode $\overline{SO}$ status at pin 34 ($\overline{SSO}$).

The IO/$\overline{M}$ signal has opposite polarity for the 8088, as compared to the 8086. This makes the 8088 compatible with the 8085.

Combining IO/$\overline{M}$, DT/$\overline{R}$, and $\overline{SSO}$, 8088 bus cycles can be decoded as follows:

IO/$\overline{M}$	DT/$\overline{R}$	$\overline{SSO}$	
0	0	0	Code segment access
0	0	1	Memory read
0	1	0	Memory write
0	1	1	No operations
1	0	0	Interrupt acknowledge
1	0	1	I/O read
1	1	0	I/O write
1	1	1	Halt

Since the 8088 has no $\overline{BHE}$ signals, nor need for any such signal, the discussion of external memory addressing and $\overline{BHE}$ given for the 8086 will not apply to the 8088.

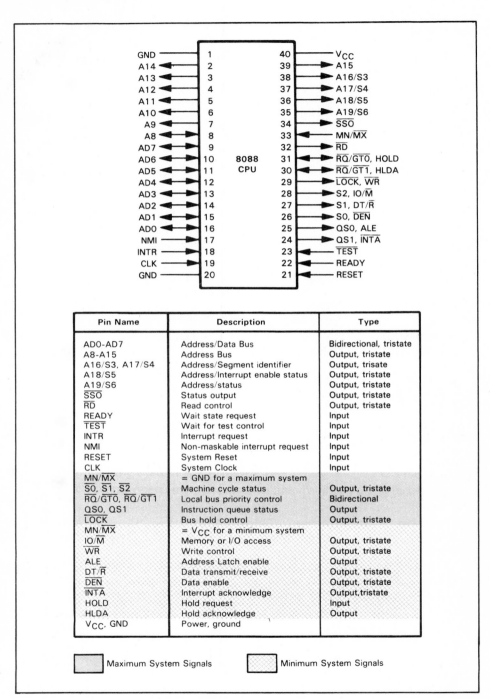

Figure D-1. 8088 Pins and Signal Assignments

8088 TIMING AND INSTRUCTION EXECUTION

The 8088 has a 4-byte instruction object code queue; the 8086, in contrast, has a 6-byte instruction object code queue. The 8088 will start executing instruction fetch bus cycles to fill its 4 byte queue as soon as one or more queue bytes are empty. The 8086, in contrast, will not start pre-fetching instruction object code bytes until two or more of its 6 queue bytes are empty. The description of bus cycles and queue logic given for the 8086 otherwise applies directly to the 8088.

Since the 8088 queue is shorter, instructions which would be totally contained in the 8086 queue may require code fetches for the 8088 to obtain the additional instruction bytes. Four clock cycles must be added for each instruction byte to be fetched. For example,

SUB TABLE[BX],300

could represent a 6-byte instruction including two bytes of displacement (TABLE) and two bytes of immediate data (300). Assuming the first four bytes are contained in the 8088 instruction queue, the two bytes of immediate data must still be fetched, adding 8 clock cycles to the instruction's execution time. This rule should be applied to derive 8088 execution times from those given for the 8086.

Additionally, since the 8088 has an 8-bit bus, two bus cycles will have to be executed wherever the 8086 would have executed a single bus cycle to fetch 16 bits of data. Appendix A provides execution times for the 8086.

8088 MEMORY AND I/O DEVICE ACCESS BUS CYCLES

Bus cycle timing for the 8088 and the 8086 differ only at the multiplexed data/address bus cycles. Timing differences are confined to the eight address bus lines A8-A15, and may be illustrated as follows:

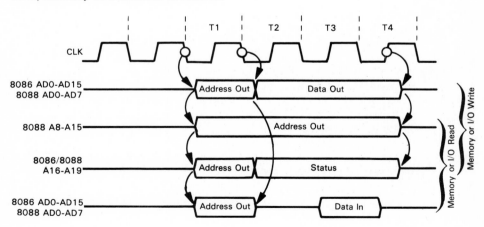

Apart from the fact that the 8088 has no $\overline{\text{BHE}}$ signal, all timing for signals other than the data/address bus is identical for the 8086 and the 8088.

THE 8088 HALT STATE

When operating in minimum mode, the 8088 delays the ALE pulse by one clock period as compared to 8086 timing. This may be illustrated as follows:

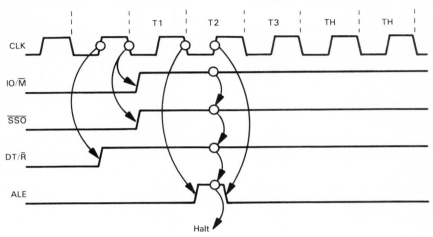

Halt state logic and timing is otherwise identical for the 8086 and the 8088.

OTHER 8086 COMPATIBLE 8088 LOGIC

8086 and 8088 logic is absolutely identical for the following states and logic:

1. The Wait state
2. The Hold state
3. $\overline{RQ}/\overline{GT}$ logic
4. Lock logic
5. Wait for test state
6. Processor escape
7. Device reset
8. Interrupt processing
9. Single stepping mode

THE 8088 INSTRUCTION SET

The 8086 and 8088 instruction sets, listed in numerous tables in this book, are identical with the exception of execution times.

Index

About the Authors

Russell Rector has been involved with computing since 1968. After receiving a B.A. in Computer Science from the University of California, he assisted in the creation of several substantial software systems before joining the technical staff at Osborne, where Mr. Rector has divided his time between software design and assisting in the writing of several Osborne publications.

George Alexy joined Intel in 1977. He is the applications manager for microprocessor products, covering all 8- and 16-bit microprocessors including the 8086, 8088, 8089, and 8087. His group at Intel is concerned with system design methodology for single and multiple processor systems, resource distribution and functional partitioning relating to CPU and system architecture and performance. Prior to joining Intel, Mr. Alexy was with Sperry Univac. He holds a master's degree in Electrical Engineering from Stanford University.

Other Osborne/McGraw-Hill Publications